The Special Educator's Guide to Assessment

Sara Miller McCune founded SAGE Publishing in 1965 to support the dissemination of usable knowledge and educate a global community. SAGE publishes more than 1000 journals and over 800 new books each year, spanning a wide range of subject areas. Our growing selection of library products includes archives, data, case studies and video. SAGE remains majority owned by our founder and after her lifetime will become owned by a charitable trust that secures the company's continued independence.

Los Angeles | London | New Delhi | Singapore | Washington DC | Melbourne

The Special Educator's Guide to Assessment

A Comprehensive Summary by IDEA Disability Category

Tara S. Guerriero
West Chester University, USA

Mary A. Houser
West Chester University, USA

Vicki A. McGinley
West Chester University, USA

Los Angeles | London | New Delhi
Singapore | Washington DC | Melbourne

FOR INFORMATION:

SAGE Publications, Inc.
2455 Teller Road
Thousand Oaks, California 91320
E-mail: order@sagepub.com

SAGE Publications Ltd.
1 Oliver's Yard
55 City Road
London, EC1Y 1SP
United Kingdom

SAGE Publications India Pvt. Ltd.
B 1/I 1 Mohan Cooperative Industrial Area
Mathura Road, New Delhi 110 044
India

SAGE Publications Asia-Pacific Pte. Ltd.
18 Cross Street #10-10/11/12
China Square Central
Singapore 048423

Acquisitions Editor: Leah Fargotstein
Editorial Assistant: Natalie Elliott
Production Editor: Gagan Mahindra
Copy Editor: Will DeRooy
Typesetter: Hurix Digital
Indexer: Integra
Cover Designer: Scott Van Atta
Marketing Manager: Victoria Velasquez

Copyright © 2021 by SAGE Publications, Inc.

Printed in Canada

Library of Congress Cataloging-in-Publication Data

Names: Guerriero, Tara S., author. | Houser, Mary A., author. | Ann McGinley, Vicki, author.

Title: The special educator's guide to assessment : a comprehensive overview by idea disability category / Tara S. Guerriero, Mary A. Houser, Vicki Ann McGinley.

Description: First edition. | Thousand Oaks, California : SAGE Publications, Inc, [2021] | Includes bibliographical references.

Identifiers: LCCN 2020017285 | ISBN 9781544344232 (paperback) | ISBN 9781544344218 (epub) | ISBN 9781544344225 (epub) | ISBN 9781544344249 (ebook)

Subjects: LCSH: Children with disabilities–Rating of–United States. | Children with disabilities–Education–Evaluation. | Disability evaluation–United States. | People with disabilities–Functional assessment–United States. | School grade placement–United States.

Classification: LCC LC4031 .G84 2021 | DDC 371.91–dc23
LC record available at https://lccn.loc.gov/2020017285

This book is printed on acid-free paper.

20 21 22 23 24 10 9 8 7 6 5 4 3 2 1

Brief Table of Contents

Detailed Contents

Preface

The Purpose and Benefits of This Textbook

The Special Educator's Guide to Assessment: A Comprehensive Summary by IDEA Disability Category is a comprehensive assessment text that seeks to deliver a practical understanding of the complexities associated with assessment. It focuses on the role that assessment plays in the diagnosis of a disability, determination of eligibility for special education services, and education of students with disabilities according to IDEA (the Individuals With Disabilities Education Act). This text provides the fundamentals of assessment, including a connection to special education legislation as well as a discussion and exploration of assessment types and techniques, components of assessment, and areas of assessment that are required knowledge for special educators. What distinguishes this text from other assessment texts is its unique point of view that provides an operational understanding of the relationship between disability, assessment, diagnosis, eligibility according to IDEA, and special education programming and instruction. *Its reader-friendly approach will help future teachers connect to assessment in a meaningful way that will directly relate to their instruction for P–12 students, thus enabling them to genuinely understand assessment as it relates to each disability category.* In order to provide a meaningful interconnection between assessment and real-world application, comprehensive case studies throughout the text provide for an authentic understanding and application of assessment concepts in relation to the diagnosis and eligibility associated with IDEA categories of disability.

The theoretical framework for this text is rooted in special education law (i.e., the Individuals With Disabilities Education Act). The Individuals with Disabilities Education Act (IDEA) is the standard by which all disabilities are evaluated and regulated in our public educational system; therefore, this framework provides a sound basis for the structure of this text.

Teachers often understand the characteristics of the disabilities but lack an understanding of the relationship between diagnostic assessment and eligibility, ongoing assessment and progress monitoring, and their relationship to instruction. It is critical to bridge this understanding, because characteristics that manifest themselves during the diagnostic and eligibility process often ultimately impact student performance in the classroom. While special education teachers are often not the ones to conduct comprehensive evaluations of students (states will vary in procedure), it is paramount that they possess genuine knowledge of their students' individual characteristics, as well as a true understanding of how assessment is used to determine diagnosis and eligibility, in order to effectively teach. It is central to their being the most informed and ultimately effective teachers that they can be and is critical to their pedagogical expertise. This text will help ensure that future teachers have the fundamental preparation needed to provide the most comprehensive instruction to P–12 students.

- Part I of the text provides the background in assessment that is necessary for comprehending and applying the components of a comprehensive evaluation for special education services under IDEA. More specifically, it includes an overall introduction to topics related to assessment, a discussion of assessment types, and an overview of assessment in different areas of student characteristics that can be used for diagnosis and eligibility purposes.
    - Chapter 1, "Introduction to Special Education History, Legislation, and Consideration for Eligibility" (McGinley, Guerriero, and Houser), provides an understanding of both the history of assessment within Special Education as well as the legislation that informs assessment decisions. Further, it helps create a link between assessment and eligibility for special education services and legislation pertaining to special education and civil rights.
    - Chapter 2, "Introduction to Assessment and Ethical Considerations" (Houser), includes an overview of assessment, assessment-related terminology, and ethical considerations surrounding assessment.
    - Chapter 3, "Assessment Types" (Guerriero), includes a description of assessment types that are commonly used in educational settings and comprehensive evaluations.
    - Chapter 4, "Assessment for Diagnosis and Eligibility: Development and Health" (Guerriero), and Chapter 5, "Assessment for Diagnosis and Eligibility: Academic Achievement and Behavior" (Guerriero), describe six areas of student characteristics (intelligence, language, social/emotional characteristics, health and medical status, areas of academic achievement, and behavior).

- Part II provides a description of the diagnostic and eligibility criteria and the assessment process associated with the IDEA categories of disability that may be diagnosed in an educational or private setting.
    - Chapter 6, "Learning Disabilities" (Guerriero)
    - Chapter 7, "Intellectual Disabilities" (Houser)
    - Chapter 8, "Autism Spectrum Disorder" (Houser)
    - Chapter 9, "Speech or Language Impairment" (McGinley)
    - Chapter 10, "Emotional Disturbance" (McGinley)

- Part III provides a description of the diagnostic and eligibility criteria and the assessment process related to disabilities, disorders, conditions, and syndromes associated with the IDEA categories of disability that are generally diagnosed not in an educational setting, but rather in a medical setting. The purpose of the chapters in Part III is to facilitate the understanding of medically related disabilities and to promote an awareness of the diagnostic criteria and its relevance to eligibility for special education services under IDEA.

- Chapter 11, "Attention-Deficit/Hyperactivity Disorder (ADHD)" (Guerriero)
- Chapter 12, "Sensory Impairments (Including Visual Impairment, Hearing Impairment, Deafness, and Deaf-Blindness)" (McGinley)
- Chapter 13, "Health-Related Disabilities (Including Other Health Impairments, Orthopedic Impairment, Traumatic Brain Injury, and Multiple Disabilities)" (Houser)

- Part IV focuses on the effective use of assessment results to make educational decisions for students.
  - Chapter 14, "Making Connections Between Diagnosis, Eligibility, and Instruction" (Houser and Guerriero)

The Suggested Course(s)/Intended Audience for This Textbook

This text is predominantly intended for special education assessment courses, which are typically required in higher education institutions that have a special education teacher preparation program that leads to teacher certification (both at the undergraduate and graduate levels). An introduction to or foundations of special education course should be a prerequisite to an assessment course that would use this text, because potential students should have a basic understanding of the categories of disability under IDEA, as well as general knowledge of special education legislation in order to truly comprehend the connection between special education and assessment. Other fields that may have coursework that would benefit from this text include school psychology, social work, and communication sciences and disorders.

The Special Features of This Textbook

An assessment text has the potential to be austere and intimidating, especially for students with a limited background in assessment. The special features will add to the goal of achieving a reader-friendly text.

Each chapter contains the following special features:

- Learning Objectives: Key learning outcomes that students should expect to achieve following the completion of each chapter are highlighted at the beginning of each chapter.

- Key Terms: Vocabulary and important concepts central to chapter content are included at the beginning of each chapter and highlighted throughout the chapter.

- Check Your Understanding Questions: Comprehension questions appear regularly throughout each chapter to gauge student understanding and help students ensure that they are following along. They also help students make sure that they are working toward achieving the learning objectives.

- Apply What You Have Learned: Application questions and suggested activities that require higher-order thinking skills, aimed at extending what students have learned, are included in each chapter. Similar to the Check Your Understanding Questions, these questions and activities will help students reach the learning objectives.

Additionally, the following special features are regularly included throughout the text, as appropriate:

- Comprehensive Case Studies: Detailed case studies are included as a means of enhancing student understanding. Authentic case studies help bring assessment to life and illustrate how assessment applies to real-life situations that students with disabilities might experience. Some chapters have one case study, while others have several. For example, Chapter 6 ("Learning Disabilities") has three case studies that are aimed at describing children with very different manifestations of learning disabilities. These different scenarios are included to portray the expansiveness and complexity associated with diagnosing a learning disability. Similarly, Chapter 13 ("Health-Related Disabilities") has multiple case studies that are aimed at showcasing the many different disabilities that it covers (e.g., orthopedic impairment, traumatic brain injury, multiple disabilities, and other health impairment). While the case studies differ in their scope and content, the following are some characteristics that you may see:
  - A student profile containing characteristics and background information (e.g., intelligence, language, academics, behavior, social/emotional, and health and medical)
  - The assessment process (e.g., assessments administered with results and interpretation)
  - The family and teacher's role in the diagnostic and eligibility process
  - The impact of diagnosis on eligibility for special education services, special education programming, and instruction

- Sample Comprehensive Evaluations: Sample evaluations are included periodically throughout the text to help the reader understand each component of a comprehensive evaluation in relation to a "real" student. For example, Chapter 12 ("Sensory Impairments") includes several sample evaluations to help the reader understand how an evaluation for a sensory impairment may be conducted and what it might entail. Chapter 14 ("Making Connections Between Diagnosis, Eligibility, and

Instruction") includes a sample re-evaluation to enhance understanding of the role of re-evaluations in the educational process.

The special features of this text are of chief importance to its effectiveness. It is through these features that the reader will gain the most comprehensive understanding of assessment as it applies to students with disabilities.

The Ancillary Supplements to This Textbook

Chapter-based PowerPoint® slides and lecture notes will help instructors set up teaching for their classes. Additionally, a complete test bank (with a variety of item types) is available for instructors. Visit **edge.sagepub.com/guerriero** for instructor resources.

Acknowledgments

We want to thank SAGE for giving us a platform to share our ideas and working with us to develop this text.

Tara Guerriero

I want to thank my husband, children, parents, and brother for your never-ending love and support. Your belief in me and encouragement mean everything to me. I also want to thank Dr. Doris Johnson and Dr. Steve Zecker of Northwestern University for helping develop my love for assessment as a means of better understanding how our students learn best. You taught me that with a true understanding of a person's strengths and needs, we can create individualized and meaningful instruction for everyone. I learned from the very best, and I will always be thankful for you and your mentorship. To my colleagues Dr. Mary Houser and Dr. Vicki McGinley, thank you for joining me in this endeavor and for your tireless work in helping turn this vision into a reality. I want to thank West Chester University for being such a wonderful place to work and for giving me the opportunity to do what I love for the last 14 years.

Mary Houser

I would like to acknowledge and thank my husband, Matt, and my children Jake, Alex, and Lauren, for their encouragement during the writing process. Your support has always allowed me to pursue my professional interests and passions with great enthusiasm. I would also like to acknowledge my parents, Rugby and Dort, who have taught me the meaning of hard work and commitment to honing my craft, with the realization that it does get better with time and dedication. Special thanks to Dr. Matthew Lindgren for sharing his medical expertise and willingness to review my medically related content. Thank you to West Chester University for being my professional home and for being supportive of my teaching and research interests. To my colleagues Dr. Tara Guerriero and Dr. Vicki McGinley, thank you for your collaborative efforts in seeing this project to a successful completion. Last, thank you so much to Dr. Tara Guerriero for your inspiration and leadership throughout this process and for being a true friend.

Vicki McGinley

I would like to thank my family for always being patient and supportive of my work. Additionally, I'd like to thank my sister and professional colleague, Paula Rollins, who is always there to answer questions, read my work, and just have fun with. Additionally, the professional work of Jill Christopher and Erica Pirolli has greatly supported this text. This text would not have been possible without the collaboration of my WCU colleagues, Dr. Tara Guerriero and Dr. Mary Houser. It has been wonderful to find other professionals who have the same passion for supporting persons with disabilities and with whom I work well, and it has been a pleasure to work with them in the completion of this text.

We would like to thank Maura Quigley for her review of the chapters.

SAGE Publishing and the authors would like to thank the following reviewers for their comments throughout the development of the book:

Kelly S. Brooksher, Ed.D., Georgia Southern University
Donna Brown, Ed.D., Texas Tech University
Susan M. Bruce, Ph.D., Professor, Department Chair, Boston College
Stephen Byrd, Associate Professor of Education, School of Education, Director of Graduate Studies at Elon University
Doug Carothers, Florida Gulf Coast University
John J. DeFrancesco, Ph.D., American International College
Nancy E. Harayama, Boston University
Deborah W. Hartman, Cedar Crest College, Allentown, PA
Caryn Huss, Ph.D., Manhattanville College
Veda Jairrels, JD, PhD., Clark Atlanta University
Dr. Mike Kelly, Dominican College
Lynn R. Larsen, Brandman University
Angela L. Patti, PhD., SUNY Buffalo State
Bruce Saddler, Ph.D., University of Albany
Neria Sebastien, Walla Walla University | Seattle University

About the Authors

Dr. Tara S. Guerriero attended Northwestern University, where she received a BS in speech, an MA in learning disabilities, and a PhD in learning disabilities, with a concentration in cognitive neuroscience. She is an associate professor in the Department of Special Education at West Chester University of Pennsylvania and has served as the faculty special assistant to the dean for assessment and accreditation. She teaches at the graduate and undergraduate level in the areas of foundations of special education, assessment, curriculum and instruction/methodology, family systems, and communication/language development and assistive technology. Dr. Guerriero was previously a clinician and supervisor in a learning clinic that focused on both the assessment and diagnosis of learning disabilities as well as the remediation of learning disabilities. Her research interests include assessment of learning disabilities, inclusive practices associated with special education, and both assessment and teaching within the areas of mathematics and reading in the field of learning disabilities.

Dr. Mary A. Houser received a BFA in related arts from Kutztown University of Pennsylvania, an MAT in special education from the College of New Jersey, and an EdD in educational leadership from Fayetteville State University. She is currently an associate professor in the Department of Special Education at West Chester University of Pennsylvania. She teaches both undergraduate and graduate courses in foundations of special education, behavior management, autism spectrum disorder (ASD), language development, and family systems. Dr. Houser has also taught graduate special education courses for Walden University, where she served as a graduate special education curriculum developer and assessor. In addition, she has taught graduate special education courses and supervised pre-service teachers for Campbell University (NC). Dr. Houser has worked as a learning disabilities specialist and has taught high school special education in both inclusive and self-contained settings to children with various disabilities. Her research interests include families of students with autism spectrum disorders and improving parent-teacher relationships for students with disabilities.

Dr. Vicki A. McGinley, professor, is a faculty member at West Chester University of Pennsylvania in the Special Education Department. She has taught both undergraduate and graduate courses in foundations, communication and behavioral disorders, action research, family systems, and legal issues. She has served in two states as a due process hearing officer and serves as a university fact finder as well as state mediator. Presently, her service and research focus on trauma-informed education, international special education, and working directly with children and teachers in schools. She was recently awarded a research and teaching Fulbright Scholarship to work in Eastern Europe. Her publications reflect her teaching and service work.

An Overview of
Assessment
in Special Education

Introduction to Special Education History, Legislation, and Consideration for Eligibility

Vicki A. McGinley, PhD, Tara S. Guerriero, PhD, and Mary A. Houser, EdD

Learning Objectives

- Identify key points and events in history that have shaped special education.

- Identify the key principles of the Individuals With Disabilities Education Act (IDEA).

- Describe the purpose of Section 504 of the Vocational Rehabilitation Act and the Americans With Disabilities Act.

- Define the categories of disability served under IDEA.

- Discuss the difference between an individualized family service plan, an individualized education program, and a Section 504 service agreement.

Key Terms

Americans With Disabilities Act (p. 8)	IDEA categories of disability (p. 11)
assessment (p. 4)	developmental delay, autism, deaf-blindness, emotional disturbance, hearing impairment, intellectual disability, multiple disabilities, orthopedic impairment, other health impairment, specific learning disability, speech or language impairment, traumatic brain injury, visual impairment
Education for All Handicapped Children Act (EAHCA/EHA) (p. 8)	
Elementary and Secondary Education Act (ESEA) (pp. 6–7)	
Every Student Succeeds Act (ESSA) (p. 7)	independent education evaluation (IEE) (p. 10)
free appropriate public education (FAPE) (p. 10)	Individuals With Disabilities Education Act (IDEA/IDEIA) (p. 9)

(Continued)

(Continued)

individualized education program (IEP) (p. 15)	procedural safeguards (p. 10)
individualized family service plan (IFSP) (p. 15)	Section 504 of the Vocational Rehabilitation Act of 1973 (p. 7)
least restrictive environment (LRE) (p. 10)	Section 504 service agreement (p. 19)
No Child Left Behind (NCLB) (p. 7)	special education (p. 16)
nondiscriminatory identification and evaluation (NDE) (p. 9)	specially designed instruction (SDI) (p. 16)
parent participation (p. 10)	Zero Reject–Child Find (p. 9)

Introduction to the Chapter

Assessment is a complicated concept that carries tremendous weight in our educational system. If done correctly, it can make a major difference in the lives of students, both those with and those without disabilities. Assessment occurs every day in early childhood settings as well as in K–12 classrooms, as teachers are continuously evaluating student performance and collecting data to gain a clear picture of where students are functioning to better determine a direction for instruction. Different types of assessment can provide insight into individual strengths and needs, which can ultimately help educators understand how a student learns best. The more comprehensive the battery of assessments is, the more beneficial it can be in providing a guide for instruction. Assessment can provide a means of evaluating students in intelligence and cognitive development, language and communication, academics, behavior, social and emotional development, physical and motor development, health and medical, and other domains. Assessments can be both formal and informal and take many forms, such as permanent products (homework, worksheets, portfolios, creative projects, etc.), norm-referenced assessments, criterion-referenced assessments, interviews, and observations. Essentially, assessment can be described as the gathering of information to make informed decisions for students.

This chapter will provide an understanding of the history of assessment within special education, as well as the legislation that informs assessment decisions. Further, this chapter will bridge an understanding of assessment and eligibility for special education services as it relates to general education legislation, civil rights legislation, and special education legislation. Many concepts that are covered in great depth throughout later chapters will be briefly introduced in this chapter, to give context to assessment as it relates to special education.

Introduction to Legislation as It Relates to Assessment in Special Education

The practice of evaluating and assessing children with disabilities or children who are suspected of having disabilities has evolved considerably over the last 50 years. From the precedents that were set in pivotal court cases (*PARC v. the Commonwealth of Pennsylvania* in 1972, *Larry P. v. Riles* in 1979, etc.), to the practices that were provided for by civil rights laws (e.g., Section 504 of the Vocational Rehabilitation Act of 1973), to the consideration of specific types of disabilities that came with the passage of the first landmark federal special education law in 1975, the Education for All Handicapped Children Act (EAHCA/EHA), or P.L. 94-142, special education assessment has made major strides.

Special Education History of Assessment and Related Court Cases

The history of special education as it relates to assessment has evolved considerably from early misconceptions of what constituted a disability (e.g., a difference in primary language) and significant differences in educational practice (segregating students with special needs and/or completely denying them access to an education) (Friend, 2018; U.S. Department of Education & Office of Special Education and Rehabilitative Services, 2010) to our current practice, which is heavily guided by law. A number of forces helped bring about change and advanced the field of special education:

- Parents of children with disabilities began advocating for better educational opportunities for their children.

- The civil rights movement brought about court cases that examined discriminatory practices in education (e.g., *Brown v. Board of Education* in 1954), and decisions made by the courts (e.g., separate but equal is not equal; segregation is not equal) ultimately extended to those with disabilities.

- The federal government, with the help of advocacy organizations (e.g., ARC), began to focus on developing educational practices for those with disabilities (U.S. Department of Education & Office of Special Education and Rehabilitative Services, 2010). Federal legislation, such as the Training of Professional Personnel Act of 1959 and the Teachers of the Deaf Act of 1961, was enacted to assist with this training. The Training of Professional Personnel Act helped train teachers and administrators to teach students with intellectual disabilities, while the Teachers of the Deaf Act focused on training teachers of those with hearing impairments and deafness (U.S. Department of Education & Office of Special Education and Rehabilitative Services, 2010). Professionals in the field of disability were being trained and starting to research student outcomes in relation to school achievement and placement (Dunn, 1968).

- Many court cases served as a catalyst for educational change for students with special needs or helped further define special education law. The following are some examples of pivotal court cases:

  ○ *Diana v. State Board of Education of California* (1970), in which the court ruled that children must be assessed in their native or primary language

  ○ *Pennsylvania Association for Retarded Children (PARC) v. The Commonwealth of Pennsylvania* (1972), in which it was ruled that children with intellectual disabilities must be provided with a Free Appropriate Public Education (FAPE)

  ○ *Mills v. Board of Education* (1972), in which the findings of PARC were extended to children with disabilities in general

  ○ *Larry P. v. Riles* (1972/1979), in which it was found that assessments such as IQ tests may be inherently racially biased and assessments that discriminate based on race can't be used to identify someone with intellectual disabilities (Yell, 2016)

  ○ *The Board of Education of Hedrick Hudson Central School Dist. v. Rowley* (1982) and *Endrew v. Douglas County School District* (2017) helped define what is meant by an "appropriate" education under the principle of Free Appropriate Public Education (FAPE) (Supreme Court of the United States, 2017).

  ○ *Oberti v. The Board of Education* (1993) addressed the complex topic of what is meant by providing education in the Least Restrictive Environment (LRE).

Check Your Understanding 1.1

1. What initial forces in our country brought about changes to the education system? How did they impact this change?

2. How did *Diana v. State Board of Education of California* in 1970 relate to assessment?

Federal Education Legislation That Impacts Students With Special Needs

As a result of advocacy and critical court cases, federal lawmakers enacted sweeping legislation on behalf of children with disabilities. One of the first federal laws in which disability was addressed was the Elementary and Secondary Education

Act of 1965 (ESEA, P.L. 89-750). This act was reauthorized in 2015 as our present law, the Every Student Succeeds Act (ESSA), which replaced the previous version of the law, the No Child Left Behind Act (NCLB), signed into law in 2002 (U.S. Department of Education, 2019; U.S. Department of Education, n.d.). While these laws are not specific to special education, being focused on education in general, they have all supported children with disabilities to some extent.

The Elementary and Secondary Education Act of 1965

The Elementary and Secondary Education Act of 1965 (ESEA, P.L. 89-750) provided support for the development of special education centers (U.S. Department of Education, n.d.).

The No Child Left Behind Act

The No Child Left Behind Act (NCLB) supported accountability measures, specifically requiring states to report on student achievement using both aggregated data and disaggregated data related to a variety of subgroups, including children with disabilities.

The Every Student Succeeds Act

The Every Student Succeeds Act (ESSA) requires states to address testing, accountability, and school improvements. The U.S. Department of Education & Office of Elementary and Secondary Education (2018, p. 3) states the following regarding assessment for students with cognitive disabilities.

> A State may adopt alternate academic achievement standards and alternate tests that measure achievement against those standards for students with the most significant cognitive disabilities. A State may administer an alternate assessment that is aligned to alternative academic standards to no more than 1 percent of its tested students. The State must demonstrate that any alternate assessment provided is aligned with the same grade-level academic content standards as the general assessment for a given grade.

Civil Rights Legislation Related to Students With Special Needs

In addition to legislation that improved the education of all students, civil rights legislation also provided new opportunities for students with disabilities to prevent discrimination.

Section 504 of the Vocational Rehabilitation Act of 1973

Section 504 of the Vocational Rehabilitation Act of 1973 was a landmark civil rights law that supported children and adults with disabilities. Among other important principles, this law addressed evaluation, identification, and assessment of children with disabilities. It prohibited federally funded programs from discriminating against people with disabilities, and it set the stage for the enactment of the Americans With Disabilities Act, which will be covered in the next section. Section 504 works together with the ADA and the Individuals With Disabilities Education Act (IDEA) to protect children with disabilities from exclusion and unequal treatment in schools, in the workplace, and in the community. In the school setting, children cannot be excluded from the general education curriculum or from activities the school offers, such as sports and musical events.

The Americans With Disabilities Act

According to the U.S. Department of Justice Civil Rights Division (n.d.), the **Americans With Disabilities Act (ADA)** (1990) is a comprehensive civil rights law that prohibits discrimination against people with disabilities. It aims to provide equal opportunities to those with disabilities. It is modeled after both the Civil Rights Act of 1964 (prohibits discrimination on the basis of race, color, religion, sex, or national origin) and Section 504 of the Rehabilitation Act of 1973 (as previously discussed).

It protects those who have a physical or mental impairment that substantially limits one or more major life activities. The ADA does not specifically name all the impairments that are covered, and a condition does not need to be severe or permanent to be a disability. The regulations provide a list of conditions that are included, such as deafness, blindness, an intellectual disability, partially or completely missing limbs or mobility impairments requiring the use of a wheelchair, autism, cancer, cerebral palsy, diabetes, epilepsy, human immunodeficiency virus (HIV) infection, multiple sclerosis, muscular dystrophy, major depressive disorder, bipolar disorder, post-traumatic stress disorder, obsessive-compulsive disorder, and schizophrenia (U.S. Department of Justice Civil Rights Division, n.d.).

The ADA protects against discrimination in areas of employment and public services (e.g., transportation, communication) and provides reasonable accommodations for access, such as changes to a work schedule, assistive technology needed to complete daily activities of living, wheelchair securement on public transportation, and accessible access in facilities (U.S. Department of Justice Civil Rights Division, n.d.).

Federal Special Education Legislation: The Education for All Handicapped Children Act (P.L. 94-142) and the Individuals With Disabilities Education Act

In 1975 the field of special education was forever changed by the enactment of the landmark federal law, the **Education for All Handicapped Children Act (EAHCA/EHA)**, or P.L. 94-142 (U.S. Department of Education & Office of Special Education and Rehabilitative Services, 2010). It was with this law that special education principles and policies really began to take hold (Yell, Katsiyannis, & Hazelkorn, 2007). With the passage of EHA, a free and appropriate public education for all children with disabilities was truly emphasized and enforced. Prior to that time, many children with disabilities were still excluded from public schools, and many were not receiving an appropriate education. Therefore, the primary concern was access to public schools for children (Katsiyannis, Yell, & Bradley, 2001). There have been many amendments and reauthorizations in the subsequent 45 years that have further defined the law and its impact on students and families with special needs, including a change in name to the Individuals With Disabilities Education Act (IDEA) in 1990 and the Individuals With Disabilities Education Improvement Act (IDEIA) in 2004. Many in the field of special education continue to refer to the law as IDEA, which is what we will use throughout this text. The name of the law changed from the Education for All Handicapped Children Act to the Individuals With Disabilities Education Act to embrace person-first language. This change came about because people with disabilities are persons first, who are part of a family that resides in society—living, working, and recreating. The language that we use when speaking about others contributes to our ideas and beliefs about them. As such, person-first language emphasizes the person first. To illustrate, we would say not "blind person," but rather "person with blindness" or "person with a visual impairment."

The following six principles are typically discussed in relation to IDEA: Zero Reject–Child Find, nondiscriminatory evaluation (NDE), FAPE, least restrictive environment (LRE), procedural safeguards, and parental participation (Heward, 2006).

- Zero Reject–Child Find: The principle of Zero Reject–Child Find encompasses the Child Find System, which requires states/local education agencies to have policies and practices in place to identify, locate, and evaluate children who are suspected of having a developmental delay or who are at risk of developmental delay. They must provide all children (from birth to age 21) with a free and appropriate public education regardless of the severity of the disability. For children served under Part C of IDEA (infants and toddlers), children may be identified at birth as having a disability and in need of services. Referrals should be made as early as possible to the appropriate agency by anyone who suspects a delay.

- Nondiscriminatory identification and evaluation (NDE): Nondiscriminatory identification and evaluation, a principle that is highly important with regard to assessment, requires schools to use assessments that are nonbiased on the basis of race, culture, and native language, as well as use multiple methods of evaluation to determine whether a child has a disability. Identification and placement decisions cannot be made on the basis of a single test score.

- Free appropriate public education (FAPE): The principle of free appropriate public education (FAPE) requires schools to provide a free appropriate public education to all children with disabilities, regardless of the severity of the disability. Appropriate services are provided at public expense and are no charge to the child's parents.

- Least restrictive environment (LRE): The principle of least restrictive environment (LRE) requires that all students with disabilities be educated in their least restrictive environment, with an emphasis on educating them together with both others with disabilities and others without disabilities to the maximum extent appropriate. States must offer a continuum of placements for children with disabilities, to ensure that they are being educated in their least restrictive environment. Students with disabilities may be placed in separate classes or schools only when their disabilities are of a severity that they cannot receive an appropriate education in a general education classroom with supplementary aids and services. The law creates a presumption in favor of inclusion in the regular classroom by requiring that a student's IEP contain a justification of the extent, if any, to which a child will not participate with nondisabled peers in the general academic curriculum, extracurricular activities, and other activities (lunch, recess, etc.).

- Procedural safeguards: The principle of procedural safeguards ensures protections of the rights of the family and child with disabilities. Thus, as part of the process, parents receive a copy of their procedural safeguard notices, which outlines parental rights within the special education system. It speaks to parental consent for initial evaluations, and subsequent evaluations, as well as placement decisions; schools must maintain the confidentiality of all records and make those records available to the parents. Additionally, it discusses the parents' rights to due process and outlines what options are available when the school and parents disagree. For example, when parents disagree with the results of an evaluation performed by the school, they may be able to obtain an independent education evaluation (IEE) at public expense. When there is disagreement on the identification, evaluation, placement, or provision of the program, a due process hearing may be requested. However, states are also required to offer parents an opportunity to resolve the matter through other avenues, such as IEP facilitation and mediation. Parents have the right to attorney's fees if they prevail in due process or judicial proceedings under IDEA.

- Parental participation: The final principle, parental participation, states that schools must collaborate with parents and students with disabilities in the design and implementation of special education services to include IEP goals and objectives, related-service needs, and placement decisions.

Check Your Understanding 1.2

1. Why do you believe the six principles associated with IDEA were included as part of the law? Choose three, and discuss how they would pertain to assessment.

2. How did ESEA/NCLB/ESSA support students with special needs?

Eligibility Criteria For Special Education Services Under IDEA

IDEA 2004 is the standard by which special education eligibility decisions are made and, further, governs special education services. As such, IDEA will be addressed globally throughout the textbook in discussions relating to evaluation, diagnosis, and eligibility. Chapters 2 and 4 will address diagnosis and eligibility in great detail; however, in this chapter, we are including a brief overview of what is required for eligibility.

To be eligible for special education services, a child must have a disability and demonstrate a need for special education services and specially designed instruction (SDI) and/or related services (Friend, 2018). Section 300.8 of IDEA (2004) has defined 14 categories of disability and, further, defines a child with a disability as

> a child evaluated in accordance with §§300.304 through 300.311 as having an intellectual disability, a hearing impairment (including deafness), a speech or language impairment, a visual impairment (including blindness), a serious emotional disturbance (referred to in this part as "emotional disturbance"), an orthopedic impairment, autism, traumatic brain injury, an other health impairment, a specific learning disability, deaf-blindness, or multiple disabilities, and who, by reason thereof, needs special education and related services.

(IDEA, 2004, § 300.8(a)(1))

IDEA recognizes the following 14 categories: developmental delay, autism, deaf-blindness, deafness, emotional disturbance, hearing impairment, intellectual disability, multiple disabilities, orthopedic impairment, other health impairment, specific learning disability, speech or language impairment, traumatic brain injury, and visual impairment.

Developmental Delay

Developmental delay refers to children aged 3 through 9 experiencing developmental delays. Child with a disability for children ages 3 through 9 (or any subset of that age range, including ages 3 through 5), may, subject to the conditions described in §300.111(b), include a child who is experiencing developmental delays, as defined by the State and as measured by appropriate diagnostic instruments and procedures, in one or more of the following areas: Physical development, cognitive development, communication development, social or emotional development, or adaptive development; and who, by reason thereof, needs special education and related services.

(IDEA, 2004, § 300.8(b))

Autism

Autism means a developmental disability significantly affecting verbal and nonverbal communication and social interaction, generally evident before age 3 that adversely affects a child's educational performance. Other characteristics often associated with autism are engagement in repetitive activities and stereotyped movements, resistance to environmental change or change in daily routines, and unusual responses to sensory experiences. Autism does not apply if a child's educational performance is adversely affected primarily because the child has an emotional disturbance.

(IDEA, 2004, § 300.8(c)(1))

Deaf-Blindness

Deaf-blindness means concomitant hearing and visual impairments, the combination of which causes such severe communication and other developmental and educational needs that they cannot be accommodated in special education programs solely for children with deafness or children with blindness.

(IDEA, 2004, § 300.8(c)(2))

Deafness

Deafness means a hearing impairment that is so severe that the child is impaired in processing linguistic information through hearing, with or without amplification that adversely affects a child's educational performance.

(IDEA, 2004, § 300.8(c)(3))

Emotional Disturbance

Emotional disturbance means a condition exhibiting one or more of the following characteristics over a long period of time and to a marked degree that adversely affects a child's educational performance:

(i). An inability to learn that cannot be explained by intellectual, sensory, or health factors.

(ii). An inability to build or maintain satisfactory interpersonal relationships with peers and teachers.

(iii). Inappropriate types of behavior or feelings under normal circumstances.

(iv). A general pervasive mood of unhappiness or depression.

(v). A tendency to develop physical symptoms or fears associated with personal or school problems.

Emotional disturbance includes schizophrenia. The term does not apply to children who are socially maladjusted, unless it is determined that they have an emotional disturbance.

(IDEA, 2004, § 300.8(c)(4))

Hearing Impairment

Hearing impairment means an impairment in hearing, whether permanent or fluctuating, that adversely affects a child's educational performance but that is not included under the definition of deafness in this section.

(IDEA, 2004, §300.8(c)(5))

Intellectual Disability

Intellectual disability means significantly sub average general intellectual functioning existing concurrently with deficits in adaptive behavior and manifested during the developmental period, that adversely affects a child's educational performance. The term 'intellectual disability' was formerly termed 'mental retardation.'

(IDEA, 2004, § 300.8(c)(6))

Multiple Disabilities

Multiple disabilities means concomitant impairments (such as intellectual disability-blindness or intellectual disability-orthopedic impairment), the combination of which causes such severe educational needs that they cannot be accommodated in special education programs solely for one of the impairments. Multiple disabilities does not include deaf-blindness.

(IDEA, 2004, § 300.8(c)(7))

Orthopedic Impairment

Orthopedic impairment means a severe orthopedic impairment that adversely affects a child's educational performance. The term includes impairments caused by a congenital anomaly, impairments caused by disease (e.g., poliomyelitis, bone tuberculosis), and impairments from other causes (e.g., cerebral palsy, amputations, and fractures or burns that cause contractures).

(IDEA, 2004, § 300.8(c)(8))

Other Health Impairment

Other health impairment means having limited strength, vitality, or alertness, including a heightened alertness to environmental stimuli, that results in limited alertness with respect to the educational environment, that is due to chronic or acute health problems such as asthma, attention deficit disorder or attention deficit hyperactivity disorder, diabetes, epilepsy, a heart condition, hemophilia, lead poisoning, leukemia, nephritis, rheumatic fever, sickle cell anemia, and Tourette syndrome; and adversely affects a child's educational performance.

(IDEA, 2004, § 300.8(c)(9))

Specific Learning Disability

Specific learning disability means a disorder in one or more of the basic psychological processes involved in understanding or in using language, spoken or written, that may manifest itself in the imperfect ability to listen, think, speak, read, write, spell, or to do mathematical calculations, including conditions such as perceptual disabilities, brain injury, minimal brain dysfunction, dyslexia, and developmental aphasia. . . . Specific learning disability does not include learning problems that are primarily the result of visual, hearing, or motor disabilities, of intellectual disability, of emotional disturbance, or of environmental, cultural, or economic disadvantage.

(IDEA, 2004, § 300.8(c)(10))

Speech or Language Impairment

Speech or language impairment means a communication disorder, such as stuttering, impaired articulation, a language impairment, or a voice impairment, that adversely affects a child's educational performance.

(IDEA, 2004, § 300.8(c)(11))

Traumatic Brain Injury

Traumatic brain injury means an acquired injury to the brain caused by an external physical force, resulting in total or partial functional disability or psychosocial impairment, or both, that adversely affects a child's educational performance. Traumatic brain injury applies to open or closed head injuries resulting in impairments in one or more areas, such as cognition; language; memory; attention; reasoning; abstract thinking; judgment; problem-solving; sensory, perceptual, and motor abilities; psychosocial behavior; physical functions; information processing; and speech. Traumatic brain injury does not apply to brain injuries that are congenital or degenerative, or to brain injuries induced by birth trauma.

(IDEA, 2004, § 300.8(c)(12))

Visual Impairment

Visual impairment, including blindness, means an impairment in vision that, even with correction, adversely affects a child's educational performance. The term includes both partial sight and blindness.

(IDEA, 2004, § 300.8(c)(13))

Special Education Services (IEP and IFSP) and Alternative Plans (Section 504 Service Agreement)

If a child is deemed eligible for special education services (the child is deemed to be a child with a disability, and there is evidence of need for special education services), an individualized education program (IEP) or individualized family service plan (IFSP) must be developed and implemented. If a child does not show evidence of need for specially designed instruction or special education services that are provided for under IDEA, he or she may receive accommodations under Section 504 of the Vocational Rehabilitation Act of 1973 (see above) through a Section 504 service agreement.

Individualized Education Program (IEP)

The individualized education program (IEP) is an educational program for children with disabilities and must by law include the following components (NASET, 2019; IDEA, 2004, § 300.320):

- *Present levels of academic and functional performance* is an indication of the student's current functioning that includes information about how the disability impacts the student's current involvement and progress in the general education curriculum.

- *Measurable annual goals* are developed as a means of determining what students should be able to accomplish during the IEP period in connection with special education services. Annual goals can be academic and/or functional goals, as appropriate. Further, short-term objectives or benchmarks are included for children who take alternative assessments instead of the regular assessments required by ESSA (as discussed earlier in the chapter).

- A statement will be made regarding *how progress toward meeting annual goals will be measured* and *when progress will be reported.*

- A statement will be made indicating *special education and related services/supplementary aids and services/program modifications* that will help students (1) attain their annual goals, (2) make progress in the general education curriculum, (3) participate in extracurricular and nonacademic activities, and (4) participate with children with and without disabilities.

  - Special education means "specially designed instruction, at no cost to the parents, to meet the unique needs of a child with a disability" (IDEA, 2004, § 300.39(a)(1)). Specially designed instruction (SDI) refers to the adaptation of content, methodology, and/or delivery of instruction for a child with a disability that will meet the unique needs of the child and ensure access to the general curriculum so that the child can meet the educational standards (IDEA, 2004, § 300.39(b)(3)).

  - *Related services* are services that support a child with a disability in benefiting from special education—such as transportation, speech-language pathology and audiology services, interpreting services, occupational therapy, physical therapy, nursing, orientation and mobility therapy, recreation, counseling services, medical services (only for diagnostic or evaluation purposes, not for ongoing treatment), social work, and parent counseling and training.

  - *Supplementary aids and services* are services to improve a child's access to the curriculum, extracurricular activities, and other nonacademic activities. They include assistive technology and paraprofessional support.

- A statement discussing the *extent of nonparticipation in the general education curriculum* will include an explanation of the extent, if any, to which the child will not participate with nondisabled peers in the regular class and in other school settings and activities.

- A description of any *testing accommodations or changes* that will be made to the student's participation in statewide or district-wide assessments. The team may decide whether the student can take the assessments as is, whether the student needs permissible accommodations (extra time, testing in another environment, etc.) to take the assessment, or whether the student needs some means of an alternative assessment (reported progress toward goals, portfolio, etc.).

- *Documentation of delivery of services* will include information about when services will begin, the frequency and duration of services, and the location in which services will be provided.

- *Transition services* will also be included in the IEP when the child turns 16, or earlier if deemed appropriate.

Individualized Family Service Plan (IFSP)

The special education law provides education and protection for infants and toddlers, ages 0 to 2, in Part C of IDEA. The program for infants and toddlers with disabilities requires states to operate a comprehensive statewide program of early intervention services. The individualized family service plan (IFSP) is the legal document that serves the child and the family, and it includes necessary supports and services. It will include strengths of both the child and the family, and it will address goals needed to support the child. Like the IEP, it must contain certain components (Parent Information Center, 2019; IDEA, 2004, § 303.344); however, there is a greater emphasis on the child, the family, and the environment. The IFSP includes:

- Information about the child's present level of physical, cognitive, communication, social/emotional, and adaptive development

- Information about the family's resources, priority, and concerns in improving the development of the child

- A statement of results or outcomes that are expected to be achieved by the child and family, along with strategies and ways in which progress will be measured

- A statement of the early intervention services that are needed to meet the needs of the child and family that includes the projected start date for services, as well as the "length, duration, frequency, intensity, and method" (IDEA, 2004, § 303.344(d)(1)(i)) for delivering the services (Services for children who are at least 3 years old will include school readiness skills, as well as pre-literacy skills, language skills, and numeracy skills.)

- A statement indicating that services will be provided in the child's natural environment to the greatest extent possible (If they aren't, a justification statement for why they can't occur in the natural environment will be made.)

- Transition services as appropriate

- A summary of documented medical services the child may need

- The contact information of the Service Coordinator and the names of all team members

Check Your Understanding 1.3

1. What is required for a child to be eligible for special education services?

2. What are the components of an IEP? Describe each.

3. Describe the components of an IFSP. How is an IFSP different from an IEP?

Alternative Means of Providing Accommodations to Children With Disabilities

Children who are not eligible for special education services because either they don't have a disability (as identified in Section 300.8 of IDEA) or they don't need special education services and specially designed instruction may receive accommodations under Section 504 of the Vocational Rehabilitation Act of 1973 (as discussed earlier in the chapter). In Section 504, "disability" is defined broadly as a physical or mental disability ("any physiological disorder or condition, cosmetic disfigurement, or anatomical loss affecting one or more of the following body systems: neurological; musculoskeletal; special sense organs; respiratory, including speech organs; cardiovascular; reproductive; digestive; genito-urinary; hemic and lymphatic; skin; and endocrine; or any mental or psychological disorder, such as [intellectual disabilities], organic brain syndrome, emotional or mental illness, and specific learning disabilities" [OCR, 2018, Question 11]) that substantially limits one or more of the following major life activities: "walking, seeing, hearing, speaking, breathing, learning, working . . . eating, sleeping, standing, lifting, bending, reading, concentrating, thinking, communicating . . . major bodily functions (functions of the immune system, normal cell growth, digestive, bowel, bladder, neurological, brain, respiratory, circulatory, endocrine, and reproductive functions)" (OCR, 2018, Question 11). An individual who might not qualify under IDEA might be considered to have a disability under these guidelines.

Students who are served under Section 504 will not have an IEP or IFSP but will instead have a Section 504 service agreement that outlines what accommodations, medications, and aids they may need. Examples of accommodations are preferential seating, extended time on tests and assignments, reduced workload, assistive technology aides, organizational materials, adapted tests, use of audio materials such as voice-output devices, excused absences, provisions for lateness, and therapies.

Check Your Understanding 1.4

1. How does a Section 504 service agreement differ from an IEP or IFSP?

2. What is included in a Section 504 service agreement?

Looking Ahead

Throughout the course of the text, the goal is to develop a better understanding of the role that assessment plays in the diagnosis of a disability, determination of eligibility for special education services, and education of students with disabilities. While special education teachers may not be the ones to conduct comprehensive evaluations of students, it is paramount that they possess a strong understanding of student characteristics in all areas, as well as a true understanding of how assessment is used to determine diagnosis and eligibility in order to effectively teach students with disabilities. It is central to their being the most informed and ultimately effective special educators that they can be and is critical to their pedagogical expertise. This text will help prepare teachers to be able to provide the most comprehensive instruction to students.

- Part I of the text provides the background in assessment that is necessary for comprehending and applying the components of a comprehensive evaluation that would be included in evaluating a student for special education services under IDEA. More specifically, it includes an overall introduction to topics related to assessment, a discussion of assessment types, and an overview of assessment in different areas of student characteristics that can be used for diagnosis and eligibility purposes.

- Part II provides a description of the diagnostic and eligibility criteria and the assessment process associated with the IDEA categories of disability that may be diagnosed in an educational or a private setting.

- Part III provides a description of the diagnostic and eligibility criteria and the assessment process associated with disabilities, disorders, conditions, and syndromes associated with the IDEA categories of disability that are generally diagnosed not in an educational setting, but rather in a medical setting. The purpose of the chapters in Part III is to facilitate the understanding of medically diagnosed disabilities and to promote an awareness of the diagnostic criteria and their relevance to eligibility for special education services under IDEA. Further, they focus on the impact that each disability may have on education, as well as differences that may occur based on the age of onset or diagnosis (prenatal, perinatal, and postnatal).

- Part IV focuses on the effective use of assessment results to make educational decisions for students.

CHAPTER SUMMARY

There is a rich history that has brought us to the present state of special education services. Special education law is very clear on procedures for the initial identification and evaluation of students who may need supports and services. It requires strict adherence to the guidelines, to ensure that students with special needs receive the most appropriate services that are unique to their needs. The law further states the importance of developing an education program (IEP or IFSP) for instruction that takes into consideration the specific characteristics of the individual. The focus of the text will now shift to the assessment, diagnosis, and eligibility of students with special needs.

APPLY WHAT YOU HAVE LEARNED

1. Select a time in history to research, and write a summary of the state of special education at that time. What was going on specifically for children with disabilities? How is it different from today?

2. Choose three of the court cases discussed in the chapter, research each of their findings, and discuss how they impacted special education legislation.

3. List the 14 IDEA categories of disability, and circle the disabilities for which you know someone personally who has the disability. Of the disabilities that you circled, choose three, and list the educational characteristics (both strengths and needs) that you have noticed about that person.

REFERENCES

Americans With Disabilities Act of 1990, Pub. L. No. 101-336, 104 Stat. 328 (1990).

Brown v. Board of Educ., 347 U.S. 483 (1954).

Dunn, L. M. (1968). Special education for the mildly retarded—is much of it justifiable? *Exceptional Children, 35*, 5–22.

Elementary and Secondary Education Act, amended by Pub. L. No. 89-750 §161 [Title VI], 80 Stat. 1204 (1966).

Endrew v. Douglas County School District, 580 U.S. (2017).

Every Student Succeeds Act, 20 U.S.C. § 6301 *et seq.* (2015).

Friend, M. (2018). *Special education: Contemporary perspectives for school professionals.* New York, NY: Pearson.

Heward, W. L. (2006). *Exceptional children: An introduction to special education* (8th ed.). Upper Saddle River, NJ: Pearson Education/Merrill/Prentice Hall.

Individuals With Disabilities Education Act, 20 U.S.C. § 1400 *et seq.* (2012).

Katsiyannis, A., Yell, M. L., & Bradley, R. (2001). Reflections on the 25th anniversary of the Individuals With Disabilities Education Act. *Remedial and Special Education, 22,* 324–334.

Mills v. Board of Education, 348 F. Supp. 866 (D.D.C. 1972).

National Association for Special Education Teachers (NASET). (2019). *IEP components.* Retrieved from https://www.naset.org/3321.0.html

No Child Left Behind Act, 20 U.S.C. § 16301 *et seq.* (2001).

Office for Civil Rights (OCR). (2018). *Protecting students with disabilities: Frequently asked questions about Section 504 and the education of children with disabilities.* Retrieved from https://www2.ed.gov/about/offices/list/ocr/504faq.html

Parent Information Center. (2019). *What's an IFSP?* Retrieved from https://picnh.org/ifsp/

Pennsylvania Association of Retarded Citizens (PARC) v. Commonwealth of Pennsylvania, 343 F. Supp. 279 (E.D. PA 1972).

Rehabilitation Act of 1973, Section 504, 29 U.S.C. § 794

Supreme Court of the United States. (2017). Endrew F., a minor, by and through his parents and next friends, Joseph F. and Jennifer F., petitioner v. Douglas County School District Re-1 580 U. S. ____ (2017). Retrieved from https://www.supremecourt.gov/opinions/16pdf/15-827_0pm1.pdf

U.S. Department of Education. (n.d.). *Every Student Succeeds Act (ESSA).* Retrieved from https://www.ed.gov/essa

U.S. Department of Education. (2019). *Every Student Succeeds Act (ESSA).* Retrieved from https://www2.ed.gov/policy/elsec/leg/essa/index.html

U.S. Department of Education & Office of Elementary and Secondary Education. (2018). *Understanding the Every Student Succeeds Act: A parents' guide to the nation's landmark education law.* Washington, DC: U.S. Department of Education & Office of Elementary and Secondary Education.

U.S. Department of Education & Office of Special Education and Rehabilitative Services. (2010). *Thirty-five years of progress in educating children with disabilities through IDEA.* Washington, DC: U.S. Department of Education & Office of Special Education and Rehabilitative Services.

U.S. Department of Justice Civil Rights Division. (n.d.). *Introduction to the ADA.* Retrieved from https://www.ada.gov/ada_intro.htm

Yell, M. L. (2016). *The law and special education.* New York, NY: Pearson.

Yell, M. L., Katsiyannis, A., & Hazelkorn, M. (2007). Reflections on the 25th anniversary of the U.S. Supreme Court's decision in *Board of Education v. Rowley. Focus on Exceptional Children, 39*(9), 1–12.

CHAPTER

2

Introduction to Assessment and Ethical Considerations

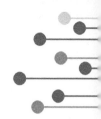

Mary A. Houser, EdD

Learning Objectives

After completion of this chapter, you should be able to:

- Define assessment in an educational context.

- Distinguish between the purposes of assessment: screening, pre-referral considerations, diagnosis, eligibility, and the relationship between instruction and assessment.

- Explain Multi-tiered System of Support (MTSS) and Response to Intervention (RTI).

- Discuss progress monitoring and benchmarks as they apply to the assessment process.

- Investigate considerations for students from culturally and linguistically diverse backgrounds during the assessment process.

- Examine ethical considerations surrounding assessment.

Key Terms

assessment loop (p. 30)	mediation (p. 48)
assessment (p. 24)	multi-tiered system of support (MTSS) (p. 33)
benchmark assessment (p. 38)	pre-referral (p. 25)
diagnosis (p. 28)	procedural safeguards (p. 46)
due process (p. 48)	progress monitoring (p. 38)
eligibility (p. 29)	Response to Intervention (RTI) (p. 34)
evidence-based strategies (p. 25)	screening (p. 24)
formative assessment (p. 31)	Section 504 plan (p. 30)
independent educational evaluation (IEE) (p. 48)	summative assessment (p. 31)

Introduction to the Chapter

Assessment is fundamental to the successful identification, placement, and programming of children with disabilities. **Assessment** in education "refers to the wide variety of methods or tools that educators use to evaluate, measure, and document the academic readiness, learning progress, skill acquisition, or educational needs of students" (Great Schools Partnership, 2015, para. 1). Assessments can take many forms, from standardized formal assessments to informal criterion-referenced assessments. No single test or assessment demonstrates a child's full range of abilities or challenges, and a variety of educators often contribute to the overall assessment process. Depending on the state, the special educator's involvement in the diagnostic evaluation can vary. Criteria differ by state as to who can conduct the various assessments in an evaluation; however, all special educators should fully understand the diagnosis, the diagnostic process, and the eligibility for each disability. Without this knowledge, there can never be a true understanding of the disability, how it affects the child, and subsequently the decisions that are made when planning for instruction. This chapter examines the screening process for potential disabilities through the comprehensive evaluation.

Purposes of Assessment

Assessment plays a critical role in helping special educators understand the strengths and challenges that our students bring to school. In realizing our students' strengths, we can capitalize on their abilities, to help them to learn more effectively. If challenges exist, assessments help us pinpoint their exact problem areas and determine whether those are academic, behavioral, or social in nature. In order for us to best educate our students with disabilities, we must first know how they are performing. The process of determining such performance begins with the screening process, then evaluation, followed by providing a diagnosis, determining eligibility for special education services, and planning for instruction.

Screening

Screening is a process that alerts educators and medical professionals to developmental problems a child may be experiencing and suggests whether a more in-depth evaluation is needed. Most public schools screen children for developmental problems that can put them at risk of school failure.

Screening occurs in large numbers and is not a precise process. There are some common characteristics among screening instruments, however: they are easy to administer, contain few items, and can be completed in a short time. They may be in the form of pencil-and-paper tests, checklists, rating scales, or even direct observations of skills and/or abilities. Examples of screening instruments are the Snellan chart for visual acuity and the Iowa Test of Basic Skills for Reading, Language, Mathematics, Social Studies, and Science (Rosenberg, Westling, & McLeskey, 2010). Educators should be cautious not to infer too much about eligibility. IDEA specifically states, "the screening of a student by a teacher or specialist to determine appropriate instructional strategies for curriculum implementation shall not be considered to be an evaluation for eligibility for special education and related services" (IDEA, 2004, § 300.302).

As mentioned in Chapter 1, public schools are required to screen students for suspected disabilities. This is a primary function of the Child Find program. Child Find requires all school districts in the United States to identify, locate, and evaluate children with disabilities from birth through age 21. Medical professionals also conduct screenings to determine how children are developing. Doctors, nurses, and other healthcare professionals are all qualified to conduct such screenings. For example, young children undergo periodic screenings at their well-child visits to the pediatrician (CDC, 2018). Such screenings are typically a brief test or a questionnaire that a parent completes about his child. These include questions addressing a child's language, movement, thinking, behavior, and emotions. In addition to those mentioned, autism-specific screenings have been added to the list of recommended screening tools. The American Academy of Pediatrics (2018) recommends developmental screenings for children during regular well-child visits at the following ages:

- 9 months
- 18 months
- 24 or 30 months

Pre-Referral Consideration

Once the screening process has occurred and specific challenges have been identified, the next step is often to begin the pre-referral process. Pre-referral is a preliminary process by which evidence-based strategies and accommodations are implemented for general education students who are having academic, behavioral, and/or social challenges. The primary goal of pre-referral is to resolve existing challenges a student is demonstrating before a referral to special education is made on his behalf. Pre-referral typically is initiated in the general education classroom by the general education teacher, who consults with other general education teachers, special education teachers, or related personnel for ideas on how to address challenges that a student is exhibiting. Sometimes, a child's difficulties can be remedied by providing him with an accommodation, such as preferential seating or use of an alternate teaching method. Other times, however, a referral to special education for a comprehensive diagnostic evaluation is needed. IDEA does not require schools to have pre-referral teams, but many times such teams do exist to help support the child and his needs. Members of a pre-referral team often include individuals similar to those on the IEP team, such as general education teachers, parents, special education teachers, administrators, and school psychologists, to name a few. It should be noted that if a parent makes an official request for a comprehensive evaluation of his child, this bypasses the pre-referral process entirely.

The pre-referral process (see Figure 2.1) occurs across a series of six distinct stages that are both sequential and developmental in nature.

Stage 1: Initial Concern Regarding Student's Progress

During this stage, the student is in a general education setting and his teacher and/or parents become concerned about his performance and/or behavior. Often, a student in this situation will lag academically behind his peers both in terms of his classwork and his performance on assessments. Teachers might notice behaviors that indicate a student is struggling, such as frustration, anxiety, or withdrawal. Parents might notice their child is not interested in going to school and might even display a poor self-concept.

Stage 2: Information-Gathering

During this stage, the teacher and parents begin to gather information about the student's performance, with the intent of using it later on to make educational decisions. Examples of information that could be gathered are test/quiz scores, observations, or even parent or teacher interviews. A pre-referral team might examine a student's educational background, or, in the case of a student with behavioral challenges, explore past classroom behavior management techniques that have been implemented and the degree to which they were successful. All of these can provide valuable insight into the challenges that a student is presenting.

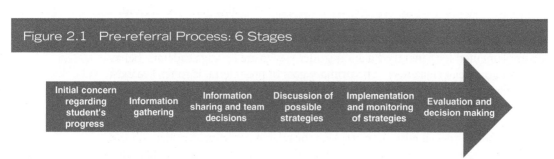

Figure 2.1   Pre-referral Process: 6 Stages

Initial concern regarding student's progress | Information gathering | Information sharing and team decisions | Discussion of possible strategies | Implementation and monitoring of strategies | Evaluation and decision making

IRIS Center. (2018). *What are the stages of the pre-referral process and what do they involve?* Retrieved from http://iris.peabody.vanderbilt.edu/module/preref/cresource/q2/p03

Stage 3: Information-Sharing and Team Decision

During this stage, the pre-referral team meets to share the information that was gathered about the student's performance and to make decisions about how to proceed. For example, the team might share and discuss test results in specific academic areas where the student is having problems, or the parent(s) might inform the team that the child has recently started taking a new medication that could be affecting his learning and/or behavior. New evidence-based classroom strategies are often used in the general education classroom to help the child succeed.

Stage 4: Discussion of Possible Strategies

The pre-referral team will identify specific interventions to implement, based on the needs of the student. These are evidence-based practices, such as direct instruction, peer-mediated instruction, and cooperative learning, to name a few. Accommodations might also be considered, such as preferential seating, extended time for test taking, and the use of a scribe. The types of strategies considered will be specific to each student and his own particular needs. The overarching idea, however, is to try different strategies that will reduce or eliminate the difficulties that the student is exhibiting.

Stage 5: Implementation and Monitoring of Strategies

During this stage, the general education teacher, with the support of special education professionals (if needed), will implement the interventions discussed. Adequate time will be allowed for the new interventions to take effect, and they will be closely monitored for effectiveness. For academics, using a curriculum-based measurement (CBM) is a fast and easy way to track data. For behavior, a data recording sheet that focuses on one or more dimensions of behavior (frequency, duration, latency, etc.) might be used to record important behavioral data. Implementation and monitoring of strategies will help the pre-referral team determine whether there is a way to manage the student's learning and/or behavioral needs in general education.

Stage 6: Evaluation and Decision-Making

During this stage, the pre-referral team will review the results of the intervention strategies. They will examine the data taken and make decisions about whether the student can be successful in the general education classroom with the changes that have been implemented or whether the interventions tried were unsuccessful. If the strategies implemented were successful, the child will remain in the general education setting using these new interventions. If the strategies were unsuccessful, the pre-referral team will discuss the need for the child to have a comprehensive diagnostic evaluation to determine whether there is a disability and, if so, whether the child is eligible for special education.

It should be stated that the pre-referral process requires quality communication between the school and the child's parents. Throughout the pre-referral process, it is important that the pre-referral team keep the student's family aware of what is happening and what next steps will be taken. Although the parents are not required to give consent for the pre-referral process to be conducted, they are key stakeholders in the process and are typically the ones most familiar with the student's development, in addition to having a vested interest in his well-being.

Check Your Understanding 2.1

1. Why is screening children for a potential disability necessary? Who is qualified to conduct screenings?

2. What is the purpose of a pre-referral team? Are all states required to have them?

Who customarily composes a pre-referral team?

3. Summarize the six stages of the pre-referral process.

Diagnosis and Eligibility

As discussed, pre-referral is the process in which general education strategies are implemented in specific ways in an attempt to resolve the academic, behavioral, or social problems a child is experiencing. If the pre-referral strategies that have been implemented are successful, the child remains in general education, having received the needed help and attention to his challenges. If the pre-referral interventions are unsuccessful, the next step is often to refer the student for a comprehensive diagnostic evaluation for special education services. According to IDEA (2004), either a parent or the public agency (school) may initiate the request for an initial evaluation to determine the presence of a disability.

Diagnosis is the process by which an individual's specific disability is identified. To date, there is no standard battery of tests or procedures that will determine whether a child has a disability. Depending on the disability, different individuals can make a diagnosis. These may include a school psychologist, a private clinician (e.g., learning specialist, mental health provider, audiologist), or a medical provider. This is the first step in determining whether a child will need special education. As discussed in Chapter 1, 14 disability categories (autism, traumatic brain injury, intellectual disabilities, etc.) are recognized under IDEA. Unless diagnosed with one of these 14 disabilities, the child will not be eligible to receive special education services. It is important to note, however, that simply having a disability, condition, or syndrome does not guarantee a child's eligibility for special education.

Eligibility for special education refers to a child being *qualified* to receive special education services. Eligibility is determined by an IEP team (aka "multidisciplinary or child study team") composed of various school professionals. The purpose of this team is to collaborate on behalf on the student to determine the reason(s) why he is exhibiting challenges.

Table 2.1 sets out the typical members of the IEP team and their respective roles.

There are three requirements for a child to be eligible to receive special education services. First, he must be diagnosed with one of the 14 disabilities under IDEA, as mentioned above. Second, the disability must negatively impact the child's educational performance. Third, the child must need and benefit from specially designed instruction.

In some cases, these requirements are easily met. To illustrate, an 8-year-old child is diagnosed with a traumatic brain injury (TBI) following a car accident. After the accident, this child, who was previously educated in the general education classroom, begins to demonstrate significant challenges in learning across his academic subjects. After pre-referral strategies are implemented with little success, he is referred for a special education evaluation, in which necessary assessments are performed. The results of the assessments indicate that the child's abilities (e.g., sensory, behavioral, or emotional abilities) have been significantly impacted by the brain injury, warranting specially designed instruction in order for him to effectively learn in school. Therefore, this child is eligible for special education services.

Table 2.1   IEP Team Members and Their Roles

Parents/guardians—a mother, father, or other person who legally raises and cares for a child

School psychologist—an individual who conducts or oversees the comprehensive evaluation, which includes a diagnostic battery of tests to determine the presence of a disability and eligibility for special education services

School administrator—an individual who oversees administrative duties at school (e.g., leadership, curriculum, goals, state regulations, testing) and who can inform the team about policy as well as enforce it

Special educator—an individual who provides instruction and support to students with disabilities

General educator—an individual who has a deep knowledge of the general education curriculum and provides instruction and support within the general education setting to both students with and students without disabilities

Related service personnel—individuals who provide services such as occupational therapy, speech therapy, physical therapy, and transportation to students with disabilities

Local education agency representative—an individual who represents the school system and possesses knowledge about its special education system and resources

Evaluation diagnostician—an individual who is trained in assessment and is able to interpret and discuss assessment results with the IEP team as they relate to designing a student's individualized educational program (Depending on the state, this individual may be able to administer a variety of assessments.)

Student—the K–12 child who is being considered for or receiving special education services

Conversely, a child can have a disability covered under IDEA and not be eligible for special education services. For example, a developmental pediatrician diagnoses a child with autism spectrum disorder (ASD). This child is considered to be high-functioning, or having many skills. His IQ is average or above average, and he performs well academically in the general education setting. In addition, he is able to manage his own behavior and has a couple of friends. Therefore, although this child has been diagnosed with a disability, ASD, he does not qualify for special education services. Why? Because his disability does not negatively impact his educational performance and he is not in need of specially designed instruction in order to be successful at school. In these types of circumstances, although ineligible for special education services, a child might be eligible for accommodations under Section 504 of the Rehabilitation Act of 1973 (as discussed in greater detail in Chapters 1, 11, and 14). These are also referred to as Section 504 plans. In this case, a Section 504 plan may be developed to provide needed accommodations because specially designed instruction and special education services are not needed or warranted.

The Relationship Between Assessment and Instruction

Once screening, diagnosis, and eligibility have been discussed, the IEP team then moves on to making instructional decisions based on both the results of the completed assessments and the characteristics of the disability or disabilities that have been identified. There are several instructional matters that will be taken into consideration in order to provide a student with the most appropriate education that addresses his particular needs. Considerations such as the educational setting(s) in which he will be educated, the duration and frequency of a particular therapy, and the degree to which he will be included in the general education setting will all be part of this planning process. All of these instructional decisions are directly linked to the results of the comprehensive evaluation, making the relationship between assessment and instruction undisputable. Once the testing has been completed, the IEP team will work closely together to create the best possible individualized educational program (IEP), including special education services and related services for the student, taking into consideration the student's personal strengths and challenges. After the IEP has been implemented and adequate time has been afforded, the IEP team will need to revisit the goals and objectives they have set forth for the student to determine whether the plan they have created is appropriate. Once again, the concept of assessment is directly linked to instruction. Chapter 14 will more thoroughly discuss the IEP and the process surrounding its development and implementation.

Assessment and instruction are interwoven in many ways. One process that is currently used by special education teachers to determine the gains that students are making at school which demonstrates this apparent connectivity is referred to as the assessment loop (see Figure 2.2). The assessment loop is the cyclical process of identifying learning goals, instructing and learning, evaluating, and reteaching or reinforcing, as appropriate.

The assessment loop begins with identifying learning goals. The special educator must ask himself: *What is it that I am trying to teach my students? What is my ultimate goal(s) for student learning?* It might be a simple concept, such as learning to count to five, or a much loftier goal, such as how to write a research paper. Once a learning goal(s) has been identified, the special education teacher will begin his instruction by employing evidence-based teaching practices, and student learning will take place. The special educator will then evaluate the students to determine whether they have sufficiently mastered the concept(s). This can be done either formally or informally, at the discretion of the teacher. Students might be administered a quiz or a test. They might be asked to write a short essay, or the special education teacher might review their portfolios or simply observe them while they work. At this point in the assessment loop, one of two things will occur: (1) the students will have not adequately learned the content presented to them and the special edu-

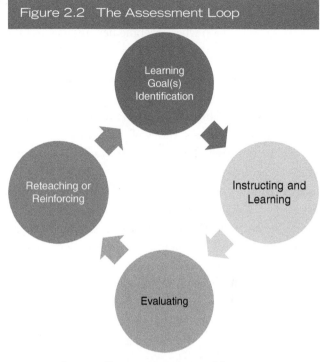

Figure 2.2 The Assessment Loop

cation teacher must reteach the content using new and more effective strategies; or (2) the students will have mastered the content and they are reinforced for a job well done. If the latter is the case, the assessment loop has been completed and will begin once again. Ultimately, the assessment loop reinforces the notion that assessment does not exist by itself; rather, it is closely tied to instruction.

There are two processes by which a student can be assessed in the assessment loop process: formative and summative. In **formative assessment**, the primary goal is to observe student progress and to provide regular feedback that can improve teaching and student learning. It is considered a low-stakes form of assessment, because it typically does not assign a point value. According to Carnegie Mellon University (2019), this process allows students to identify areas of strengths and weaknesses as well as pinpoint areas that need improvement. Additionally, formative assessment provides teachers knowledge of students who are struggling and allows them to address their problems in an expedited manner (para. 1). Examples of formative assessments are journaling, exit tickets, "vote with thumbs," self-assessment, one-minute essays, and observation.

Summative assessment, on the other hand, is used for the purpose of evaluating student learning. In summative assessment, the teacher is looking at the student's culminating progress in a high-stakes manner by comparing it against a benchmark or standard and assigning point value (Carnegie Mellon University, 2019). Examples of summative assessments are chapter tests, standardized tests, portfolios, and achievement tests.

In the following case study, depicting the cyclical nature of an assessment loop, a middle-school math teacher demonstrates the steps in a typical assessment loop when teaching her students the algebraic concept of integer factorization.

Case Study 2.1: Pre-Algebra Instruction via the Assessment Loop

Mrs. Auer is an eighth-grade pre-algebra teacher at Nottingham Middle School. This week she is teaching her students integer factorization. She carefully plans out her lessons for the week, allowing ample time for instruction and guided practice. After all, this has been a concept that her students have struggled with in the past. When her students come to class on Monday morning, she introduces the topic and provides explicit instruction on how to factor integers. Her students listen attentively as she goes over each step in the process. The following day, Mrs. Auer has the students engage in guided practice problems factoring integers. Carefully, she works her way around the classroom, answering questions and checking her students' understanding to ensure that they are on the right track when solving these practice problems. As class time moves on, Mrs. Auer feels more confident that her students are able to factor integers. On Tuesday, Mrs. Auer assigns homework problems on this pre-algebraic concept. Mrs. Auer begins class on Wednesday by going over each of the homework questions. She asks for volunteers to go to the whiteboard to share their answers with others. The students spend the remainder of the class period working through these problems. At the end of class, Mrs. Auer announces that the following day there will be a quiz on integer factorization. On Thursday, she gives her students a 10-item quiz. As she looks around the room, she can see her students busily solving the quiz problems. This gives her a sense of relief, because she has worked hard to teach them this challenging concept. Upon grading her quizzes, Mrs. Auer calculates that more than the majority of the students have earned a score of mastery or higher. She rewards her students with free computer time at the end of class and tells them that she is proud of their progress. This pleases her students, because they enjoy playing educational games on the classroom computers. Realizing that her students have grasped integer factorization, Mrs. Auer plans to teach a new algebraic concept the following day. She will follow the same teach/assess process as she did with integer factorization.

Check Your Understanding 2.2

1. What is the assessment loop? How it is demonstrated in Mrs. Auer's pre-algebra classroom?

2. How does Mrs. Auer ensure that her students will want to do well on the next quiz?

3. Think back to your own P–12 educational experiences. Provide an example of when one of your teachers used the assessment loop when teaching a concept.

Multi-Tiered System of Support (MTSS)

It is paramount that special education teachers understand the notion that students with disabilities need to be adequately supported in their learning process. When teaching students with disabilities, we cannot simply deliver content to them in the same way as we do typically developing students, because they will need extra assistance to reach their academic, behavioral, and social goals. Multi-tiered system of support (MTSS) is a *framework* of standards-aligned, comprehensive school improvement that began as an effort to improve the way that educators were identifying and supporting children who need special education services. This broad-based approach addresses the academic, social, emotional, and behavioral development of children through their school experiences. MTSS incorporates Response to Intervention (RTI), curriculum design, positive behavior intervention and supports (PBIS), teacher-learner collaboration, and home-school collaboration in problem-solving (Lexia, 2018, para. 6). In order to procure the best outcome, MTSS also requires considerable collaboration between general education and special education teachers. All educators are responsible for maintaining their specific roles and responsibilities in order to support continuous improvement.

The concept behind MTSS is to document student performance as a means of indicating their need for additional services once the pre-referral changes have been made to classroom instruction. Table 2.2 gives examples of MTSS components.

Response to Intervention (RTI)

Another way that we can support the learning needs of students with disabilities is to identify their challenges in a timely manner. The sooner that we are able to identify students' challenges, the sooner we will be able to intervene and make

---

Table 2.2 MTSS Components

1. *High-quality, differentiated instruction*—every student receives high-quality instruction by highly qualified teachers in the general education classroom. There is a focus on culturally and linguistically relevant instruction.

2. *Systemic and sustainable change*—continuous improvement is evident at all levels (district, school, grade).

3. *Integrated data system*—districts and schools create an integrated data-collection system that includes state tests, universal screenings, diagnostics, and progress monitoring to help inform decisions about student placement in the tiered system.

4. *Positive behavioral support*—districts and schools focus on implementing both schoolwide and classroom positive behavioral support so that their students will increase their social and learning outcomes.

California Department of Education. (2019). MTSS components. Retrieved from https://www.cde.ca.gov/ci/cr/ri/mtss-components.asp

their educational programming more effective in meeting their needs. **Response to Intervention (RTI)** is another multi-tiered support system used when identifying students with learning and behavioral needs during the early years of their education. The purpose of this approach is to (1) provide all students with the best opportunities to succeed in school, (2) identify students with learning and behavioral problems, and (3) ensure that they receive appropriate instruction and related services (National Center on Response to Intervention, 2010).

RTI is one component of MTSS. It was founded in the 1970s when researchers were trying to determine a better way to identify students with specific learning disabilities. At this time, schools relied on the discrepancy model to identify students with potential learning disabilities. This model assessed students by determining whether there was a discrepancy between their IQs and their achievement in particular subject areas. A discrepancy suggested the presence of a learning disability (this will be discussed more in Chapter 6). RTI, on the other hand, has offered a relatively new approach to targeting students with learning difficulties through the use of "tiered" instruction. This approach has proven to be both effective and possibly faster than the discrepancy model alone at identifying potential learning problems. In 2004, IDEA not only included RTI as a process by which school districts could identify students with specific learning disabilities (SLDs) but also began to provide funding to start RTI programs at both the district and the state level (NEA, 2017).

RTI has many features that aid in identifying students who might need special education services. As previously mentioned, RTI is an approach that occurs in the general education setting, and typically students are not considered for a referral to special education until they have been unsuccessful at Tier 3 (the three tiers will be discussed in depth in the next section). Table 2.3 lists four essential requirements of a successful RTI classroom.

Table 2.3 Response to Intervention (RTI) Components
1. *High quality, scientifically based instruction*—teaching that employs systematic, empirical methods that use rigorous data analysis, relies on reliable and valid data, and is validated using an experiment
2. *Ongoing student assessment*—a continual process of determining a student's progress through evaluation. This type of progress monitoring helps teachers keep track of a student's academic performance, quantify a student rate of improvement or responsiveness to instruction, and evaluate the effectiveness of instruction (Center for Response to Intervention, n.d., para. 1). Parents may also request a psycho-educational evaluation for special education services at any point in the RTI process.
3. *Tiered instruction*—differentiating instruction to meet the child's needs
4. *Parent involvement*—communication with parents/guardians to inform them of their child's progress as well as obtain suggestions for supporting the child's progress

RTI Action Network. (2018). *What is RTI?* Retrieved from http://www.rtinetwork.org/learn/what/whatisrti

RTI uses a tiered approach to identifying students with academic and behavioral concerns. There are typically three tiers (see Figure 2.3). Each tier dictates a specific amount, intensity, and frequency of instruction and support a student will need to be successful. The following is the common sequence of RTI:

Before a child enters an RTI placement, a universal screening should occur. Universal screenings usually are conducted a few times a year to identify students who are at risk of academic, behavioral, or social challenges. A universal screening is a brief assessment of targeted skills to determine early on whether a child will need additional support and instruction. If a child's scores fall below a specific cutoff point on the universal assessment, he will then be assigned to Tier 1 in an RTI program. The following is a discussion of the three different tiers.

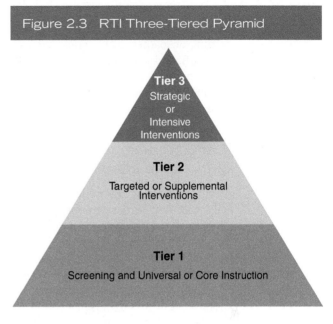

Figure 2.3   RTI Three-Tiered Pyramid

Tier 1 (Primary Level of Prevention): Universal or Core Instruction

All students assigned to general education placements in an RTI classroom will begin their education in Tier 1. Tier 1 placements constitute the majority of the public school students receiving this intervention (approximately 80%). In this placement, all students receive high-quality classroom instruction by highly qualified teachers. This tier is sometimes referred to as the "universal or core" instructional intervention and is considered the least intense level of RTI. Typically, the goal of Tier 1 is for all students to meet minimal proficiency on benchmark assessments reflecting state standards. Students who are not academically and/or behaviorally successful in Tier 1 will move up to Tier 2.

Tier 2 (Secondary Level of Prevention): Targeted or Supplemental Interventions

Tier 2 allows for more targeted or supplemental intervention. Students who are placed in this tier have demonstrated lower than expected proficiency on benchmark assessments. Therefore, they are performing below grade level and require intervention. This constitutes approximately 15% of the student population. While in Tier 2, students receive small-group instruction (three to five students per group) and individualized instruction (as needed) in the areas of academic skills (typically reading or mathematics) and/or behavior. Sessions are generally 20 to 40 minutes in length, and students typically meet three to four times a week (National Center on Response to Intervention, 2010). This is considered a moderate-intensity intervention that uses evidence-based interventions. Progress is monitored weekly or biweekly. If students are not successful in Tier 2, they will be moved up to Tier 3.

Tier 3 (Tertiary Level of Prevention): Strategic or Intensive Interventions

Tier 3 is the most intense level of the RTI model. Approximately 5% of students will need Tier 3 interventions. At this level, students are performing well below their expected grade level, requiring intensive support and instruction. In this tier, group size is usually one to three students. Students will have longer sessions and will meet more frequently with their instructors than in Tier 2. In most cases, the individuals responsible for the intervention session require specialized training, such as a reading specialist, counselor, or special education teacher. Progress monitoring occurs weekly. If a child is unsuccessful at Tier 3, it is then appropriate to refer him for a comprehensive diagnostic evaluation to determine whether he should receive special education services.

It is relevant to note that students may be in different tiers for different subjects. To illustrate, a student may be in Tier 1 for mathematics and Tier 2 for reading. Not all students will remain in the more intense RTI tiers: Tier 2 or Tier 3. For some students, it might be appropriate to discontinue Tier 2 or Tier 3 intervention if they have demonstrated required progress. In order for this to occur, students must typically achieve predetermined criteria prior to implementing the RTI approach. Special education teachers should be cautious not to discontinue intervention too early, as this can result in undesirable outcomes if a student is not ready to resume his learning in a more typical setting.

The following case study depicts a student's journey through the RTI process. It discusses the student's learning challenges prior to entering RTI and explains his progress as he moves throughout this intervention, which eventually suggests that a referral to special education is warranted.

Case Study 2.2: Sonny's RTI Journey

Sonny is a friendly, happy student in Mr. Markel's first-grade class. He lives with his three brothers, his two sisters, and his mother and father. Sonny is excited to be at school and to learn. He told Mr. Markel last week that he wants to grow up to be an astronaut. This has been a difficult school year for Sonny, however. In particular, he has been struggling with reading comprehension. Recently, Sonny and his classmates partook in a universal screening at school. As it turned out, Sonny failed a portion of the screening, demonstrating problems in reading. Mr. Markel spoke with Sonny's parents about the results of the assessment and suggested that he be moved to an RTI classroom to support his reading needs in the coming days. He stated this might be a good way to see whether Sonny's reading challenges could be resolved in a regular education classroom or whether there were more significant reading problems at hand. Sonny's parents were surprised, because they were not aware that he was struggling, but they agreed to get the help that he needed to be successful in school. Sonny began his Tier 1 RTI classroom placement the following week and met his new teacher, Mrs. Harry.

Mrs. Harry's classroom was very different from Mr. Markel's classroom. In this classroom, the teacher was differentiating reading instruction for her students. It was a busy classroom, and Mrs. Harry worked hard to meet each student's needs. Although she worked diligently with Sonny, he was not able to make adequate progress. He still struggled and was not able to achieve his reading comprehension goals. After several weeks of Tier 1 intervention, Sonny was moved to a Tier 2 reading classroom taught by Ms. Davis. During his time in Ms. Davis's class, Sonny received reading instruction in small groups, and the instruction occurred more frequently than in Mrs. Harry's reading class. Sonny attended Ms. Davis's class four times a week, and his parents were glad that the school was providing quality instruction to their son, but they could tell that Sonny was still frustrated when reading. The pre-referral team met once again and decided that if by the end of the month Sonny was not making adequate progress it would be necessary for him to be moved up to Tier 3, the most intensive RTI reading classroom. Unfortunately, Sonny's progress was minimal at the Tier 2 level, and so he was moved to Mrs. Henrichson's Tier 3 reading classroom. Most of Sonny's time with Mrs. Henrichson was spent in one-on-one instruction. Together, Mrs. Henrichson and Sonny worked hard to close some of the learning gaps and to increase his ability to comprehend and retain the information that he read. After a few weeks, Mrs. Henrichson indicated that she had significant concerns about Sonny's reading skills. She noted that he could not remember sight words or homonyms. He could not easily create rhymes. His handwriting was very poor, and she was concerned about the possibility of both dyslexia and dysgraphia. Sonny's mother indicated that her brother had dyslexia, and she wondered whether Sonny also had a reading learning disability. The pre-referral team decided that a comprehensive assessment of his skills would be necessary to determine the presence of a disability. The next step was to obtain written consent from Sonny's parents to perform a comprehensive diagnostic evaluation.

Check Your Understanding 2.3

1. Briefly describe the differences between Tier 1, Tier 2, and Tier 3 in Response to Intervention (RTI).

2. Explain Sonny's parents' reaction when Mr. Markel told them about the results of his universal screening and his apparent difficulties with reading.

3. Recount Sonny's journey through the various RTI tiers leading to the likelihood of a comprehensive diagnostic evaluation.

Progress Monitoring and Benchmarks

Another way to ensure students with disabilities are supported at school is to regularly check the progress they are making. This means that instead of waiting until the end of the semester, grading cycle, or year, to see what they have learned, we evaluate their progress on a more systematic basis. **Progress monitoring** is a process by which students' academic, behavioral, and social gains, setbacks, and plateaus are observed and recorded. Whether you are assessing for screening, eligibility, or achievement students will demonstrate throughout the school year, progress monitoring is needed. While progress monitoring is beneficial to all students, progress monitoring for students with disabilities is particularly critical to ensuring that they have meaningful IEP goals and are receiving special education and related services that will aid in their respective development.

There are two distinct types of progress monitoring: mastery measurement and curriculum measurement. *Mastery measurement* is based specifically on a curriculum's scope and sequence. In mastery measurement, the special education teacher teaches a skill to students and assesses it until students demonstrate mastery of this skill. In other words, special education teachers will continue to reteach a specific skill until the skill has been mastered. To illustrate, a child must master each reading level before he is able to move up to the next reading level. *Curriculum measurement* or *curriculum-based measurement (CBM)* is the other type of progress monitoring. This method does not adhere to a curriculum sequence. Instead, regular assessments (probes) measure all skills in the curriculum. This form of progress monitoring is commonly used, as it allows special education teachers to incorporate many skills and subsequently tailor their teaching to meet the needs of their diverse students. Progress monitoring benefits special education professionals, because it often aligns to the progress of annual goals identified on a student's IEP. In addition, it can drive instruction, providing opportunity for increased flexibility and differentiation, which is not possible when using the mastery measurement model (Winfree, 2018).

There are various types of progress monitoring tools. One commonly used example of a progress monitoring tool is a **benchmark assessment**. A benchmark assessment, or interim assessment, is used to evaluate where students stand in their learning progress and to also determine whether they are on track to performing well on future assessments (Glossary of Education Reform, 2013). It is a locally determined district-wide assessment designed to measure the achievement of standards (Bergan, Bergan, & Burnham, 2013). Such assessments provide feedback to both the teacher and the students. Benchmark assessments have several distinct purposes, as detailed in Table 2.4.

In most cases, benchmark assessments are offered periodically throughout the year, such as every six to eight weeks. All students, including both general education and special education students, participate in benchmark testing.

Table 2.4 Purposes of Benchmark Assessments

1. *To communicate expectations for learning*

   Students need a clear understanding of what the special educator expects from them with respect to learning. One way a special educator can communicate expectations is by writing daily objectives on the board. Communicating expectations for learning is best expressed by the special educator in a clear and direct manner. If a teacher does not communicate his expectations for their learning, students will be unclear what the goals and objectives for the lesson are.

2. *To plan curriculum and instruction*

   In order for students to achieve their goals, careful attention must be made to planning for curriculum and instruction. Choosing a curriculum that is closely tied to the students' learning goals and state standards is paramount. Once a quality curriculum has been selected, special educators can then create an instructional plan that will result in mastery of the material.

3. *To monitor and evaluate instructional and/or program effectiveness*

   The special educator's job is not complete once instruction occurs. After instruction, he is responsible for monitoring students' progress to determine whether his instruction was effective and to also determine the overall effectiveness of the program. If students are not performing adequately, the special educator must reexamine his methods and implement new ones in an attempt to heighten student understanding.

4. *To predict future performance*

   Benchmarks allow both general educators and special educators an idea of how students will perform on final district or state assessments. These assessments are able to predict future performance, because they serve as a snapshot of the students' performance to date.

Herman, J., Osmundson, E., & Dietel, R. (2010). *Benchmark assessment for improved learning: An AACC policy brief.* Retrieved from https://files.eric.ed.gov/fulltext/ED524108.pdf

Check Your Understanding 2.4

1. Define progress monitoring, and explain its significance.

2. What is another name for a benchmark assessment? How often are benchmark assessments usually performed?

3. Indicate the various purposes of using benchmark assessments when monitoring student progress.

Considerations for Students With Emotional, Behavioral, and Social Differences During the Assessment Process

When assessing students with disabilities, educational professionals are aware that some students have emotional, behavioral, and/or social differences that can impact their performance during the assessment process. Such behaviors can include attentional difficulties, test anxiety, impulsivity, aggression, lack of interest in "pleasing" the test administrator, lack of motivation, or general disinterest in the testing process. To illustrate, it is common for a typically developing child to want to "please" the test administrator by showing off his knowledge of a particular subject. This desire to please the test administrator motivates the child to perform as best he can during the assessment process. For example, a typical first-grader might want to show the test administrator that he knows how to read well, because doing so makes him feel smart and important. Consider a child with autism spectrum disorder (ASD), on the other hand, who possesses distinct social challenges. She might have little to no interest in "pleasing" the test administrator and become agitated or throw a tantrum at having to complete a given test. These behaviors would likely generate less desirable results than that of the typical first-grade student. A child with attention-deficit/hyperactivity disorder (ADHD) might have extreme difficulty sitting still during an evaluation. This could increase the number of testing sessions required for him to complete the assessment and affect the validity of his test performance. A child with a conduct disorder might aggress at the test administrator during testing, making test administration challenging once again. A child with testing anxiety might second-guess his answers, be nervous that he is being evaluated, or shut down completely during this process. These are just some examples of how possessing certain disabilities can impact assessment results. It will be important for the special educator or other educational professional assessing such students to have an awareness of the challenges they might face and how to best resolve them in order to glean the most positive and accurate assessment results. If this person is unsuccessful in managing students' emotional, behavioral, or social differences, there is a likelihood that the assessment results will not be a true representation of the students' abilities.

Considerations for Students From Culturally and Linguistically Diverse (CLD) Backgrounds

When assessing students with disabilities, it is critical that we be aware that students come from varied backgrounds with diverse experiences. The United

States is widely regarded as a "melting pot," which refers to the concept that our society comprises many different people, cultures, and languages. Because of the heterogeneity of our society, special educators need to be sure that they are accurately assessing students who differ culturally and linguistically from the norm. Culturally and linguistically (CLD) diverse students are those individuals whose culture or language is different from that of the dominant culture or language in American society (Murry, 2012). These students might also be referred to as limited English proficient, English language learners (ELLs), or language minority students. Historically, CLD students have been disproportionally represented in special education (as implied in Chapter 1). This means that there has been an over-representation of CLDs in special education relative to the presence of this group in the overall student population. Several factors have contributed to this over-representation, including test bias, poverty, lack of adequate training in working with CLD students, and poor general education instruction.

Federal legislation, namely IDEA, states that assessment and evaluation materials must be appropriate to the individual taking the assessment (aka nondiscriminatory evaluation). Assessments may not be racially or culturally discriminatory. This legislation also requires that evaluation materials be provided in the child's native language or other mode of communication, unless this is not feasible. Therefore, assessment of culturally and linguistically diverse students should occur in their dominant language, or the language an individual reads, writes, and speaks the best. Failure to properly assess CLD students in this manner can result in inaccurate test results and inappropriate educational placements.

Assessing CLD students has proven challenging at times. One limitation across assessment procedures and measures for English language learners (ELLs) is a restricted range of measures appropriate for ELL children despite an increase in this student population. Ongoing assessments prove to be particularly meaningful to ELLs. This is because unlike standardized measures, ongoing assessments are able to measure their content knowledge and abilities. To illustrate, a child might speak any number of languages. The language he primarily speaks could be one that is commonly known and used, such as English or Spanish, or it might be one that is not commonly known, such as Belarusian or Koro. If the language the child speaks is not commonly spoken, it can be daunting to find an appropriate assessment in that particular language that can be used to accurately assess him. This makes ongoing assessments a better indicator of the student's strengths, challenges, and progress.

According to Burnette (2000), there are four principles that serve as best practices for ensuring proper assessment of culturally and linguistically diverse (CLD) students (see Table 2.5).

Table 2.5 Best Practices for Assessing Culturally and Linguistically Diverse (CLD) Students

- Gather a full, multidisciplinary assessment team. This team should include parents, educators, assessors, interpreters, bilingual educators, and a person who is familiar with the student's culture and language. All of these individuals are essential members of the team who bring their own distinct skills and expertise to assessing the child and helping make the best educational decisions for him.

- Implement pre-referral strategies and interventions. Information should be obtained to determine whether the CLD student's difficulties stem from cultural or language differences, inadequate instruction, or a disability. It is critical to know whether the child's challenges are due to not being assessed in his own language or whether an actual disability exists. This is the difference between a language difference and a language disability (discussed later in the text). For example, if a school assesses a student in English and his first language is Spanish, this student will have great difficulty demonstrating his actual knowledge of what is being assessed.

- Determine the language(s) to be used in testing. Assessment of language dominance and proficiency should be completed *before* testing for the CLD student whose dominant language is not English. Knowing the child's dominant language and proficiency will help the assessor select the appropriate assessment(s) to be administered. It is also relevant to note that the student's dominant language might vary across subject matter. To illustrate, a student's dominant language in reading might be English, whereas his dominant language in writing might be Spanish.

- Conduct a tailored, appropriate assessment of the child and environment. This should consist of nonbiased, appropriate instruments in combination with other sources of information (e.g., observations, interviews) from a variety of environments (e.g., school, home, community). No one test will accurately determine the presence of disability. For example, a child might be assessed using teacher observations, rating scales, and parent interviews. Such assessments might occur both at home and at school.

Check Your Understanding 2.5

1. How might a student possessing an emotional, a behavioral, and/or a social disability demonstrate differences in a testing situation? Provide an example.

2. How are students who are considered culturally and linguistically diverse protected in the assessment process? What must schools consider when assessing this student population for special education services?

3. Identify two challenges of assessing students who are culturally and linguistically diverse. How might these challenges be resolved?

Ethical Considerations Surrounding Assessment

In addition to the various concepts surrounding assessment in this chapter, it is also essential to discuss the importance of ethical behavior as it relates to students with disabilities. Ethics refer to a code of moral standards. These moral standards dictate what is deemed acceptable or good, as opposed to what is unacceptable or poor. There are various types of ethics that people possess which govern the way in which they behave toward a particular group or situation. As special educators, we have our own code of ethics that we are called on to adhere to both as classroom teachers and as individuals who assess students with disabilities on a regular basis. Special education teachers are required to abide by the Council for Exceptional Children's (CEC) professional ethical principles, practice standards, and professional policies. These standards outline ways that certified special education teachers must respect the diverse characteristics and needs of individuals with exceptionalities and their families. This code of ethics drives all ethical decisions special educators make with regard to assessment, as well as everyday classroom practice (see Table 2.6). The code is as follows (CEC, 1993, p. 4):

> We declare the following principles to be the Code of Ethics for educators of persons with exceptionalities. Members of the special education

Table 2.6 CEC Code of Ethics for Educators of Persons With Exceptionalities

1. Special education professionals are committed to developing the highest educational and quality of life potential of individuals with exceptionalities.

2. Special education professionals promote and maintain a high level of competence and integrity in practicing their profession.

3. Special education professionals engage in professional activities that benefit individuals with exceptionalities, their families, other colleagues, students, or research subjects.

4. Special education professionals exercise objective professional judgment in the practice of their profession.

5. Special education professionals strive to advance their knowledge and skills regarding the education of individuals with exceptionalities.

6. Special education professionals work within the standards and policies of their profession.

7. Special education professionals seek to uphold and improve where necessary the laws, regulations, and policies governing the delivery of special education and related services and the practice of their profession.

8. Special education professionals do not condone or participate in unethical or illegal acts, nor violate professional standards adopted by the Delegate Assembly of CEC.

Council for Exceptional Children. (1993). *CEC policy manual*. Reston, VA: Author.

profession are responsible for upholding and advancing these principles. Members of the Council for Exceptional Children agree to judge and be judged by them in accordance with the spirit and provisions of this Code.

As mentioned, this code of ethics dictates the special educator's responsibilities required when assessing and/or educating students with disabilities. It mandates that special education teachers be highly accountable for their professional behavior. In doing so, they must not only be committed to setting the bar high when working with students with disabilities but also must maintain their own personal integrity by adhering to laws, regulations, and policies. In addition, they must remain current in their knowledge of the field of special education.

Check Your Understanding 2.6

1. Consider each of the eight provisions listed in Table 2.6 in the CEC Code of Ethics. Why do you think it is important that special education teachers adhere to these standards of behavior? Explain.

2. Select any two of the provisions listed above. Explain how you, as a special education teacher, will demonstrate these provisions in your practice as an educator.

In addition to being responsible for their own professional behavior as educators, special education teachers must be cognizant of the importance of ethics regarding the assessment of students with disabilities. This is particularly important when examining students with disabilities' right to nondiscriminatory identification and evaluation under IDEA (2004). This law has set forth several requirements:

- Unbiased, multi-factored evaluation methods should be used.

  An unbiased evaluation is one that is impartial or neutral and shows no preference. A multi-factored evaluation is one that consists of several components or areas to be assessed. Therefore, a child must be assured that the evaluation methods provided him show no preference and assess several areas of his learning.

- Testing and evaluation procedures must not discriminate on the basis of race, culture, or native language.

  As discussed above, all tests must be administered in the child's native language. To illustrate, a child whose first language is German must be given an assessment written in German.

- Placement decisions cannot be made on the basis of a single test score.

When determining where a child will receive his education, educators must consider the results of several assessments and not just one assessment.

(Heward, 2013, para. 3)

It is also relevant to note that in order for the evaluation to be considered ethical, more than one test examiner should participate, because this reduces the chance of examiner bias. In addition, special education professionals are required to use multiple assessment methods when assessing a child for a disability. No one single data source is appropriate for determining whether a child has a disability. Supplemental assessments may take the form of observations, background information, and/or information provided by educational professionals. In addition to all of these ethical considerations, is it critical that schools frequently and effectively communicate with the families of students with disabilities to make them aware of the assessment process.

The Importance of Communication Between Home and School During the Assessment Process

Assessing students with disabilities is a complex process. Great consideration goes into how, when, and where such evaluations will take place. Because of the unique demands of assessing students with academic, behavioral, and social challenges, it is paramount to involve the parents of students as much as possible.

Earlier in this chapter, we discussed the need to maintain good communication with parents during the pre-referral process. Communication with parents needs to continue throughout other times of assessment as well. Parents play an integral role in decision-making with regard to their child and how he will be educated. Therefore, it is necessary for appropriate communication to be maintained between home and school before, during, and after the assessment process. Parents provide essential input into the evaluation process, as they typically have the most complete understanding of the whole child. For example, parents are able to speak to their child's past educational experiences, his ability to complete homework, his attitude toward school, and so on. This information will be valuable as the IEP team works to determine the presence of a possible disability.

Schools are also required to provide parents with a description of the assessments that will be used, as well as their intended purpose, when evaluating their child. Moreover, parents should be provided with an explanation of the test results by a school psychologist or other qualified person, as well as an explanation of any proposed educational decisions based on those test results. This should occur before the parents meet with the IEP team, so that they are able to review the results and develop any questions that they might have about the evaluation results.

Parents are entitled to what are referred to as "parental rights," which must be communicated to them by the school. Parental rights are legal rights that serve as a protection or safeguard during the special education process. Often parents are given these in a written format, referred to as a "parent handbook of rights." It is pertinent to note that parents are typically not aware of their rights until the school discloses them, because for many parents this is the first time they have had a child assessed for a disability. This parent handbook addresses specific procedural safeguards and requires parents to verify by their signature that they have received it. The following is a list and description of procedural safeguards that parents are afforded:

- Parental consent to evaluate

- Confidentiality of students' records (FERPA)

- Prior written notice

- Disciplinary procedures

- Independent evaluations

- Mediation

- Due process

Parental Consent to Evaluate

One of the core components of IDEA is parental consent to evaluate. Parental consent means that parents must give permission in order for their child to be tested to determine whether a disability is present. According to IDEA (2004), this means the parents are giving permission only to evaluate and are not yet giving the school permission to begin special education and related services (IDEA, 2004, § 300.300). In special education, parental consent is needed respectively to conduct the comprehensive diagnostic evaluation and to begin special education services, if warranted. In the case of the comprehensive diagnostic evaluation, parents must agree in writing to their child's being evaluated to determine the presence of a disability. If parents deny the school the ability to conduct such an assessment, the school must document all attempts made to obtain such consent. If an agreement to evaluate is not reached between the parties, the school may request mediation or due process. It is relevant to note, however, that in some states this is not permissible, due to inconsistencies in the state law related to parental consent.

Confidentiality of Students' Records

FERPA, or the Family Educational Rights and Privacy Act of 1974, was designed to protect the confidentiality of students' educational records. This is also known as the "Buckley Amendment." Essentially, FERPA maintains that a student's educational records should be kept confidential and prohibits the improper disclosure of personally identifiable information. Once a child turns 18 or begins attending a postsecondary institution, the student is granted access, the right to control the disclosure of personally identifiable information, and the right to seek to have his records amended. FERPA applies to all educational agencies and institutions (e.g., schools) that receive funding under any program administered by the Education Department (U.S. Department of Education, 2015).

Prior Written Notice

Parents have the right to receive prior written notice from their child's school every time the school proposes to make a change to the child's education. This might include (Center for Parent Information & Resources, 2017, para. 1):

- a proposal to initiate or change the identification, evaluation, or education placement of the child;

- a proposal to initiate or change the provision of FAPE (free appropriate public education) to the child;

- refusal to initiate or change the identification, evaluation, or education placement of the child; or

- refusal to initiate or change the provision of FAPE to the child.

Disciplinary Procedures

Another right that parents possess is in relation to their child's behavior while at school. Parents should be informed that if their child is subject to disciplinary procedures while he is receiving special education services, several provisions must be in place:

1. School personnel must make a case-by-case determination about discipline.

2. The child is entitled to a manifestation determination hearing that will determine whether his violation is the direct result of his disability.

3. Schools may not remove a child from his current placement for more than 10 school days during the same school year.

4. If discipline does change the child's placement for more than 10 consecutive days and the violation is determined not to be a manifestation of the child's disability, all relevant disciplinary procedures as would be applied to students without disabilities will be implemented.

5. The child should continue to receive educational services while removed from his current placement.

Independent Evaluations

Parents have additional rights with respect to the outcome of their child's comprehensive diagnostic evaluation. If the parents do not agree with the results of the assessments performed by the school district, they have the right to obtain an independent educational evaluation (IEE). This occurs when the parents seek a qualified outside evaluator. In some cases, the school district will pay for the outside evaluation. In other districts, the parents are expected to cover the cost of the evaluation.

Mediation and Due Process

Mediation and due process are legal avenues that parents may pursue if they cannot come to an agreement with the school district about decisions regarding educational placement and special education services (these were discussed in Chapter 1). The first step in resolving a dispute between home and school is often mediation. This process allows the parents/guardians, along with an impartial mediator, to meet and discuss possible solutions to the dispute. At times, the parties are able to reach a compromise. In the event the dispute is not resolved, due process might occur. Due process, available under IDEA, provides a regulatory basis for a formal set of policies and procedures that school districts are required to implement for children receiving special education services. Due-process hearings are administrative hearings held on behalf of the child.

Check Your Understanding 2.7

1. Describe the importance of schools maintaining effective communication with students' households during the assessment process. What steps must they take to inform parents as they progress through this process?

2. Select any two of the procedural safeguards discussed. If you were a parent, discuss why you think it would be important to be afforded these rights. Be sure to mention the impact they might have on protecting the child. Give examples.

CHAPTER SUMMARY

This chapter highlighted the key elements of the assessment process in special education, beginning with the screening process and ending with diagnosis and eligibility for special education services.

It also examined the concepts of progress monitoring and benchmarks, as well as multi-tiered system of support (MTSS) and Response to Intervention (RTI). Considerations for students with emotional, behavioral, and social disabilities were examined. Culturally and linguistically diverse students and assessment and ethical considerations surrounding assessment were explored. Parental rights and procedural safeguards in special education were also highlighted.

APPLY WHAT YOU HAVE LEARNED

1. If a child you knew was going through the process of diagnosis and eligibility, what questions might you ask the IEP team members? Why would it be important to gain answers to these questions?

2. How could you organize the information you learned about the pre-referral process to create a presentation on the pre-referral process to a group of new teachers who know little about this process?

3. What key concepts would you use to explain mediation and due process? Which of the two do you think is a preferable first step in resolving a dispute? Why?

REFERENCES

American Academy of Pediatrics. (2018). *Screening recommendations*. Retrieved from https://www.aap.org/en-us/advocacy-and-policy/aap-health-initiatives/Screening/Pages/Screening-Recommendations.aspx

Bergan, John Richard, Bergan, John Robert, & C. G. Burnham. (2013). *Benchmark assessment in standards-based education: The Galileo K-12 Online Educational Management System*. Retrieved from https://www.ati-online.com/pdfs/researchK12/BenchmarkAssessment.pdf

Burnette, J. (2000). *Assessment of culturally and linguistically diverse students for special education eligibility*. ERIC Digest. Retrieved from http:// https://www.ericdigests.org/2001-4/assessment.html

California Department of Education. (2019). *MTSS components*. Retrieved from https://www.cde.ca.gov/ci/cr/ri/mtsscomponents.asp

Carnegie Mellon University. (2019). *What is the difference between formative and summative assessment?* Retrieved from https://www.cmu.edu/teaching/assessment/basics/formative-summative.html

Centers for Disease Control and Prevention. (2018). *Developmental monitoring and screening*. Retrieved from https://www.cdc.gov/ncbddd/childdevelopment/screening.html

Center for Parent Information & Resources. (2017). *Rights to receive prior written notice*. Retrieved from http://www.parentcenterhub.org/notice-prior

Center for Response to Intervention. (n.d.). *Progress monitoring*. Retrieved from https://www.rti4success.org

Council for Exceptional Children. (1993). *CEC policy manual*. Reston, VA: Author.

Glossary of Education Reform. (2013). *Interim assessment*. Retrieved from https://www.edglossary.org/interim-assessment

Great Schools Partnership. (2015). *The Glossary of Education Reform*. Retrieved from https://www.edglossary.org/assessment

Herman, J., Osmundson, E., & Dietel, R. (2010). *Benchmark assessment for improved learning: An*

AACC policy brief. Retrieved from https://files.eric.ed.gov/fulltext/ED524108.pdf

Heward, W. (2013). *Six Major Principles of IDEA.* Retrieved from https://www.education.com/reference/article/six-major-principles-idea

Individuals with Disabilities Education Act, 20 U.S.C. § 1400 (2004).

IRIS Center. (2018). *What are the stages of the pre-referral process and what do they involve?* Retrieved from http://iris.peabody.vanderbilt.edu/module/preref/cresource/q2/p03

Lexia. (2018). *RTI and MTSS: Do you know the differences between these support systems?* Retrieved from https://www.lexialearning.com/blog/rti-and-mtss-do-you-know-difference-between-these-support-systems

Murry, K. (2012). Cognitive development, global learning, and academic progress: Promoting teacher readiness for CLD students and families. *Journal of Curriculum and Instruction (JoCI),* 6, 11–24.

National Center on Response to Intervention. (2010). *RTI 101: Frequently asked questions.* Retrieved from https://rti4success.org/sites/default/files/rtiessentialcomponents_042710.pdf

NEA. (2017). *Education for all: An introduction to RTI.* Retrieved from https://www.neamb.com/professional-resources/introduction-rti.htm

Rosenberg, M., Westling, D., & McLeskey, J. (2010). *Types of tests in used in special education.* Retrieved from https://www.education.com/reference/article/types-tests-used-special-education

RTI Action Network. (2018). *What is RTI?* Retrieved from http://www.rtinetwork.org/learn/what/whatisrti

U.S. Department of Education. (2015). *FERPA general guidance for students.* Retrieved from https://www2.ed.gov/policy/gen/guid/fpco/ferpa/students.html

Winfree, L. (2018). *Types of progress monitoring in special education.* Retrieved from https://study.com/academy/lesson/types-of-progress-monitoring-in-special-education.html

Assessment Types

Tara S. Guerriero, PhD

Learning Objectives

After the completion of this chapter, you should be able to:

- Discuss the similarities and differences between formal and informal assessments.

- Explain the purpose of the following types of assessment: Norm-referenced, criterion-referenced, curriculum-based, performance-based, portfolio, error analysis, interview, direct observation, checklists, and behavior rating scales.

- Identify the differences between the terms norm-referenced and criterion-referenced.

- Describe the different types of scores (raw score, standard score, scaled score, percentile, stanine, range, standard error of measurement, confidence interval, and age/grade equivalence) that can be obtained for norm-referenced assessments.

- Evaluate the effectiveness of using multiple types of assessment to examine student performance.

Key Terms

behavior rating scale (p. 88)	formal assessment (p. 53)
checklist (p. 87)	informal assessment (p. 53)
criterion-referenced assessment (p. 76)	interview (p. 83)
curriculum-based assessment (p. 78)	norm-referenced assessment (p. 55):
direct observation (p. 84):	mean, median, mode, distribution of scores, normal distribution, bell curve, chronological age, starting point (basal rule), stopping point (ceiling rule), raw score, standard score, average, standard deviation, scaled score, percentile (percentile rank), stanine, range, standard error of measurement, confidence interval, age-equivalence, grade-equivalence, reliability, validity
anecdotal recording, event recording/ frequency recording, interval recording/ time sampling, duration recording, latency recording, inter-response time	
error analysis (p. 81)	

(Continued)

(Continued)

performance-based assessment and authentic assessment (p. 79)	standardized (p. 53)
portfolio assessment (p. 80)	

Introduction to the Chapter

All students have their own set of capabilities and qualities that make them uniquely different from one another. How can educators better understand these characteristics so that they can help students learn in the best way possible? Assessment gives educators the opportunity to explore every student's capabilities and better understand their individual strengths and needs. Further, assessment provides information that will help teachers make decisions about how to best teach their students. When thinking about the concept of assessment, an educator may wonder:

- "Why are there so many different types of assessments?"

- "What is the difference between each type of assessment?"

- "Why is it so important to understand the purpose of different types of assessment?"

- "How do I decide what assessment to give?"

- "How does student performance on different assessments lead us to better understand student characteristics?"

- "How do I use assessment results to improve my instruction?"

There isn't an easy answer to any of these questions. While every assessment can provide some insight into a student's skills and knowledge, there isn't one measure or type of assessment that, alone, can give a complete profile of a student. Whether you are evaluating a student for purposes of screening, diagnosis and eligibility, or instructional considerations, it is necessary to carefully consider the different types of assessment and the purpose of each. A combination of assessments may ensure that you conduct a well-rounded, comprehensive evaluation, as required by law. Throughout the course of this chapter, we will discuss many types of assessment that are commonly used in educational settings.

Formal and Informal Assessments

Before we delve into each specific type of assessment, it is important to note that assessments can be classified into two broad categories: formal assessments and informal assessments. Formal and informal assessments differ in the way that they are developed, administered, scored, and interpreted. This is an overview section that will discuss broad terminology that will be defined and discussed in greater depth and with more specificity throughout the chapter.

Formal Assessments

Formal assessments allow for the measurement of a student's overall performance, either in comparison to the performance of others of the same age or grade level (i.e., norm-referenced assessments) or to a specific set of criteria or standards (i.e., criterion-referenced assessments). They may also be used to identify comparable strengths or weaknesses with peers (Weaver, 2018). Formal assessments are developed in such a way whereby all test-takers answer the same questions, in the same way, with the same time constraints (if appropriate), and then the test is scored in a consistent manner. This makes it possible to compare the relative performance of individuals. Formal approaches to assessment practices allow for comparison of both educational quality and student performance across regions, states, and countries.

It is common to see the term "standardized" used synonymously with the concept of formal assessment; however, you should take caution when using the term "standardized." It is often used in one of two ways:

1. It may be used more generally to refer to all formal assessments that are "administered, scored, and interpreted in a standard, consistent manner" (Mertler, 2007, p. 3).

2. Alternatively, the term "standardized" may be used much more specifically to refer to assessments that have also been statistically normalized so that they conform to a normal distribution across the overall, general population; this definition of "standardized" is often used when referring to the concept of norm-referenced assessments, which will be highlighted later in the chapter.

Since the term can be used so differently, it is important to know how it is being used in order to have a good understanding of how to interpret the "standardized" assessment.

Informal Assessments

Informal assessment is another form of assessment often used by educators to evaluate student performance. Unlike formal assessment, informal assessment is typically teacher-created or textbook-generated and governed by content and performance, rather than a formal comparison to the overall population or to state or federal standards. Informal assessments are frequently relevant to instruction and content across the curriculum. Information about many different areas of performance (e.g., academics, behavior, social/emotional) can be gained through informal assessments. Some examples of assessments that can be informal are criterion-referenced assessments, curriculum-based assessments, performance and portfolio assessments (e.g., projects, experiments, presentations, demonstrations, performances), error analyses, interviews, observations, checklists, and behavior rating scales. The following are examples of ways that an educator could use informal assessments:

- To test students' understanding of a math unit that was taught recently

- To evaluate a collection of a student's best work that highlights specific skills

- To examine a student's ability to generalize functional skills learned in the classroom to a job setting

Concluding Thoughts on Formal and Informal Assessments

It is important to note that while some assessment types are classified as either formal or informal based on the underlying nature of the assessment type (e.g., norm-referenced assessments being formal), others can be either formal or informal (e.g., a behavior rating scale can be norm-referenced or teacher-created). It depends on how the assessment is developed, administered, scored, and interpreted. This chapter will describe many different types of formal and/or informal assessments that can be used to build a better understanding of a student's strengths and needs in all areas of performance.

Check Your Understanding 3.1

1. Describe the difference between a formal and an informal assessment.

2. Give some examples of informal assessments.

3. Describe an instance when a formal assessment might be more beneficial than an informal assessment.

4. Describe an instance of the reverse (when an informal assessment might be more beneficial than a formal assessment).

Norm-Referenced Assessments

One of the most common types of assessment that is used to compare the performance of students to each other and evaluate a student's areas of strength and need are norm-referenced assessments. **Norm-referenced assessments**, also referred to as norm-referenced tests (NRTs), are standardized, formal assessments that are

> designed to compare and rank test takers in relation to one another. Norm-referenced tests report whether test takers performed better or worse than a hypothetical average student, which is determined by comparing scores against the performance results of a statistically selected group of test takers, typically of the same age or grade level, who have already taken the exam.
>
> (Glossary of Education Reform, 2015, para. 1)

If a test is well-normed, the group of test-takers on which the test is normed is often referred to as the general population, because it is representative of the characteristics of the whole population, which include age, grade, culture, geographical location type (e.g., urban, suburban, rural), and other demographics. Norm-referenced assessments can measure numerous areas of performance (e.g., intelligence, academic areas of achievement, behavior, social/emotional characteristics) and can involve a variety of response types (multiple-choice items, open-ended and/or short-answer questions, fill-in-the-blank, etc.) that lead to the evaluation of a student in those various areas. Further, scores on these assessments can be reported in a number of ways (e.g., raw score, standard score, scaled score, percentile, stanine, age-equivalence, grade-equivalence). The following are examples of norm-referenced assessments that are commonly used:

- Wechsler Intelligence Scale for Children (WISC)
- Woodcock-Johnson Tests of Cognitive Abilities
- Stanford-Binet Intelligence Scales
- Wechsler Individual Achievement Test (WIAT)
- Kaufman Test of Educational Achievement (KTEA)
- Peabody Individual Achievement Test (PIAT)
- Peabody Picture Vocabulary Test (PPVT)
- Wide Range Achievement Test (WRAT)
- Woodcock-Johnson Tests of Achievement
- the Conners
- the AAMR Adaptive Behavior Scales

Distribution of Scores and the Bell Curve

In order to really understand the concept of norm-referenced assessments, it is important to first examine concepts and statistical measures that are associated with the distribution of scores, or the continuum of scores in a given set of data. When you are examining the distribution of scores on any given measure, there are a number of ways to compare the performance of different students to one another. For example, you may be familiar with the concepts of mean, the average of a group of scores; median, the middle score in a group of scores; and mode, the score that occurs the most frequently in a group of scores. In order to better understand mean, median, and mode, consider the following explanations that are based on the group of scores 8, 3, 5, 3, 8, 7, and 8:

- Mean: The mean is calculated by adding up all the scores and dividing them by the total number of scores. The following steps would be used to calculate the mean based on the given group of scores:

    1. Add all the scores together: 8 + 3 + 5 + 3 + 8 + 7 + 8 = 42.

    2. Divide the total sum of the scores (42) by the number of scores (7): 42 ÷ 7 = 6.

    3. The mean score, or average score, is 6.

- Median: The median is calculated by putting the scores in ascending (or descending) order and determining which score is the middle score. To determine the median for the given group of scores, you would take the following steps:

    1. Put all the scores in order from smallest to largest: 3, 3, 5, 7, 8, 8, 8.

    2. Identify the middle score in the group: 3, 3, 5, <u>7</u>, 8, 8, 8.

    3. The median score, or middle score, is 7.

- Mode: The mode is determined by counting the frequency of each of the scores. To determine the mode for the given group of scores, you would take the following steps:

    1. List all the scores that were obtained in the set of scores.

        3

        5

        7

        8

    2. Count how many times each score was obtained in the group of scores.

        3: 2 times

5: 1 time

7: 1 time

8: 3 times

3. Identify the score that was obtained the most frequently.

8: 3 times

4. The mode, or most frequently occurring score, is 8.

Depending on the data set and how you want to analyze the distribution of scores, it can be beneficial to find each of the three statistics.

Developing a graphic representation of data could also be a good way to provide a visual depiction of the distribution of scores on any given measure. For example, a graphic representation of performance across students could be developed whereby the x-axis represents the range of scores that can be achieved on the assessment and the y-axis represents the number of students who obtained each score. The following are examples of what a distribution of scores might look like, depending on student performance. Figures 3.1, 3.2, 3.3, and 3.4 represent four different examples of the patterns that might demonstrate student performance on any given measure.

- Figure 3.1 is an example of a distribution of scores where the scores are predominantly at the upper end of the range. A graph might look like this if most of the students scored between 50% and 100% instead of across the full range, which would be from 0% to 100%.

- Figure 3.2 is an example of a distribution of scores where the scores are predominantly at the lower end of the range. A graph might look like this if most of the students scored between 0% and 50% instead of across the full range, which would be from 0% to 100%.

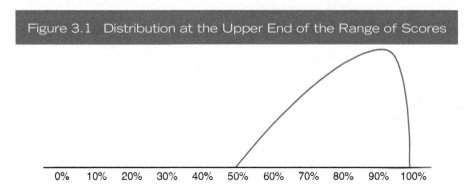

Figure 3.1 Distribution at the Upper End of the Range of Scores

0%   10%   20%   30%   40%   50%   60%   70%   80%   90%   100%

- Figure 3.3 is an example of a distribution that is wide and shallow because the scores are evenly distributed along the full continuum of scores (i.e., 0%–100%).

- Figure 3.4 is an example of a distribution that is very narrow and steep because many students received a similar score. For example, nearly all the students received a 50% on the assessment.

Examining a distribution of scores can be done in a number of ways, but how does this information relate to a norm-referenced assessment? What does norm-referenced really mean? One way to better understand the concept of a norm-referenced test is to think about a **normal distribution**, which can be

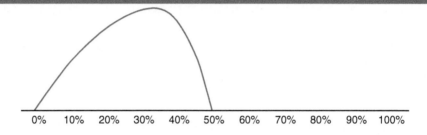

Figure 3.2   Distribution at the Lower End of the Range of Scores

Figure 3.3   Wide Distribution of Scores Across the Full Continuum of Scores

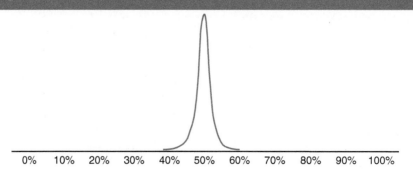

Figure 3.4   Narrow Distribution of Scores

represented by a **bell curve**. In reference to standardized, norm-referenced assessments, a standardized bell curve (also referred to as a normal curve or a normal bell curve) takes the shape of a "bell" and represents a normal distribution of scores that characterizes the general population. All norm-referenced assessments statistically conform to a normal bell curve; they are symmetrical in nature, and they have the same value for the mean, median, and mode. Figure 3.5 is an example of a normal bell curve that includes standard deviations, standard scores, percentages, and ranges.

Bell curves can be used to determine in which range a student scores (e.g., average, above average, superior, very superior, below average, well below average) as compared to the general population of the same age and/or grade level. Performance on assessments that are either non-standardized or informal typically results in a non-normal distribution of scores (see those examples represented in Figures 3.1–3.4), while performance on assessments that are norm-referenced can be compared to a normal distribution of scores or normal bell curve (see Figure 3.5).

Check Your Understanding 3.2

1. Mrs. Jones gave a math test to her third-grade class of 20 students. Out of a possible score of 100 points, the students obtained the following scores: 97, 88, 79, 100, 95, 93, 93, 97, 90, 88, 97, 100, 97, 92, 87, 85, 94, 97, 96, 81.

   a. Find the mean, median, and mode.

   b. Develop a graph that represents the data.

2. Does the graph you created in 1(b) resemble a normal bell curve? If not, does it resemble any of the graphic representations in Figures 3.1–3.4?

3. Why might a graphic representation of the distribution of scores from a teacher-created test look different than a normal bell curve based on a norm-referenced assessment?

4. Why might it be beneficial to refer to a visual of a bell curve when discussing a student's scores on a standardized assessment?

Age-Level vs. Grade-Level Norms

Norm-referenced assessments frequently allow for a comparison of a student's performance to peers either of the same age or in the same grade. While differences in scores between the two types of norms may be very minimal in many circumstances, it is still important to be purposeful about which norms to use. Many factors can be considered in determining whether age-level or grade-level norms would be more appropriate; however, there may not be a definitive answer about which to use in every circumstance. When determining which norms to refer to (age-level or grade-level):

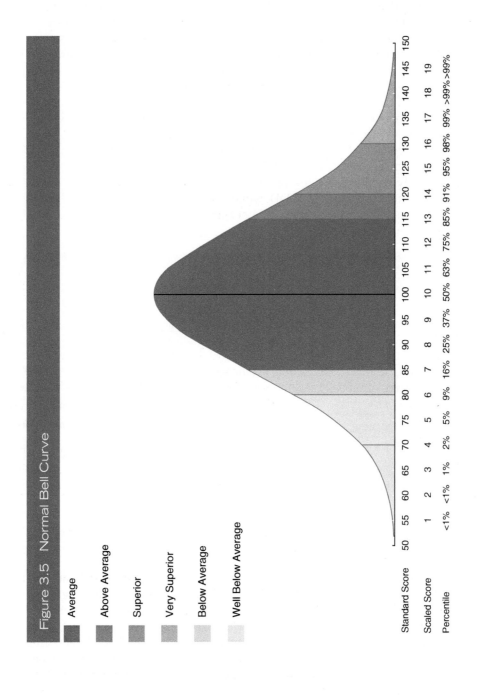

Figure 3.5 Normal Bell Curve

| | Average | Above Average | Superior | Very Superior | Below Average | Well Below Average |

Standard Score	50	55	60	65	70	75	80	85	90	95	100	105	110	115	120	125	130	135	140	145	150
Scaled Score			1	2	3	4	5	6	7	8	9	10	11	12	13	14	15	16	17	18	19
Percentile			<1%	1%	2%	5%	9%	16%	25%	37%	50%	63%	75%	85%	91%	95%	98%	99%	>99%	>99%	

- Consider the purpose and content of a particular assessment. For example, if the information being tested is developmental in nature and independent of grade-level learning (e.g., intelligence, memory), it may be appropriate to compare to age-level norms. Alternatively, if the information being tested is based on content that is typically taught at a particular grade level (e.g., mathematics), it may be beneficial to refer to grade-level norms.

- Consider specific circumstances associated with the student. For example, a situation in which grade-level norms may be appropriate is when a student is older than most typical children in his grade level; however, he may have only learned the information that is appropriate to that grade level. If he were compared to age-level peers, it may look like his skills are lower than that of the general population, because he has not learned the content yet. Similarly, it may be more appropriate to compare a student who is younger than most typical children in a grade level to the age-leveled norms, because the student may not be developmentally caught up to same-grade peers.

- Consider the purpose of the evaluation. For example, if you are doing a screening to examine performance in various areas of academic achievement in comparison to what has been taught (to determine whether a further evaluation is necessary), it may be appropriate to use grade-level norms. However, if completing a full, comprehensive psychoeducational evaluation for purposes of diagnosis and eligibility, examiners often may choose to refer to age-level norms.

In thinking about these examples, it is important to note that there are many instances in which you should be cautious when using age-level and grade-level norms, to ensure that they are not misinterpreted based on the circumstances associated with the student. For example, depending on the curriculum that is used, students in different school districts and different states may learn different skills at different times. The grade-level norms may not be in keeping with what has been taught according to a particular curriculum. The same can be said for age-level norms.

Age-Level Norms

When you are comparing the performance of a student to that of same-aged peers, it is necessary to determine the student's precise age, because performance, especially at younger ages, can vary considerably from month to month and even from day to day. This age is often referred to as the **chronological age** of a student. Chronological age is calculated and reported as the number of years, number of months, and number of days that a student is aged on the day(s) that the tests were administered. In order to calculate the chronological age, you need two dates: the date that the assessment is administered and the date of the student's birth. For purposes of this example, the date of administration will be January 1, 2020, and the date of the student's birth will be July 21, 2005.

The following are the guidelines for calculating chronological age:

1. Set up the calculation like a subtraction problem.

	Year	Month	Day
Test Date	2020	01	01
Birth Date	– 2005	– 07	– 21
Chronological Age	# years	# months	# days

2. Subtract the student's day of birth (21) from the day of the evaluation (01). If the day of birth exceeds the day of the evaluation, borrow 30 days from the month column; borrow 30 days regardless of how many days are in that particular month. In this example, the initial problem would be 01 – 21; after borrowing 30 days, the resulting problem would be 31 – 21 = 10 days.

	Year	Month	Day
Test Date	2020	00	31
Birth Date	– 2005	– 07	– 21
Chronological Age	# years	# months	10 days

3. Subtract the student's month of birth (07) from the month of the evaluation (01); if you borrowed a month to calculate days in the previous step, subtract 1 from the month. Next, if the month of birth exceeds the month of the evaluation (minus the month borrowed to calculate days), borrow 12 months from the year column. In this example, the initial problem was 01 – 07; a month was borrowed to calculate days, resulting in 00 – 07. After borrowing 12 months from the year column, the resulting problem would be 12 – 07 = 5 months.

	Year	Month	Day
Test Date	2019	12	31
Birth Date	– 2005	– 07	– 21
Chronological Age	# years	5 months	10 days

4. Subtract the student's year of birth (2005) from the year of the evaluation (2020); if you borrowed a year to calculate months in the previous step, subtract 1 from the year. In this example, the initial problem was 2020 – 2005; a year was borrowed to calculate months, resulting in 2019 – 2005 = 14 years.

	Year	Month	Day
Test Date	2019	12	31
Birth Date	– 2005	– 07	– 21
Chronological Age	14 years	5 months	10 days

5. The chronological age of the student in the example is 14 years, 5 months, and 10 days.

Grade-Level Norms

Grade-level norms allow for the comparison of same-grade peers across the general population. For example, grade-level norms would give you the opportunity to compare a second-grader's reading performance to the performance of other second-graders (regardless of chronological age). Although no calculations are needed to determine the student's grade level (as was the case for age-level norms), norm-referenced tests (NRTs) may have differences in how grade level is classified. Some NRTs are normed by full grades (first grade, second, grade, third grade, etc.), while others are more precise in their grade-level norms, and they specify the time during the year (fall of first grade, spring of first grade, fall of second grade, etc.). The reason for this is to account for growth during the course of a grade. Particularly at earlier grade levels, it can be tricky to compare student performance at a particular grade level, because so much change often occurs during each grade level.

Concluding Thoughts on Age-Level and Grade-Level Norms

It is important to interpret age- and grade-level norms carefully so as not to develop misconceptions about a student's performance. As was previously mentioned, it is important to take caution when using age-level and grade-level norms to ensure that they are not misinterpreted based on the circumstances associated with the student. For example, depending on the curriculum that is used, students in different school districts or states may learn skills at different times. The grade-level norms may not be in keeping with what has been taught according to a particular curriculum. The same can be said for age-level norms.

Check Your Understanding 3.3

1. Calculate your own chronological age.
2. What is the difference between an age-level norm and a grade-level norm?
3. Why would it be important to differentiate between an age-level norm and a grade-level norm?
4. Describe a scenario where a grade-level norm might be more appropriate than an age-level norm.

Administration of Norm-Referenced Assessments

Because NRTs are standardized, formal tests, they typically have clearly articulated guidelines for administration, scoring, and interpretation of test results.

Required Materials

Norm-referenced assessments have standard materials that are associated with the assessment; the following are common materials associated with NRTs:

- *A test manual or examiner's manual.* A test manual, or examiner's manual, provides general information about the test that commonly includes
  - a general description of the test,
  - the purpose of the test,
  - the population (i.e., age range) for which the test is intended,
  - a description of what the test is measuring,
  - the level at which an examiner must be trained and the qualifications that an examiner must have in order to administer the assessment,
  - administration procedures,
  - scoring rules,
  - different ways that individual performance is reported (e.g., raw score, standard score, scaled score, percentile, stanine, age-equivalence, grade-equivalence), and
  - norming procedures (e.g., information on the population on which the test was normed, discussion of the test's reliability and validity).

- *A protocol*. Protocols, or response forms, allow the examiner to record responses during or after test administration. Additionally, protocols often include sections for recording demographic information and completing scoring and score interpretation. Protocols can be as short as one page, or they may be many pages long.

- *Test items or stimuli*. A test book, stimulus book, or materials containing test items to be administered are included in the materials.

It is very important that test materials be carefully guarded, to ensure the integrity of the test. For example, the test items and protocol shouldn't be copied or given to anyone who is not directly involved with the testing, to prevent the actual test items from being compromised.

Administration Guidelines

Before an individual can administer an NRT, he or she must become familiar with the rules of administration, as well as scoring procedures and interpretation. It is important that everyone who administers the test administer it, score it, and interpret the scores in the same way, so that performance can be compared across individuals. The following are some examples of rules associated with test administration that may be specified:

- Whether the examiner can indicate if an answer is correct or incorrect during test administration

- Whether the examiner should follow up an individual's response with a query or an additional prompt

- Whether the test should be timed or untimed

- Whether the test-taker should be given scrap paper or a pencil to use during the test

- Whether practice items and item training are completed prior to test items

- Whether a question can be repeated

- Whether there are rules pertaining to starting points (basals)/stopping points (ceilings)

Starting Points (Basals) and Stopping Points (Ceilings)

To elaborate on the last point (rules pertaining to starting and stopping points), norm-referenced assessments are often designed to be administered to a wide age range (e.g., the KTEA is normed for individuals between the ages of 4 and 25). However, it would typically not be appropriate to give the same set of items to individuals who are 4 as compared to those who are 25, unless they are at similar developmental or ability levels. Therefore, many NRTs develop starting and stopping rules that ensure that test items are appropriate at different age, ability, and/or competency levels. The purpose of developing starting or stopping points is to shorten the test administration and to ensure the administration of the most appropriate items to each student. Knowledge of starting and stopping rules prior to test administration is very important, because not adhering to them can greatly impact the score that a student achieves.

Starting Points (Basals)

A **starting point** is the item(s) that an examiner should begin administering to an individual. Many NRTs get more difficult as the test progresses. On those types of tests, it may be appropriate for some students to start at the beginning, and it might be equally appropriate for others to begin at more advanced items. Starting points can take many different forms across tests; the following are some examples of how a starting point may be specified:

- *Common starting point for all test-takers*: All individuals begin with Item 1.

- *Blocked starting/stopping points*: There is a specific block of items that is to be completed based on age or grade level, and the student completes only those items, regardless of performance on those items. For example, a student who is in third grade should begin with Item 11 and complete all items through Item 25, and a score is based on just those items that are administered.

- *Starting point based on a basal rule*: A **basal rule** is used to determine a starting point (higher than Item 1) that aims to reduce the number of items that a student must complete, while still ensuring that the items are developmentally appropriate for the student. A typical basal rule indicates that testing begins at a recommended starting point (other than Item 1) that is based on the student's age or grade level. If a student gets a specified number of items correct at the starting point, earlier items can be considered correct, and the student can progress to more advanced items in the test. The following are two examples of a basal rule with a recommended starting point of 11; note how differently the basal rules are applied across these two examples:

  1. If the student obtains four consecutive correct responses on the first four items given (Items 11 through 14), more advanced items may be administered. All items prior to the starting point are counted as correct (Items 1 through 10). If four consecutive correct responses are not achieved on Items 11 through 14, previous items must be

given in reverse order until four consecutive responses are achieved or until the student has completed Item 1.

2. If the student obtains three correct responses on the first five items given (Items 11 through 15), more advanced items may be administered. All items prior to the starting point are counted as correct (Items 1 through 10). If the student does not achieve correct responses on three out of the first five items (Items 11 through 15), the examiner must go back and administer all items prior to the starting point, beginning with Item 1.

Many NRTs provide guidelines for adjusting recommended starting points for students with special needs who may be at different developmental levels.

Stopping Points (Ceilings)

Similar to the concept of starting points is the idea of stopping points. A **stopping point**, or ceiling item, is the point at which the examiner stops administering items in a test. As was previously mentioned in relation to starting points, many tests get progressively more difficult as the test items advance. For these types of NRTs, stopping rules help ensure that individuals do not become frustrated with items that are above their level or that were developed for older individuals. Like starting points, stopping points can be very different across tests. Consider the following examples of stopping points:

- *Common stopping point for all test-takers.* The stopping point for all individuals is the last item on the test.

- *Blocked starting/stopping points.* In the earlier example of a specific block of items that is to be completed based on age or grade level, the student completes only those items, regardless of performance on those items. The stopping point would be Item 25.

- *Stopping point based on a ceiling rule.* Similar to a basal rule, a **ceiling rule** also helps ensure that students complete developmentally appropriate items and aren't asked to complete items that are well beyond their level of capability. The ceiling rule is typically based on the individual's performance on the test. Once the student reaches the ceiling item, no subsequent items are administered. The following are two examples of different ways of specifying a ceiling rule:

  1. Once the student gives four consecutive incorrect responses, subsequent items should not be administered.

  2. Once the student gives three out of five incorrect responses, subsequent items should not be administered.

Concluding Thoughts on Administration of Norm-Referenced Assessments

In order for performance on a norm-referenced assessment to truly be able to be compared among individuals, strict adherence to the administration guidelines is crucial. Examiners must become familiar with how the test is administered, in order to administer it correctly and obtain an accurate score on the assessment. Frequently, when evaluating for purposes of diagnosis and eligibility, a statement about whether norm-referenced assessments were administered in a standardized manner is often required, to ensure that the results are accurate.

Check Your Understanding 3.4

1. What is a starting point? What is a stopping point?

2. Why might the inclusion of a basal rule that indicates a starting point other than Item 1 be beneficial for the test-taker? For the examiner?

3. How can a ceiling rule that specifies the stopping point help alleviate frustration for test-takers?

Scoring and Interpretation of Norm-Referenced Assessments

One of the most important considerations when using norm-referenced assessments to learn about a student's strengths and needs is understanding the different types of scores that are available and how to interpret those scores. As was previously mentioned, there are a number of ways to calculate scores on an NRT and subsequently compare performance across individuals. The ones we will discuss are raw score, age-equivalence, grade-equivalence, standard score, scaled score, percentile, and stanine.

Raw Score

The raw score is the total number of points received on the assessment. For example, if each item on a test is given a value of 1, the raw score represents the total number of items correct (including items not administered according to the basal rule, as appropriate). The following are examples of ways that a raw score may be calculated:

- The starting point is Item 1, and the last item administered is Item 37. The student gives six incorrect responses during the course of the assessment. The resulting raw score would be 31 (based on the total number of correct responses given).

- The starting point is Item 15, and the ceiling item is Item 75. Between Items 15 and 75, the student obtains 10 incorrect responses. The student achieves the criteria for the basal rule, so all items before Item 15 (Items 1–14) are considered correct. The raw score in this example would be 65.

- All items are worth 0, 1, or 2 points. The student completes Items 1–28 and demonstrates the following performance:

  ○ The student receives 0 points on three items, which would contribute 0 points to the raw score.

  ○ The student receives 1 point on seven items, which would contribute 7 points to the raw score.

  ○ The student receives 2 points on all remaining items (18 items), which would contribute 36 points to the raw score.

  ○ The resulting raw score would be 43 points.

Raw scores can be compared across individuals who have taken the same assessment; however, they are relative to a particular test and difficult to use in a meaningful way to interpret or report an individual's performance.

Raw scores can also be statistically converted and used to obtain derived scores that allow for a better comparison to the normal population. In order to better interpret a student's performance and make comparisons to the general population, NRTs employ a standardization process by which raw scores are converted to fit the standardized bell curve for each age and grade level for which the test is normed. The following is a discussion of different types of derived scores that can be obtained by converting the raw score:

Standard Score

One such conversion results in a **standard score**. A standard score has a mean, or **average**, and a **standard deviation**, or a value that represents the amount of variation in a set of numbers, that is consistent across age and grade levels. Norm-referenced assessments commonly calculate standard scores based on a mean of 100 and a standard deviation of 15 (i.e., scores between 85 and 114 would be considered average). Standard scores are beneficial because they provide a reference score that is a comparison to the normed population of the same age or grade level. Once a standard score is obtained, it can be compared across individuals and across tests. Consider a 6-year-old and a 14-year-old who have taken the same assessments. It is not likely that they will have the same raw score, because a 14-year-old is typically more advanced; however, with the conversion to a standard score, performance between the two can be compared. For example, if both were to have a standard score of 115, that means that the 6-year-old is scoring 1 standard deviation above the mean as compared to other 6-year-olds, and the 14-year-old is scoring 1 standard deviation above the mean as compared to other 14-year olds. Both have scored in the above-average range. The concept of range will be further discussed below.

Scaled Score

Scaled scores are similar to standard scores in that they are obtained by converting raw scores to conform to the normal curve, with a score of 10 being the mean and a standard deviation of 3. Some NRTs use scaled scores as a way to report scores on subtests that are contained within a larger assessment. For example, on an assessment that has 10 subtests, the evaluator may be able to calculate 10 different scaled scores (one for each individual subtest), but scores on those subtests may be combined to obtain a standard score for the test as a whole.

Percentile

Percentile, or percentile rank, provides another reference point for comparing students of the same age or grade level. The percentile at which a student scores is out of 100 and refers to the percentage of same-age or grade-level peers in the general population (on which the test was originally normed) who scored below the student's score. For example, if a student's percentile score is 85, it means that 85% of the students (in the normative sample) who were the same age or grade level scored below the student's score.

Stanine

Raw scores can also be converted into stanines in order to compare students on the same scale. Stanines allow for all scores to be divided into nine equal units, with a mean of 5 and a standard deviation of 2 (Mertler, 2007).

Range

Derived scores can be discussed in terms of a range of performance (e.g., average, above average, superior, very superior, below average, well below average). The terminology used to discuss ranges often changes depending on the norm-referenced assessment. For example, some use the term "high average" and some use the term "above average"; some use "well below average" and others use "borderline." Regardless of the terminology that is used, it is important to understand how the range describes the student's performance. Of more importance is to maintain consistency in the use of terminology and its relationship to the derived scores that were obtained. For example, if a student scores a standard score of 116 on two different assessments, and one assessment refers to it as "high average" while the other refers to it as "above average," it may be beneficial to define what the term means and use it consistently each time (e.g., scores ranging from 115 through 119 are going to be referred to as "above average").

A Comparison of Derived Scores

In norm-referenced assessments, the previously discussed scores (standard score, scaled score, percentile, stanine, and range) that allow for a comparison to the normal population can also be compared to one another. Table 3.1 provides the conversions between standard score (not all standard scores are included, only

Table 3.1	Standard Score, Scaled Score, Percentile, Stanine, and Range Equivalence			
Standard Score	Scaled Score	Percentile	Stanine	Range
145	19	>99%	9	Very Superior
140	18	>99%	9	Very Superior
135	17	99%	9	Very Superior
130	16	98%	9	Very Superior
125	15	95%	8	Superior
120	14	91%	8	Superior
115	13	84%	7	Above Average
110	12	75%	6	Average
105	11	63%	6	Average
100	10	50%	5	Average
95	9	37%	4	Average
90	8	25%	4	Average
85	7	16%	3	Average
80	6	9%	2	Below Average
75	5	5%	2	Well Below Average
70	4	2%	1	Well Below Average
65	3	1%	1	Well Below Average
60	2	<1%	1	Well Below Average
55	1	<1%	1	Well Below Average

quintiles), scaled score, percentile, stanine, and range. Being aware of these conversions can really help you make sense of the data. For example, if a student has a standard score of 130, that would be equivalent to a scaled score of 16, a percentile of 98%, and a stanine of 9, and it would be considered to be in the very superior range. Earlier, it was mentioned that many tests use different terminology for the ranges. By understanding the conversions and being able to look at the other score values in relation to the range, you can better understand differences in terminology between the different tests. Additionally, this ability to see equivalent scores can be very beneficial when a test doesn't provide a means of calculating all of these different types of derived scores.

Standard Error of Measurement and Confidence Intervals

Norm-referenced assessments have a certain amount of built-in measurement error, which is referred to as the standard error of measurement. The standard error of measurement is used "to determine the effect of measurement error on individual results" (Huang & Leong, 2016, p. 1). It is "a function of both the standard deviation of observed scores and the reliability of the test" (Leong & Huang, 2010, p. 1428). This error means that the obtained score that a student receives on an assessment might not be completely accurate. For example, if a raw score of 45 on a particular test converts to a standard score of 100, the error associated with that assessment might mean that the student actually scored a 98. To account for the standard error of measurement, norm-referenced assessments often include confidence intervals. In this example, the particular assessment might provide confidence intervals at different percentages (e.g., 95% and 99%). A 95% confidence interval might be ±4, meaning that even in considering the standard error of measurement, one can say with 95% confidence that the student who achieved a standard score of 100 actually scored between 96 and 104. A 99% confidence interval might be ±6, meaning that one can say with 99% confidence that the student who achieved a standard score of 100 actually scored between 94 and 106.

Age-Equivalence and Grade-Equivalence

Insight into approximate age-equivalence or grade-equivalence based on a student's performance on an NRT can also be obtained by converting raw scores. NRTs often examine the raw scores that were obtained by the normative sample in relation to their age/grade levels and calculate approximate ages and grades associated with each raw score. Age and grade equivalence is then determined by comparing the raw score that a student obtains to the approximate ages and grades that are associated with that raw score from the normative sample. For example, on a test that has a possible raw score of 60, students who are in the fall of their first-grade year may have gotten an average of 15 points on the assessment. Any student, regardless of age, who receives a raw score of 15 on the same assessment can be considered to have a grade-level equivalence of fall of first grade. As with the age-level and grade-level norms that were discussed earlier in the chapter, it is important to interpret age- and grade-level equivalents with caution, to avoid misconceptions about student skill level.

Concluding Thoughts on Scoring and Interpretation of Norm-Referenced Assessments

Just as important as it is to ensure that norm-referenced tests are being administered according to guidelines, it is equally important to fully understand what a score refers to before using that score to describe a student's performance. All of these different types of scores mean something different and therefore need to be interpreted differently. For example, if someone does not understand the difference between a percentile and a standard score, he or she might think that a student with a standard score of 100 scored higher than everyone else in the population, when in actuality the standard score is exactly at the mean; that is, the student scored higher than 50% of the population. Similarly, if an individual has a scaled score of 9, he or she has scored in the average range; however, a stanine score of 9 is the highest stanine that can be achieved. Throughout this text, terminology surrounding different types of scores will be used, and it is important to proper diagnosis and determination of eligibility that you understand this terminology.

Check Your Understanding 3.5

1. What is a percentile rank?

2. What is a derived score?

3. What is a raw score?

4. Why would it be beneficial to know in what range a student scores?

5. Why would it be beneficial to see a score represented as both a standard score and a percentile? What is the difference?

6. What is an age-equivalence?

7. Why might a raw score be more difficult to interpret than a derived score?

Norming Procedures

The process by which a norm-referenced assessment is developed and normed is extensive and is usually described in great detail by the test developer in the manual that typically accompanies each assessment. Of particular importance is a description of the population on which the test was normed (e.g., total number of individuals, age level, grade level, race, ethnicity, geographic regions across the country, geographical location types [e.g., urban/suburban/rural], presence of disability). Additionally, since the purpose of a norm-referenced assessment is to compare student performance across the population, irrespective of the region in which the student lives, it is imperative that the measure demonstrate high levels of reliability and validity. **Reliability** refers to "the degree to which scores from a test are stable and results are consistent" (Institute of Medicine, 2015, p. 95), while **validity** refers to the assessment's ability to measure the concepts and skills that it purports to measure.

Reliability

When interpreting scores on an assessment, examiners need to be confident in the results and assured that those results will allow them to develop an accurate interpretation of the student's performance. Measures of reliability allow for stability and consistency across time, among different evaluators, and across test items and forms. There are several types of reliability that are typically provided in an NRT, including test-retest reliability, inter-rater reliability, alternate-form reliability, and split-half reliability.

Test-retest reliability measures the consistency of scores between two administrations of the same assessment. If the same assessment were to be given to the same population of students a second time, an assessment that has high levels of test-retest reliability would yield consistent results. The amount of time between administrations can influence the test-retest reliability if the assessment is measuring something that may inherently change over time (e.g., reading ability, math skills, height/weight). If the time between administrations is very short, there should be little change in performance; however, if there is a large gap in time, students may show increased performance as a result of changes in the child.

Inter-rater reliability refers to the idea that if two qualified evaluators were to score the same assessment, the scores should be consistent. In order to ensure that an individual student's scores can be compared to the general population, it is important to have strong inter-rater reliability in scoring. There are typically very specific guidelines governing how a test should be scored; within those guidelines, there should be limited subjectivity and variation in scoring. This becomes increasingly difficult for assessments that include open-ended items that may not have a definitive correct answer (e.g., written samples, drawings samples). Even in these instances, if a test has good inter-rater reliability, the scoring system will be specific enough that two evaluators would yield consistent results in scoring.

Alternate-form reliability is relevant when an assessment has been developed in more than one form. Equivalent or alternate forms allow for variability among items while ensuring the same level of difficulty. If equivalent or alternate forms are to be considered equal, scores across forms should be consistent.

Split-half reliability is similar to alternate-form reliability; however, only one form is developed. The assessment can be split in half, and scores can be compared between the two halves. Assessments with high split-half reliability would result in consistent scores if the two halves are equal. Split-half reliability measures internal consistency or "consistency of different items intended to measure the same thing within the test (homogeneity)" (Institute of Medicine, 2015, p. 95).

When determining whether a test demonstrates each of these different types of reliability, it is necessary that you understand how reliability is reported. Reliability is measured on a 1.00 point scale, with 0 being the least reliable and 1.00 being the most reliable. Reliability is generally considered to be adequate if it is .6 or greater and high if it is greater than .8 (Overton, 2016).

Validity

In addition to being assured that an assessment is reliable, examiners need to be assured that an assessment is actually measuring what it says that it measures. For example, if a test claims to measure reading comprehension, the items on the assessment need to truly relate to reading comprehension. Measures of validity allow for a clear picture of what the assessment is actually measuring in relation to what it claims to measure. Validity is "the degree to which evidence and theory support the interpretations of test scores for proposed uses of tests" (American Educational Research Association, American Psychological Association, & National Council on Measurement in Education, 2014, p. 11). The Institute of Medicine (2015) further states that "To be considered valid, the interpretation of test scores must be grounded in psychological theory and empirical evidence that demonstrates a relationship between the test and what it purports to measure" (p. 96).

Similar to reliability, several types of validity are evaluated for NRTs, including content validity, construct validity, criterion validity, concurrent validity, and predictive validity.

Content validity occurs when the test items are representative of the specific content (e.g., academic area, behavior, social/emotional) purported to be measured on the assessment. Content validity refers to the "degree to which the test content represents the targeted subject matter and supports a test's use for its intended purposes" (Institute of Medicine, 2015, p. 96). For example, if a measure claims to assess mathematical computation skills, content validity refers to whether the actual items on the test truly measure mathematical computation skills and whether there are enough items to adequately measure skill in mathematical computation. The content and skills also need to be appropriate for the level of the individuals for which the test was normed. For example, if a test purports to be appropriate for children between the ages of 6 and 16, there would need to be appropriate items to measure that particular skill at each of those ages.

Construct validity refers to the "The degree to which an individual's test scores correlate with the theoretical concept the test is designed to measure" (Institute of Medicine, 2015, p. 96). A construct is an attribute that an individual has that is not in and of itself directly observable (e.g., intelligence, creativity, memory) (Cronbach & Meehl, 1955; Westen & Rosenthal, 2003).

Criterion-related validity, or *criterion validity*, refers to the "degree to which the test's score correlates with other measurable, reliable, and relevant variables thought to measure the same construct" (Institute of Medicine, 2015, p. 96). An example of this may be a correlation with another test or measure of that same criterion.

Concurrent validity and predictive validity are often thought of under the umbrella of criterion-related validity. *Concurrent validity* evaluates the extent to which the test demonstrates criterion-related validity with a measure of related criterion that is administered on or around the same day. *Predictive validity* evaluates the extent to which the test can predict future performance on a measure of related criterion.

Concluding Thoughts on Norming Procedures

In order to ensure that a norm-referenced test will yield good data, it is important to examine the norming procedures to better understand the population on which the test was normed, as well as how reliable and valid the test is. The results of an assessment are only as good as the test itself.

Check Your Understanding 3.6

1. Why would it be important to use a norm-referenced test that is reliable? Valid?

2. What is the difference between reliability and validity?

3. Choose one type of reliability, and discuss a testing situation when it would be relevant.

Concluding Thoughts on Norm-Referenced Assessments

In summary, there are many elements that go into the development, administration, scoring, and interpretation of a norm-referenced assessment. NRTs tend to be used heavily when determining whether a student has a disability, because they allow the evaluator to examine that student's performance in comparison to the general population in many different areas (e.g., intelligence, academic areas of achievement, behavior, social/emotional). The majority of the terms that have been discussed within this section will be referred to in some capacity throughout the textbook as assessment, diagnosis, and eligibility for each of the different disabilities is discussed.

Criterion-Referenced Assessments

Another type of assessment that is commonly used to understand a student's level of competence in any given area is a criterion-referenced assessment. Criterion-referenced assessments, also referred to as CRTs, can be either formal or informal measures that "compare a student's performance to some pre-established criteria or objectives. The resulting scores are essentially interpreted as the degree of accuracy with which a student has mastered specific content" (Mertler, 2007, p. 83).

> Underlying the concept of achievement measurement is the notion of a continuum of knowledge acquisition ranging from no proficiency at all to perfect performance. An individual's achievement level falls at some point on this continuum as indicated by behaviors he displays during testing. The degree to which his achievement resembles desired performance at any specified level is assessed by criterion-referenced measures of achievement or proficiency.

> (Glaser & Darley, 1963, p. 519)

Consider an example where the standard states that students will be able to solve two-digit by two-digit addition problems that require regrouping. A criterion-referenced assessment would contain two-digit by two-digit addition problems that require regrouping. The test is a true measurement of what the standard states.

In differentiating criterion-referenced assessments from norm-referenced assessments, criterion-referenced assessments examine performance against a set of criteria, whereas norm-referenced assessments examine performance against the performance of others. It is possible to have an assessment that is based on specific criteria (criterion-referenced) and also allows for comparison to the general population (norm-referenced). It depends on the intended purpose of the assessment, the way in which it was developed, and the way in which the scores are interpreted.

Federal legislation (i.e., IDEA, ESSA) has established requirements for ensuring that students are learning according to what is deemed important at various age/grade levels or standards. Standards "set goals for what students should know and be able to do while learning academic content" (U.S. Department of Education, n.d., p. 1). The mechanism by which this occurs is through high-stakes tests that are criterion-referenced assessments. Each state establishes or adopts a set of standards in several different areas of achievement (e.g., reading, mathematics, written language, science) that specify what should be achieved at each age/grade level. Subsequently, each state identifies or develops a formal, criterion-referenced assessment that evaluates student performance each year from third through eighth grade and at least once during high school. Reading and mathematics standards are evaluated each time, while standards in other areas are evaluated at certain intervals.

Criterion-referenced assessments can also be informal assessments that measure a student's performance based on specific criteria or objectives. For example, if an educator wants to evaluate whether a student has attained mastery of a particular skill, he or she can develop a criterion-referenced assessment that measures that skill. Similarly, if a textbook chapter establishes particular objectives to be met following the completion of the chapter, a criterion-referenced assessment can be developed to specifically measure those objectives.

Check Your Understanding 3.7

1. What is a criterion-referenced test?

2. Why would it be useful to compare a student's performance to established criteria or standards?

Curriculum-Based Assessments

Curriculum-based assessments (CBAs) are measures of a student's achievement in the curriculum. The curriculum refers to "what" information is taught and, in some instances, "how" that information is taught (or the method of instruction). Curriculum-based assessments can be teacher-created or textbook-generated. Additionally, they can measure broad concepts or very narrow concepts taught in the curriculum. For example, if the social studies curriculum includes a unit on the Revolutionary War, a curriculum-based assessment could relate to one battle associated with the war, or it could be a unit assessment that encompasses the whole topic.

There is no set format that CBAs must adhere to. They can take many forms, including informal assessments that are teacher-created as well as formal assessments. For example, curriculum-based measurement (CBM), as described by Deno (1985), is a formal type of CBA whereby teachers are able to monitor progress according to what has been taught in the curriculum. Refer back to Chapter 2 for a more extensive discussion of curriculum-based measurement, or curriculum measurement, and how it relates to the progress monitoring of skills that are taught within the curriculum. Regardless of the format, ultimately, the goal of using CBAs is to obtain information about what a child has learned according to what has been taught. Educators can be very deliberate about their course of instruction based on student performance on curriculum-based assessments. Hargis (2005, p. 21) stated that

> if curriculum based assessment is to be used well, a curriculum should be laid out on a seamless continuum. The scope and sequence of skills or objectives should be borderless. It should be sequenced by order of difficulty and by readiness relationships. . . . Curriculum-based assessment is used to find the correct place on a continuum that will permit student success.

Some may ask what the difference is between criterion-referenced assessments (see previous discussion) and curriculum-based assessments. Criterion-referenced assessment is a method of evaluating performance according to standards, and curriculum-based assessment focuses on what is being taught in the curriculum. "Standards represent the goals for what students should learn. They are different from curriculum, which means what teachers teach, and how" (U.S. Department of Education, n.d., para. 2). Both are beneficial in different ways and can give you insight into a student's strengths and needs.

Refer back to the discussion of an assessment loop in Chapter 2; CBAs provide a good mechanism for engaging in the continuous process of teaching information in the curriculum, evaluating what the student has learned, and using that information to guide instruction and make improvements, as appropriate. Curriculum-based assessment is "a tuning process where level of instruction is continually matched with student skill" (Hargis, 2005, p. 40).

Check Your Understanding 3.8

1. Can a teacher create a curriculum-based assessment? If so, provide an example. If not, explain why not.

2. What information can a curriculum-based assessment provide?

Performance-Based and Portfolio Assessments

Throughout their education, students are frequently asked to complete various types of tasks that relate to what they are learning. For example, they may be asked to write an essay describing their favorite animal, complete a book report on a book that they read, or show their classmates how to solve a problem that they are working on in math. With these types of tasks in mind, let us introduce the concepts of performance-based assessment and portfolio assessment.

Performance-Based Assessments

Performance-based assessment, or performance assessment, refers to products or work samples that are created by a student to demonstrate his or her skills or knowledge. Examples of performance-based assessments may include pieces of writing, performances, presentations, art projects, debates, experiments, and demonstrations. An authentic assessment is an assessment that requires real-world applications (e.g., assessing students' understanding of measurement by asking them to measure out a liquid in a measuring cup; assessing the ability to tie shoes by asking a student to demonstrate how to tie her shoe). Some use the terms "performance assessment" and "authentic assessment" synonymously, whereas others see one as a subset of the other (Frey & Schmitt, 2007). Performance-based assessments and authentic assessments allow students to apply their knowledge or skills in a meaningful way. Additionally, they provide many different possible mechanisms for demonstrating a skill. For example, one student may, having read a narrative, be really proficient at writing an essay that compares and contrasts the main characters. Another student may prefer to give an oral report to the class. Still another student may be able to demonstrate her understanding by acting out the story. Performance assessments allow educators to utilize various approaches to assessing their students to best understand their students' skills or knowledge.

Portfolio Assessments

A portfolio is a collection of performance assessments that serves to "review the progress of a learner's work over time" (Janesick, 2001, p. 7). Since a portfolio is composed of a number of individual performance assessments, it provides a good look at a student's strengths and needs in that area. Portfolios are often developed in a number of different areas (writing portfolio, art portfolio, music portfolio, etc.) for different purposes. The following are some of the different ways that selections for a portfolio can be made:

- All work samples in the portfolio topic can be included.

- Students may choose their favorite or best products.

- Teachers may select what they deem the most representative products.

- One product from each of several skill categories may be chosen (for example, a writing portfolio may contain a sample of a narrative, a poem, a description, a persuasive essay, and a letter).

- Products can be randomly selected.

- Similar products from different points in time may be selected.

It is important to consider the selection process when evaluating a portfolio, because there may be differences in the quality of performance, depending on how the pieces were chosen.

Overall, performance assessments and portfolio assessments can give useful information about how a student might apply his or her knowledge. Further, the numerous types of performance assessments that may be used can help an educator find the best way that a student can demonstrate his or her skills.

Error Analysis

When you are evaluating a student's responses on an assessment, it may be very straightforward to determine whether the student provided correct or incorrect responses. That may yield a percentage correct and give you a sense of how the student performed. However, that does not provide insight into *why* the student responded correctly or incorrectly. An **error analysis** is a close examination or analysis of a student's errors or mistakes to determine whether a pattern emerges that may give you insight into the student's level of understanding. Errors can be random in nature and reveal very little about what a student understands; alternatively, they can reveal patterns that are a window into a student's strengths and needs, as well as which strategies the student is using to approach a particular type of question. If a pattern emerges, it is possible to use that information to tailor instruction to meet the student's unique needs.

There are a number of ways in which to complete an error analysis, and error analysis can be performed on any type of assessment in which a student is providing an answer or response. Consider the following examples of errors where patterns may be evident:

- A student completes an assessment of mathematical computation that measures single-digit by single-digit multiplication facts. If the student gives an answer of 48 each time he is given the problem 7 × 8, that may give you insight into the fact that he is demonstrating table errors or errors in recalling math facts. Instead of thinking of 7 × 8 = 56, he may be incorrectly associating the problem 7 × 8 with the answer for 6 × 8.

- A student is reading a passage aloud and makes several errors in oral reading. It is possible to closely examine those errors and determine both the type of error (substitution error, omission error, insertion error, self-correction, etc.) and the impact of the error (e.g., syntax error). That can give you insight into how the student approaches an unknown word. For example, the student reads the sentence: *We wanted to go to the park to play on the slide and swings, but Mom said that we had to go to the store before we could go to the park* as "*We want to go to park to pay on the slid and swing, but Mom say that we had go to stove before we could go to the pack.*" In this sentence, there are several mistakes that the student has made. There are some trends, such as leaving off morphological endings (*want* instead of *wanted*; *swing* instead of *swings*), substituting words for visually similar words (*pay* instead of *play*; *stove* instead of *store*, *pack* instead of *park*), and omissions (<u>the</u> park; <u>to</u> go; <u>the</u> store).

- In a writing sample about a child's upcoming birthday party, a student penned the following passage . . .

Our birthday party is going to be in August. We are allowed to invite 10 friends each and we are having our party at our house. We are going to play lots of games and we will have prizes too. Last night, we were so excited about our party that we wrote all of our invitations and begged mom and dad to take us to the post office so that we could mail them to our friends.

in the following way:

are berthday party is gowing to be in ogust we are a lowd to invit 10 frends each and we are haveing are party at are hows. we are gowing to play lots of gams and we will have prizez to. Last nit, we were so exited about are party that we rote all of are invatashuns and beged mom and dad to tack us to the post ofis so that we cood mail them to are frends

In this example, the student demonstrates several error patterns within spelling (e.g., misspellings are generally phonetically accurate, not demonstrating an understanding of the v-c-e rule). There are also difficulties with capitalization and punctuation. While this is not a long sample, it is possible to see some trends; it would be important to look at more than one sample, or a much longer sample, to really determine a true pattern; but this may give you some direction or insight.

These are just a few examples of how patterns of errors may provide insight into a student's understanding. Error analyses are often very time-consuming, because they typically involve systematic methods of determining patterns; however, the benefits can greatly outweigh the time commitment. Error analyses can be highly beneficial for pinpointing the source of the difficulty and providing a very specific direction for instruction.

Check Your Understanding 3.10

1. What does an error analysis measure?

2. Describe the benefits of looking for patterns in a student's mistakes.

Interview

When conducting an evaluation of a student, it may be impossible for the examiner to learn everything that he or she needs to learn about that student through direct assessments. An interview provides the examiner an opportunity to learn about the student from another's perspective. It may be beneficial to ask questions of teachers, parents, and the student himself or herself to gain a better understanding of the student's performance and ability in different areas (e.g., academics, behavior, social, emotional, physical/medical), as well as his or her likes, dislikes, and future plans. It is typically not possible to glean enough information to determine whether a student has a disability without conducting interviews with people who have had different types of experiences with the student (or conducting interviews with the student himself or herself).

Interviews can be formal or informal. When creating an interview, there are many ways of developing interview questions; however, it is typically beneficial for you to generate open-ended questions that encourage the interviewee to provide information. For example, instead of asking a student "Do you have a favorite subject?" (to which the answer may be simply yes or no), you could change the question to "What is your favorite subject?"

A benefit to conducting interviews about the same student with multiple individuals is that you can compare perspectives. For example, a teacher and a parent may have very different perspectives on a student's academic performance. Consider the concept of homework and the completion of each homework assignment. A teacher would typically have insight into the following information:

- What was assigned

- The expectations of the assignment

- The information that was taught in preparation for the assignment

- Whether the student submitted the assignment

- The quality of the assignment

The parent would typically have insight into the following information:

- Whether the parent observed the child working on the assignment

- Whether the child asked for help and whether the parent provided help

- How long the assignment took to complete

- Whether the child showed confusion or frustration regarding the assignment

These two perspectives on homework may be very different and provide different views of homework that should be considered when evaluating a student's academic performance.

Overall, interviews provide a great opportunity to better understand a student's strengths and needs in many areas of evaluation (e.g., academics, behavior, social, emotional, physical/medical). Interviews offer an indirect view of a student's skills, and this alone would typically not be sufficient to make educational decisions; however, using information gained from an interview as a complement to information that has been directly measured (by norm-referenced assessments, criterion-referenced assessments, curriculum-based assessments, direct observations, etc.) can help you create a more complete picture of a student.

Check Your Understanding 3.11

1. What are some questions that you could ask parents about their child's academics? Social skills? Behavior?

2. Discuss possible benefits of interviewing a student about his or strengths and needs.

Direct Observation

Another commonly used method of assessing students is direct observation. In a direct observation, a special education professional or other qualified observer sits and watches a student in his or her environment while recording data about the behaviors the child is demonstrating. Direct observation is considered non-intrusive and passive, meaning that the observer is not engaging with the student during the time of the observation. A primary purpose of direct observation is to gain insight into the student's behavior. For example, a special educator might be having behavioral difficulties with a student in class. He or she may conduct direct observations of the student to better understand the function of, or reason for, the student's behavior. During the observations, the observer might notice that the student appears to be acting out because he or she wants attention from classmates.

There are many types of direct observation, including observations that produce data that is more qualitative in nature (e.g., anecdotal recording), as well as those that produce data that is more quantitative in nature (e.g., event recording/frequency sampling, interval recording/time sampling, duration recording, latency recording, inter-response time). Both qualitative and quantitative observations can be beneficial, depending on the purpose of the observation.

Anecdotal Recording

An **anecdotal recording** is one in which the observer records all the behaviors that a student demonstrates, as well as any interactions that the student has, during a specified period of time. Those observations can then be evaluated to identify all undesirable behaviors and determine the events immediately surrounding the behavior, to identify possible trends. These events are known as the *antecedent* to the behavior and the *consequence* of the behavior. The antecedent is the event that takes place immediately before the behavior occurs. The consequence is the event that takes place immediately following the behavior. (It is important to note that this usage of the term "consequence" is very different from the conventional connotation of the term, which is negative and typically refers to a punishment.) Following the observation, the observer develops an ABC chart (A stands for antecedent; B stands for behavior; and C stands for consequence.). This gives him or her the opportunity to look for trends in behavior. Consider the following examples of ABC sequences:

- Each time a teacher calls on a student to answer a question (antecedent), the student puts his head on the desk (behavior), and the teacher moves on to another student (consequence). In this situation, it is possible that the behavior is a function of wanting to avoid having to answer a question. The fact that the teacher moves on may reinforce the behavior, because the student knows that if he puts his head down, the teacher will move on and he won't have to answer the question.

- The teacher is having a discussion with students in the class (antecedent), the student calls out and tells the teacher that she had cereal for breakfast (behavior), and the teacher tells the student that she likes cereal also (consequence). Later during the observation, the teacher is meeting with a small reading group and the student is not part of that group (antecedent); the student calls out to the teacher to ask if she can sharpen her pencil (behavior), and the teacher walks over to the student to see if the pencil really needs to be sharpened (consequence). In both of these instances, the teacher is focused on students other than the student being observed (antecedent), and the teacher gives attention to the student (consequence) following the behavior. The student may be engaging in this behavior because she is seeking attention, and the consequence may be reinforcing the attention-seeking behavior.

Event Recording

An **event recording**, sometimes referred to as a frequency recording, is an observation in which the observer records the number of times that a student engages in a previously identified behavior over a prolonged period of time. "Frequency or event recording is most useful when observing behaviors that have a discrete beginning and ending" (Hintze, Volpe, & Shapiro, 2002, p. 997). For example, the observation may take place over a two-hour time period, and the behavior of interest might be the student's getting up out of her seat when remaining seated is expected. An event recording would yield a number of events (the number of times that the student got out of her seat) over that time period (two hours).

Interval Recording

An interval recording, or time sampling, is an observation in which the observer watches the student's behavior during particular intervals for a specified period of time (e.g., 30-second intervals for 1 hour, totaling 120 intervals) to see whether the student is engaging in the behavior of interest. The behavior of interest is often a behavior that the student engages in frequently. For example, if the behavior of interest involves the student picking at his wrist, the observer may record the number of intervals (e.g., each period lasting 30 seconds) in which the student is picking at his wrist. The data would then be calculated as the total number of intervals or the percentage of intervals in which the student picks at his wrist. In this scenario, if the student was observed for two hours, there would be 120 intervals of observation. Hintze et al. (2002) described three methods of completing interval recordings: whole-interval recording (interval is counted if the behavior spans the duration of the interval), partial-interval recording (interval is counted if the behavior occurs at any time during the interval), and momentary time sampling (interval is counted if the behavior occurs at the moment that the interval begins).

Duration Recording

A duration recording is one in which the observer records the duration or length in time of an identified behavior from when the student first engages in the behavior to when the student stops engaging in the behavior. For example, if the identified behavior is the student crying when her parent drops her off in the morning, the observer would watch the child during several instances when she is dropped off. If the child cries, the observer would note the length of time that the child cries. After several instances, the observer would determine an average duration of the behavior.

Latency Recording

A latency recording is one in which the observer records the amount of time that it takes a student to engage in a behavior after a direction is given. For example, if the teacher asks the student to take out his homework, the observer would record how long it takes for the student to do so. If the teacher tells students to line up for lunch, the observer would record how long it takes the student to line up. After observing several different instances of directions being given, the observer could then determine an average latency.

Inter-Response Time

Inter-response time is a measure of the amount of time that occurs between two instances of a behavior. If the identified behavior is that the student calls out without raising her hand, the observer would measure the amount of time that elapses between one instance of calling out and another instance of calling out. After measuring the elapsed time between several instances, the observer could then calculate an average amount of elapsed time, or inter-response time.

Concluding Thoughts on Direct Observation

Each of these types of observation could be beneficial both in isolation and in combination. There may be particular behaviors that are more conducive to a particular type of recording, but many behaviors could be measured in a number of ways, using different types of recordings.

Check Your Understanding 3.12

1. What are antecedents, behaviors, and consequences?

2. Compare/contrast three types of direct observation.

Checklists and Behavior Rating Scales

Chances are good that you have used or will use a checklist at some point (to-do list, packing list, etc.). Checklists can be really beneficial as an assessment, because they provide you the opportunity to look at a list of skills and/or characteristics and determine whether a student has demonstrated evidence of the skill or characteristic. Checklists provide for a basic "yes" (check) or "no" (don't check) response. Additionally, if you are completing a series of checklist assessments, they allow you the opportunity to look at the skills/characteristics over time to see whether the student demonstrates consistent performance, a decline in performance, or growth in performance. The following are some examples of when a checklist may be appropriate:

- Determining whether a child has met age-appropriate developmental milestones in the various developmental domains (e.g., social/emotional, cognitive, language, physical/movement).

- Assessing a student's writing sample to determine whether he or she has included particular elements.

- Assessing a set of appropriate behaviors in a specific setting.

Behavior rating scales are similar to checklists; they just have a different form of response. While checklists require a yes/no response, behavior rating scales, often reported on a Likert scale, have a range of performance. They may be beneficial when there isn't a definitive yes/no answer to a question. For example, "On a scale of 1 to 5, how would you rate the child's ability to follow a set of directions when they are given?" Both behavior rating scales and checklists can help you better understand a student's abilities or skills.

Check Your Understanding 3.13

1. What are some skill areas that you could assess using a checklist?

2. How do checklists and behavior rating scales differ?

CHAPTER SUMMARY

This chapter highlights many types of formal and informal assessment that can be used to better understand a student's strengths and needs. A combination of these types of assessment can provide data and information that can give you great insight into student performance and level of ability. When trying to determine which types of assessment to use, it is important that you really consider the purpose of conducting an assessment (e.g., screening, diagnosis and eligibility, instructional considerations). Further, when interpreting assessment results, always take into consideration the characteristics of the assessment (e.g., the type of assessment, the purpose of the assessment, the way in which it was administered, the way that it was scored, the way that it is supposed to be interpreted). The multitude of assessments to choose from can seem daunting; however, a systematic approach to assessment selection will make the process seem much more manageable. In Chapters 4 and 5, a discussion relating to the different areas of student characteristics will be considered in the context of the assessment types that were discussed in this chapter. Further, throughout each chapter on disabilities, reference will be made to various types of assessment.

APPLY WHAT YOU HAVE LEARNED

1. Look back at Figures 3.1 through 3.4 and the description of the distribution of scores that they represent. Draw a distribution based on the following: the scores are predominantly at the upper end of the range of scores (possible scores range from 0% to 100%) and most students received a similar score (90%).

2. Research the topic of curriculum-based measurement (CBM). Give an example of a test that is considered to be a CBM, and

explain why it would be helpful to better understanding student performance.

3. Explain the difference between criterion-referenced and norm-referenced tests. What are the benefits of each?

4. Why would it be beneficial to conduct both interviews and direct observations? What possible information could interviews provide that direct observations could not, and what possible information could direct observations provide that interviews could not?

5. Make a chart of the following assessment types: Norm-referenced assessments, criterion-referenced assessments, curriculum-based assessments, performance/portfolio assessments, error analyses, interviews, direct observations, and checklists/behavior rating scales. Give a description of each, and explain why each could help you better understand student performance.

REFERENCES

American Educational Research Association, American Psychological Association, & National Council on Measurement in Education. (2014). *Standards for educational and psychological testing.* Washington, DC: Author.

Cronbach, L., & Meehl, P. (1955). Construct validity in psychological tests. *Psychological Bulletin, 52*(4), 281–302.

Deno, S. (1985). Curriculum-based measurement: The emerging alternative. *Exceptional Children, 52*(3), 219–232.

Frey, B., & Schmitt, V. (2007). Coming to terms with classroom assessment. *Journal of Advanced Academics, 18*(3), 402–423.

Institute of Medicine (IOM). (2015). *Psychological testing in the service of disability determination.* Washington, DC: The National Academies Press.

Glaser, R., & Darley, J. (1963). Instructional technology and the measurement of learning outcomes: Some questions. *American Psychologist, 18*(8), 519–521.

Glossary of Education Reform. (2015). *Norm-referenced test.* Retrieved from https://www.edglossary.org/norm-referenced-test

Hargis, C. (2005). *Curriculum based assessment: A primer* (3rd ed.). Springfield, IL: Charles C. Thomas.

Hintze, J., Volpe, R., & Shapiro, E. (2002). Best practices in the systematic direct observation of student behavior. In A. Thomas & J. Grimes (Eds.), *Best practices in school psychology* IV (pp. 993–1006). Bethesda, MD: National Association of School Psychologists.

Huang, J., & Leong, F. (2016). *Standard error of measurement.* Encyclopaedia Britannica. Retrieved from https://www.britannica.com/science/standard-error-of-measurement

Janesick, V. (2001). *The assessment debate: A reference handbook (Contemporary education issues).* Santa Barbara, CA: ABC-CLIO.

Leong, F., & Huang, J. (2010). Standard error of measurement. In Salkind, N. J. (Ed.), *Encyclopedia of research design.* Thousand Oaks, CA: SAGE Publications. Retrieved from https://search-ebsco-host-com.proxy-wcupa.klnpa.org/login.aspx?direct=true&db=nlebk&AN=474297&site=bsi-live

Mertler, C. (2007). *Interpreting standardized test scores: Strategies for data-driven instructional decision making.* Los Angeles, CA: SAGE Publications.

Overton, T. (2016). *Assessing learners with special needs* (8th ed.). Upper Saddle River, NJ: Pearson Education.

U.S. Department of Education. (n.d.). *College- and career-ready standards*. Retrieved from https://www.ed.gov/k-12reforms/standards

Venn, J. (2014). *Assessing students with special needs* (5th ed.). Upper Saddle River, NJ: Pearson Education.

Weaver, B. (2018). *Formal vs. informal assessments*. Retrieved from https://www.scholastic.com/teachers/articles/teaching-content/formal-vs-informal-assessments

Westen, D., & Rosenthal, R. (2003). Quantifying construct validity: Two simple measures. *Journal of Personality and Social Psychology, 84*(3), 608–618.

Assessment for Diagnosis and Eligibility

Development and Health

Tara S. Guerriero, PhD

Learning Objectives

After the completion of Chapters 4 and 5, you should be able to:

- Summarize the IDEA guidelines for conducting an evaluation.

- Discuss the difference between intelligence and achievement.

- Define the five elements of language and differentiate between them.

- Identify the five main areas of academic achievement and describe each of the related subareas.

- Explain how language is related to each of the five areas of achievement.

- Discuss methods for evaluating behavior and why it is important to determine the function of behavior.

- Examine the benefits of completing a comprehensive diagnostic evaluation that includes assessment of students in all of the following areas: intelligence, language, areas of achievement, behavior, social/emotional characteristics, and health/medical status.

Key Terms

component categories of language (p. 101)	diagnostic and/or eligibility process (p. 92)
language form, language content, and language use	comprehensive evaluation, comprehensive diagnostic evaluation, psycho-educational evaluation, multidisciplinary evaluation
diagnosis (p. 93)	

(Continued)

(Continued)

elements of language (p. 101)	language (p. 100)
phonology, phoneme, morphology, morpheme, syntax, semantics, pragmatics	receptive language, expressive language
eligibility (p. 93)	language difference, language delay, language disorder (p. 106)
health and medical (p. 110)	social and emotional characteristics (p. 107)
intelligence (p. 96)	
intelligence quotient (IQ), mental ability, mental capacity, cognitive ability	

Introduction to the Chapter

The diagnostic and/or eligibility process for each disability is unique, as well as complicated. In order to better understand the extensive scope of a comprehensive evaluation, it may be beneficial to think of the diagnostic and/or eligibility process as a giant jigsaw puzzle. There are many pieces that need to be evaluated, but it doesn't fully make sense until all the pieces are put together to reveal the whole picture. An effective diagnostic and/or eligibility process needs to be comprehensive enough to depict a clear picture of the student that includes strengths and needs across the full continuum of characteristics associated with the student. Further, it has to be specific enough to allow for differentiation between different categories of disability, to ensure an accurate diagnosis.

Throughout this text, the following four terms will be used interchangeably to refer to the **diagnostic and/or eligibility process**:

- **Comprehensive evaluation**
- **Comprehensive diagnostic evaluation**
- **Psychoeducational evaluation**
- **Multidisciplinary evaluation**

Each of these terms is used in education; however, different areas of the country and/or different areas of specialty might prefer one over another.

Diagnosis vs. Eligibility and the Role of the Multidisciplinary Team

The use of the terms "diagnosis" and "eligibility" in an educational setting can be difficult to understand. When do we use the term "diagnosis," when do we use the term "eligibility," and what is the role of the multidisciplinary team in the process? Diagnosis involves a determination of whether an individual demonstrates the required diagnostic criteria that are associated with a particular disability (disorder, condition, syndrome, etc.). Eligibility relates to the determination of whether an individual qualifies for special education services and subsequently needs specially designed instruction as the result of a diagnosed disability.

Depending on the disability (disorder, condition, syndrome, etc.), the diagnostic process may take place in an educational setting, or it may take place in a private or medical setting. There are several disabilities—such as learning disabilities, intellectual disabilities, and speech and language impairments—that may be diagnosed in an educational setting by a school psychologist or other school specialist (e.g., speech-language pathologist). However, other disabilities—such as ADHD, hearing impairments, visual impairments, health and medical conditions (heart conditions, cancer, type 1 diabetes, etc.), and physical conditions (cerebral palsy, spina bifida, etc.)—are more frequently diagnosed in a private or medical setting by a mental health professional (e.g., clinical psychologist), specialist (e.g., audiologist), or medical professional (e.g., primary care physician, psychiatrist, ophthalmologist).

The role of the team will differ depending on whether they are diagnosing a disability and determining eligibility for special education services or whether a diagnosis has already been made and they are only determining whether the student is eligible for special education services. If a student has already been diagnosed in a private or medical setting, the purpose of the multidisciplinary team is not to diagnose, but rather to determine eligibility for special education services. Alternatively, if it is a disability that can be diagnosed in an educational setting and the student is not coming with an already diagnosed condition, the role of the team is to evaluate for a possible diagnosis, and then, if a diagnosis is made, to further determine whether the student is eligible for special education services. Consider the following scenarios as a means of highlighting the differences:

- Hunter has been referred for an evaluation by the multidisciplinary team for a suspected learning disability. The multidisciplinary team (typically led by a school psychologist or other professional who specializes in conducting evaluations) conducts a comprehensive diagnostic evaluation and determines that Hunter does in fact qualify for a diagnosis of a learning disability and that he is eligible for special education services based on need.

- Olivia was diagnosed (by her pediatrician) with cerebral palsy. Her parents have requested an evaluation by the multidisciplinary team to determine her eligibility for special education services.

In both of these scenarios, the role of the multidisciplinary team is to determine eligibility; however, only in Hunter's situation is the team also determining whether he qualifies for a diagnosis of a disability. This chapter and Chapter 5 will highlight important areas in which information is gathered in a multidisciplinary evaluation. Regardless of whether the team is diagnosing a student and determining eligibility, or whether it is only determining eligibility, the evaluation involves the gathering of information in the same areas of student characteristics.

IDEA Regulations for Evaluation of Disabilities

IDEA Section 300.304 (2004) provides the following guidelines for conducting an evaluation:

- Evaluators must use more than one measure to determine whether a child has a disability; gather functional, developmental, and academic information about the child from a variety of different tools and sources (including the parents); and use assessments that are technically sound.

- As was discussed in Chapter 2, evaluators must choose and administer assessments that are nondiscriminatory based on race and culture, that utilize the child's primary language or mode of communication (unless it is not feasible to do so), and that take into consideration any deficits (e.g., sensory, motor, and communication) that the student may have, to ensure that the results accurately reflect the child's capabilities.

- Assessments must be administered by trained personnel in a way that is consistent with the instructions that accompany the assessment tool and for the purposes for which they were intended.

- Students must be assessed in "all areas related to the suspected disability, including, if appropriate, health, vision, hearing, social and emotional status, general intelligence, academic performance, communicative status, and motor abilities" (IDEA, 2004, § 300.304(c)(4)).

The purpose of Section 300.304 of IDEA is to ensure that students are being evaluated in such a way that will allow for reliable and valid results. It is very important that the results of a comprehensive evaluation be done in such a way that it allows for a true picture of a student's strengths and needs and that it, further, leads to recommendations for instruction.

In addition to obtaining new information about a student through multiple assessments, it is valuable to review existing data that has already been obtained. IDEA Section 300.305 (2004) further delineates guidelines for reviewing existing data as part of a comprehensive evaluation that includes the following: information provided by the parents; results from classroom-based, local, and state assessments; and observations conducted by teachers and related service providers.

IDEA Section 300.306 (2004) provides the following guidelines for determining eligibility for special education services following the completion of the comprehensive evaluation:

- A team of qualified professionals and the parents evaluate the assessment information to determine whether the child has a disability according to one of the 14 categories of disability defined under IDEA (see Chapter 1 for a complete list) and to evaluate the educational needs of the child.

- A child will not be considered eligible for services if the determining factors include a lack of appropriate instruction in reading or math or limited English proficiency. Additionally, if the student does not meet the eligibility criteria related to the IDEA categories of disability, he or she will not be eligible for services.

- Information from a number of different sources (e.g., assessments that measure aptitude and achievement, information provided by parents and teachers) and information relating to the child's physical condition, social or cultural background, and adaptive behavior must be gathered, documented, and carefully considered.

- If it is determined that a student has one of the 14 IDEA disabilities and there is evidence of need for special education and related services, a child will be considered eligible, and an IEP will be developed.

The overarching takeaway from each of the previously stated IDEA guidelines should be to understand the extensive nature of a comprehensive evaluation and its role in determining whether a student has a disability and whether he or she is eligible for special education services. Careful attention must be placed on selecting a battery of assessments that will allow the examiner to develop a thorough set of results that is truly able to shed light on all the unique characteristics that each student possesses and to lead to good instructional recommendations. Accomplishing this requires examination of many aspects of student performance, through a variety of assessment types. The assessment types that were discussed in Chapter 3 can all be valuable in better understanding student performance. Thus, connections to the assessment types and examples of specific measures that were discussed in Chapter 3 will be made throughout this chapter and Chapter 5.

Throughout the course of this chapter and Chapter 5, information relating to evaluating student characteristics in the following six areas will be discussed, to provide a better understanding of what is factored into a comprehensive evaluation that allows for a well-rounded examination of the student:

- Intelligence

- Language

- Social and emotional characteristics

- Health and medical status

- Areas of academic achievement

- Behavior

The present chapter will focus on the areas that are typically more developmental in nature or relate to health (intelligence, language, social and emotional characteristics, and health and medical status), while Chapter 5 will focus on the areas that are typically learned (areas of academic achievement and behavior). Many comparisons will be made between the areas discussed in this chapter and those included in Chapter 5.

Intelligence

Intelligence is a widely discussed concept that often yields much disagreement, in terms of both what constitutes intelligence and how intelligence should be evaluated. For purposes of this text, **intelligence** will be discussed in relation to an individual's level of mental capacity or potential for learning. The following terms are often used interchangeably to describe intelligence: **intelligence quotient (IQ)**, **mental ability**, **mental capacity**, and **cognitive ability**. Intelligence is thought to be innate to an individual. That is, it isn't something that is directly taught; rather, it is something that is unique to each individual and the way in which each individual's mind works. Additionally, it is thought to remain stable over time. For example, an individual should have the same level of intelligence (as compared to those of the same age) at the ages of 5, 35, and 85, if it is accurately measured.

The concept of intelligence means different things to different people, and it can be measured in a variety of ways. A number of theories (e.g., Carroll's Three Stratum Theory (Carroll, 1993), the Cattell-Horn-Carroll model (Flanagan & Dixon, 2013), Gardner's Theory of Multiple Intelligences (Gardner, 2011)) aim to explain the complex concept of intelligence. The Cattell-Horn-Carroll model, or CHC model, often serves as the foundation for many intelligence tests (Flanagan & Dixon, 2013). The CHC theory describes several factors, often referred to as G-factors, that are often associated with or contribute to an individual's level of intelligence. These include, but are not limited to, the following:

- *Fluid reasoning (Gf)* is "The use of deliberate and controlled mental operations to solve novel problems that cannot be performed automatically. Mental operations often include drawing inferences, concept formation, classification, generating and testing hypothesis, identifying relations, comprehending implications, problem solving, extrapolating, and transforming information. Inductive and deductive reasoning are generally considered the hallmark indicators of Gf" (McGrew, 2009, p. 5). When people are faced with situations that they haven't encountered before, they might use fluid reasoning to problem solve or develop a plan for how to proceed in the situation.

- *Comprehension-knowledge (Gc)* is "The knowledge of the culture that is incorporated by individuals through a process of acculturation. Gc is typically described as a person's breadth and depth of acquired knowledge of the language, information and concepts of a specific culture, and/or the application of this knowledge" (McGrew, 2009, p. 5). Comprehension-knowledge allows for the understanding of cultural or interpersonal norms. An example of comprehension-knowledge may be the knowledge that in some cultures, it is expected that one make eye contact when having a conversation.

- *Short-term memory (Gsm)* is "The ability to apprehend and maintain awareness of a limited number of elements of information in the immediate situation (events that occurred in the last minute or so). A limited-capacity system that loses information quickly through the decay of memory traces, unless an individual activates other cognitive resources to maintain the information in immediate awareness" (McGrew, 2009, p. 5). Short-term memory is considered immediate memory that is temporary. For example, short-term memory would be required in order to look at a phone number and enter it into one's phone from memory, without looking at it again.

- *Long-term storage and retrieval (Glr)* is "The ability to store and consolidate new information in long-term memory and later fluently retrieve the stored information (e.g., concepts, ideas, items, names) through association. Memory consolidation and retrieval can be measured in terms of information stored for minutes, hours, weeks, or longer" (McGrew, 2009, pp. 5–6). Long-term storage and retrieval involves the ability to store memories and retrieve those memories at a later time. For example, if someone were asked what they had for dinner the night before, he or she would need to have stored that information in long-term memory and be able to retrieve it in order to answer the question.

- *Processing speed (Gs)* is "The ability to automatically and fluently perform relatively easy or over-learned elementary cognitive tasks, especially when high mental efficiency (i.e., attention and focused concentration) is required" (McGrew, 2009, p. 6). An example of processing speed would be the speed at which a person could answer a question once it was asked. That person would need to take in the information, process it, and think of a response.

- *Auditory processing (Ga)* is "Abilities that depend on sound as input and on the functioning of our hearing apparatus. A key characteristic is the extent an individual can cognitively control (i.e., handle the competition between signal and noise) the perception of auditory information. The Ga domain circumscribes a wide range of abilities involved in the interpretation and organization of sounds, such as discriminating patterns in sounds and musical structure (often under background noise and/or distorting conditions) and the ability to analyze, manipulate, comprehend and synthesize sound elements, groups of sounds, or sound patterns" (McGrew, 2009, p. 5). Once information has come into the auditory system, auditory processing allows the brain to make sense of the stimuli that have entered the system. For example, if a song were to come on the radio, auditory processing would be needed to recognize the song.

- *Visual processing (Gv)* is "The ability to generate, store, retrieve, and transform visual images and sensations. Gv abilities are typically measured by tasks (figural or geometric stimuli) that require the perception and transformation of visual shapes, forms, or images and/ or tasks that require maintaining spatial orientation with regard to objects that may change or move through space" (McGrew, 2009, p. 5). Similar to auditory processing, visual processing occurs when the brain processes information that comes in through the visual system. For example, being able to detect a visual pattern within a larger design is an example of a task that would require visual processing.

While the specific methodology associated with any given intelligence test may differ, the common purpose under the CHC model is to measure the general intelligence of an individual, as well as several factors that are commonly associated with intelligence. The following assessments are often used to measure intelligence: the Wechsler Intelligence Scale for Children (WISC), the Wechsler Preschool and Primary Scale of Intelligence (WPPSI), the Wechsler Adult Intelligence Scale (WAIS), the Woodcock-Johnson Tests of Cognitive Abilities, the Stanford-Binet Intelligence Scale, the Comprehensive Test of Nonverbal Intelligence (CTONI), the Wechsler Nonverbal Scale of Ability (WNV), and the Detroit Tests of Learning Abilities (DTLA). Intelligence tests can measure both verbal ability (stimuli that involve words and language) and nonverbal ability (stimuli that do not require the use of language, such as analyzing a visual representation). Further, they can differ in the type of input (e.g., auditory, visual) and required output or response (e.g., oral, pointing). However, regardless of the type of intelligence test that is given, it is essential that intelligence be measured accurately, to give a true picture of the student's capabilities. For example, if a student is unable to communicate verbally, it wouldn't be appropriate to give her an IQ test that requires verbal responses. Similarly, if a student has a visual impairment that prohibits his ability to view specific details, it wouldn't be appropriate to measure his IQ using materials that require the interpretation or evaluation of pictures or objects with fine detail.

Intelligence often carries so much importance in the diagnostic process that the guidelines surrounding who can administer and interpret intelligence tests are very stringent. For this and other reasons, many IQ tests require extensive training to administer and interpret. As is true for all standardized, norm-referenced tests, most tests specify what qualifications are required for administration. In addition to specifications indicated by the assessment itself, each state provides specific guidelines about who can administer and interpret intelligence tests. Some states require degrees/certification in specific fields (e.g., school psychology, clinical psychology), while other states require proven training but are not so exacting about the particular degree or certification.

Concluding Thoughts on Intelligence

While there may be differences between theories of intelligence, and many ways to measure intelligence, the idea that intelligence is a complex concept that carries much importance in the diagnostic process remains fairly consistent. One may ask why there is so much emphasis placed on intelligence. The following notions in education may help shed light on why intelligence is thought to be such an important marker (assuming that it is measured accurately):

- It helps guide our understanding of a student's mental capabilities and provides a window into how each individual's mind functions.

- It isn't thought to be something that a person learns; rather, it is thought to be innate and specific to each individual.

- It provides a marker for better predicting a student's potential for learning and can give us insight into why students may be showing certain developmental and educational patterns.

An understanding of an individual's intellectual functioning can be used in combination with other information to form a more complete understanding of an individual's capabilities. Many of the following chapters in this text will focus on identifying and describing links between a student's intellectual functioning and other characteristics (e.g., achievement, behavior, social/emotional characteristics). For some disabilities (e.g., learning disabilities, intellectual disabilities), intelligence and its relationship to other areas actually serve as defining diagnostic criteria.

1. Explain what it means to say that "Intelligence is innate."

2. What is an example of an activity that requires processing speed? Auditory processing? Long-term storage and retrieval?

3. Describe one possible reason why the results of an intelligence test may not reflect a student's true capabilities.

4. List four commonly used intelligence tests.

Language

The American Speech-Language-Hearing Association (ASHA) defines language as "the comprehension and/or use of a spoken (i.e., listening and speaking), written (i.e., reading and writing) and/or other communication symbol system (e.g., American Sign Language)" (ASHA, n.d., para. 1). Merriam-Webster defines language as "a systematic means of communicating ideas or feelings by the use of conventionalized signs, sounds, gestures, or marks having understood meanings" (Merriam-Webster, n.d., definition of language 1(b)(2)).

Evaluating a student's language proficiency as part of a comprehensive evaluation is instrumental in developing a complete picture of that student's capabilities; it can provide windows into many of the other areas that are discussed throughout this chapter and Chapter 5. The following are examples of how language intersects with other areas:

- Intelligence

  As was discussed in the previous section on intelligence, language proficiency should be taken into consideration when determining what type of intelligence test to administer, to make sure that the student's real capabilities are being measured.

- Social characteristics

  In thinking about social and emotional characteristics of students, it should be noted that a child's facility with language is often at the center of social interactions. It is difficult to discuss social proficiency without taking into consideration how the child uses and understands language.

- Academic achievement

  Language is often at the root of academic achievement (which will be discussed in depth in Chapter 5), as some form of language is required in most academic and achievement-related activities. Language can be discussed in terms of receptive language and expressive language. **Receptive language** is language that a person receives and can optimally understand; **expressive language** is meaningful language that an individual produces. When thinking about the basic areas of academic achievement, consider the role of receptive and expressive language:

○ *Oral language.* Oral language has elements of both receptive (listening) and expressive language (speaking).

○ *Reading.* Reading requires receptive language, because the individual is taking in the words on the page.

○ *Written language.* Written language, or writing, involves expressive language through written expression.

○ *Mathematics.* Depending on how mathematics is conveyed, there are often elements of oral language (receptive and expressive language), reading (receptive language), and written language (expressive language).

○ *Nonverbal abilities.* The premise behind nonverbal abilities is that they include the ability to understand information that doesn't involve language; however, nonverbal abilities relate to language in that they are often associated with the use of language and communication in a social context and how it is perceived within society.

Elements of Language

Knowledge of the underlying elements of language is also important when evaluating a student's level of proficiency associated with language, as it can allow for a more complete understanding of student performance. Bloom and Lahey (1978) identified three main **component categories of language**: language form, language content, and language use. These main categories can further be delineated into five main **elements of language** (refer to Table 4.1), which include the following: phonology (language form), morphology (language form), syntax (language form), semantics (language content), and pragmatics (language usage).

Phonology

Phonology is the study of the sound structure and sound patterns within a language. Within oral language, phonology involves the ability to both hear the different sounds and produce the different sounds in the language. Within reading, it involves the ability to connect the visual letters to the sounds that they make (e.g., the visual letter B makes the /b/ sound). Alternatively, for written language,

Table 4.1 Model of Language

Language Form	Phonology	The study of the sound structure and sound patterns within a language
	Morphology	The study of the form or structure of words within a language and how words are formed
	Syntax	The study of the grammatical structure and rules used for combining words, phrases, and clauses into sentences
Language Content	Semantics	The study of meaning within the language
Language Usage	Pragmatics	The study of the use of language for social interaction and the rules that govern the social use of language

Bloom, L., & Lahey, M. (1978). *Language development and language disorders*. New York, NY: Wiley.

it involves the ability to hear the sounds and relate them to possible letter patterns (e.g., the sounds /s/-/i/-/t/ could be written using the letters SIT).

In discussions of phonology, the term **phoneme** is often used. A phoneme is the smallest unit of sound within a language. While there are 26 letters in the English alphabet, there are approximately 44 phonemes that make up words in the English language. For example, the letters T and H can be used in isolation or in combination to make many more than two phonemes.

- /t/ sound as in <u>t</u>op and <u>t</u>ake

- /d/ sound as in le<u>tt</u>er and wa<u>t</u>er

- /h/ sound as in <u>h</u>at and <u>h</u>ost

- /th/ sound as in wi<u>th</u> and <u>th</u>ink

- /th/ sound as in <u>th</u>e and <u>th</u>at

Phonemes relate to the number of sounds in a word, not the number of letters. For example, the word "dog" has both three letters and three phonemes, /d/-/o/-/g/, while the word "thought" has seven letters but only three phonemes, /th/-/o/-/t/. Within this chapter, there will be many examples of phonemes and how they make up the words in our language. The International Phonetic Alphabet (IPA) is a symbol system that is often used to symbolize each of the different phonemes. However, please note that the scope of this chapter is not to teach the IPA system, so it will not be used to represent examples of phonemes. Instead, any examples of phonemes will be represented in a way that will help the reader best identify the sounds. For example, the "long e" sound in *sleep* would be written as /i/ in IPA, but it will be written as /ē/ in this chapter. In Chapter 5, further discussion surrounding phonological awareness will give further meaning to the concept of phonology.

Morphology

Morphology is the study of the form or structure of words within a language and how words are formed. A morpheme is each individual unit of meaning; morphemes can be individual words (e.g., "dog") that can stand alone, or they can be parts of words (the -s in "dogs" indicates plurality; the -ed in "jumped" indicates past tense) that are added to a word and carry meaning. According to Gleason and Ratner (2017), Berko (1958) described an assessment called the Wug Test, which is an assessment that evaluates a student's understanding of morphology and word parts through nonwords.

Syntax

Syntax is the study of the grammatical structure and rules used for combining words, phrases, and clauses into sentences. For example, there are specific syntactic rules that are used to turn a statement ("I went to the store") into a question ("Did you go to the store?"). Syntax also encompasses the different parts of speech within a language (noun, verb, adjective, adverb, conjunction, etc.). Syntax can be measured through oral language, reading, and written language.

Semantics

Semantics is the study of meaning within the language. When you are thinking about semantics, it may be important to understand vocabulary and the meaning associated with words both in isolation and in combination with one another (needed for language comprehension). One's vocabulary is very important to the way in which an individual is able to use language and communicate with others. Each individual has his or her own lexicon, which can be thought of as a personal word bank. To better understand vocabulary proficiency, we can measure vocabulary on dimensions of *breadth*, *depth*, and *flexibility*:

Breadth involves the number of words that an individual knows, or the size of his or her vocabulary. For example, individuals with very broad or wide vocabularies have many words that they know and are able to use in communication. However, someone with a very narrow vocabulary may not have as much facility with language, because he or she doesn't have the same repertoire of words to choose from. For example, the word "rain" is a very common word that many people would consider part of their vocabulary. However, "rain" could have a wide range of meaning when it is used. Breadth within vocabulary may allow the concept of "raining" to be described with greater specificity using different terms, such as "pouring," "sprinkling," "spitting," "raining cats and dogs," and "drizzling." Each of those words/expressions may conjure a different visual representation and improve meaning; however, if that level of breadth isn't part of one's vocabulary, that type of specificity may be more difficult to attain.

Depth relates to knowledge of the meaning and use of words. How much is a word understood? For example, an individual may know the definition of a particular word (its denotation) but not know the underlying meaning that society places on that word (its connotation). For example, the dictionary definition of the word "average" is "a level (as of intelligence) typical of a group, class, or series" (Merriam-Webster, n.d., definition of average 2[b]). The definition is that it is typical; however, some members of society often place a negative connotation on the word "average." If students had knowledge of only either the dictionary definition *or* the connotation that society associates with the word, they might lack a complete understanding of how the word is used.

Flexibility involves the ability to choose or adapt the meaning of a word to suit different contexts. For example, there are many ways in which the word "warm" can be used in context. It can be used to refer to the outdoor temperature, a friendly personality, a feeling of comfort, a somewhat spicy food, the temperature of someone's body, the temperature of food, and so on. Flexibility in language allows for the ability to adapt the meaning of a word to suit the context.

Another way to better understand an individual's facility with the meaning of language is to evaluate underlying concepts associated with words. Consider the following ways that words can be characterized:

- *Taxonomy or superordinate categories* are overarching categories that a word may belong to. For example, when asked, "What is an orange?" an individual may respond, "An orange is a type of fruit." This would show that he or she has an understanding of the category that the word would fall into.

- *Synonyms* are words that are similar in meaning to another word. In defining the word "jump," it could be said that "jump" is similar to "hop."

- *Antonyms* are words that have the opposite meaning. For example, "down" is the opposite of "up."

- *Part/whole relationships* refer to the relationship that exists between a whole object and the parts that compose it. For example, a "car" has wheels, doors, bumpers, and so on.

- *Modification or description* is a way to describe words. For example, an "apple" can taste sweet or sour; it is round in shape; it can be red, green, or yellow in color; it feels hard; and so on.

- *Function/use* characterizes what an object is used for or how it functions. For example, a "fork" is something that we can use to eat.

Pragmatics

Pragmatics is the study of the use of language for social interaction and the rules that govern the social use of language. Pragmatics goes beyond the actual structure of the language and relates more specifically to how language is used and understood within society. For example, understanding that when someone says, "Hi, how are you today?" it would be appropriate to show reciprocity and respond with something like "I'm doing well. How are you?" As another example, good pragmatics skills might help a person know the appropriate distance to stand from another person when having a conversation.

When you are thinking about pragmatics, it is often beneficial to break communication down into the following components that were described by Austin (1962): the locutionary act (the actual language that is used in the communication); the illocutionary act (the speaker's intent associated with that language); and the perlocutionary act (the impact that the language has on the communicative partner, or the way that the communicative partner interprets the language). In many instances, these three components match up; the locutionary act conveys the intent of the speaker (illocutionary act), and it is correctly received by the listener (perlocutionary act). However, there are many situations when the three components don't match up. For example, if it is cold in a building and a person says, "Wow, is it snowing in here?" (locutionary act), the intent of the speaker may be to point out that it is really cold (illocutionary act); if the listener doesn't pick up on that intent, he or she may be confused by the question and say, "No; of course it doesn't snow inside."

Deficits in language usage (pragmatics) could impact a student to such an extent that it hinders overall language and communication with others, even if there are no problems with language form (phonology, morphology, and syntax) or language content (semantics).

The five elements of language provide a deeper understanding of the complexities associated with language. When you are assessing language skills, it isn't enough to simply say that a student has deficits in language. Delving into the different elements of language can be a means of getting a better picture of specific strengths and needs associated with language. For example, if it is clear that a student has deficits in pragmatics, steps can be taken to specifically improve pragmatics skills. If specific elements weren't assessed, and it was merely said that there were deficits in language, it may not be apparent that pragmatics is the main element of concern, and it wouldn't lead to an obvious jumping-off point for instruction. The following are examples of assessments that assess multiple elements of language: the Comprehensive Assessment of Spoken Language (CASL) and the Oral and Written Language Scales (OWLS) measure semantics, syntax, and pragmatics; and the Test of Language Development–Primary (TOLD-P) measures phonology, morphology, syntax, and semantics.

Language Difference, Language Delay, and Language Disorder

When you are evaluating language, it is important to distinguish between the following three concepts:

- Language difference: A language difference is when an individual's primary language (e.g., Spanish, Italian, Mandarin, American Sign Language) is different from that of the dominant culture in a school. Individuals with a language difference may also be diagnosed with a disability, but they can't be diagnosed based on their language difference. See Chapter 2 for a more thorough discussion of language difference.

- Language delay: A language delay is when a child does not acquire language as quickly as would be considered developmentally typical. A language delay could be just that—a delay—and the child may develop language in the typical way, but at a slower rate. Or, a child with a language delay may have an underlying disorder that may be diagnosed later in the child's development.

- Language disorder: A language disorder is an actual disorder or disability that an individual may have. Language disorders will be discussed in depth in Chapter 9.

It is important when thinking about language not to confuse language difference, language delay, and language disorder, to assume that they are all the same, or to assume that they all are synonymous with a language disability.

Concluding Thoughts on Language

Language is at the base of assessment for students, and it is necessary that a student's language skills be understood as a means of better evaluating proficiency, strengths, and needs in all areas of achievement. The elements of language (i.e., phonology, morphology, syntax, semantics, and pragmatics) allow us a meaningful way to better understand all the complexities associated with language and get to the core of a student's level of language proficiency.

Check Your Understanding

1. List the five elements of language, and discuss the meaning of each.

2. How many phonemes are in the following words: "stop," "sleep," "three"?

3. Describe and give examples of how morphology might relate to oral language, reading, and written language.

4. Define "breadth," "depth," and "flexibility" as they relate to vocabulary.

5. Why would it be beneficial to break down the components of language and assess a student's skills in each of the five elements of language?

6. How would assessing language help explain a student's performance in reading or written language?

7. Differentiate between language difference, language delay, and language disorder.

Social and Emotional Characteristics

Social and emotional characteristics are patterns of social skills and emotional functioning that an individual exhibits that are critical in everyday functioning. However, they may be overlooked in favor of academics, because academics are typically more of a focus in the curriculum. As a result, in the evaluation process, more attention may be given to measuring intelligence, language, and academics than social and emotional functioning. Evaluating social and emotional characteristics is necessary to a comprehensive evaluation, as there are several disabilities that include social and emotional functioning as part of the diagnostic criteria. Throughout this text, we will highlight possible social and emotional patterns that may accompany each disability and should therefore be evaluated.

Social Characteristics

Social skills speak to the way in which individuals relate to others in the world around them. Many of the previously discussed concepts—such as language skills (e.g., receptive and expressive oral language, pragmatics), nonverbal abilities, and behavior—are relevant when considering an individual's social skills and interactions. Social skills may develop as a result of learned behavior (e.g., watching others interact socially), as well as from one's own personality traits (being an introvert or extrovert, being outgoing or shy, etc.). They are part of the diagnostic criteria for several disabilities (e.g., autism spectrum disorder, intellectual disabilities) and may be considered secondary effects of other disabilities.

Examining social skills as part of a comprehensive diagnostic evaluation is crucial, because the more that can be learned about a student's social skills, the more can be done to subsequently find ways to improve social skills that are considered deficient. Having good social skills is a trait that may be considered invaluable throughout an individual's life. Social skills can be evaluated across a number of different dimensions (e.g., circumstances or settings), including the following:

- *Peer interaction.* Children will spend much of their lives interacting with peers in many different settings and contexts. The following are different ways that peer interactions may be examined:

  o Examining a student's interaction with peers both in a school setting and outside of a school setting can shed light on how that individual may function with others in the world. A student may act differently at school as compared to outside of school, for a number of reasons. Therefore, observations and perceptions about a student's peer interactions from both the teachers and the parents/guardians can provide insight into the student's level of proficiency in social skills. Neither the teachers nor the parents alone would likely have enough insight across all settings to give a complete picture of a child's social interactions with peers. This is because teachers don't typically know how children interact with others outside of a school setting, and parents may not know how their child interacts in school.

  o It is also useful to distinguish between social interactions with peers who are friends as compared with peers who are acquaintances, across both settings. Children may respond differently with someone whom they consider a friend as compared to someone whom they know but are not as close to.

  A good understanding of peer interactions can help in determining a means of improving social skills, if needed.

- *Family interaction.* Depending on the child's specific situation, individuals may act very differently when they are with family, as compared to when they are with friends, acquaintances, or strangers. For example, a person may show reduced social proficiency with family, because the family may compensate for the individual in a variety of ways (e.g., speak for the child in a social setting). Alternatively, individuals may demonstrate better social skills with family if their comfort level is higher. Further, comparing social interactions with siblings to interactions with parents could also be revealing.

- *Age-based interaction.* When you are evaluating social skills and interactions, it can be beneficial to examine any differences that occur between different age ranges. For example, if you are evaluating social skills among children, it is beneficial to examine interactions with same-aged peers, younger children, and older children. It is important to note whether a student changes his or her social behavior depending on the age of the individual with whom he or she is interacting. Similarly, comparing an individual's social skills and interactions with children to his or her social skills and interactions with adults can reveal similarities or differences.

- *Interactions with figures in positions of authority.* When you are examining interactions with adults, evaluating similarities and differences between interactions with adults in positions of authority (e.g., parent, teacher, coach) and interactions with adults who are not in positions of authority for the individual could provide insight. Individuals may relate differently to those who are authority figures as compared to those who aren't.

As will be further discussed in Chapter 5 with nonverbal abilities, observing an individual's social interactions in a natural social setting may yield different information than a testing situation. Interviews, direct observations, checklists, and rating scales can all be good mechanisms for examining social skills. The Social Skills Improvement System (SSIS) Rating Scales are an example of a norm-referenced assessment that assesses social skills. Social skills are an important part of how a student functions in the world, and there are many different dimensions in which social skills should be evaluated to obtain a true picture of how an individual relates socially to the world around him or her.

Emotional Characteristics

There are many mechanisms for evaluating the emotional characteristics of a student, such as interviews, direct observations, checklists, and rating scales. However, assessment results relating to feelings or emotions may need to be interpreted very cautiously and take into consideration who is doing the reporting.

Indirect reports made by others. Obtaining information about emotional status from someone other than the student may not be completely valid, because no one can truly know how another person is feeling. It is possible for others to speculate on a person's emotional status, and to make assumptions based on behavior that a person exhibits, but that isn't always true to what is actually happening within the individual. For example, if a person is observed to be laughing, it may be assumed that the person thinks that something is funny. However, if the person has a nervous laugh, the laugh may actually be a sign of discomfort rather than a sign that something is funny.

Self-reports made by the student. An accurate self-report may be difficult to attain, because an individual may not always fully recognize or understand his or her own feelings and emotions. Further, an individual may not be able to communicate his or her feelings and emotions accurately. For example, many children use the term "boring" to describe an activity that they don't want to do or that is hard for them. If a student uses the word "boring" to describe his or her feelings about reading, it may be that the child doesn't like reading or that it is difficult, rather than boring. Whether a student is completing a rating scale or providing information through an interview, the student may not be able to express those feelings to others.

When you are evaluating emotional characteristics, it may be helpful to determine whether the emotions that an individual is demonstrating are pervasive (i.e., present across settings and situations) or whether they are situational (i.e., present only under particular conditions or circumstances). For example, people may feel high levels of anxiety in settings that are stressful to them (e.g., school or work) but may not have those same feelings in a setting that is less stressful for them (e.g., an extracurricular activity that a student enjoys). That is very different from circumstances where a person feels the same emotion (e.g., anxiety) in all settings.

The more that a student's emotional characteristics can be understood and interpreted through an evaluation, the easier it will be to develop a plan to help the student. The DSM-5 (APA, 2013) provides guidelines that enable medical professionals and psychologists to evaluate and diagnose mental disorders that may impact the emotional well-being of a child. In Chapter 10 ("Emotional Disturbance"), the evaluation of emotional status will be highly discussed, as it relates to a number of types of disorders or conditions.

Check Your Understanding 4.3

1. Why may it be difficult to evaluate emotional characteristics of a student?

2. Explain why it would be beneficial to assess social skills in different types of settings, with individuals of different age ranges, and with friends as compared to acquaintances.

Health and Medical Status

Evaluating and providing information about an individual's health and medical status is an important component of a comprehensive diagnostic evaluation. Medical professionals typically evaluate health and medical status, as well as make any specific health or medical diagnoses. As part of a comprehensive diagnostic evaluation, a student's vision and hearing will be evaluated to determine whether there are sensory deficits that are impacting his or her performance. Additionally, motor capabilities will be evaluated, as appropriate. While medical professionals will be the ones to evaluate information regarding health and medical status, as well as diagnose a health or medical condition, both the parents and the school nurse may assist in interpreting health and medical information and communicating that information to the multidisciplinary team when determining eligibility for special education services.

Students may present with a variety of health and medical conditions that will impact them in school, and Chapter 13 will focus heavily on a variety of such conditions. The following are often considered for health and medical conditions:

- *Type of condition.* Health or medically related conditions are often categorized as either *chronic* conditions (e.g., type 1 diabetes), which persist over time, or *acute* conditions, which have a very sudden onset and are usually severe (e.g., a sudden heart attack). Knowing whether a condition is chronic or acute may help you determine the types and duration of special education services that a student may need, so it is important to note as part of the evaluation.

- *Acquisition of the condition.* Health and medical conditions can be either *congenital* (onset is before birth, at birth, or just after birth) or *acquired* (onset can be any time during a person's life). The following are some examples of possible causal factors of congenital conditions:

  - Biological/genetic factors

  - Maternal behavior during the pregnancy (e.g., poor nutrition, use of alcohol or drugs, environmental factors)

  - Maternal illness during the pregnancy

The following are possible causes of acquired conditions:

  - Illness/disease

  - Environmental factors (e.g., trauma, poor health-related habits)

While the school will not diagnose health or medical conditions, it will evaluate the impact that the condition has on the student in the school setting. Therefore, this information is crucial in evaluating the student. Throughout the text, a discussion of health and medical characteristics will be discussed as they relate to each disability. Some disabilities won't have any health or medical characteristics that are associated with the disability, while others will depend heavily on the individual's health or medical conditions.

Check Your Understanding 4.4

1. Why would it be beneficial to know whether a condition is chronic or acute?

2. Who diagnoses medical or health-related conditions?

CHAPTER SUMMARY

Countless characteristics combine to make every individual unique. A comprehensive evaluation must be completed in such a way that the multidisciplinary team can analyze the results and truly develop a clear picture of a student's strengths and needs. This chapter focused on evaluation of characteristics in areas that are developmental in nature (e.g., intelligence, language, social/emotional characteristics) and health or medically related. Chapter 5 will focus on areas that are typically learned, including academic achievement and behavior.

APPLY WHAT YOU HAVE LEARNED

1. If parents were to ask you why their child needs to be assessed in so many different areas when the child seems to have difficulties only with math, how would you explain to them the need for a comprehensive evaluation?

2. If you have a new student in your class who has been diagnosed with a disability and is eligible to receive special education services, explain why it would be important for you to fully read and understand the comprehensive evaluation.

3. Review the guidelines for conducting an evaluation provided by IDEA Section 300.304 (2004) at the beginning of the chapter, and explain why the guidelines are necessary in order to complete a comprehensive evaluation.

4. What is the difference between diagnosis and eligibility? What is the role of the multidisciplinary team in diagnosis and eligibility? What other types of professionals may be involved in diagnosis? What are the components of determining eligibility?

REFERENCES

American Psychiatric Association (APA). (2013). *Diagnostic and statistical manual of mental disorders: DSM-5* (5th ed.). Arlington, VA: Author. Retrieved from https://dsm-psychiatryonline-org.proxy-wcupa.klnpa.org/doi/book/10.1176/appi.books.9780890425596

American Speech-Language-Hearing Association (ASHA). (n.d.). *Language in brief.* Retrieved from https://www.asha.org/Practice-Portal/Clinical-Topics/Spoken-Language-Disorders/Language-In--Brief

Austin, J. (1962). *How to do things with words* (William James lectures; 1955). Cambridge, MA: Harvard University Press.

Average. (n.d.). In *Merriam-Webster.com.* Retrieved December 28, 2019, from https://www.merriam-webster.com/dictionary/average

Berko, J. (1958). The child's learning of English morphology. *WORD, 14*(2–3), 150–177.

Bloom, L., & Lahey, M. (1978). *Language development and language disorders.* New York, NY: Wiley.

Carroll, J. B. (1993). *Human cognitive abilities: A survey of factor-analytical studies*. Cambridge, UK: Cambridge University Press.

Flanagan, D. P., & Dixon, S. G. (2013). The Cattell-Horn-Carroll theory of cognitive abilities. In C. R. Reynolds, K. J. Vannest, & E. Fletcher-Janzen (Eds.), *Encyclopedia of special education: A reference for the education of children, adolescents, and adults with disabilities and other exceptional individuals* (4th ed.). Hoboken, NJ: Wiley. Retrieved from http://proxy-wcupa.klnpa.org/login?https://search.credoreference.com/content/entry/wileyse/the_cattell_horn_carroll_theory_of_cognitive_abilities/0?institutionId=649

Gardner, H. (2011). *Frames of mind: The theory of multiple intelligences* (3rd ed.). New York, NY: Basic Books.

Gleason, J. B., & Ratner, N. B. (2017). *The development of language* (9th ed.). Boston, MA: Pearson Education.

IDEA (Individuals With Disabilities Education Act). (2004). *Section 300.304*. Retrieved from https://sites.ed.gov/idea/regs/b/d/300.304

IDEA (Individuals With Disabilities Education Act). (2004). *Section 300.305*. Retrieved from https://sites.ed.gov/idea/regs/b/d/300.305

IDEA (Individuals With Disabilities Education Act). (2004). *Section 300.306*. Retrieved from https://sites.ed.gov/idea/regs/b/d/300.306

Language. (n.d.). In *Merriam-Webster.com*. Retrieved December 28, 2019, from https://www.merriam-webster.com/dictionary/language

McGrew, K. S. (2009). CHC theory and the Human Cognitive Abilities Project: Standing on the shoulders of the giants of psychometric intelligence research. *Intelligence, 37*(1), 1–10.

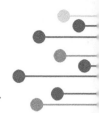

CHAPTER 5

Assessment for Diagnosis and Eligibility

Academic Achievement and Behavior

Tara S. Guerriero, PhD

Learning Objectives

After the completion of Chapters 4 and 5, you should be able to:

- Summarize the IDEA guidelines for conducting an evaluation.

- Discuss the difference between intelligence and achievement.

- Define the five elements of language and differentiate between them.

- Identify the five main areas of academic achievement and described each of the related subareas.

- Explain how language is related to each of the five areas of achievement.

- Discuss methods for evaluating behavior and why it is important to determine the function of behavior.

- Examine the benefits of completing a comprehensive diagnostic evaluation that includes assessment of students in all of the following areas: intelligence, language, areas of achievement, behavior, social/emotional characteristics, and health/medical status.

Key Terms

behavior (p. 148)	oral language (p. 118)
	phonological awareness, phonemic awareness
mathematics (p. 134)	reading (p. 124)
early math skills, computation, word problem solving	emergent literacy skills, phonics, decoding, word recognition, reading fluency, reading vocabulary, reading comprehension
nonverbal abilities (p. 146)	written language (p. 128)
	handwriting, spelling, written vocabulary, syntax, written expression/discourse

Introduction to the Chapter and Connection to Chapter 4

This chapter is the second part of our discussion on assessment for diagnosis and eligibility. As was previously mentioned, Chapters 4 and 5 contain information pertaining to the evaluation of student characteristics in the following six areas as a means of helping you develop a thorough understanding of what is factored into a comprehensive evaluation:

- Intelligence
- Language
- Social and emotional characteristics
- Health and medical
- Areas of academic achievement
- Behavior

Recall that Chapter 4 focused on the areas that are typically more developmental in nature (intelligence, language, social and emotional characteristics, and health and medical), while this chapter focuses on the areas that are typically learned (areas of academic achievement and behavior). Many comparisons and connections between the areas discussed in Chapter 4 and those included in this chapter will be made. For instance, distinctions will be made between intelligence and achievement, and connections will be made between language development and academic achievement.

Areas of Academic Achievement

In contrast to intelligence (as discussed in Chapter 4), achievement involves what has been learned in a particular subject or area, and it can change over time, depending on how a student is progressing. There are five main areas of basic academic achievement: oral language, reading, written language, mathematics, and nonverbal abilities (note that this category isn't always included as an area of academic achievement). These five areas of basic academic achievement should not be compared to subjects within school, as they often are included in many subjects. For example, within the subject area of science, the following are examples of how each of the areas of achievement may be required in an activity (in this case, completing a science lab):

- *Oral language:* Students would need to listen to their teacher explain the steps for completing the lab and ask any questions that they have before or during the lab.

- *Reading*: They may need to read directions associated with completing the lab; they may need to read labels of different materials associated with the lab.

- *Written language*: Students are often asked to record observations during a lab and write a lab report following the lab.

- *Mathematics*: If there is specific data associated with the lab, the student may have to calculate results or graph the data.

- *Nonverbal abilities*: Students may have to watch a physical reaction and interpret what is happening without an explanation.

At the core of achievement is the concept of language, which was highlighted in Chapter 4. An understanding of language provides a base for better understanding each area of achievement.

Benefits of Assessing Language Proficiency in Relation to the Areas of Achievement

Developing a good understanding of an individual's language skills through assessment may be a window into performance across each area of achievement. The Clinical Evaluation of Language Fundamentals (CELF) is an example of an assessment that allows for a comparison of language across different areas of achievement. The following example is a possible illustration of how a deficit in phonology may manifest itself across different areas of achievement:

- *Oral language*: Within oral language, it may be evident that a student is having difficulties perceiving different sounds within the language because he or she is appearing to misperceive what is being said. Consider the following examples:

  - A student is asked to describe what a "pen" looks like. The student says, "It is a large object that has a round bottom with edges and a long handle" (description of a "pan").

  - A student is asked to "Use the following word in a sentence: 'thanks.'" The student says, "The water was held in large tanks."

- *Reading*: In reading, the student may show deficits in decoding unknown words or words that are not real words, because that skill relies heavily on phonological skills. For example, the student may be given the nonword "lesk" and asked to read it. Since it isn't a real word, the student can't rely on meaning and must instead rely on the ability to sound it out (using phonological skills). One may ask why it would matter whether a student can read nonwords. The fact is, it doesn't truly matter whether a student can read a nonword; however, until any real word is part of a student's lexicon, it essentially is a nonword to that student. Thus, the ease with which a student can use phonological skills to sound out words will likely impact reading fluency and comprehension.

- *Written language*: In written language, the student may spell words incorrectly because he or she can't correctly perceive the sounds. In using the same example that was used for oral language, if a student is asked to write the word "pen" and writes "pan," the student will have an incorrect response, not because he or she doesn't understand the conventions of spelling (although that may also be the case), but because he or she didn't accurately perceive the sounds in the word.

Further, evaluation of language skills across each area of achievement may indicate whether patterns are global (across all areas) or specific to a particular area (e.g., reading but not oral language). For example, if a student has difficulties with language comprehension, assessing oral language comprehension and reading comprehension and comparing performance between the two may give insight into whether there is a global deficit in comprehension or whether the comprehension difficulties are specific to a particular area. This type of knowledge can help you make a more informed decision about instruction. If a student shows deficits in both oral comprehension and reading comprehension, instruction may need to focus on comprehension strategies to enhance comprehension, in general. Alternatively, if comprehension is only a deficit when the child is reading, as compared to when he or she is listening, there may be another factor associated with the child's reading that is impacting the ability to comprehend.

When you are assessing a student for diagnostic or eligibility purposes, looking at proficiency in each of the five areas of achievement will help you understand what he or she has learned in each area. Additionally, each of the five areas has numerous subareas that can be evaluated to more fully determine a student's capabilities. Information about each area and related subareas can be collected across multiple types of assessments (norm-referenced assessment, criterion-referenced assessment, curriculum-based assessment, etc.) that were discussed in Chapter 3.

Oral Language

Oral language is language that is expressed through sound, and it can be evaluated in terms of receptive oral language (listening) and expressive oral language (speaking).

Receptive vs. Expressive

Receptive oral language, or listening, involves the following: the ability to hear the stimuli that comes in through the auditory sensory system; auditory perception, or the brain's ability to perceive and interpret a sound that comes in through the auditory sensory system; and comprehension, or the application of meaning to the sounds (phonemes/words/sentences) that are perceived. Students use receptive oral language throughout the school day. Consider the following instances where receptive oral language must be used:

- If a teacher is reading a story to the class, the students need to use receptive oral language to understand the story.

- If students are told to get their lunchboxes and get into line for lunch, they need to hear the stimuli and process it to understand the directions.

- If two people are talking by phone, each must employ receptive oral language to comprehend what the other is saying.

When examining receptive oral language, you may find it necessary to first examine whether students can hear and perceive each sound before delving deeper into whether they understand what is being said within a language. Then, receptive oral language can further be measured through vocabulary and listening comprehension skills. The following are examples of different norm-referenced measures that can examine receptive language at the level of the word, sentence, and/or discourse: the Peabody Picture Vocabulary Test (PPVT), the Receptive One-Word Picture Vocabulary Test, the Woodcock-Johnson, the Kaufman Test of Educational Achievement (KTEA), and the Wechsler Individual Achievement Test (WIAT).

Expressive oral language, or speaking, refers to the ability to produce or pronounce the sounds and combinations of sounds (syllables, words, sentences) associated with the language. Additionally, it refers to the usage of vocabulary and the way that words are organized into phrases, sentences, and discourse so that they are meaningful to the listener. The following are examples of activities where expressive oral language is needed:

- If a family is sitting at the dinner table and the parents ask the children what they did in school today, the children need to use expressive oral language to describe their day.

- If a teacher reads a story to the class and asks the class to retell the story, the students would use expressive oral language to give the retell.

- Expressive oral language is required for a person to greet another person by saying "Hi! It's nice to meet you."

Similar to receptive oral language, there are many measures that evaluate expressive oral language skills; these include the Expressive Vocabulary Test (EVT), the Expressive One-Word Picture Vocabulary Test, the Woodcock-Johnson, the KTEA, the WIAT, and the Goldman-Fristoe Test of Articulation.

Phonological Awareness

An important component of oral language (both receptive and expressive) is phonological awareness, or awareness of the sound structure of phonemes, syllables, words, and sentences. Phonological awareness skills often show a pattern of development that progresses from larger units (e.g., whole word) to smaller units (e.g., phoneme) (Vaughn & Bos, 2012). The reasoning behind this progression is that words carry meaning, whereas phonemes (in and of themselves) do not; therefore, a student can use background knowledge and vocabulary to perceive a word but not necessarily a single phoneme. There are many different types of phonological awareness skills that relate to a student's proficiency with the sound structure associated with the language, including discrimination, counting, rhyming, alliteration, blending, segmentation, deleting sounds, adding sounds, substituting sounds, and transposing sounds (Vaughn & Bos, 2012). The following are some examples of tasks by which an educator may evaluate phonological awareness:

- *Discrimination.* Discrimination is the concept that determines whether a student can listen to two or more sounds, syllables, or words within the language and discriminate, or differentiate, between them and/or determine whether they are the same or different. Discrimination can be measured at many levels. The following are some examples of phonemes/syllables/words that might be used in a discrimination task:
  - The /t/ sound and the /d/ sound: The only difference between these two sounds is the presence of voicing (vibration of the vocal cords while saying the /d/ sound).
  - The words "stick" and "sick": The difference between them is one sound and the presence of a consonant blend.
  - The words "bat" and "pat": These words differ in the sound in the initial position.
  - The words "bat" and "bit": These words differ in the sound in the medial position.
  - The words "bat" and "bad": These words differ in the sound in the final position.

If a student has difficulty discriminating between sounds, it could cause problems when he or she is trying to understand conversation and may lead to further complications at such time as he or she learns to read and write.

- *Counting.* Counting refers to the ability to determine the number of phonemes or syllables in a word and possibly the number of words in a phrase or sentence. The following are some examples:
  - How many phonemes are in the word "cat"? (three)

- How many syllables are in the word "constitution"? (four)

- How many words are in the sentence "I went to the store"? (five)

- *Rhyming.* Rhyming words are words that have matching ending sounds, such as "bat"/"cat"/"hat"/"mat"/"pat"/"rat"/"sat."

- *Alliteration.* Alliteration is a group of words that begin with the same sound. In terms of assessment, it is often beneficial to see whether a student can hear the initial sounds in words. For example, consider John Harris's Peter Piper riddle (Phillips, 1911): "Peter Piper pick'd a peck of pickled peppers . . ." In this riddle, each word starts with the /p/ sound. Students who can hear and recognize alliteration may find this type of riddle to be funny or interesting, because of the presence of alliteration. Others, such as those with difficulty perceiving or recognizing alliteration, may not acknowledge it as anything different from any other passage.

- *Blending.* Blending occurs when phonemes/syllables are combined sequentially to form a whole word (e.g., /k/-/a/-/t/ → "cat"; /ev/-/rē/-/wən/ → "everyone") or when words are combined sequentially to form phrases and/or sentences (e.g., I-went-to-the-store → I went to the store).

- *Segmentation.* Segmentation is when the flow of speech is broken into words, syllables, and phonemes (e.g., "cat" → /k/-/a/-/t/; "everyone" → /ev/-/rē/-/wun/; I went to the store → I-went-to-the-store)

- *Phonemic awareness.* **Phonemic awareness** is a type of phonological awareness in which a student is asked to manipulate phonemes in words. The following are examples of phonemic awareness tasks:

  - Deleting sounds: Say "shout" without /sh/ → out

  - Adding sounds: Add /sh/ to "out" → shout

  - Substituting sounds: Change the /sh/ in "shout" to /p/ → pout

  - Transposing/reversing sounds: Reverse the sounds in "top" → pot

Difficulty with phonological and phonemic awareness tasks may not in and of itself present substantial problems for a student; however, it may signal deficits that will impact oral language, reading, and written language proficiency. For example, a person typically doesn't need to count the number of sounds in a word in everyday life; however, if a student can't count the sounds, it may signal that the student is having difficulties perceiving the sounds in the language. This may make the facility with which the student accesses language more difficult and thus lead to further deficits in reading and written language.

Concluding Thoughts on Oral Language

Understanding an individual's oral language proficiency is often a window into other areas of achievement, because it is typically considered a precursor to other areas of achievement. When engaging in a conversation, the listener is typically very forgiving and will often try to interpret what the speaker is trying to convey. Therefore, it may be difficult to truly gauge an oral language deficit through everyday language. That is why it is so important to break down the components of receptive and expressive oral language, as well as phonological awareness, to gain a full understanding of oral language skills.

Check Your Understanding 5.1

1. Describe a classroom activity or scenario in which students would use both receptive oral language and expressive oral language.

2. Why would it be beneficial to assess a student's rhyming skills?

3. What is phonological awareness? Describe three types of phonological awareness that can be assessed.

Reading

In order to assess reading skills in a student, it is imperative to evaluate many dimensions, to get a true picture of what is happening with the student. The following subskills may contribute to reading proficiency: emergent literacy skills; phonics, decoding, and word recognition; reading fluency; vocabulary; and comprehension (refer to Figure 5.1).

Emergent Literacy Skills

Often well before children are able to read, they are developing emergent literacy skills, or reading readiness skills and/or early literacy skills that will ultimately help them as they learn to become proficient readers. The Test of Early Reading Ability (TERA) is an assessment that examines several dimensions of early reading skills. Assessing the following skills may provide insight into reading readiness, as well as why a student may be having difficulties learning to read:

- *Oral language proficiency.* A child's oral language capabilities, including phonological awareness, may contribute heavily to reading development. For example, if a child has difficulties perceiving sounds, that may likely cross over into learning to connect letters with the sounds that they make. Similarly, a child's oral vocabulary and comprehension of oral language may cross over to reading vocabulary and reading comprehension.

Figure 5.1 Subskills of Reading

- Emergent literacy skills
- Phonics, decoding, and word recognition
- Reading fluency
- Reading vocabulary
- Reading comprehension

- *Conventions of print.* There are a number of skills that aid in being able to read (Reid, Hresko, & Hammill, 2018; Texas Education Agency, 2019). The following are some examples of conventions that are precursors to reading:

  ○ Knowing that text is read from the left to the right and from the top to the bottom

  ○ Knowing that pages turn from right to left

  ○ Knowing how to hold a book right side up instead of upside down

  ○ Understanding capitalization at the beginning of a sentence and end punctuation at the end of a sentence

  ○ Understanding what a word is (as compared to a letter)

  ○ Understanding spacing between words

- *Letter names.* Being able to visually recognize each of the letters in the alphabet and determine the name of the letter is an early literacy skill that is needed for learning to read.

- *Alphabet.* A child's knowledge of the alphabet is an important precursor to reading. While the "ABC" song can be just that, a song that a child is familiar with, it can also be a step toward knowing letters and being able to apply that "song" to reading skills.

- *Sight word vocabulary.* Often before students are able to sound out words and truly read, they are able to recognize certain words. They may be able to recognize their own name, or the logo of a favorite restaurant. This helps them develop the visual memory that they will ultimately need to develop automatic word recognition as they learn to read.

Phonics, Decoding, and Word Recognition

Phonics, decoding, and word recognition are the building blocks of learning to read (Reutzel & Cooter, 2012). They can then lead to fluency within reading, vocabulary acquisition associated with reading, and reading comprehension.

- **Phonics** refers to mapping sounds to print (e.g., "What sound does the letter P make?").

- **Decoding** is the application of phonics skills to sound out unknown words (e.g., "Sound out the word 'dog.'").

- **Word recognition** occurs when an individual can look at a word and automatically (on sight) know what it is without having to decode. Typically, this also comes with an association with meaning.

Decoding and word recognition skills can be measured in a number of ways. Students can be asked to read single words that are out of context, in assessments such as the Wide Range Achievement Test (WRAT), or words that are in context, in assessments such as the Gray Oral Reading Test (GORT). For example, a child can be shown the word "dog" and asked to read it. The child may either sound it out and decode it or read it automatically. Alternatively, the student can be given the sentence, "I love my pet dog." In both instances, the student is being asked to read the word. In one instance, there is context information that may assist (or deter) the student in determining the word. In the other, knowledge of that vocabulary word may assist the student. When assessing student reading proficiency, you may find it difficult to differentiate between decoding skills and word recognition skills unless the child is reading out loud and actively decoding or sounding out words. One way to assess decoding skills in isolation without the influence of the meaning, vocabulary, or background knowledge that is associated with real words is to ask the student to sound out nonwords (e.g., "mok," "zan," "foon," "vook," "ruch," "vight," "gask"). There are many standardized tests, such as the Woodcock-Johnson, that measure nonword reading. Comparing a student's performance on real-word reading with nonword reading tasks can give you a better sense of the underlying difficulty. If a student does much better with real words than nonwords, that may be evidence that the student is using vocabulary, visual memory, and/or automatic word recognition to access the words. If there is similar performance between the two, it may mean that the student is using the same strategy (possibly decoding) to read both real words and nonwords. Either way, it can inform areas of strength and need as well as inform instruction.

Reading Fluency

Reading fluency is a combination of accuracy, speed, and prosody (intonation) that comes with improved reading skills. For example, an individual can sound out each word very slowly and be able to decode all the words in a sentence; however, a lack of word recognition or automaticity may reduce the reading rate, thus impacting the fluency. Similarly, a student could read very quickly but make many mistakes in the words that he or she reads, therefore demonstrating reduced fluency. Prosody involves the inflection and tone of voice that is taken while reading. If an individual is reading out loud, the ability to adjust the inflection and adjust to the punctuation cues can improve fluency. Increased reading fluency is often thought to relate to increased reading comprehension, because the reader makes fewer errors and spends less time trying to decode the words.

Reading Vocabulary

Evaluating an individual's reading vocabulary is important, as it may be different from that of oral or written language. In addition to one's knowledge of words, reading vocabulary also depends on the facility with which the individual can decode or recognize words while reading, the context in which the words are used, and the background knowledge that the individual is able to apply during reading. For example, consider the following sentence: "The boy was two." A student may have a complete understanding of the number 2 and may be able to recognize it in numerical form; however, when presented with the written word "two," the child might not know what it is, because of difficulty reading (or decoding) the word.

Reading Comprehension

Reading comprehension involves the ability to understand what is read in the text and to develop a mental representation of the details in the text. Comprehension can be broken up into literal comprehension and inferential comprehension. Literal comprehension is an explicit understanding of the information that can be found directly in the text. It doesn't require interpretation or the need to "read between the lines." Alternatively, inferential comprehension is an implicit understanding of the text that requires the reader to use inferencing skills to interpret what is occurring in the text. It requires the reader to infer meaning that is not explicitly stated. For example, consider the following brief passage:

> Three friends went to the park to have lunch and spend the afternoon. They were really excited that the weather turned out the way that it did, because they were able to enjoy their time at the park.

The following are possible literal comprehension questions that could be asked:

- "Where did the friends go?"
- "How many friends went to the park?"

The following are possible inferential comprehension questions that could be asked about the same passage.

- "What do you think the weather might be?"
- "Why did the weather impact the friends' ability to enjoy their time at the park?"

The first two questions could be answered with information found directly in the text. The second two questions rely on the reader's ability to put the information together and interpret what type of weather might be desirable for a park outing. Both require the student to comprehend, but the differences between the two sets of questions require different types of thinking and understanding.

An important consideration during assessment of reading comprehension is whether the student is demonstrating comprehension deficits as a result of underlying decoding, word recognition, or fluency deficits. Since comprehension is based on having read the text, it can sometimes be difficult to analyze. However, a well-rounded battery of assessments can assist you in breaking down the components to determine where the underlying difficulties occur. Additionally, comprehension difficulties may result from underlying memory deficits, so it can be beneficial to examine any differences in comprehension when students can refer back to the text as compared to when they have to answer from memory. The following are all examples of methods that can be used to measure reading comprehension (using the earlier story about the park):

- *Open-ended comprehension questions.* Open-ended questions, such as those asked earlier (e.g., "How many friends went to the park?"), require recall or interpretation of information in the text.

- *Multiple-choice questions.* Multiple-choice questions measure recognition of information found directly in the text or that can be interpreted from the text. The following is a multiple-choice question the requires the same information as the previous open-ended question:

  How many friends went to the park?

    A. One friend

    B. Two friends

    C. Three friends

    D. Four friends

- *Retell of the story.* Students can be asked to provide a retell of the story. The goal of this type of approach is for the students to tell as much information as possible about what they remember from the story.

- *Cloze procedure.* The cloze procedure is a method where a statement is made with one or more blank spaces. The student is given choices within the context of the sentence and is asked to determine the correct choice. The following is an example of the cloze procedure:

  _____ (Two, Three) friends went to the park.

In this example, the correct answer would be for the student to choose (Three).

Several different types of comprehension questions can be asked, and comparisons can be made to help determine a student's underlying strengths and/or needs associated with reading comprehension.

Reading Level

An important component of assessment in the area of reading is to determine a student's reading level both for accuracy and comprehension. For some students, accuracy and comprehension may be at the same level, but for many other students, there may be a difference between the two. A student's reading level can be evaluated in a variety of ways, both formal and informal. When you are determining a student's reading level, it is often beneficial to evaluate his or her proficiency at different grade levels and determine the following: what level of material is too difficult for the student, what level is a good place for instruction (can read with assistance), and what level is considered an independent level (can read without assistance) for the student. That will help you tailor your instruction.

Concluding Thoughts on Reading

Reading, often referred to as literacy, is considered a capability that is highly valued in society. Schools are constantly trying to improve reading skills to aim for higher rates of literate individuals, or individuals who can read. If an individual is illiterate or has difficulty reading, it will be beneficial to assess multiple aspects associated with skilled reading. There are many types of assessments (norm-referenced, criterion-referenced, curriculum-based) that measure one or more aspects of reading. The following are some examples of specific assessments or types of assessments that are frequently used to evaluate reading proficiency in a diagnostic evaluation: the Gray Oral Reading Test (GORT), the Woodcock-Johnson, the Gates-MacGinitie Reading Test (GMRT); AIMSweb, aimswebPlus, DIBELS, the Qualitative Reading Inventory (QRI), the Informal Reading Inventory (IRI), the WIAT, the KTEA, the Woodcock Reading Mastery Tests (WRMT), the Gray Diagnostic Reading Tests, the Gray Silent Reading Tests, the Scholastic Aptitude Tests (SAT), most of the state criterion-referenced tests that are given annually (third through eighth grade), curriculum-based assessments that are found in classroom textbooks or workbooks, and teacher-created assessments. When selecting which reading assessments to administer to any given individual, you should give careful consideration to choosing appropriate assessments that will lead to a true depiction of reading skills for that particular student.

1. Why is it important to measure a student's reading level?

2. What is the difference between decoding and word recognition? If a student is having difficulties with reading, what is one way of determining whether it is a problem with decoding or word recognition?

3. What is the difference between literal and inferential comprehension? Why is it

beneficial to assess differences in performance between the two?

4. List and describe three different emergent literacy skills. Why is it appropriate to evaluate emergent literacy skills for a student who is having difficulty reading?

5. Describe the cloze procedure for assessing reading comprehension.

Written Language

Written language is a complex area that encompasses many different aspects that come together to enable an individual to write in an effective way that will be understood by a reader. In contrast to what was said earlier about oral language, it isn't as easy for a reader to understand written language when there are many errors. Errors in written language often lead to a great disconnect between the writer and the reader that might not be as evident in oral language (between a speaker and a listener). In order to truly evaluate written language, you will likely need to develop an understanding of each of the following areas: handwriting, spelling, written vocabulary, syntax, and written discourse, as seen in Figure 5.2.

Handwriting

While there are many avenues of expressing written language (typing, talk-to-text, etc.), the importance of developing handwriting skills should be considered and evaluated. There are a number of different types of handwriting that students may engage in, including manuscript (i.e., print), cursive, D'Nealian, and a combination of different types. When you are evaluating handwriting, it is necessary to examine it in different ways to be able to understand the various dimensions (e.g., letter formation, spacing, size, pencil grip, and writing pressure) that are associated with handwriting proficiency. Additionally, it is important to examine handwriting at the level of the letter (upper case and lower case), word, phrase/sentence, and discourse.

Letter formation. One aspect of handwriting that is especially important when it comes to evaluating the legibility of a student's handwriting is the assessment of letter formation. All letters are made up of only a few different formations, including circles

(O), partial circles (c) or curves, vertical lines (|), horizontal lines (—), diagonal lines (/ and \), and dots (.). What differs is the size, orientation, and combinations in which those formations are used. It can be beneficial both to focus on the parts that make up the letters and to view each letter in a holistic way. For example, when looking at a student's handwritten letter H, consider the following questions:

Figure 5.2 Subskills of Written Language

- **Handwriting**
- **Spelling**
- **Written vocabulary**
- **Syntax**
- **Written expression/ discourse**

- Did the student accurately represent each part of the letter (i.e., two parallel vertical lines and a horizontal line bisecting the two)?

- Does the whole product visually resemble the letter H?

Those questions could yield different results. It is possible that the student can correctly write the parts but can't put them together in a way that conveys the whole picture accurately (e.g., ⊢). Alternatively, what the student has written could resemble an H, but the individual parts may not be completely correct (Ⱶ).

Spacing. Consider spacing both at the level of the word (spacing between letters) and at the level of the phrase or sentence (spacing between words). A student may have no difficulties forming individual letters, but when these are combined into words, inconsistent or improper spacing may reduce legibility. For example, it may be difficult to read the word "hand" if it is written as *ha n d* or *hand* Similarly, if word combinations are not spaced properly, it may be hard for the reader to recognize which letters go together to form words. For example, if the sentence "I am going to go on vacation" were written as "Iamgoingtogoonvacation," it would be much less legible.

Size. Size, and more specifically consistency of size, can play a role in handwriting proficiency and legibility. A student may write very well with larger letters but have extreme difficulty when writing smaller letters.

Pencil grip. Look at the pencil grip (both the type of grip and the strength of the grip) to determine whether it is effective for the student. If the pencil grip isn't appropriate for the student, it may be difficult for the student to form letters properly. Additionally, if the student has a weak grip, the formation may not be precise.

Writing pressure. The pressure with which the student writes may make a difference in legibility, because if there is too much pressure, the letters could be too dark or imprecise. Additionally, the writing implement could break. If there is not enough pressure, the writing may be too light to see.

Overall, while there are many ways to express written language, handwriting is an important skill that likely will make a difference in the student's ability to communicate through written language. Another important reason for evaluating the student's handwriting is to determine whether another avenue (e.g., assistive technology) may be a better option than continued handwriting instruction for him or her.

Spelling

Spelling is an aspect of written language that is often at the root of written language assessment. One reason for this is that accurate spelling can be a determining factor in whether a student's written language is going to be understood by the reader. There are many ways that spelling can be examined to better understand proficiency. Consider the following examples of ways to assess spelling proficiency:

- *Assessing spelling in and out of context.* Sometimes contextual clues can either help or hinder the spelling process for a student, so measuring spelling skills both in and out of context may yield different results.
    - Out of context: Write the word "yellow."
    - In context: Write "The school bus is yellow."

- *Assessing oral vs. written spelling.* There may be a difference when writing the correct spelling of a word and orally providing the spelling of the same word.

- *Assessing spelling recognition or recall.* Recognizing the correct spelling of a word is a different process than recalling it from memory. Many spelling assessments require recall (e.g., the Wide Range Achievement Test, or WRAT); however, evaluating spelling recognition (e.g., the Peabody Individual Achievement Test, or PIAT) might also give insight into spelling abilities, because recognizing accurate spelling is an important step in the spelling process. It is possible that a student is able to recognize the correct spelling of a word when he or she sees it, but that same student may not be able to come up with the spelling of a word from memory. Consider the following examples:
    - Recognition: When presented with possible choices (e.g., Yelo, Yellow, Yellow, Yello), can a student recognize the correct spelling of the word?
    - Recall: "Spell the word *yellow*."

- *Assessing accuracy*. Is the word spelled correctly or incorrectly?
  - Correct: yellow
  - Incorrect: yello
- *Assessing error patterns*. In Chapter 3, the concept of an error analysis was discussed as a means of better understanding a student's level of proficiency. There are several spelling systems that require the examiner to evaluate the student's spelling patterns to better understand his or her spelling ability. The following are examples of patterns that might emerge when looking at spelling errors:
  - Phonological: Spelling that resembles the sound of the original word (e.g., *yello*)
  - Orthographic: Spelling that visually resembles the original word (e.g., *yellaw*)
  - Misuse of spelling rules or patterns that are known within the language (e.g., *lik* instead of *like*)

Spelling can be assessed in several ways. Some examples of standardized methods that are often used are AIMSweb, the Wide Range Achievement Test (WRAT), the Peabody Individualized Achievement Test (PIAT), and the KTEA. It is very common for teachers to develop weekly spelling lists and informal tests to measure spelling proficiency. Evaluating spelling proficiency is often much more complex than whether a student spelled a word correctly or incorrectly. One thing to remember is that the more complex the information that is gained from the assessment, the easier it is to determine the student's underlying strengths and needs, which will assist both in the diagnostic process and in recommendations for instruction.

Written Vocabulary

It can be beneficial to evaluate vocabulary in different areas of achievement to determine whether it is similar across areas of achievement. As was mentioned in the areas of reading and oral language, an individual's vocabulary usage may be very different across areas of achievement, likely because of the underlying skills that may accompany the use of vocabulary. For example, written vocabulary involves the dimension of spelling. A vocabulary word may be part of a student's lexicon, but uncertainty about its spelling may dissuade the student from using the known word. If a student doesn't use a wide range of words, we should not assume that he or she has a limited vocabulary; it may be a function of other underlying factors.

Syntax

When evaluating written language, you may find it useful to develop an understanding of an individual's syntax. This includes evaluating sentence form (e.g., fragments, run-ons, simple sentences, complex sentences, compound sentences); sentence function (declarative, interrogative, imperative, exclamatory); and sentence length.

Sentence form represents the make-up of the sentence. Sentence fragments and run-on sentences are examples of incorrect sentence forms.

- A *sentence fragment* is not a complete sentence in that it doesn't have all the required elements needed to stand alone (e.g., "If I go to the park." or "The puppy.").

- *Run-on sentences* are two or more independent clauses that are not combined with a conjunction (and, or, but, for, nor, so, yet) and are therefore grammatically incorrect (e.g., "I went to the park I saw a puppy.").

In addition to determining whether a student has written incorrect sentence forms, it is useful to look at the correct sentence forms and distinguish between them to better understand written syntax capabilities. Simple sentences, complex sentences, compound sentences, and combinations of different forms are often evaluated.

- *Simple sentences* are made up of one independent clause (e.g., "The puppy is little."), but may also contain various different phrases (e.g., "I saw a puppy at the park.").

- *Complex sentences* contain at least one independent clause and one dependent clause (e.g., "The puppy, who I saw at the park, lives in my neighborhood.").

- *Compound sentences* contain two or more independent clauses that are combined by a conjunction (e.g., "I went to the park, and I saw a puppy.").

- *Compound-complex sentences* are a combination of the two types (e.g., "I went to the park, and the puppy, who I know from my neighborhood, was there.").

It may be beneficial to first determine whether a student is writing grammatically correct sentences or whether he or she is writing fragments or run-ons. Then, when looking at correct sentences, look at the complexity of sentence forms. Are most of the sentences simple sentences? Does the student know how to write complex sentences? Is there variety within the sentence forms?

Sentence function refers to the purpose of the sentence.

- *Declarative sentences* are statements that are made (e.g., "I like going to school.").

- *Interrogative sentences* are questions (e.g., "Do you like going to school?").

- *Imperative sentences* are commands (e.g., "Go to school.").

- *Exclamatory sentences* are statements that show enthusiasm and are marked with an exclamation point (e.g., "I get to go to school today!").

Students may be very proficient with one sentence function (e.g., declarative sentences), but have difficulties using the other types of functions in a grammatically accurate way. Some written samples lend themselves to a specific type of sentence function. For example, expository writing often includes a multitude of declarative sentences. Therefore, gaining different types of written samples that would lend themselves to different sentence functions (e.g., narrative) could help you evaluate a student's capabilities with respect to sentence function.

Sentence length (e.g., average number of words or average number of morphemes across sentences) is another component of written language that may give insight into syntax ability. Students may have grammatically accurate sentences, but they may be very short. As students' writing capabilities improve, it is typical for sentence length to increase.

Written Expression/Discourse

When you wish to examine written expression and discourse as a whole, it can be beneficial to evaluate several styles of written language (e.g., expository, journals, narratives, poetry), because students may be more capable in certain styles. For example, a student may feel very comfortable writing a less formal journal as compared to writing a narrative, or story. One of the most important aspects of evaluating written expression is to get multiple samples of different types to truly gain an accurate picture of written expression.

Within written expression, it is important to evaluate the different levels associated with writing a composition, including word or vocabulary choice, sentence development, paragraph development, and essay or composition development. It can also be beneficial to evaluate the different stages associated with the writing process, including prewriting (brainstorming, use of graphic organizers, checklists for ideas, etc.), writing the draft, and post-writing (revising, editing). Additionally, examining the student's ability to take the audience into consideration and adjust his or her writing appropriately is an important aspect of written expression.

Many assessments examine syntax, content, spelling, capitalization/punctuation, and other areas of written expression. The Test of Written Language (TOWL), the KTEA, the Oral and Written Language Scales (OWLS), and the Test of Early Written Language (TEWL) are examples of norm-referenced assessments.

Concluding Thoughts on Written Language

Written language allows individuals to communicate over time and space. We can read something that a person wrote hundreds of years ago and still be able to understand it (with possible differences in vocabulary usage or meaning associated with words). Similarly, the writer and reader can be in completely different locations and have no contact with one another and still be able to communicate through written language. Becoming a capable writer allows for greater communication between individuals, and it can also allow a person to write things that he or she can refer to later. However, in order for written language to truly be effective, many components need to come together.

Check Your Understanding 5.3

1. Why might handwriting difficulties cause reduced written language productivity?

2. How can assessing sentence forms (fragments, run-ons, simple sentences, etc.) inform instruction in the area of syntax?

3. What type of information might you look for with an error analysis in the area of spelling?

4. What is the difference between assessing spelling recognition and spelling recall?

Mathematics

Mathematics is an area of achievement that often conjures up much emotion for students. When asked what their most favorite or least favorite subject is, they often name mathematics as one or the other. Math isn't typically an area of achievement to which students are indifferent. Why is this the case? One reason may be that since math is so rule-based and concepts continue to build on one another, either students often understand it and can move forward, or they have difficulties that make it hard to progress. Evaluations of mathematical skills can often be difficult to interpret, because proficiency is often related to what has been taught. In math, unlike in some of the other areas of achievement, it is often more difficult to independently gain skills, because math is so heavily driven by complex procedures and concepts. Students often are unable to perform math problems independently unless they have been taught the underlying concepts or algorithms that are needed to solve them. Therefore, when evaluating math skills, keep in mind what should be expected, based on what has been taught. There are several subareas of mathematics that must be evaluated to better understand mathematical proficiency, including early mathematical skills, computation, word problem solving, and other math skills (time, measurement, pattern development, etc.) Refer to Figure 5.3 for the subskills associated with mathematics.

Early Mathematical Skills

Early mathematical skills often pave the way for later math skills, and deficits or delays in early math skills can make it much harder to learn more advanced math concepts. The Test of Early Mathematics Ability (TEMA) is a norm-referenced assessment that measures early mathematical competency. Consider the following concepts that would be considered early mathematics skills:

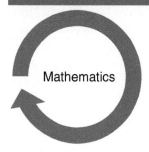

Figure 5.3 Subskills of Mathematics

Mathematics

- Early mathematical skills
- Computation
- Word problem solving
- Other math skills (e.g. measurement, time)

- *Counting.* While counting seems to be a fairly straightforward skill, there are many aspects of counting that should be considered. Rote counting is much like saying the ABCs; it can often be memorized but not truly understood for what it represents. However, to truly understand a child's proficiency in counting, it is important to consider many factors.

  Guerriero (2010) reported that Gelman and Gallistel (1978) presented five principles that children must understand before becoming truly proficient in counting: one-to-one correspondence, stable order, cardinality, abstraction, and order irrelevance (Geary, 1996).

  ○ *One-to-one correspondence* is "the idea that each object is represented by one verbal label or number" (Guerriero, 2010, p. 47). For example, when a student is counting a set of five objects, evidence of one-to-one correspondence would be giving one verbal label to each object (e.g., "1, 2, 3, 4, 5"). It doesn't matter if the verbal label is not accurate (e.g., "1, 2, 4, 5, 6"); it just matters that one label is given to each object.

  ○ *The stable order principle* "states that each time a child counts, he or she uses the same sequence of verbal labels" (Guerriero, 2010, p. 47). For example, a student would demonstrate stable order if every time she counted to 10, she said, "1, 2, 3, 4, 5, 6, 7, 8, 9, 10." It would still be considered a stable order even if the order wasn't correct (e.g., "1, 2, 4, 5, 7, 8, 9, 10"), as long as that same order was used every time.

  ○ *Cardinality* is "the principle in which the total number of objects is equal to the last number or verbal label that was used when counting" (Guerriero, 2010, p. 47). For example, if a child counted five objects "1, 2, 3, 4, 5" and then was asked how many objects there were, he would demonstrate cardinality if he said "five," because it was the last verbal label given to an object.

○ *Abstraction* "refers to the understanding that counting can be generalized to different sets of objects" (Guerriero, 2010, p. 47). For example, if a child learns how to count a specific set of objects in a book, but cannot count a different set of objects, that child would not exhibit abstraction.

○ *Order irrelevance* is "a principle that states that a given set of objects can be counted in any order and result in the same amount" (Guerriero, 2010, p. 47). For example, if a child counted a set of items from left to right and then again from right to left, the child should understand that there would be the same number of objects.

Guerriero (2010) further stated that "there are several levels of complexity within skilled counting including counting with manipulatives, finger counting, and verbal counting" (p. 47). Guerriero (2010) reported that Geary (1996) discussed several strategies for counting that make it more complex, including the following strategies: the *counting-all* strategy, the *adding-on* strategy, and the *min* strategy:

○ The *counting-all* strategy is "one in which both addends are counted on the fingers" (Guerriero, 2010, p. 47). For example, if there were two sets of objects, and the first set had three objects and the second set had five objects, a student would count both sets of objects: "1, 2, 3 → 4, 5, 6, 7, 8."

○ The *adding-on* strategy is "a developmentally more complex strategy in which children start with the first addend and add the second addend by counting the number of fingers of the second addend" (Guerriero, 2010, pp. 47–48). In this scenario, when given the same sets of objects as the previous example, the student would start with 3 (since the first set had three objects) and add on: "3 → 4, 5, 6, 7, 8."

○ The *min* strategy is "more complex and is an extension of the *adding-on* strategy, in which the smaller addend is added to the larger addend. The *min* strategy is a more advantageous approach because it minimizes the number of fingers that must be counted" (Guerriero, 2010, p. 48). By using the *min* strategy, the student would complete as little counting as possible. He or she would start with the largest group of objects (5) and add on to that with the other set of objects: "5 → 6, 7, 8."

Assessing counting proficiency and the different precursors and levels of complexity could be important in better understanding math proficiency in different areas. Sometimes, it may not be enough to determine simply whether a student is able to count, because that could mean any of a number of things.

- *Number sense*. Number sense refers to a child's understanding of numbers, what they represent, and how they relate to one another. For example, understanding which is more, 3 or 4, may demonstrate number sense.

- *Recognition of written numerals*. Being able to recognize numerals is an important step in learning mathematics. For example, a student may be able to count two objects, but she may not recognize the numeral 2 as the same as two objects. Assessing whether a child is able to recognize the numerals and relate them to the values that they represent can give insight into the child's understanding within math.

These early math skills often pave the way for later math learning, and assessing children's proficiency in each of them can help you develop a better understanding of their skill strengths and needs.

Computation

Guerriero (2010) reported that "Computations or calculations can be represented as isolated numerical problems as well as problems that are embedded in context (word problems)" (p. 46). All mathematical computations require one or more of the following four operations: addition, subtraction, multiplication, and division. However, computation problems can differ in their level of complexity, and they may be referred to as "simple" or "complex." While the terms "simple" and "complex" are often used in different ways by different people, for purposes of this text, complexity will be discussed in the following way: Addition and multiplication computations will be considered "simple" if the computation problems contain two single-digit numbers (e.g., "6 + 5" or "4 × 3"). Subtraction and division problems that are the reciprocal of simple addition and multiplication problems, respectively, would also be considered simple (e.g., "11 − 5" or "12 ÷ 3"). Alternatively, "complex" computation includes addition or multiplication problems with one or more values that have at least two digits (e.g., "3 + 12") and the reciprocal subtraction or division problems (e.g. "15 − 3"), as well as problems that have more than two values in the problem (e.g., "7 + 2 + 5").

As was discussed in Chapter 3, and earlier in this chapter, closely examining a child's error patterns can give insight into overall difficulties that the child may be having. There are many patterns of computation errors that are often seen in children's computations. Guerriero (2010) indicated that Ashcraft (1992) discussed four types of errors that frequently occur in simple computational problem solving: wild guesses, near misses, operation confusions, and table errors.

Wild guesses "occur early in development and they are seen in various forms. A frequently observed error that is characterized as a wild guess is one in which the addends in the problem are combined as in '4 + 1 = 41.' Another type of error that is classified as a wild guess is a restatement of one of the addends in the problem as the solution to the problem as in '4 + 1 = 1'" (Guerriero, 2010, p. 50).

Near misses "frequently occur when children miscount while using counting strategies, or when they incorrectly use a strategy such as the add-on strategy. For example, when given the problem '4 + 5,' they may incorrectly use the adding-on strategy and count '4, 5, 6, 7, 8' instead of counting on from the '4' as in '5, 6, 7, 8, 9'" (Guerriero, 2010, p. 50).

Operation confusions "result when children retrieve the answer to a problem with the wrong sign as a result of a failure to consider the sign. For example, when given the problem '5 − 4,' they might answer '9' because they did not attend to the sign, and assumed that it was an addition problem. Another example of operation confusion occurs when two numbers are associated with a particular sign, and the child incorrectly recalls the solution using the wrong sign. For example, when given the problem '4 × 2,' a child who makes an error that is classified as an operation confusion might give a solution of '6' instead of '8' because the numbers '4' and '2' may be more highly associated with the problem '4 + 2' rather than '4 × 2.' Operation errors of this type frequently occur when children are first learning a new operation, and they substitute an answer from an already learned operation using the same digits" (Guerriero, 2010, pp. 50–51).

Table errors are "errors in which children provide an answer from the table that involves one of the numbers in the problem. For example, when given the problem '7 + 8,' they may give a solution of '13,' which corresponds to the problem '7 + 6.' Table errors suggest either the inconsistent input or storage of the problem and/or answer in long term memory or the inconsistent retrieval of the answer from long term memory" (Guerriero, 2010, p. 51).

Guerriero (2010) further indicated that "As children's level of mastery in solving computational problems increases, the types of errors change as well; however, one should be cautious when analyzing error patterns because a particular answer could signal more than one type of error. For example, consider the previously described counting error '4 + 5 = 8.' In this instance, the error could actually be a table error, in which the child retrieved the answer to '4 + 4 = 8'" (p. 51).

Guerriero (2010) further discussed several types of errors with regrouping that may result from a lack of understanding associated with the base-10 system or procedural errors that are associated with regrouping strategies. Consider the following examples from Guerriero (2010, p. 53):

	5 2	8 10	10		10 10
7 3	7̸ 3	9̸ 0 3	7 3	6 0	5 0 5
− 3 5	− 3 5	− 4 0 5	− 5 4	− 2 7	− 2 8 7
4 2	2 0	4 0 8	2 9	4 7	3 2 8

In the first example, the smaller number is always subtracted from the larger number, regardless of whether the number is on the top or the bottom. In the second example, a "2" is borrowed from the tens column to add to the "3" in the ones column. This will lead to "5 − 5 = 0" in the ones column. In the third example, the place holder in the tens column is ignored. In the fourth example, a "10" is borrowed from the tens column, but "1" is not removed from the tens column. In example 5, the "0" is ignored. In the last example, borrowing is required in both the ones column and the tens column, but "1" is not taken away from the hundreds column. These are the more common errors that exist in complex subtraction problems; however, children make other errors that do not seem to fit any of these patterns

(p. 53).

Computation skills can be measured in isolation and in context, and students may perform differently based on whether there is context associated with the computation. Similar to decoding in reading and spelling in written language, computation is often at the base of mathematical proficiency. A student may have no problem understanding the concepts and being able to solve word problems, but if he or she can't compute the problem accurately, the solution will be incorrect. There are many assessments that examine computation skills, such as the Wide Range Achievement Test (WRAT), the KeyMath, the Woodcock-Johnson, the KTEA, the WIAT, and the Test of Mathematical Ability (TOMA).

Word Problem Solving

"Mathematical problem solving, often referred to as word problem solving, is a process that allows children to understand how mathematics can be applied to real world situations. A word problem is a real world instance in which numbers are manipulated in order to answer a question" (Guerriero, 2010, p. 20). Word problem solving often poses difficulties, because solving problems often requires so many underlying skills. In evaluating word problem solving proficiency, looking at various components can help you determine where an individual's difficulties lie. Guerriero (2010) reported that word problem solving proficiency can be evaluated across a number of different dimensions, including classification of word problem structure, linguistic components, and stages of word problem solving.

Problem classification. "Word problems have been classified into four general classes based on the relationship between the problems' actions and agents: 1) change, 2) combine, 3) compare, and 4) equalize" (Guerriero, 2010, p. 22). Table 5.1 gives descriptions and examples of each of the four classes of word problems.

Change problems. "Change problems involve an action to, or change in, the value of a single set that occurs over time. There is an initial condition (Time 1), which changes when an action is performed (Time 2), and results in a final state (Time 3). An example of an addition change problem is: *John had 2 apples. Bob gave John 6 apples. How many apples does John have?* In this example, the single set, or initial condition, is John's set of apples. The change occurs when Bob gives John additional apples. The final state is the number of apples that John has after receiving apples from Bob" (Guerriero, 2010, p. 22).

Combine problems. "Combine problems present a static relationship and do not involve an action as the change problems do. They involve the combination

Table 5.1 Problem Classification

Problem Classification	Description	Example
Change problems	An action to, or change in, the value of a single set that occurs over time	*John had 2 apples. Bob gave John 6 apples. How many apples does John have?*
Combine problems	The combination of two subsets into a whole set (addition) or the decomposition of a whole set into two subsets (subtraction)	*Jen had 3 kittens. Jen had 1 puppy. How many animals did Jen have?*
Compare problems	A static relationship that involves the comparison of two isolated sets	*Kathy washed 9 plates. Kathy washed 5 more bowls than plates. How many bowls did Kathy wash?*
Equalize problems	An action or change that occurs between two isolated sets that must be compared	*Chris ate 8 crackers. If Chris ate 4 more crackers, Chris would eat as many as Tom. How many crackers did Tom eat?*

of two subsets into a whole set (addition) or the decomposition of a whole set into two subsets (subtraction). An example of an addition combine problem is: *Jen had 3 kittens. Jen had 1 puppy. How many animals did Jen have?* In this example, the kittens are one subset and the puppies are the second subset. The two subsets combine to form the whole set, which is animals" (Guerriero, 2010, p. 22).

Compare problems. "Compare problems convey a static relationship that involves the comparison of two isolated sets. An example of an addition compare problem is: *Kathy washed 9 plates. Kathy washed 5 more bowls than plates. How many bowls did Kathy wash?* In this example, the two isolated sets to be compared are plates and bowls" (Guerriero, 2010, p. 23).

Equalize problems. "Equalize problems are the most complex because they are a combination of change problems and compare problems. They involve an action or change that occurs between two isolated sets that must be compared. An example of an addition equalize problem is: *Chris ate 8 crackers. If Chris ate 4 more crackers, Chris would eat as many as Tom. How many crackers did Tom eat?* In this example, the two isolated sets that must be compared are the crackers that Chris ate and the crackers that Tom ate. The change that occurs is the number of crackers that Chris would have to have eaten to equal the number that Tom ate" (Guerriero, 2010, p. 23).

Linguistic components. Components can be added to a word problem that may change the complexity and difficulty of the problem. The following are examples of linguistic components that may change the complexity: consistency of relational terms, extraneous information, extra steps, and pronoun usage. Consider the following word problem: "Scott picked 4 apples. Jane picked 5 more apples than Scott. How many apples did Jane pick?" It is a compare problem that requires addition to solve. Now consider variations of this original problem that have different linguistic components. See Table 5.2 for examples of linguistic components and example word problems.

Consistency of relational terms. "Relational terms are often used to compare elements in a word problem. These include terms such as *more* or *less* that indicate the operation to be used to solve the problem. When they are used consistently with their traditional meaning, *more* and *less* signal addition and subtraction, respectively. Conversely, when they are used inconsistently with their typical meanings, *more* and *less* signal subtraction and addition, respectively" (Guerriero, 2010, p. 24). Consider the following problem: "Scott picked 4 apples. Scott picked 5 less apples than Jane. How many apples did Jane pick?" In this example, the relational term

Table 5.2 Linguistic Components in Word Problems

Linguistic Component	Example Word Problem
Original compare problem	Scott picked 4 apples. Jane picked 5 more apples than Scott. How many apples did Jane pick?
Consistency of relational terms	Scott picked 4 apples. Scott picked 5 less apples than Jane. How many apples did Jane pick?
Extraneous information	Scott picked 4 apples. Jane picked 5 more apples than Scott. Jane also picked 10 oranges. How many apples did Jane pick?
Extra steps	Scott picked 3 apples. Later, Scott picked 1 more apple. Jane picked 5 more apples than Scott. How many apples did Jane pick?
Pronoun usage	Scott picked 4 apples. Jane picked 5 more apples than him. How many apples did she pick?

"less" is used inconsistently to signal addition. When used inconsistently, these types of signal words can increase the level of difficulty associated with a problem. Further, if children are specifically taught to look for signal words, they may be misled in a problem that uses inconsistent relational terms.

Extraneous information. "Extraneous information is irrelevant linguistic or numerical information that is inserted into a problem but not used to compute the answer to the problem. It can distract the reader or influence the reader to misinterpret the question that is presented in the problem" (Guerriero, 2010, p. 25). The following problem contains extraneous information that may cause difficulties for the student. "Scott picked 4 apples. Jane picked 5 more apples than Scott. Jane also picked 10 oranges. How many apples did Jane pick?" If children think that they should use all the numbers in the problem, they will not construct the appropriate equation for this problem.

Extra steps. Extra steps require individuals to complete more than one computation in order to solve the word problem. Consider the following: "Scott picked 3 apples. Later, Scott picked 1 more apple. Jane picked 5 more apples than Scott. How many apples did Jane pick?" Children often have difficulties with problems that require more than one step. Even if the operation is not difficult, children will often make errors. Children with poor working memory may have difficulties with problems that require extra steps and may subsequently make errors because reasoning through the problem and planning a solution is more taxing on their mental resources.

Pronoun usage. Pronouns (e.g., he/him, she/her, it, them) are often used in place of proper nouns; however, pronouns can be ambiguous (e.g., names that could be traditionally male or female being used with pronouns). Even if pronouns are not ambiguous, understanding them may not be automatic for a child. Children may have difficulties placing the pronoun with the appropriate referent. This could lead to misunderstandings in the problem. In the following example, the student is required to interpret pronouns to solve the problem: "Scott picked 4 apples. Jane picked 5 more apples than him. How many apples did she pick?" If the student has difficulties determining who him or she refers to, it may be a difficult problem to solve.

Stages of word problem solving. Word problem solving requires both reasoning (comprehension and equation construction) and computation. According to Guerriero (2010), "Several models have emerged that aim to explain the process of solving word problems. . . . Many of these models describe in some detail various cognitive and execution phases that are associated with solving a word problem" (p. 25). Guerriero (2010) further discussed Mayer's four-stage model of word problem solving (Hegarty, Mayer, & Green, 1992), which includes problem translation, problem integration, solution planning, and solution execution:

- *Problem translation* requires mental interpretation of each sentence in the problem, as well as literal comprehension of information given in the text. Inconsistent signal words or ambiguous pronouns could hinder this stage.

- *Problem integration* requires integration between sentences in the problem. It also requires inferential comprehension through the interpretation of the text and the ability to synthesize all the information in the text in a meaningful way. Inconsistent signal words and extraneous information could hinder this stage.

- *Solution planning* involves the development of a plan or equation that will be used to solve the problem. This stage requires an understanding of place value, as well as the ability to correctly align numbers.

- *Solution execution* requires the computation needed to obtain an accurate solution to the problem. Children must be able to compute the solution to the equation or else they will have an incorrect answer to the word problem, even if they understand the word problem.

Guerriero (2010) developed the Word Problem Comprehension Task, which aims to evaluate word problem solving proficiency at each stage of word problem solving by asking comprehension questions that mimic the stages of word problem solving. In the Word Problem Comprehension Task, the following types of questions are asked:

- Literal comprehension questions that do not contain relational terms (require problem translation)

- Literal comprehension questions that contain relational terms (require problem translation)

- Inferential comprehension questions (require problem integration)

- Questions about equation construction (require solution planning)

- Computation accuracy (require solution execution)

This type of assessment would enable the evaluator to determine at what stage of word problem solving the student is having difficulties. It also allows for patterns to emerge based on different linguistic components.

Word problem solving is highly complex and involves a great many possible stages and components. In order to evaluate proficiency in word problem solving, it is important to examine the characteristics of each problem to determine what is really being required of the student. That will help you gain insight into where difficulties may be occurring through analyzing patterns of performance. Figure 5.4 depicts the components of word problem solving.

The following are examples of assessments that evaluate word problem solving: the Woodcock-Johnson, the KTEA, the KeyMath, and the WIAT.

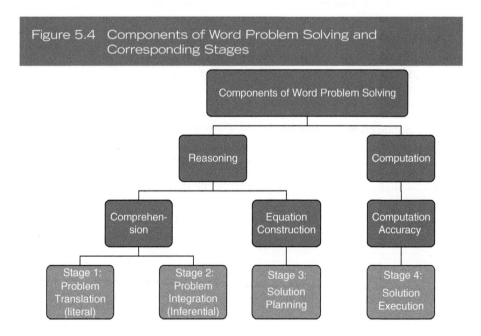

Figure 5.4   Components of Word Problem Solving and Corresponding Stages

Other Math Skills

Math skills that are related to concepts such as time, measurement, and money are vital functional skills that individuals will need to use often. Assessing students' capabilities in these areas is valuable, because if they are areas of difficulty, focused instruction may be necessary.

The ability to understand concepts related to time is needed daily. The following are examples of skills associated with time that may be evaluated:

- The ability to tell time at the level of the hour, ½ hour, ¼ hour, 5 minutes, and minute (on a digital and/or analog clock)

- Measuring elapsed time (e.g., "What is the elapsed time between 4:30 and 8:00?")

- The concept of time (e.g., "How long does it take to brush your teeth?")

- Relating time to a calendar (hours in a day, days in a week/month, days/weeks/months in a year, etc.)

- Understanding the concept of time management

A variety of measurement skills, such as length, weight, temperature, and volume, are useful skills to have for everyday functioning. Measurement skills are used for cooking, understanding the weather to determine appropriate clothing, understanding distance, and so on.

There are many concepts associated with money that should be evaluated, such as identifying coins/bills and knowing the value of each; being able to use fractions and decimals to represent amounts that are not whole dollar amounts; determining how much money is needed to purchase a particular item and how much is left after that purchase; and understanding the value of money. An individual's ability to work with money and understand money is of extreme importance in the scope of his or her life.

While it is important to understand all aspects of mathematical ability, if these types of skills are not directly assessed, it may not be evident that instruction needs to address those areas.

Concluding Thoughts on Mathematics

Mathematics involves many interrelated concepts that often build off of one another. The wide scope of mathematical skills needs to be examined (as appropriate for the individual's age and grade) to fully understand actual mathematical deficits. There are many norm-referenced assessments (e.g., the KeyMath, the WIAT, the Woodcock-Johnson, the KTEA) that examine math proficiency. However, since math is so skill-based and often intersects very closely with what was taught, curriculum-based assessments or criterion-referenced assessments can be really beneficial, as well.

1. Describe how you could assess one-to-one correspondence.

2. What is the min strategy, and why is it more complex than counting all?

3. Develop three questions that would help you determine whether a student has good number sense.

4. Give an example of a table error in computation.

5. What are the four operations that are used in mathematical computation?

6. Consider the following word problem: "Jack went to the store and bought 5 green apples, 6 red apples, and 5 yellow apples. He also bought a fruit bowl to put them in. How many apples did Jack buy?"

   a. Which of the four problem classifications is this problem an example of?

   b. Which of the linguistic components that are described in the chapter are present in this problem?

7. What is the difference between problem translation and problem integration?

8. If a student consistently answers word problems incorrectly, what can you do to determine where the difficulties lie?

9. Why is it important to measure a student's understanding of time? List three scenarios where competency in the area of time might be beneficial for a student.

10. Mathematics is a very rule based-area of achievement. What impact might this have on the assessment process?

Nonverbal Abilities

Nonverbal abilities involve the interpretation of information that does not directly relate to words within the language. For example, interpreting pictures, solving puzzles, interpreting sounds heard in nature, and understanding spatial relationships would all be considered nonverbal abilities. Further, as was mentioned earlier in this chapter, nonverbal abilities often do relate to language and pragmatics in that they are frequently associated with the way that language is used in a social context and how it is perceived within society. The following are examples of how nonverbal abilities may impact language and communication:

- Interpreting visual cues such as gestures, body language, facial expressions, and eye contact is an important skill that often allows communication partners to better understand each other. Difficulty gauging the visual cues that another person is exhibiting can cause misunderstandings and lead to possible social difficulties for an individual.

- Interpreting auditory cues within language—such as *prosody*, or "the rhythmic and intonational aspect of language" (Merriam-Webster.com, s.v. "prosody"); *intonation*, or "the rise and fall in pitch of the voice in speech" (Merriam-Webster.com, s.v. "intonation"); *volume of speech;* and *inflection*, or "change in pitch or loudness of the voice" (Merriam-Webster.com, s.v. "inflection")—also require nonverbal abilities. Misunderstandings associated with these types of auditory cues can result in awkward conversations.

- Rules associated with turn-taking and maintaining an appropriate distance from a communicative partner also take place within the context of language, but they are not associated with the words of the language. Failing to adhere to these types of social conventions could result in others feeling uncomfortable with the person who doesn't understand these unwritten rules.

- Understanding sarcasm and figurative language often requires nonverbal skills, because the listener has to interpret language differently from the way that it is presented. As children grow into older children and adolescents, this type of language is often used socially, and it can be difficult for an individual to socially interact with same-aged peers if it isn't fully understood.

Nonverbal abilities is an area of achievement that is seen across academics, and better understanding an individual's capabilities associated with nonverbal abilities provides great insight into how that individual will relate to the world around him or her. There are assessments that evaluate pragmatics; however, evaluating nonverbal abilities is often very tricky, because it is typically more beneficial to evaluate them in an authentic setting than in a contrived setting or testing situation. For this reason, direct observations and interviews (refer back to Chapter 3) may be very useful tools for better understanding nonverbal abilities.

Concluding Thoughts on Areas of Academic Achievement

The discussion of the five main areas of academic achievement and their relationship with language was extensive, as it really impacts student performance across all subject areas in relation to what has been taught. Throughout later chapters, much attention will be paid to language, achievement, and how students perform academically across different disability categories. For example, Chapter 6, "Specific Learning Disabilities," will rely heavily on this chapter as a means of discussing different characteristics associated with learning disabilities.

1. If a student has difficulties in reading, is it important to evaluate any other areas of achievement? Explain.

2. Why does language need to be evaluated in conjunction with the different areas of achievement?

3. Describe a scenario that might show that a student possesses impaired nonverbal abilities.

Behavior

In contrast to intelligence and academic ability, behavior may be something that is both innate to an individual and something that can be shaped. Behavioral patterns often impact the way that an individual interacts with others and functions across many different contexts (home, school, extracurricular activities, etc.). Evaluating behavior is often instrumental to better understanding the characteristics of various disabilities, since behavioral patterns are often discussed as part of the criteria for diagnosis of many disabilities (e.g., autism spectrum disorder, emotional disturbance, and ADHD) and eligibility for special services.

In Chapter 3, interviews and direct observations were discussed as possible mechanisms for evaluating behavior. Interviews serve as an indirect means of obtaining information about behavior from a variety of sources (parents, teachers, etc.). Direct observations are a direct method of observing behavior, whether meant to inventory behavior and look for patterns or to specifically observe positive behaviors or behaviors of concern. The Behavior Assessment System for Children (BASC), the Motivation Assessment Scale (MAS), the Functional Analysis Screening Tool (FAST), and the Functional Assessment Interview Form (FAIF) are all examples of assessments that can be used to examine behavior and determine behavioral patterns. When a student demonstrates behavior that is of concern, a Functional Behavior Assessment (FBA) can help you determine the possible function of that behavior or reason for engaging in it (e.g., to seek attention, to avoid something, to gain sensory stimulation). Functional Behavioral Assessment (FBA) is "a process for identifying problem behaviors and developing interventions to improve or eliminate those behaviors" (PaTTAN, 2018, p. 1). The following is an example of the types of information that may be included in a FBA and is adapted from PaTTAN's *Functional Behavioral Assessment Process* (2018).

- Student profile: The student profile often contains information about strengths and needs associated with academics, social skills, and behavior. It also may include information about the student's personal interests and family.

- Interviews: Interviews can provide insight into behaviors of concern, as well as possible antecedents and consequences associated with those behaviors (as reported by the interviewee). They can also provide information about any patterns of behavior that are evident and ideas about possible functions of those behaviors.

- Direct observations: Direct observations provide a means for the examiner to directly observe behaviors of concern and examine antecedents, consequences, and any patterns that emerge (see Chapter 3 for examples of antecedents, behaviors, and consequences).

- Development of a hypothesis regarding the function of the behavior of concern: The ultimate goal is to determine why a student is demonstrating the behaviors of concern and find a means of reducing and optimally eliminating behaviors of concern. Developing a hypothesis about the function of the behavior is supported through the data that was obtained in the interview and direct observations.

Concluding Thoughts on Behavior

Evaluating behavior, examining behavioral patterns, and determining functions of those behaviors can be a crucial factor in effectively evaluating student performance. Behavior can heavily impact language, areas of achievement, and social/emotional status. For example, while it may seem that a student is having difficulties with reading, observations of the student may reveal that the actual problem is related to the individual's behavior during the reading process (as opposed to ability to read). Getting to the root of behavioral patterns is essential for fully evaluating a student and determining how to move forward with instruction.

Check Your Understanding 5.6

1. What benefits can be gained from examining behavior both through interviews and through direct observation?

2. Why would it be useful to determine the function of a student's behavior?

3. Describe a situation where negative behaviors could impact the functioning of a classroom.

CHAPTER SUMMARY

Countless characteristics come together to make every individual unique. A comprehensive diagnostic evaluation must be completed in such a way that the diagnostic team can analyze the results and develop a clear picture of a student's strengths and needs. The expansiveness of information in Chapters 4 and 5 should help convey the extensive and complex nature of the diagnostic and eligibility process. There are numerous pieces to the puzzle, and the multidisciplinary team must ensure that the results are an accurate reflection of an individual. Closely examining characteristics associated with (1) intelligence, (2) social and emotional status, (3) health and medical status, (4) language, (5) areas of academic achievement, (6) and behavior can provide the information necessary to make a truly informed decision about diagnosis and eligibility.

In subsequent chapters, the focus turns to examining each disability category in relation to the areas highlighted in Chapters 4 and 5. It is recommended that you refer back to these chapters frequently as you focus on the various disabilities. Each disability has specific criteria for diagnosis and may focus more heavily on some areas as compared with others. For example, Chapter 6, "Learning Disabilities," will refer heavily to discussions from this chapter on intelligence and areas of academic achievement and language, while Chapter 8, "Autism Spectrum Disorder," will focus very specifically on communication/language, behavior, and social skills. However, regardless of the disability, all areas will be addressed, as all are required elements of a comprehensive diagnostic evaluation. Additionally, case studies related to each disability will highlight many of the concepts from these chapters.

APPLY WHAT YOU HAVE LEARNED

1. Compare and contrast the difference in vocabulary across oral language, reading, and written language. Why might a student show different vocabulary skills across these areas of achievement?

2. Throughout the chapter, reference was made to many norm-referenced assessments. Choose three assessments in the area of reading, research them, and provide a description of what they assess.

3. Read the following written sample and evaluate it for spelling, vocabulary, content, syntax, and written expression. Why is it important to look at each component when you are evaluating the sample?

Squirel

An animal that I research and learn about was squirl. A squirl is not very rare creacher. A squirel has a lot of critcal infermation that you mint like to lern about.

The squirl has a range of color the colors that is can be are red brown and back. They have booshy tales. Squirels are little, but biger than a chipmunk mouse or rat.

The food the squirl eats are plant and meat. dont feed squirrels becuz they will not leave you alon they want more food.

The squrl live everywhere in the cuntry. You see them a lot in park or at home in tree. Thay like to run up trees and play. They make skweeky noiz to. Sometime you can here them playing and chase each uther. They are funy but you dont want them for pet.

That is what I lern about squirrels.

REFERENCES

Ashcraft, M. (1992). Cognitive arithmetic: A review of data and theory. *Cognition, 44,* 75–106.

Geary, D. (1996). *Children's mathematical development.* Washington, DC: American Psychological Association.

Gelman, R., & Gallistel, C. R. (1978). *The child's understanding of number.* Cambridge, MA: Harvard University Press.

Guerriero, T. (2010). *The Role of Language Comprehension and Computation in Mathematical Word Problem Solving Among Students with Different Levels of Computation Achievement (Doctoral Dissertation).* Northwestern University in Evanston, Il. Department of Communication Sciences and Disorders

Hegarty, M., Mayer, R., & Green, C. (1992). Comprehension of arithmetic word problems: Evidence from students' eye fixations. *Journal of Educational Psychology, 84,* 76–84.

Pennsylvania Training and Technical Assistance Network (PaTTAN). (2018). *Functional Behavioral Assessment (FBA) process.* Retrieved from https://www.pattan.net/getattachment/ Publications/Functional-Behavioral-Assessment-Process/FBA_ProcessBklt0516-pdf/FBA-Process-Bklt-10-18-wba.pdf?lang=en-US&ext=.pdf

Phillips, L. (1911). *Peter Piper's practical principles of plain & perfect pronunciation.* Boston, MA: Le Roy Phillips.

Reid, D. K., Hresko, W., & Hammill, D. (2018). *TERA-4: Test of Early Reading Ability* (4th ed.). Retrieved from https://www.proedinc.com/Products/14635/tera4-test-of-early-reading-ability-fourth-edition.aspx

Reutzel, D. R., & Cooter, R. (2012). *Teaching children to read: The teacher makes the difference* (6th ed.). Upper Saddle River, NJ: Pearson Education.

Texas Education Agency. (n.d.). *Print awareness: Guidelines for instruction.* Reading Rockets. Retrieved from http://www.readingrockets.org/article/print-awareness-guidelines-instruction.

Vaughn, S., & Bos, C. (2012). *Strategies for teaching students with learning and behavior problems* (8th ed.). Upper Saddle River, NJ: Pearson Education.

Assessment and Diagnosis of Disabilities

Learning Disabilities

Tara S. Guerriero, PhD

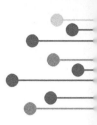

Learning Objectives

After the completion of this chapter, you should be able to:

- Define a specific learning disability according to IDEA.

- Explain the purpose and components of the exclusionary clause.

- Discuss the relationship between intelligence, academic achievement, and psychological processing that exists among individuals diagnosed with a learning disability.

- Identify the different types of deficits related to psychological processing that contribute to the diagnosis of a learning disability.

- Identify the components that are included in a comprehensive diagnostic evaluation, or psychoeducational evaluation, to determine whether a student has learning disabilities.

- Explain each of the three methods that are most widely used for diagnosing learning disabilities (discrepancy model, Response to Intervention, and patterns of strengths and weaknesses).

- Evaluate the merits of each of the three methods for diagnosing learning disabilities (discrepancy model, response to intervention, and patterns of strengths and weaknesses).

- Apply what has been learned about the diagnostic process associated with learning disabilities to three case studies.

Key Terms

attention (p. 163)	auditory perception (p. 171)
coming to attention, sustained attention, selective attention	auditory discrimination, auditory blending, auditory figure-ground discrimination, auditory memory, auditory closure

(Continued)

(Continued)

discrepancy model (p. 178)	Response to Intervention (RTI) (p. 179)
exclusionary clause (p. 158–159)	speed of processing (p. 167)
haptic perception (p. 173)	visual/auditory/motor integration (p. 173)
visual/motor integration, visual/auditory/motor integration	
memory (p. 164)	visual perception (p. 167)
immediate memory, short-term memory, working memory, long-term memory, encoding, storage/organization, retrieval	visual discrimination, visual figure-ground discrimination, object recognition, spatial relations, visual memory, visual closure
patterns of strengths and weaknesses (PSW) (p. 180)	word finding (p. 173)
psychological processing (p. 156)	

Introduction to the Chapter

Learning disabilities are characterized by deficit(s) in **psychological processing**, or the way that the mind works with information that comes in through the sensory system. Processing deficits hinder those with learning disabilities from achieving academically in the same way that they would if they didn't have processing deficits. Traditionally (prior to the inclusion of RTI and patterns of strengths and weaknesses as criteria for diagnosis in IDEA), students with learning disabilities had at least an average or anywhere above level of intelligence. They demonstrated a significant discrepancy, or difference, between intelligence and one or more areas of academic achievement that could only be explained by one or more deficit(s) in processing. While many states continue to recognize the discrepancy model, in more recent years, alternate means of diagnosing learning disabilities (e.g., Response to Intervention, patterns of strengths and weaknesses) have also become prevalent.

The type(s) of processing deficits, along with the impact of those deficits, can vary so widely between individuals that there isn't one set of characteristics that easily defines the population. Each individual with a learning disability has a different set of circumstances that is based on the underlying processing deficits in combination with processing strengths that the student exhibits. Difficulties in one or more of the following five basic areas of academic achievement are a hallmark of learning disabilities:

- Oral language

- Reading

- Written language

- Mathematics

- Nonverbal ability (note that this category isn't always included as an area of academic achievement)

Students with specific learning disabilities make up the largest population of students with disabilities who receive services under IDEA; according to the 2018 Annual Report to Congress on the Individuals With Disabilities Education Act (2018), 38.6% of students ages 6–21 who received special education services under IDEA in 2016 received services for specific learning disabilities. Although learning disabilities are prevalent among those receiving services, they continue to be one of the most misunderstood types of disability by the general population and even some in the field of education. Why are learning disabilities so difficult for many to understand? One possible reason is the name itself; since the name may seem nonspecific, one may assume that any difficulties associated with a child's learning must be the same as a learning disability. Another possible reason is that there are different methods of diagnosing learning disabilities, and the diagnostic criteria surrounding those methods can differ from state to state, making it somewhat difficult to navigate the underlying premise of the disability. A third possible reason is that each student with a learning disability is so different that it is difficult to clearly describe identifying characteristics that are common to all students with learning disabilities.

The purpose of this chapter is to apply the concepts learned in Chapter 2 (e.g., RTI), Chapter 3 (norm-referenced tests, criterion-referenced assessments, etc.), and Chapters 4 and 5 (intelligence, academic achievement, behavior, etc.) to the diagnostic process associated with learning disabilities and develop a solid understanding of the true foundation of learning disabilities. One of the benefits of truly understanding the underlying processing deficits associated with an individual's diagnosis of a learning disability is that it can serve as the basis for teaching the student in a different way, one that can ultimately capitalize on their processing strengths. Students with learning disabilities are capable of learning in their academic area(s) of difficulty; however, they may need to learn in a different way depending on their specific processing deficit(s). Ultimately, the success that a student will attain through instruction relies heavily on the information that is gained through the diagnostic and eligibility process.

IDEA Definition of Specific Learning Disability

Specific learning disability means a disorder in one or more of the basic psychological processes involved in understanding or in using language, spoken or written, that may manifest itself in the imperfect ability to listen, think, speak, read, write, spell, or to do mathematical calculations, including conditions such as perceptual disabilities, brain injury, minimal brain dysfunction, dyslexia, and developmental aphasia.

Specific learning disability does not include learning problems that are primarily the result of visual, hearing, or motor disabilities, of intellectual disability, of emotional disturbance, or of environmental, cultural, or economic disadvantage.

(IDEA, 2004, § 300.8(c)(10))

Diagnostic Criteria

According to Section 300.309 of IDEA (2004), a child has a specific learning disability if

- "the child does not achieve adequately for the child's age or to meet State-approved grade-level standards in one or more of the following areas, when provided with learning experiences and instruction appropriate for the child's age or State-approved grade-level standards: Oral expression, listening comprehension, written expression, basic reading skill, reading fluency skills, reading comprehension, mathematics calculation, and mathematics problem solving" (§ 300.309(a)(1));

- "the child does not make sufficient progress to meet age or State-approved grade-level standards . . . when using a process based on the child's response to scientific, research-based intervention" (§ 300.309(a)(2)(i)); or

- "The child exhibits a pattern of strengths and weaknesses in performance, achievement, or both, relative to age, State-approved grade-level standards, or intellectual development, that is determined by the group to be relevant to the identification of a specific learning disability, using appropriate assessments" (§ 300.309(a)(2)(ii)).

Further, one of the most important aspects of the diagnostic process for determining whether a student has a learning disability is to rule out other conditions as primary causes of learning difficulties. This is referred to as an **exclusionary** clause. Section 300.309(a)(3) of IDEA (2004) describes an exclusionary clause that states that specific learning disabilities can't primarily be the result of:

- a visual, hearing, or motor disability;
- an intellectual disability;
- emotional disturbance;
- cultural factors;
- environmental or economic disadvantage; or
- limited English proficiency.

It has to be clearly demonstrated that each of the exclusionary criteria in the previous list can't be considered to be a causal factor of the child's learning disability. For many of the exclusionary criteria, it is possible that a student may have it in conjunction with a learning disability, but not as a causal factor. Consider the following examples of the exclusionary clause:

- *Vision and hearing disability*. If the underlying premise of a learning disability is that a student has processing deficits that hinder the mind from processing information that comes in from the sensory system, sensory deficits could not be at the root of the learning difficulties, because they wouldn't then be related to processing. Instead, it would be a sensory deficit, such as a visual impairment or a hearing impairment, that would be causing the learning difficulties. However, it is possible for a student to have both a sensory impairment and a learning disability. For example, a student who has a visual impairment can also have a learning disability, but only if it is based on difficulty processing information that comes in through another sensory system (e.g., hearing).

- *Emotional disturbance*. An individual with an anxiety disorder (or other disorder classified under emotional disturbance) might have difficulties achieving academically, but for very different reasons than a student with a learning disability. The person could have an anxiety disorder as well as a learning disability, but it would have to be shown that it is not the student's emotional disturbance that is causing the difficulties.

- *Limited English proficiency*. Limited English proficiency can't be the cause of a learning disability, because it has to be demonstrated that there are difficulties processing the language, rather than difficulties understanding the language due to a language difference. It stands to reason that an individual whose primary language is not English would have difficulty learning to read or write in English. A language difference is not a disability; it is just that, a difference. For an individual with a primary language other than English to be diagnosed with a learning disability, the student has to be evaluated in such a way as to eliminate any difficulties that are associated with the language difference. The student would need to be evaluated for intelligence, achievement, and processing in the language that is the most appropriate based on his or her language capabilities.

In addition to the limitations for diagnosis that are described in the exclusionary clause, it must also be demonstrated that learning difficulties are not resulting from a lack of appropriate instruction in reading or math. It is necessary to show evidence that the child has received appropriate instruction that has been "delivered by qualified personnel" (IDEA, 2004, § 300.309(b)(1)). Additionally, the team must also consider "Data-based documentation of repeated assessments of achievement at reasonable intervals, reflecting formal assessment of student progress during instruction, which was provided to the child's parents" (IDEA, 2004, § 300.309(b)(2)).

Now that you have a better understanding of what does *not* cause a learning disability, let us shift to discussion of the three main components of student performance that are typically associated with learning disabilities: intelligence, academic achievement, and psychological processing. Student performance in each of these areas, and the relationship between the performance in each of these areas, is often at the core of the diagnostic evaluation. Gathering information about intelligence, academic achievement, and psychological processing is paramount to determining whether there is a learning disability.

Intelligence

In Chapter 4, intelligence was described as an individual's level of mental capacity or potential for learning that is unique to that individual and the way in which his or her mind works. Students with learning disabilities have traditionally demonstrated a level of intelligence that is at least in the average range or anywhere above the average range. Students may have gifted levels of intelligence and still be diagnosed with a learning disability. However, in some circumstances, a student's level of intelligence doesn't play a role in the diagnosis of a learning disability. As was mentioned previously, learning disabilities are diagnosed differently in different states, and some states don't use intelligence tests to diagnose learning disabilities.

Additionally, the importance of accurately measuring intelligence was discussed in Chapter 4. Because of the characteristics associated with a learning disability, accuracy in determining intelligence becomes exceedingly more difficult depending on the instrument that is used to measure intelligence. A student's processing deficits can hinder performance on the intelligence test and, thus, make his or her intelligence appear lower than it actually is. As a result of this, different types of intelligence tests may be used to produce a more accurate reflection of the student's mental capacity or potential for learning. Refer back to the discussion in Chapter 4 of the different types of intelligence tests that can be administered to help ensure that an accurate representation of intellectual functioning is attained. Additionally, as was previously mentioned, different methods of diagnosis (e.g., patterns of strengths and weaknesses) can be employed to diagnose learning disabilities and account for possible limitations associated with obtaining a true indication of intelligence.

Academic Achievement

Students with learning disabilities demonstrate deficits in one or more areas of academic achievement, due to the way that their minds process information that comes in through the sensory system. Academic achievement was described in Chapter 5 as what has been learned in a particular subject or area that can change over time depending on how a student is progressing.

In the previous chapter, we highlighted five areas of academic achievement (oral language, reading, written language, mathematics, and nonverbal ability), along with subareas that are associated with each area of achievement (e.g., early literacy skills, decoding, fluency, and comprehension in the area of reading). Refer to Chapter 5 for examples of specific assessments that are used to measure performance in each of the five areas of achievement, as well as the related subareas.

Please note that while we focus on five basic areas of academic achievement in this text, IDEA lists eight more specific areas that would fall under the five umbrella areas of academic achievement in the following way:

- Oral language:
  - Oral expression
  - Listening comprehension
- Reading:
  - Basic reading skill
  - Reading fluency skills
  - Reading comprehension
- Written language:
  - Written expression
- Mathematics:
  - Mathematics calculation
  - Mathematics problem solving

- Nonverbal ability:

    Nonverbal ability is not expressly included as one of the IDEA areas; however, many in the field of learning disabilities consider it as a basic academic area of achievement in which one may have a learning disability.

For a student with a learning disability, a diagnostic process that is well-planned and extensive enough to give insight into which of the five basic areas of achievement (along with the subareas of achievement) are impacted can ultimately benefit the student greatly, by acting as a source of information used to inform instruction. To illustrate, many students have learning disabilities in the area of reading; however, a student with a learning disability that primarily impacts decoding will benefit from a different instructional plan than a student whose learning disability primarily impacts reading comprehension. Since academic achievement is learned and can change over time, students can often become very successful in their former areas of academic weakness, through targeted instruction that aims to teach them in a different way. However, if the diagnostic process is not precise enough to pinpoint the difficulties, instruction may not be as beneficial for the student. Further, depending on the type(s) of processing deficits that are present, different patterns of performance across each area of academic achievement will likely emerge and, thus, require different methods of instruction. The following are some examples of teaching the same concept in different ways to achieve similar results, depending on the types of processing strengths and needs that a student may have:

- In the area of reading, some students learn using a phonics-based approach, which focuses on sounding out words using phonological awareness skills in conjunction with written letters and words. A focus is placed on developing good letter-sound correspondence and using that knowledge to decode, or sound out, unfamiliar words. Another approach that is often used to teach reading is a more holistic approach which focuses on learning words as a whole entity instead of breaking them down and sounding them out. Depending on a student's processing strengths and deficits, one method may be more effective than another.

- In the area of math, there are many different ways to learn multiplication facts. Some rely heavily on using a multiplication table; some focus on memorization through repetition or use of flash cards; some employ "finger tricks"; some use a variety of written algorithms; some use arrays; and so on. Similar to the example for reading, all can be effective and lead to the same outcome (knowing multiplication facts), but different students may find one method more effective, depending on their processing strengths and weaknesses.

Concluding Thoughts on Academic Achievement

Deficits in academic areas of achievement are typically the first signs that may prompt a referral for an evaluation to determine whether there is a learning disability. For example, it is typically much easier to see that a student is having difficulties learning to read than it is to see that he or she has difficulties processing information. Additionally, academic achievement typically directly relates to school performance. Many of the areas of academic achievement, such as English Language Arts (which includes oral language, reading, and written language) and mathematics, are included as the subject areas in the early years. Further, state criterion-referenced tests (see Chapter 3 for discussion) are often direct measures of reading, math, and written language.

Check Your Understanding 6.1

1. Why is it beneficial to examine performance in the subareas (e.g., handwriting, spelling, grammar) associated with each area of academic achievement rather than just the overall area of academic achievement (e.g., written language)?

2. Why would a deep analysis of performance on academic achievement assessments help inform instruction?

Psychological Processing

Psychological processing refers to the way that the mind makes sense of and works with information that has entered the sensory system through the five senses: hearing, vision, touch, taste, and smell.

Components of Psychological Processing

Before we discuss specific types of processing, such as visual or auditory perception, let us examine the role of (1) attention, (2) memory, and (3) speed of processing as components of psychological processing. Individuals with learning disabilities typically have difficulties in one or more of these components in addition to one or more types of processing.

Attention. Once information has entered through the sensory system, the brain has to give **attention** to it before it can be processed. For an individual with learning disabilities, it is important to note whether there are attentional deficits that hinder the individual from being able to process information. Attention can be discussed in a number of different ways. The following three types of attention are often considered important to evaluate.

- *Coming to attention*. When an individual becomes alert to or aware of stimuli, it is often referred to as **coming to attention**. The mind cannot process information from the sensory system until one has become alert to the stimuli.

- *Sustained attention*. **Sustained attention** refers to the ability to maintain attention on stimuli for a period of time.

- *Selective attention*. **Selective attention** is the ability of the mind to choose between competing stimuli and focus on one stimulus.

If a student being evaluated for a learning disability has attentional difficulties, you should be careful to ascertain that the underlying reason for his or her learning difficulties is truly the way that the student processes information as opposed to a diminished ability to attend to stimuli. While difficulties with attention are typical in students with learning disabilities, if attentional deficits are not accompanied by one or more processing deficits, the underlying cause of learning difficulties may not be a learning disability.

Memory. When it comes to processing information within the brain, **memory** often serves as a foundation. The way that an individual can use his or her memory will ultimately impact how information is processed within his or her brain. Memory refers to the mind's ability to recall something that has already occurred or been experienced. It is necessary to develop an understanding of a student's memory capacity when evaluating him or her for a learning disability. Memory can be classified into two categories: immediate memory and long-term memory (see Figure 6.1).

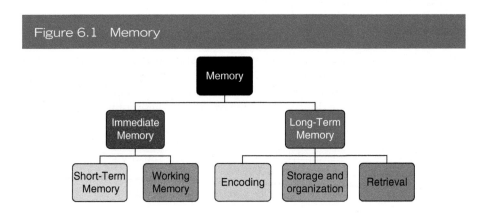

Figure 6.1   Memory

- **Immediate memory** refers to the ability to remember information in the here and now. For example, if someone were to hear a phone number and recite it back within seconds of hearing it, he or she would be accessing immediate memory. Immediate memory can be subdivided into short-term memory and working memory (Raymond, 2012).

  ○ **Short-term memory** is temporary storage of information that is passive. The earlier example of being given a phone number and being asked to repeat it right after hearing it would be an example of short-term memory. The individual does not have to manipulate the information or do anything with it; he or she just has to remember it. Short-term memory is instrumental in all aspects of learning. If short-term memory is weak, it may be difficult to get to a place where individuals can use other components of their memory system. The short-term memory is heavily engaged for all areas of achievement. For example, in the area of reading, short-term memory is instrumental for literal comprehension, which requires an explicit understanding of the information that can be found directly in the text. If a student with short-term memory deficits were to read the following sentence: "John and Emily went to the store to buy apples, grapes, strawberries, and lemons," and be asked "Who went to the store?" or "What did John and Emily buy?" the student may have extreme difficulty remembering the names or the list of fruits.

  ○ **Working memory** is temporary storage that requires active manipulation of sensory information, typically in combination with information received from long-term memory. For example, if an individual were to hear a list of five objects and asked to repeat them back in alphabetical order, the student would have to both remember the objects and mentally manipulate them to put them in alphabetical order. Working memory can impact performance in all areas of achievement. For example, in the area of math, a student would need to access working memory to work through different steps of a problem. In the area of reading, the student would need to remember what has just been read, relate it to background knowledge, and then be able to relate it to new information that follows in the text. These types of connections require working memory.

- **Long-term memory** refers to anything beyond the here and now. As in the earlier example of hearing a phone number and being able to recall it, if a person can recall it five minutes later, or three days later, or one year later, that would all be considered part of the long-term memory. Anything that is beyond the immediate here and now becomes part of the long-term memory. If you still remember what the exclusionary clause is that you learned about earlier in the chapter, you are now accessing it from your long-term memory. Long-term memory is complex and includes three components: encoding, storage/organization, and retrieval (Raymond, 2012). If a person has a hard time remembering the name of the street that he or she lived on as a child, or the food that he or she had for breakfast, it isn't as simple as thinking about long-term memory as a whole. These different components, in combination with one another, allow for long-term memories to be recalled.

- ○ **Encoding** refers to how information gets into long-term memory. How does the brain input information in order to create a new memory that will be stored in long-term memory? Is there other information that accompanies an event that gets encoded with it? For example, is there a particular smell associated with an event that gets encoded with the memory? In another example, if a person is studying for a test and associates a new piece of information with where it appears on the page or what color was used to color-code it, that information becomes part of the encoding process and, thus, part of the memory. If we compare our mind to a computer, the encoding process would resemble the input of data into a computer.

- ○ **Storage and organization** refers to the way in which the information is stored or organized in the memory. In continuing with the comparison to a computer, a person can enter information into the computer (encode it), but it then needs to be put somewhere. Is it put in a particular file, within a particular folder? How are those folders organized? Storage associated with long-term memory works in a similar way. Where is the information stored, and how is it organized within the memory system?

- ○ **Retrieval** refers to the ability to get the memories back. Does the brain recognize where the memories were stored or how they were organized? Can individuals get them back when they need to? In the computer analogy, once the information has been input into the computer (encoded) and stored in a folder (stored), there needs to be a way of getting it back at the time that it is needed (retrieving it).

Difficulties with any of the three components associated with long-term memory would hinder overall long-term memory. For example, deficits in encoding would make it hard to then store the information and recall it correctly. If a student could encode, but had difficulty storing or organizing the information, it would make it hard to recall the information. Similarly, a student may have no difficulty encoding or storing the information but have trouble retrieving what has been encoded and stored.

Both immediate memory (short-term memory and working memory) and long-term memory are very important to the learning process, and difficulties in any aspect of memory can contribute to deficits across all five areas of academic achievement for students with learning disabilities. Information about each type of memory can give great insight into student strengths and needs associated with learning disabilities.

Speed of processing. Before we delve into the many different ways that that the mind processes information, it is important to discuss **speed of processing** and the impact that it may have on learning. Speed of processing is the speed at which the mind can process information that comes into the system. In combination with deficits in processing information that comes into the sensory system, many individuals with learning disabilities have deficits in the speed at which they process that information. If a student's brain is not able to process information quickly, he or she may have difficulties across many different areas of achievement. For example, in the area of oral language, if a student has a slower speed of processing, it may be difficult for that student to listen to a teacher talking and process the information at the same speed as the other students. The student may still be processing a question that a teacher has asked when other students have already processed the question and determined an answer. If a student is listening to a lecture, he or she may miss parts of the lecture because he or she can't process the information quickly enough. In the area of reading, a slower speed of processing can hinder a student's level of fluency and thus impact comprehension. If a student is trying to complete a math problem, slower speed of processing can impact the number of problems that can be completed and, thus, impact the level of experience associated with each problem type. Regardless of how well an individual can process information, processing speed may be a barrier to success.

Types of Psychological Processing

Attention, memory, and speed of processing are all required components of an effective processing system. However, what happens when the brain tries to process information that comes in through the sensory system? What does psychological processing truly mean? To help shed light on the concept of psychological processing, following are some of the many ways that the brain processes information.

Visual perception refers to the complex processing of information that comes in through the visual sensory system and the way that the mind perceives that information. Stimuli are named and given meaning, then associated with representations in long-term memory. The following are different aspects of visual perception (Raymond, 2012) in which a student with learning disabilities may have deficits (see Figure 6.2):

- **Visual discrimination** is the ability to determine whether two visual stimuli are the same or different. That could be verbal stimuli, such as written letters or words, or it could be nonverbal stimuli, such as

Figure 6.2 Types of Visual Perception

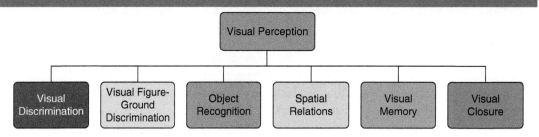

facial expressions or gestures. Think of what is required in the reading process. In order to be a successful reader, it is necessary to be able to discriminate between letters and words. Can a student discriminate between the lowercase letters p, b, d, and q? All four of those letters have the same visual characteristics (a line and a circle). The only difference is the position of the circle in relation to the line. Could he or she discriminate between two words, such as "bat" and "pat"? "dip" and "did"? "best" and "pest"? "dad" and "dab"? "bib" and "bid"? Similarly, think about the letters a and o. The only difference between the two is the presence or absence of a line to the right of the circle. If the student can't perceive the difference, could he or she discriminate between the words last and lost? stack and stock? Similar to the previous examples, many other English letters, forms of punctuation, and math symbols and shapes are very similar to one another. Consider the following:

- Similarities between the following pairs of letters: T and I, M and N, Y and V, U and V, Q and O, R and K, E and F, l and i.

- Similarities between the following pairs of punctuation symbols: colon (:) and semicolon (;), colon (:) and period (.), semicolon (;) and comma (,), beginning quotes (") and ending quotes ("), ending quotes (") and apostrophe (').

- Similarities between the following pairs of math symbols and shapes: division (÷) and addition (+), approximately (≈) and equals (=), less than (<) and greater than (>), circle (O) and oval (0), rectangle (▮) and square (■).

Think about the following additional examples of activities that require visual discrimination:

- *Perception of color.* When children are very young, they typically learn their colors. They see a color and are told that it is a particular color. Is there any guarantee that every individual sees the exact same thing? If someone can't perceive a difference between the colors green and red, he or she will be confused about those two colors and not understand why two seemingly similar colors are called two different things.

○ *Orientation.* Most objects can be held in any orientation and still be considered the same object. For example, a pen can be held vertically, horizontally, or diagonally and still be considered a pen. However, when it comes to many of the arbitrary symbols that make up the English language, the orientation of the symbols becomes a factor. For example, if a W is rotated 180 degrees, it resembles an M. Similarly, in the area of math, the only difference between the numbers 6 and 9 is the orientation (if one is rotated 180 degrees, it becomes the other). Also in the area of math, if the symbol for addition (+) is rotated 45 degrees, it resembles a multiplication symbol (x). If a square (■) is rotated 45 degrees, it resembles a diamond (◊). For an individual who has difficulty perceiving orientation, the ability to discriminate between these symbols/letters will be hindered.

○ *Directionality.* Perceiving differences in directionality, such as right-left orientation, is important throughout life. Consider the many different activities that might be impacted by deficits with right-left orientation. Within the English language, text is read and written from left to right. If a person does not know the difference between left and right, it may be difficult to follow text or create meaningful text. In the area of math, many computation problems require a set of steps to solve the problem that involve starting from the right or left and moving in a particular direction as the problem solving progresses. Right-left orientation can also make a difference for more functional activities, such as determining which shoe goes on which foot, how to set a table, which hand to use when shaking hands with another person, which side of the road to drive on, and which hand to use when writing or throwing a ball.

○ *Perception of nonverbal stimuli.* The ability to discriminate between nonverbal stimuli is also an important ability for students to possess. For example, could a person look at two faces and tell whether they are the same or different? Could a student look at two different facial expressions (e.g., happy and angry) and tell whether they are the same or different? Could a person look at two houses and tell whether they are the same or different?

• **Visual figure-ground discrimination** involves the ability to differentiate an object in the foreground from its background. If there are words on a piece of paper, can a person distinguish the words from the background of the paper? If there are flowers in the grass, could someone pull out the flowers from the grass background? If a person were standing up against a wall, could an individual distinguish the person from the wall?

The color and/or brightness contrast between the object and the background can make a big difference in perception associated with visual figure-ground discrimination. For example, it might be more difficult to see a black word on a gray page than a black word on a white page. It might be more difficult to distinguish a green flower in a field of grass than a red or yellow flower. It might be more difficult to distinguish a person wearing the same color as the wall in the background than a person who is wearing a contrasting color.

- **Object recognition** is the ability to look at an object and determine what it is. For example, when shown a car, can an individual recognize that it is a car just by what it looks like? Can he or she visually perceive what it is?

- **Spatial relations** involve the relationship between visual stimuli in space. What is the distance between two objects? Can a person perceive how far an object is from him or herself? Can a person perceive three-dimensional relationships? The following activities are examples of situations that typically require an understanding of spatial relations:

  ○ Many aspects of driving require spatial relations; some examples are changing lanes, keeping a safe distance behind another vehicle, merging onto a highway, driving into a parking space, parallel parking, and being able to make a left-hand turn when there is oncoming traffic.

  ○ Catching a ball requires an understanding of where the ball is in relation to oneself, and throwing a ball to another person requires an understanding of the spatial relationship between oneself and the receiver.

  ○ Individuals who have difficulties with spatial relationships may have difficulty perceiving the distance between themselves and another person. If they stand too close to another person, it may be uncomfortable for the other person and, thus, may cause social difficulties.

  ○ Trying to read a map and determine one's current location on it may be very difficult for those with deficits in perceiving spatial relationships.

- **Visual memory** involves the ability to recognize an object even when it is no longer present. If an individual were to see an object and that object were then removed from view, would he or she retain a memory of that object when it is no longer visible? This could involve either verbal or nonverbal stimuli. For example, if someone were to see a picture of a face, and then that face were no longer there, would that person be able to recognize the face? When driving to a place that they had been before, would individuals be able to recognize that they had been there before?

Would they have a visual memory for the landmarks they had seen? Reading requires a tremendous visual memory for verbal stimuli. For example, instant word recognition requires visual memory. Further, the visual representation of sight words or word parts that can't be sounded out ("the," "of," "from," "-tion," etc.) requires visual memory. This is often referred to as orthographic awareness or orthographic processing.

- **Visual closure** is the ability to see an incomplete object or part of an object and to mentally fill it in to determine the object without seeing the whole object.

The previous examples should show that processing associated with visual perception can mean many different things. Therefore, when you are evaluating a student for learning disabilities, evaluating different aspects of visual perception may give you insight into the student's specific difficulties. What is the nature of the visual perceptual deficits? The Motor-Free Visual Perception Test (MVPT), the Test of Visual Perceptual Skills (TVPS), and the Developmental Test of Visual Perception (DTVP) are examples of norm-referenced tests that measure many of the above aspects of visual perception. Individuals with learning disabilities who have processing deficits associated with visual perception may demonstrate deficits in any or all of the five areas of achievement; it would depend on the specific deficit(s).

Similar to visual perception, **auditory perception** refers to the complex processing of information that comes in through the auditory sensory system and the way that the mind perceives that information. Most people are familiar with the game "telephone" or "Whisper Down the Lane," in which one person gives a message to another and the message is passed from person to person until the final person in line reveals the message. The point is to determine whether the original message is the same as the final message. More often than not, the beginning message and ending message are different in some way. Various different aspects of auditory perception are likely at the root of this phenomenon. In another example, how is it possible for five different people to listen to a lecture and have five different sets of notes based on what they thought they heard? As with visual perception, there are many different subcategories of auditory perception (Raymond, 2012) that may impact an individual with learning disabilities (see Figure 6.3):

Figure 6.3 Types of Auditory Perception

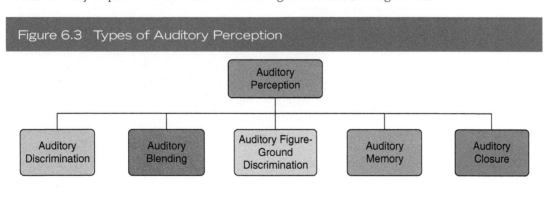

- **Auditory discrimination** is similar to visual discrimination. If two sounds are heard, can an individual determine whether they are the same or different? In Chapter 5, phonological awareness—and, more specifically, phonemes—were discussed. There are some phonemes that are so close in sound to another phoneme that it can be very difficult to discriminate between them. An example that was given in Chapter 5 was the presence or absence of voicing. The only difference between the sounds /t/ and /d/ is vibration of the vocal cords that exists with the sound /d/. If a person can't discriminate between sounds that are voiced as compared with those that are unvoiced, he or she would likely have difficulties discriminating between many words (bat/bad, tip/dip, try/dry, push/bush, pup/pub, pat/bat, fast/vast, fail/veil, great/crate, class/glass, etc.).

- **Auditory blending** involves the ability to hear a series of isolated sounds and put them together as a whole. For example, if a person were to hear /c/ /a/ /t/, could that person put those sounds together to determine that they create the word "cat"? Auditory blending is typically used very heavily when a person is decoding unfamiliar words.

- **Auditory figure-ground discrimination** is the same idea as visual figure-ground discrimination. Is a person able to distinguish between a sound and background sounds? For example, if driving in a very congested area, would a person be able to hear a siren among the sounds of the traffic in general? If someone were in a loud restaurant, would he or she be able to discriminate between the person talking to him or her and the background voices of others in the restaurant?

- **Auditory memory** is similar to visual memory. Can a person hear a sound and remember it when it is no longer present? Similar to visual memory, auditory stimuli can be either verbal or nonverbal. If an individual were to hear a dog barking, would he or she be able to remember what that bark sounds like? After hearing the pronunciation of a word, could a person remember how that word sounds? Can someone remember what it sounds like when a telephone rings?

- **Auditory closure** is, again, very similar to visual closure. If only part of an auditory signal is heard, is it possible to fill in the rest and tell what the sound is? Think about a phone call where there is poor cell reception. Only parts of words may be heard. How does that impact the understanding of what is being said? Can the listener fill in the missing sounds to make sense of the conversation?

Similar to visual perception, auditory perception could impact all areas of academic achievement, depending on the nature of the deficit. The Developmental

Test of Auditory Perception (DTAP) and the Woodcock-Johnson are examples of norm-referenced tests that measure a variety of auditory perception skills. In Chapter 5, the concept of phonological awareness was heavily discussed as it relates to oral language, reading, and written language. An individual with phonological processing deficits has underlying deficits in auditory perception that hinder the understanding of sounds specific to language.

Visual/auditory integration involves the ability to integrate or combine information that is perceived through the visual system with information that is perceived through the auditory system. An individual may have no difficulties with visual perception or auditory perception in isolation; however, when the two must be integrated, it becomes problematic. Reading and spelling are both examples of skills that require visual/auditory integration. In reading, it is necessary to perceive the visual stimuli and relate them to auditory signals. In spelling, it is necessary to think about the auditory sounds in the word to develop a visual representation, which is the letters.

Haptic perception relates to the sense of touch. Can an individual place meaning on tactile and kinesthetic stimuli (Raymond, 2012)? Tactile information relates to the sense of touch, and kinesthetics involves the sense of touch associated with movement. This also relates to the integration between other senses and the sense of touch, such as visual/motor integration. Can a person relate information that comes in through the visual system with information involved with touch or kinesthetic movement? This would be involved in activities such as catching a ball, drawing, and typing. The Beery-Buktenica Developmental Test of Visual-Motor Integration (Beery VMI) is an example of a norm-referenced test that measures visual/motor integration. Even more complex are activities such as writing words or reacting to a moving car that is honking that require visual/auditory/motor integration.

Most people have experienced that "tip of the tongue" phenomenon when they can't remember a word that they want to say. It can be the most basic word that they are very familiar with, but they just can't recall it. It might be the name of a friend or the name of a particular object. It can be any word, but somehow the word eludes them at the time that they need it. A student with a word finding deficit frequently has those types of experiences. It isn't that the student has a limited vocabulary; rather, it is that the student has difficulty accessing the words from his or her lexicon when they are needed. Word-finding deficits could impact each area of achievement in different ways. In the area of oral language, if a person is trying to have a conversation with another person and relaying a situation that has happened, a word-finding deficit may make it difficult to be specific in the relaying of the story. For example, think about how difficult it might be to tell another person that you had cereal for breakfast if you couldn't come up with the word "breakfast" or "cereal." Think about what you might say to try to convey your ideas. In the area of reading, if a person has word-finding deficits, it may be difficult to have automatic word recognition because the individual might not be able to readily come up with each word that is in the passage. Similar to oral language, if someone were trying to write a story, it would be very difficult to do so if he or she couldn't remember the specific words needed to tell the story. Assessments that measure rapid automatic naming (RAN) can give good insight into whether a student has word-finding deficits. An example of an activity that could be included in a RAN assessment would require the student to name as many things within a category (e.g., types of fruit, animals, names of towns, states, foods, names of books) as possible (typically within 1 minute).

Concluding Thoughts on Psychological Processing

Processing deficits can have so many impacts on an individual's ability to learn that the diagnostic process associated with a learning disability is very complex. A single processing deficit (e.g., a visual perception deficit) can cause serious deficits in any of the five areas of achievement. What happens when one processing deficit is coupled with another or even several others? How can that change the way that the student achieves, academically? Further, what if there are added difficulties with attention, memory, or speed of processing? The possible combinations of difficulties is considerable, so it is important to be as thorough as possible with the psychoeducational evaluation. There are a multitude of norm-referenced tests (See Chapter 3 for a discussion of norm-referenced tests) that can give insight into a student's level of processing skills. There are some that specifically measure the different areas of processing, and there are others in which the measuring of processing skills is embedded within other measures. If intelligence or academic achievement were tested in isolation, the true underlying deficits associated with a student's learning disability might not be realized. That is, the reason why the student is having difficulties with academic achievement might not be evident. Therefore, a comprehensive evaluation of a child's level of processing is instrumental in evaluating learning disabilities.

Check Your Understanding 6.2

1. What does psychological processing mean?

2. Describe the differences between short-term memory and working memory. Give one activity that would require short-term memory and one activity that would require long-term memory.

3. Define coming to attention, sustained attention, and selective attention.

4. Differentiate between visual closure and visual memory.

5. Name one task that would use visual/motor integration.

6. What is a word-finding deficit?

Concluding Thoughts on Diagnostic Criteria

The diagnostic criteria related to the exclusionary clause, intelligence, academic achievement, and processing are highly important to the assessment of learning disabilities. The reason that learning disabilities are so complex is that the outcome can be very different for every individual, depending on his or her combination of deficits in relation to strengths. A good diagnostic evaluation for learning disabilities will highlight processing strengths and weaknesses and give insight into why the student has difficulties with basic areas of academic achievement. Students with learning disabilities can try to overcome processing deficits, use processing strengths to bypass the need for processing deficits, and find strategies for more effective processing. However, if the diagnostic process is not extensive enough to really examine specific patterns of performance, a plan for instruction may not be as effective as it could be. Ultimately, the goal for a student with a learning disability is to reach his or her learning potential despite processing deficits that may present a barrier to success. Developing a true picture of a student through a comprehensive diagnostic evaluation serves not only as a means of diagnosis, but also as a means of eliminating those barriers to success.

Check Your Understanding 6.3

1. Why would a processing deficit impact academic achievement? Give an example.

2. Describe why it is important to make sure that intelligence has been accurately measured.

3. Why might speed of processing hinder academic achievement?

4. Why are the characteristics associated with learning disabilities so different from person to person?

How the Diagnosis Is Made

While the diagnostic criteria for learning disabilities usually involve intelligence, academic achievement, and psychological processing, the way in which a diagnosis is made in relation to those criteria may differ from state to state. Section 300.307 of IDEA (2004) indicates that it is the responsibility of each state to develop specific diagnostic criteria for determining whether an individual has a specific learning disability. In developing those criteria, states may not choose to solely use the discrepancy model, which is the most traditional means of diagnosing a learning disability. States must also include other possible criteria for diagnosing learning disabilities that allow for an examination of other factors, such as a student's response to interventions that are scientifically and research-based as well as other research-based procedures. As was previously discussed, the fact that a learning disability diagnosis can differ from state to state makes for some confusion surrounding learning disabilities within the general population. It is possible that a student may be diagnosed with a learning disability in one state, but not in another state, depending on the specific criteria developed by each state.

Components of a Comprehensive Psychoeducational Evaluation for Learning Disabilities

Section 300.311 of IDEA (2004) states several components that must be included in a comprehensive evaluation for a learning disability (italicized in the list below). In order to determine whether a student has a learning disability, a complete psychoeducational evaluation typically includes the following information:

- Intelligence (based on a norm-referenced assessment)
- Academic achievement

    Norm-referenced assessment of academic achievement in each of the five basic areas of academic achievement (including subareas as appropriate)

    Current classroom-based assessments (current grades, progress-monitoring data, error-analysis information, data related to performance assessments and portfolio assessments, etc.)

    Performance on state criterion-referenced assessments

    Performance on any local assessments administered by the school or district

    Performance in academic achievement that indicates whether the child:

    ○ *"does not achieve adequately for the child's age or to meet State-approved grade-level standards"*

    ○ *"does not make sufficient progress to meet age or State-approved grade-level standards"*

    ○ *"exhibits a pattern of strengths and weaknesses in performance, achievement, or both, relative to age, State-approved grade level standards or intellectual development"*

- Psychological processing

    Norm-referenced assessment associated with processing and related mental activity

Any classroom-based information related to processing

- *Medical findings/history that are relevant to the student's education*

- Family history relevant to education and/or learning disabilities

- Interviews of parents, teachers, and the student (as appropriate) including information about academics, behavior, and social/emotional status

- *Behavior as observed in direct observations as well as the relationship of that behavior to the student's academic functioning*

- *Exclusionary factors including the impact(s) of sensory deficits (i.e., visual and hearing), a motor disability, an intellectual disability, an emotional disturbance, cultural factors, environmental or economic disadvantage, or limited English proficiency on the child's academic achievement level*

- *Whether the child has participated in Response to Intervention that includes the employment of instructional strategies and the collection of student-centered data, as well as the documentation ensuring that parents were notified about the state policies "regarding the amount and nature of student performance data that would be collected and the general education services that would be provided; strategies for increasing the child's rate of learning; and the parents' right to request an evaluation" (IDEA, 2004, § 300.311)*

Methods of Diagnosing Learning Disabilities

The diagnostic process associated with learning disabilities is complex, and the goal is to ensure that the diagnostic process yields an accurate result. The following three methods have emerged as the most typical ways to diagnose a learning disability (see Figure 6.4):

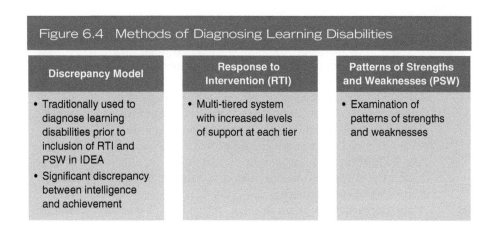

Figure 6.4   Methods of Diagnosing Learning Disabilities

Discrepancy Model	Response to Intervention (RTI)	Patterns of Strengths and Weaknesses (PSW)
• Traditionally used to diagnose learning disabilities prior to inclusion of RTI and PSW in IDEA • Significant discrepancy between intelligence and achievement	• Multi-tiered system with increased levels of support at each tier	• Examination of patterns of strengths and weaknesses

The Discrepancy Model

The discrepancy model was the traditionally accepted way of diagnosing learning disabilities before the 2004 changes to IDEA allowed for diagnosis through Response to Intervention (RTI). In this model, an individual with a learning disability demonstrates a significant discrepancy between intelligence and one or more areas of academic achievement that is caused by one or more deficits in psychological processing. The determination of whether there is a significant discrepancy is based on the student's performance on norm-referenced tests used to measure intelligence and achievement. A significant discrepancy is thought to be a difference that is so large that it seems to go beyond what is typical of performance associated with individual strengths and weaknesses that are frequently seen within any given individual. For example, it may be expected that a student could show a slight difference between intelligence and achievement in any given area of achievement (e.g., at the high end of the average range as compared with the middle of the average range). However, if a student has a level of intelligence that is in the average range, but the student is achieving well below average in the area of reading, it is cause to wonder why the student isn't reaching his or her potential for learning as indicated by his or her intelligence. If all the considerations included in the exclusionary clause have been evaluated and found not to be causes, if the student has received an appropriate education from qualified personnel, and if the student demonstrates processing deficits, it is possible that the student does, in fact, have a learning disability in the area of reading that is causing such a large difference between intellectual functioning and achievement.

Many professionals in the field continue to use the discrepancy model and find it effective, and it continues to be a widely accepted way to diagnose learning disabilities; however, many also feel that it isn't effective enough to diagnose all students who have learning disabilities. The following are some examples of concerns surrounding the use of the discrepancy model as the sole means of diagnosing learning disabilities:

- *Different definitions of significance.* The actual difference that is required to be considered significant enough to be diagnosed with a learning disability differs by state. Many states are not specific about what defines a significant discrepancy (Maki, Burns, & Sullivan, 2018). Some states define significant as 1.5 standard deviations (approximately 23 points); others consider 2 standard deviations (30 points) to be significant. As an example, if a student has a level of intelligence that is at a standard score of 100 (which is higher than 50% of the population and directly in the middle of the average range), the student would need to demonstrate achievement that is at or below a standard score of 77 (which is higher than 6% of the population and well below average) to have a 1.5-standard-deviation discrepancy. Similarly, that same student with a 100 IQ would need to demonstrate achievement at or below a standard score of 70 (which is higher than 2% of the population and well below average) to demonstrate a 2-standard-deviation discrepancy. Some were concerned that this type of difference among states did not make for a clear-cut diagnosis. Those students who live in a state where 2 standard deviations are required may not qualify for a diagnosis of a learning disability and special education services, while the same student in another state would qualify. In another example, if a student were to move from one state to another, the evaluation would follow with the student; however, once the student is re-evaluated in the new state, it could change that student's diagnosis.

- *The wait-to-fail method.* It is well known that the earlier in life that interventions can begin, the better the outcome for students with disabilities. Some consider the discrepancy model to be a "wait to fail" model, meaning that if a student does not have a large enough discrepancy to be considered significant, the student will not be diagnosed with a learning disability or receive services until the student can show a larger discrepancy. This would hinder the student who ultimately is diagnosed with a learning disability from receiving special education services until achievement is low enough to be considered significantly discrepant.

- *Difficulties with demonstrating true intelligence.* As was previously discussed, processing deficits may hinder individuals from demonstrating their true intelligence, depending on the type of processing deficit(s) in combination with the type of intelligence test that is used. Students in this situation may not have been diagnosed with a learning disability, because their academic achievement was not shown to be significantly different from their intelligence.

Response to Intervention (RTI)

RTI was discussed in Chapter 2 as a multi-tiered system used to aid in identifying students with learning and behavioral needs. Recall that RTI is a three-tiered system, with increased levels of support at each tier, that allows for students to receive targeted instruction using research-based or scientifically based strategies. Some schools have implemented a formal RTI system, while others informally implement RTI. It has been proven effective in providing an alternate means of diagnosing learning disabilities in children who might not have been diagnosed using the discrepancy model. RTI often allows for students to receive interventions quickly, once difficulties are recognized, rather than wait to receive targeted instruction until there has been a diagnosis. While there are many positive attributes of RTI, as with the discrepancy model, there are possible drawbacks of using RTI as the sole method of diagnosing learning disabilities. The following are some examples of difficulties that may exist:

- *Strategy selection.* When a student undergoes a comprehensive diagnostic evaluation, a great deal of information is gathered to help the team make an informed decision about the direction of instruction. Without comprehensive information about the student to help support the selection of strategies, the team may not have a clear direction for strategy selection. As was previously mentioned, there are many different strategies that can be used to help a student with learning disabilities to achieve despite processing deficits. It may be difficult to determine the best choice if processing deficits are unknown. The team may spend a long time trying different strategies and subsequently make limited progress.

- *Implementation of strategies.* Special educators are trained to work with students with disabilities. Students may receive strategy instruction from teachers who are highly qualified to teach within their area of certification, but who may not be trained to work with students with special needs.

- *Completion of a psychoeducational evaluation.* Even when RTI has been implemented, a student with a possible learning disability will typically still need to undergo additional testing that is included in a comprehensive psychoeducational evaluation. While evidence from the RTI process can be used as a means of diagnosis, it typically would not replace a full battery of tests.

- *Formal vs. informal implementation of RTI.* Schools that have adopted a formal means of implementing RTI may have a much more guided approach to implementing RTI, whereas those who informally use it may not implement it in the same way or in a consistent manner from teacher to teacher. This may impact its effectiveness as a means of diagnosing learning disabilities.

Patterns of Strengths and Weaknesses (PSW)

The concept behind the process of diagnosing learning disabilities according to patterns of strengths and weaknesses (PSW) involves the examination of the patterns of strengths and weaknesses within cognitive processing in conjunction with patterns associated with academic achievement (Hale et al., 2010; McGill, Styck, Palomares, & Hass, 2016; Miciak et al., 2014; Phipps & Beaujean, 2016). According to Miciak et al. (2014) and McGill et al. (2016), three predominant theories of PSW have been proposed:

- The concordance/discordance model

- The Cattell-Horn-Carroll operational model (see Chapter 4 for a discussion surrounding this model)

- The discrepancy/consistency model

McGill et al. (2016) reported that while there are differences between these models, all three models indicate that "evidence of cognitive weaknesses must be present, an academic weakness must also be established, and there must be evidence of spared cognitive–achievement abilities" (McGill et al., 2016, p. 160). Further, Phipps and Beaujean (2016) indicated that all three methods "collect data from multiple sources across multiple time points using a variety of assessment tools and strategies; analyze the data to look for patterns, rely on predictive and treatment validity literature; and use logical and empirical evidence to guide decision making" (Phipps & Beaujean, 2016, p. 20).

Miciak et al. (2014) indicated that the three models differ with respect to the following: "how achievement deficits and cognitive weaknesses are theoretically linked; the role of exclusionary factors that may preclude LD [learning disability] identification (e.g., emotional, economic factors); specified thresholds for achievement deficits; and methods for establishing a cognitive discrepancy" (p. 2).

Similar to the discrepancy and RTI models for diagnosing learning disabilities, there are many merits associated with the PSW model. For example, in examining the best means of diagnosing learning disabilities, Hale et al. (2010) provided support for the PSW model through the results of a study that surveyed experts in the field of learning disabilities about the diagnostic procedures associated with learning disabilities. The following is a summary of the experts' recommendations surrounding the methods used for diagnosing learning disabilities:

1. Maintain the SLD (specific learning disability) definition and strengthen statutory requirements in SLD identification procedures.

2. Neither ability-achievement discrepancy analyses nor failure to respond to intervention (RTI) alone is sufficient for SLD identification.

3. To meet SLD statutory and regulatory requirements, a "third method" approach that identifies a pattern of psychological processing strengths and weaknesses, and achievement deficits consistent with this pattern of processing weaknesses, makes the most empirical and clinical sense.

4. An empirically validated RTI model could be used to prevent learning problems in children, but comprehensive evaluations should occur for SLD identification purposes, and children with SLDs need individualized interventions based on specific learning needs, not merely more intense interventions designed for children in general education.

5. Assessment of cognitive and neuropsychological processes should be used not only for identification, but for intervention purposes as well, and these assessment-intervention relationships need further empirical investigation.

(Hale et al., 2010, pp. 225–226)

While there are many proponents of the PSW model, there are some noted concerns, as well. For example, there is a concern that that there isn't one uniform method that is used to define PSW, that there are inconsistencies in diagnosis between different theories, and that there is a lack of agreement on how to operationalize what constitutes a cognitive weakness (McGill et al., 2016; Miciak et al., 2014; Phipps & Beaujean, 2016).

Concluding Thoughts on Methods of Diagnosing Learning Disabilities

IDEA (2004) requires states to determine other means of diagnosing learning disabilities than solely using the discrepancy model. This ultimately encourages states to consider possible research-based alternatives for diagnosing learning disabilities. All three methods that have been described in this chapter (the discrepancy model, Response to Intervention, and patterns of strengths and weaknesses) are considered by many to be effective in diagnosing learning disabilities. However, all three methods have some noted concerns that may not make them a truly effective means of diagnosing *all* students with learning disabilities. The thought is that by having a variety of possibilities for diagnosis, the team has the best chance of truly detecting the presence or absence of a learning disability.

There isn't an easy answer to the best way to diagnose learning disabilities. Unfortunately, based on the fact that there are multiple methods that could yield different results as well as different diagnostic criteria from state to state, there is bound to be some confusion associated with diagnosing learning disabilities. However, regardless of the specifics of the diagnostic criteria, the goal of all diagnostic evaluations is to find the best means possible of making an accurate diagnosis for each individual. Students with learning disabilities have great potential; however, they typically need to learn in different ways to be able to be as successful as possible. The diagnostic procedure is critical to the ultimate success of these students.

Check Your Understanding 6.4

1. Describe the discrepancy model for diagnosing learning disabilities.

2. For each of the three methods of diagnosing learning disabilities, give one strength and one weakness of the method.

Subtypes Associated With Learning Disabilities

When diagnosing a learning disability, many special educators look at the specific characteristics of the student and focus on particular subtypes of learning disabilities that demonstrate patterns of performance in combination with specific processing deficits (dyslexia, dysgraphia, phonologically based, etc.). There are different theories associated with subtyping learning disabilities and different sets of subtypes depending on the different theories. Others prefer not to refer to subtypes when diagnosing learning disabilities and instead focus on the student as an individual. Both approaches have been shown to have merit within the field of learning disabilities. However, it is important to note whether there is a reference to a subtype, because if a diagnosis specifies a subtype, it is necessary to truly understand the characteristics of that subtype and the associated terminology.

As was previously mentioned, different theorists and others in the field may refer to subtypes in different ways. For example, some use the term *dyslexia* to refer to any learning disability that results in a reading disability. Others use the term very specifically to refer to students who have reading deficits that are associated with phonological processing deficits. It would be important to be clear on what is meant by the term if it is used as part of the diagnosis.

Who Makes the Diagnosis

Section 300.308 of IDEA (2004) indicates the following individuals as members of the team that are included in the diagnosis of a learning disability:

- The child's parent(s)

- The child's regular teacher or general education teacher, or a regular teacher or general education teacher who is qualified to teach children of the same age; if the child is younger than school-age, the team must include an individual who is qualified by the state educational agency (SEA) to teach children of the same age

- An individual who is qualified to conduct the assessments required for diagnosing learning disabilities, such as a school psychologist, speech-language pathologist, or remedial reading teacher

Concluding Thoughts on How the Diagnosis Is Made and Who Makes the Diagnosis

The process associated with the diagnosis of a learning disability is complex and must be completed in such a way that can detect whether a student is truly a student with a learning disability. The importance of a true diagnosis is critical to ensure that students with learning disabilities receive the best education possible to help them to achieve their potential. In Chapter 4, the process of diagnosing students with disabilities was compared to the completion of a jigsaw puzzle. Students with learning disabilities exhibit so many different component characteristics, and the determination of whether there is a learning disability relies heavily on how all those characteristics relate to one another. In order for a student to be diagnosed with a learning disability, all the "pieces of the puzzle" have to be evaluated and pieced together to reveal students who have deficit(s) in processing that hinder their ability to achieve their full potential.

Check Your Understanding 6.5

1. Why are there three different methods of diagnosing learning disabilities?

2. How might different diagnostic criteria among states make the diagnosis of a learning disability more complex?

3. Why is it important to understand the terminology used to define a subtype of learning disabilities (e.g., dyslexia) if subtypes are included in the diagnosis?

Other Characteristics

While the main characteristics associated with learning disabilities relate to intelligence, academic achievement, and psychological processing, there are other characteristics that may need to be considered for students with learning disabilities, including behavior, social and emotional characteristics, and health and medical status.

Behavior

Students with learning disabilities may exhibit behaviors that result from their learning disabilities, such as acting out, withdrawing, or seeking attention from others to validate performance. The psychoeducational evaluation for learning disabilities requires a direct observation to determine whether there are any noted behaviors that impact the student educationally (IDEA, 2004, § 300.310). Even if the cause of behavioral difficulties may be the learning disability (as opposed to another disability that results in behavioral deficits), it still may be important to work toward improving those behaviors that the student is exhibiting.

Social and Emotional Characteristics

Social and emotional characteristics are important to consider for students who have learning disabilities.

Processing deficits may make social interactions more difficult for a student with learning disabilities, depending on the processing deficits that the student has. For example, if a person has difficulties with visual perception associated with nonverbal stimuli, he or she may not be able to recognize facial expressions, gestures, or body language that helps most individuals better understand those with whom they are communicating. Further, deficits in word finding may hinder the ability to have meaningful conversations with others. Additionally, deficits in auditory perception may make communication difficult for students with learning disabilities.

Recall that according to the exclusionary clause, it has to be demonstrated that emotional difficulties are not the cause of a learning disability; however, it is possible for emotional difficulties to be secondary to learning disabilities. For example, a student with learning disabilities may develop an anxiety disorder or symptoms of depression that are associated with experiences related to the learning disability. As another example, many students with learning disabilities understand that they have a high capability level (i.e., intelligence); however, they may not understand why they can't learn in certain ways or why they can't understand academic information in the same way that their peers can. This may cause students to develop emotional difficulties. Similarly, it is important when diagnosing a learning disability to rule out a lack of motivation as a cause of a learning disability. However, some students with learning disabilities lose motivation because they have had difficulties being successful academically.

Health and Medical Status

While there aren't specific medical conditions that are associated with learning disabilities, it is still important to recognize any medical findings that may impact the student's education. If there are any medical conditions that are impacting the student's academic achievement, they may need to be addressed in conjunction with the learning disability.

Case Studies and Extension to Instruction

Three different case studies will be discussed, to highlight the individual nature of a learning disability and differences that exist based on the connection between intelligence, academic achievement, and the nature of the processing deficits. Following is a brief summary of each one, followed by each case study in full.

- **Case Study 6.1:** Joseph is 8 years old and in the third grade. His intelligence is in the above-average range. He has been diagnosed with a learning disability in the areas of reading and written language, with weaknesses in auditory perception (impacting phonological awareness) as well as speed of processing. He has relative strengths in visual perception.

- **Case Study 6.2**: Courtney is 13 years old and in the eighth grade. Her intelligence is within the very superior range, and she is considered to be intellectually gifted. She has been diagnosed with a nonverbal learning disability that impacts aspects of reading, written language, and nonverbal abilities. She demonstrates processing weaknesses in visual processing of nonverbal stimuli and visual/motor integration. She has strengths in visual and auditory processing of verbal stimuli, visual/auditory integration of verbal stimuli, and memory for verbal information.

- **Case Study 6.3**: George is 9 years old and in the fourth grade. His intelligence is in the average range, and he has been diagnosed with a learning disability in the area of mathematics, with weaknesses in visual processing and memory. He has strengths in speed of processing, auditory perception, and haptic perception.

Following the discussion of the educational background and diagnosis associated with each case study, an extension to instruction will be highlighted for each. Instruction for students with learning disabilities may differ widely depending on intelligence, patterns of performance across areas of academic achievement, and psychological processing. Therefore, the goal is to connect instructional methods with specific patterns of difficulty that an individual would possess.

Case Study 6.1: Joseph

Joseph, an 8-year-old boy who is currently in the third grade, has recently been diagnosed with a learning disability in the areas of reading and written language.

Educational and Diagnostic Evaluation

Joseph was originally diagnosed with a speech and language impairment when he was 4 years old. At that time, he began receiving special education services for his language difficulties and articulation deficits. Receptive language was an area of weakness for him, because he often misunderstood words that were said to him. Additionally, his articulation deficits made his language somewhat difficult to understand. As he progressed into the school-age years, his teachers and parents became concerned that he wasn't learning to read as easily as the other children. Other aspects of school came easily to him, but reading and spelling were proving to be very difficult. By the end of his kindergarten year, he was starting to read common sight words such as "the" and "of." He was very good at reading logos on restaurant and store signs, and he could easily recognize his own name. As he moved into first grade, it was starting to become evident that he was having difficulties learning to sound out words; however, benchmark testing indicated that he was performing at grade level. His difficulties continued through first and second grade, until the beginning of his third-grade year, when his benchmark testing and classroom performance in reading and writing had gotten considerably worse, in relation to the other students. He was also starting to voice his concerns about how hard it was to read. He was referred by his general education teacher for an evaluation to determine whether he had a learning disability.

The results of the psychoeducational evaluation indicated that Joseph had a learning disability in the areas of reading and written language. He was found to have an IQ of 116, which is in the above-average range. However, he demonstrated a significant discrepancy between intelligence and achievement in reading (single-word reading, decoding, and reading fluency) and written language (spelling and writing fluency). The following is a description of Joseph's performance in each of the five areas of academic achievement according to norm-referenced tests:

- Oral language: In the area of oral language, Joseph's receptive and expressive oral language were within the upper end of the average range (standard scores of 109 and 106, respectively). He continued to have slight difficulties with his articulation deficits; however, his speech was much easier to understand. Additionally, his receptive language had improved considerably, because he was able to use his strong background knowledge to better understand words in context.

- Reading: Within the area of reading, Joseph's performance was in the average range on measures of word reading

(standard score of 85), reading fluency (standard score of 87), and reading comprehension (standard score of 103). His weakest performance was on measures of nonword reading (standard score of 70), which is in the well-below-average range.

- Written language: In the area of written language, Joseph's performance was in the well-below-average range for measures of spelling (standard score of 69) and the average range for measures of writing fluency (standard score of 89) and written expression (standard score of 107).

- Mathematics: In the area of mathematics, all scores were within the above-average range, with the exception of math fluency (standard score of 93), which was in the average range.

- Nonverbal ability: Joseph's performance on all measures of nonverbal ability was within the above-average range.

Joseph's performance on measures of processing and related mental activities yielded the following findings:

- Joseph demonstrated well-below-average performance on measures of phonological awareness and auditory perception (auditory discrimination, auditory blending, and auditory closure).

- Joseph's performance was in the lower end of the average range across all measures of fluency, which measures a combination of speed and accuracy. His pattern of performance on both the reading and writing fluency measures showed errors in accuracy as well as slower speed. Within the area of math, his performance showed that his accuracy was very high, but his

(Continued)

rate was slower. While neither his teacher nor his parents noted any difficulties with his processing speed during the diagnostic process, the fact that his math fluency was lower than other math scores suggested that processing speed might be a factor.

- Joseph demonstrated above-average performance in measures of attention, memory, and all other areas of processing. Visual perception was found to be a relative strength for him.

As part of the diagnostic process, all exclusionary criteria were ruled out as causal factors for Joseph's difficulties associated with reading and written language. Additionally, it was shown that he had received a good education in the areas of reading and math and that it was delivered by qualified teachers who were certified in elementary education.

Extension to Instruction

Following his diagnosis, the IEP team determined that Joseph would be included in the general education classroom for most of the school day, with the exception of two hours per week, when he would receive one-on-one remediation from a special education teacher in the areas of reading and written language. Additionally, it was determined that he would receive special education services in the areas of reading and written language in the general education classroom for an additional five hours per week. Joseph began receiving services soon after his diagnosis, and the focus of instruction for his learning disability included the following:

- As a result of Joseph's difficulties with auditory processing, a multisensory phonics-based reading program was implemented, with the hopes that it would help him connect his strong visual perceptual skills and kinesthetic movement to the improvement of his auditory perception and phonological awareness skills. The goal was to use his areas of strength to help train his ear to better discriminate between the different phonemes.

- Additionally, emphasis was placed on learning patterns within words, to help Joseph improve his word recognition without relying as heavily on decoding. His visual processing skills were so strong that learning visual patterns was a method that could be very beneficial for him. In order to do this, he learned to apply different types of morphological patterns, along with their meanings, to word reading (-tion, -ed, -ing, -ness, -sion, etc.). Further, he was taught to recognize and use the following six syllable types: Closed, open, vowel team, vowel-consonant-e (often called "magic e" or "silent e"), consonant-le, and r-controlled syllables (Reading Rockets, n.d.) (see Figure 6.5).

- Although Joseph's speed of processing was in the average range, it was a relative weakness in comparison to other skills. An emphasis was placed on improving his fluency skills within reading, writing, and math. For example, in the area of reading, the following strategies were used to help him improve fluency (Jennings, Caldwell, & Lerner, 2010; Polloway, Patton, Serna, & Bailey-Joseph, 2018):

Wide reading of easy text

Use of patterned books with repeated phrases

Figure 6.5   Syllable Types

Closed: In closed syllables, the vowel makes a short vowel sound →The vowel is followed by one or more consonant (VC, CVC, CVCC) -This is the most common syllable type
Examples: it, pat, best

Open: in open syllables, the vowel makes a long vowel sound → Consonant(s) are followed by a single vowel letter (CV)
Examples: go, be, so, she

Vowel Team: The vowel sound associated with a vowel team can be short (e.g, br**ea**d), long (t**ea**m), or a dipthong (e.g, c**oi**n)→A vowel team is when 2 or more vowels are connected (a vowel team may contain consonants as in "ough")
Examples: team, snow, may, though

Vowel-Consonant-e: The vowel makes a long vowel sound→A single vowel letter is followed by a consonant,which is then followed by e (Vce). These syllable types may also be called magic-e or silent-e.
Examples: make, ride, mode, scheme

R-Controlled: R-controlled syllables have a single vowel that is followed by an r. The vowel sound doesn't resemble a short or long vowel sound. Instead, it takes on the properties of the r sound, (V-r)
Examples: short, for, first, park, fern

Consonant-le
 -Can only occur in words with 2 or more syllables
 -The final syllable consists of a consonant followed by an le (C-le)
Examples: a**ble**, cy**cle**, lit**tle**

Repeated readings

Echo reading (Joseph reads a sentence after it has been read to him by a fluent reader)

Unison reading (Joseph reads at the same time as a fluent reader)

Overall, Joseph had many strengths that he could rely on to help build up his weaker areas. Focus was placed on both improving his weak areas and using his areas of strength to learn in a different way that wouldn't rely as heavily on his weak areas.

1. Based on the information in the case study, which of the three methods (could be more than one) was likely used to diagnose Joseph?

2. What are some activities that would help improve Joseph's speed of processing in the areas of written language or mathematics?

3. Why would a multisensory, phonics-based approach to reading be beneficial for Joseph?

4. Why didn't the teachers or parents refer Joseph for an evaluation for learning disabilities until third grade?

Case Study 6.2: Courtney

Courtney, a 13-year-old girl who is currently in the eighth grade, has recently been diagnosed with a nonverbal learning disability that impacts aspects of oral language, reading, and nonverbal ability.

Educational and Diagnostic Evaluation

By about the age of 2, it became very apparent to both her parents and her pediatrician that Courtney's cognitive development and language skills were well beyond what is considered typical. She was speaking in complete sentences that averaged four or five words per sentence, and her vocabulary was very strong. Recognizing her enjoyment of language and books, Courtney's parents taught her to read at the age of 4. Courtney seemed to love learning, but there were certain things that frustrated her, such as completing puzzles. She had extreme difficulty figuring out how the pieces fit together and determining what the puzzle should look like when it was completed. When she entered kindergarten at the age of 5, she was reading at the second-grade level. She was a very strong student, and the teacher constantly tried to find ways to enrich her learning. The only difficulties that the teacher noted was that she didn't really like coloring and that she was having difficulty learning to write her letters. By the

beginning of second grade, she was placed in the school's gifted program, and she began receiving more targeted enrichment. As she continued through elementary school and into middle school, she was continuing to thrive as a student, but she began to have more difficulties with her peers. She was having a hard time relating to them. She didn't seem to understand some of the social rules that kids at that age were following. For example, when she talked to other kids, she would stand really close to them, and it often made them feel uncomfortable. When her peers would tell jokes or use sarcasm, she would tell them that they didn't make any sense and that they weren't funny. She didn't seem to respond to their facial reactions or gestures; it was as though she didn't notice them. Her peer relationships started to become more and more strained as she continued through middle school. Further, she was beginning to have some academic difficulties. As more difficult literature was introduced in the curriculum and the books that she was reading became more complex, she began having a hard time interpreting the literature. She told her parents that she wasn't really enjoying reading as much anymore and that she preferred to just read nonfiction books. By the middle of her eighth-grade year, it was becoming evident that her difficulties were having more and more of an impact on her. Courtney's parents discussed the difficulties with her teachers, and together they decided that she would be evaluated by the school's MDT for a possible learning disability.

The results of the psychoeducational evaluation indicated that Courtney had a nonverbal learning disability that impacted her in the areas of reading, written language, and nonverbal ability. She was found to have an IQ of 135, which is in the very superior range. However, she demonstrated a significant discrepancy between intelligence and achievement in reading comprehension, written language (handwriting and writing fluency), and nonverbal ability. The following is a description of Courtney's performance in each of the five areas of academic achievement according to norm-referenced tests:

- Oral language: In the area of oral language, Courtney's scores for both receptive and expressive oral language were within the superior or very superior range (standard scores ranging between 125 and 140).

- Reading: Within the area of reading, Courtney scored in the very superior range on measures of word reading, nonword reading, and reading fluency (standard scores of 137, 134, and 140, respectively). She demonstrated reduced performance on measures of reading comprehension (standard score of 102). An analysis of her error patterns in reading comprehension revealed very strong literal comprehension and weaker inferential comprehension.

- Written language: In the area of written language, Courtney's performance was again in the superior or very superior range for spelling and written expression (standard scores of 132 and 127, respectively). However, on measures of handwriting and

writing fluency, she scored in the average range (standard scores of 99 and 103, respectively).

- Mathematics: In the area of mathematics (computation, math fluency, and word problem solving), all scores were within the very superior range (standard scores ranging from 130 to 137).

- Nonverbal ability: Courtney's performance on all measures of nonverbal ability were within the lower end of the average range or average range (standard scores ranging from 91 to 105). In addition to norm-referenced tests, some informal tests were completed, to help learn more about Courtney's difficulties in nonverbal ability.

  o Courtney was given written situations and asked to match them with a basic emotion. She had little difficulties matching the emotions. See the following examples:

Excited	A little girl lost her puppy and she misses it.
Happy	I'm going to the park and I can't wait.
Surprised	The boy can't understand the math problem.
Confused	A friend throws a party that you weren't expecting.
Sad	Someone said something that made you laugh.

  o However, when asked to act out the emotions, Courtney had difficulties. She used her hands to try to manipulate

(Continued)

(Continued)

her face to make her face resemble a particular emotion. For example, she curved her mouth up with her hands to show the emotion "happy."

○ When asked when she would feel some of these basic emotions, Courtney responded that she didn't know.

○ The evaluator used body language in addition to facial expression to convey basic emotions and asked Courtney to name the emotion. Courtney indicated that she was unaware that body language could also indicate an emotion. She also said that it was hard for her to tell the difference between different facial expressions. She knew what the mouth was supposed to do (e.g., curve up for happy, curve down for sad, look round for surprised), but she couldn't really see the difference when she looked at someone's face.

○ When shown photographs, and asked to interpret and explain what was happening in the picture or what a person in the picture might be feeling, Courtney had considerable difficulties using her background knowledge to interpret the photographs.

Courtney's performance on measures of processing and related mental activities yielded the following findings:

• Courtney demonstrated processing weaknesses (standard scores in the average range) in visual processing of nonverbal stimuli and visual/motor integration. She showed clear difficulties on measures that required picture interpretation, visual discrimination of designs that didn't have a clear verbal label (e.g., if she were to see two designs that she didn't recognize as a specific shape or object that she could name, she had difficulty discriminating between them), visual closure (e.g., if shown only part of an object, she had difficulty determining what it was), puzzle completion, spatial relationships, and understanding directionality (e.g., understanding direction on a map). She also had difficulties with handwriting speed, which likely influenced her writing fluency, as well as difficulties on tasks that required the drawing or copying of nonverbal stimuli (e.g., copying a figure that wasn't a typical shape, such as a square).

• Courtney was strong in attention, processing speed (except on measures that involved writing or drawing), and memory for verbal information, as well as visual and auditory processing of verbal stimuli and visual/auditory integration of verbal stimuli.

As part of the diagnostic process, all exclusionary criteria were ruled out as causal factors for Courtney's difficulties associated with reading comprehension, writing fluency, and nonverbal ability. Additionally, it was shown that she had received a good education in the areas of reading and math and that it had been delivered by qualified teachers who were certified in elementary education and, later, in middle-grades education.

Extension to Instruction

Following her diagnosis, the IEP team determined that Courtney would benefit from some targeted time outside of the general education classroom. She would participate in small social-skills groups for 40 minutes, twice a week, to help improve her social skills in a more authentic way. During the social-skills group, the group participated in many role-plays, where they focused on typical social rules (conversational rules, maintaining appropriate personal space, etc). Additionally, she received one-on-one learning support in a separate classroom for 40 minutes, three times a week, which was aimed at improving her nonverbal ability and visual/motor integration.

- Courtney worked on picture interpretation and learning how to use her verbal skills to talk through the pictures.

- She completed many types of puzzles, with verbal mediation from the special educator.

- She worked on navigating the school building and grounds using visual maps with no verbal information. She also focused on awareness of spatial relationships within and outside of the building.

- She worked on looking at pictures of real faces and learning to identify their expressions through the features associated with each expression.

- A focus was placed on better understanding spatial relationships and judging distance.

- Courtney worked on improving her visual/motor integration and handwriting, with an emphasis on tracing and copying a visual model. She also worked on throwing and catching objects as a means of improving visual/motor integration.

- Another focus of instruction was to improve Courtney's inferential comprehension and understanding of figurative language. Courtney hadn't realized that there were different ways to read text and to "read between the lines." She knew that she could read all the words; it just didn't seem to make sense to her. The teacher spent time working on how to better interpret information using short stories, jokes, comic strips, and videos. Courtney used her strong verbal skills to better understand the true meaning behind them.

It is often difficult to teach nonverbal skills in a meaningful way that feels authentic and real. Courtney's special education teacher found hands-on activities and manipulatives really beneficial in helping Courtney better understand visual stimuli. It was also important to draw on Courtney's intelligence and strong verbal skills to help her learn how to process nonverbal and other visual stimuli.

Check Your Understanding 6.7

1. Based on the information in the case study, which of the three methods (could be more than one) was likely used as a basis for diagnosis and eligibility for Courtney?

2. Why did it take until eighth grade for her parents and teachers to realize that Courtney should be evaluated for a learning disability?

3. How does Courtney's level of intelligence factor into her instruction?

4. Describe Courtney's processing deficits, and give examples of tasks that she might have difficulties with.

5. Why did the team decide to involve Courtney in a social-skills group?

Case Study 6.3: George

George, a 9-year-old boy who is currently in the fourth grade, has recently been diagnosed with a learning disability in the area of mathematics.

Educational and Diagnostic Evaluation

When George was in preschool and kindergarten, his early math skills (e.g., counting and number sense) seemed to be developing appropriately. However, as the focus in school started to move toward the development of computation skills and word problem solving, math became much harder for him. He was able to get through his math with a lot of help from his teacher and his parents during first grade and part of second grade, but as the concepts and problems became more difficult, he started to really struggle. As he continued in second and into third grade, he became more and more discouraged in the area of math, and, when asked about his most and least favorite subjects, he always said that math was his least favorite subject. He was a motivated student who did well in all of his other subjects, but he just couldn't seem to understand math concepts. During his parent-teacher conference in November of fourth grade, George's teacher and parents spent much of the time talking about his difficulties in the area of math. George's parents indicated the following information related to math:

- George has math homework almost every night, and it is becoming more and more burdensome on him and the family. Even though he spends a lot of time on all of his homework, he doesn't seem to have difficulties in any area except math. In math, he spends a lot of time trying to figure it out, but he often asks for help and says that he has a hard time remembering how he learned it in school.

- George often tells his parents that he is worried about math and that he doesn't think that he will be able to learn how to do math.

- George seems to have problems with his memory; when they ask him to do something that has a lot of steps, he has trouble remembering the steps.

The teacher noted the following with respect to math:

- George appears to be self-motivated; he always does work when asked and seems to want to improve math skills.

- The school engages in a Response to Intervention (RTI) program, and George has been receiving tier-3 interventions in the area of math for much of the school year. Through this process, the teacher has tried several research-based interventions for math, but George hasn't shown a lot of progress and continues to have difficulty with computations and word problem solving.

In the area of computation, George demonstrates the following:

- He often mixes up the signs (+, −, ×, ÷) and has said that he has difficulties telling the difference between them.

- He has difficulties with procedural skills for addition and subtraction. He uses his fingers to count when he adds and subtracts and is having a hard time learning how to regroup (i.e., carry and borrow).

- He hasn't been able to learn his math facts for multiplication; he seems to be having great difficulty remembering the facts. Instead, he uses his fingers to do repeated addition. He has also learned a "trick" for remembering the 9's math facts.

- Word problem solving has been a struggle for him, especially as the problems get more complex; he often has to reread the problem many times to figure out what operation should be completed.

By the end of the conference, his parents and teacher came to the conclusion that George's math proficiency was continuing to decrease, and they were concerned that there might be some other reason why he was having so many difficulties in the area of math. He was referred for an evaluation to determine whether he had a learning disability and whether he was eligible for special education services.

The results of the psychoeducational evaluation indicated that George had a learning disability in the area of mathematics and that he was eligible for services under IDEA. He was found to have an IQ of 102, which is in the average range. However, he demonstrated a significant discrepancy between intelligence and achievement in math (computation, word problem solving, and math fluency). The following is a description of George's performance in each of the five areas of academic achievement according to norm-referenced tests:

- Oral language: In the area of oral language, all of George's scores were within the average range; however, there was a slight weakness on a measure of receptive vocabulary (when given a word, he had to point to a picture that represented that word) that was at the low end of the average range (standard score of 88). Standard scores on all other measures of receptive oral language and expressive oral language ranged between 99 and 105.

- Reading: Within the area of reading, George's performance was in the average range on measures of word reading and nonword reading (standard scores of 105 and 99, respectively), reading fluency (standard score of 103), and reading comprehension (standard score of 99). Reading was generally regarded as an area of strength for him.

- Written language: In the area of written language, George's performance was again in the average range for measures of writing fluency (standard score of 95) and written expression (standard score of 97); however, his spelling performance was at the lower end of the average range (standard score of 89).

- Mathematics: In the area of mathematics (computation, math fluency, and word problem solving), all scores were within the well-below-average range (standard scores of 63, 66, and 68, respectively).

- Nonverbal ability: George's performance on all measures of nonverbal ability was within the lower end of the average range.

George's performance on measures of processing and related mental activities yielded the following findings:

- He demonstrated well-below-average performance on measures of visual perception (specifically visual discrimination, spatial relations, and visual memory).

- His performance on all measures of long-term memory and immediate memory (short-term and working memory) was in the well-below-average range and, thus, considered areas of weakness for him; however, his memory for auditory information was stronger than his memory for visual information.

(Continued)

(Continued)

- He demonstrated average performance on measures of attention, processing speed, and all other areas of processing. Auditory perception and haptic perception were found to be relative processing strengths for George.

As part of the diagnostic process, all exclusionary criteria were ruled out as causal factors for George's difficulties associated with mathematics. Additionally, it was shown that he had received a good education in the areas of reading and math and that it had been delivered by qualified teachers who were certified in elementary education. Additionally, his teacher had tried several research-based interventions for math that didn't result in significant progress.

Extension to Instruction

Following his diagnosis and determination of eligibility, the IEP team determined that George would be fully included in the general education classroom.

- George participated in small-group instruction (delivered by the special education teacher) in a separate area of the general education classroom for 40 minutes, five days per week, during the regular math period. The other members of his group had similar difficulties in mathematics.

- Additionally, George received one-on-one learning support with the special educator for 60 minutes per week in the general education classroom. They focused on learning strategies aimed at improving George's long-term and working memory as well as enhancing his visual perception. While math was the only area in which George showed a significant discrepancy between intelligence and achievement

and that he showed real difficulties with in school, the evaluation showed that he had relative weaknesses in receptive vocabulary, likely related to deficits in long-term memory and visual perception (as the assessment required picture interpretation). Additionally, he had a relative weakness in spelling, which likely related to difficulties with visual memory. Further, his relatively weak nonverbal ability was likely associated with difficulties in visual perception.

The focus of the small-group instruction included the following:

- As a result of George's difficulties with visual processing, instruction in the area of symbol recognition focused on analyzing the different visual parts (vertical lines, horizontal lines, diagonal lines, dots, etc.) that made up each math symbol. The symbols were color-coded with the different visual parts (e.g., | – \ / .). George focused on saying the parts and tracing the parts with his fingers to help him visually discriminate between them. He also did exercises in which he looked at several lines of symbols and had to circle a particular symbol (e.g., +). Further, he completed worksheets that had a mixture of operations; however, before completing any problems, he circled the operation and wrote the operation (e.g., circled + and wrote "addition"). These interventions helped him better recognize the different symbols associated with each operation.

- George's working-memory deficits make it difficult for him to use the traditional algorithm for regrouping in addition and subtraction problems, because he often has difficulties with the steps. To improve his procedural skills for addition and subtraction, he used manipulatives (e.g., base-10 blocks) to help him to focus on place value for regrouping. He was able to build the numbers to be added and subtracted with the manipulatives. Once he felt comfortable with the manipulatives, he learned to draw pictures to represent the blocks and completed problems using the pictures. This helped reduce his working-memory load and helped improve his addition and subtraction computation.

- Similarly, George's working-memory deficits had an impact on word problem solving. He had a hard time making connections between the different parts of the problem. To help alleviate these difficulties, the teacher developed comprehension questions (similar to those discussed in the Word Problem Comprehension Task in Chapter 5) that helped George work through and understand the different parts of the problem, as well as the stages of word problem solving. The teacher also helped him analyze the problems by discussing the different types of complexities (extraneous information, extra steps, etc.) associated with problem solving (see Chapter 5). Once George learned how to focus on and make sense of each part of the problem, as well as different elements that are often incorporated into such problems, his confidence in his ability to problem solve really started to grow. The comprehension questions allowed for a step-by-step approach that helped alleviate the burden on his working memory.

- The teacher worked with George on improving his multiplication fact retrieval with several different types of activities.

George learned how to use arrays to represent multiplication facts. Additionally, the teacher employed the following strategies that drew heavily on George's areas of processing strength (haptic perception and auditory perception).

- ○ George learned songs that helped him remember a variety of math facts.

- ○ Since a finger trick had helped George learn his 9's facts, the teacher taught him additional finger methods that worked for 6, 7, and 8.

- ○ The teacher employed a multisensory approach, in which George traced the numbers in the air while he said the multiplication fact (e.g., "6 times 5 equals 30") out loud. Because he had learned to read with a multisensory approach, the IEP team reckoned that a multisensory approach to remembering his math facts might also be beneficial.

In George's one-on-one sessions, the instruction focused on strategies aimed at improving his memory, which would help him in all academic areas. Additionally, they focused on visual perception.

- To help improve his memory, George engaged in a lot of verbal repetition. This allowed him to engage his stronger auditory perception skills to help him encode memories.

- He was taught mnemonic acronyms, and he learned or made up songs that would help him remember information.

- He learned to "chunk" information that he wanted to remember.

- He worked on making associations (e.g., relate it to a song, associate it with something personal) with information that

(Continued)

(Continued)

he was learning, to help encode it into his long-term memory.

- He worked on talking through and writing down steps that he wanted to remember, so that he could refer to his notes instead of having to remember the steps.

- Since George's reading skills were strong, the teacher used those skills to help him improve his spelling. Within spelling, there often aren't rules to help determine the spelling of the word. For example, the word "bowl" could be spelled *bole*, *boal*, or *boul* and still resemble other words with the same sounds (e.g., "hole," "coal," "soul," respectively). Visual memory often has to take over when we are thinking of the spelling of a word. George learned to develop possible spellings of words and then use his reading skills to help him choose which one looked correct. He would then look at the actual spelling of the word (provided by either the teacher or a spell-checker) to confirm whether he was correct. This was important, because the teacher didn't want to reinforce incorrect spellings.

George's progress in the area of mathematics was greatly improved with the use of these and other methods. Additionally, his memory and visual perception was showing improvement. Information that was gained during the diagnostic evaluation helped the team understand his strengths and needs and, thus, allowed them to specifically tailor instruction to his specific needs.

As mentioned earlier in the chapter, there are a great many ways to teach different math concepts; however, there isn't one method that is effective for everyone. Developing an understanding of a student's specific strengths and needs allows for instruction that will both help build up the student's weak areas and draw on his or her areas of strength.

Check Your Understanding 6.8

1. Based on the information in the case study, which of the three methods (could be more than one) was likely used as a basis for diagnosis and eligibility for George?

2. Find a research-based method for teaching word problem solving. Based on George's areas of strength and need, determine whether that method would be a good learning strategy for him, and explain why or why not.

3. Why was focusing on visual parts of math symbols (e.g., color-coding) beneficial for George?

4. Describe why you think deficits in working memory could impact word problem solving.

CHAPTER SUMMARY

Students with learning disabilities are the most widely served disability population under IDEA; however, the specific characteristics associated with learning disabilities can vary greatly among individuals. Students with learning disabilities typically demonstrate a level of intelligence that is at or anywhere above the average range; however, they have difficulties learning in one or more of the five areas of academic achievement (oral language, reading, written language, mathematics, and nonverbal ability). These difficulties occur because of deficits in the way that their minds process information. There are several different methods that can be used to diagnose learning disabilities, including the discrepancy model, Response to Intervention (RTI), and patterns of strengths and weaknesses (PSW). However, ultimately, regardless of which method is used, the findings from each individual's diagnostic evaluation should serve as a basis for delivering instruction. Instruction for a student with learning disabilities can't be truly effective unless the specific characteristics associated with his or her own personal patterns of performance are taken into consideration. Thus, the diagnostic process is crucial for a student with learning disabilities.

APPLY WHAT YOU HAVE LEARNED

1. Design an informal assessment that would measure visual discrimination associated with letters.

2. Explain why the exclusionary clause is important in diagnosing learning disabilities. Choose two of the following exclusionary criteria and describe why it would not be appropriate for them to be considered primary causes of a learning disability:

    a) Motor disability

    b) Intellectual disability

    c) Economic disadvantage

    d) Cultural factors

3. Compare and contrast the three methods of diagnosing learning disabilities, and make an argument for which one is the best model (in your opinion).

4. Research the method that your state/district uses for diagnosing learning disabilities, and explain which one (or more) of the three methods of diagnosing learning disabilities (discrepancy model, RTI, and PSW) is employed.

5. Make a table that characterizes each of the students in the case studies (Joseph, Courtney, and George). Within your table, include information about intelligence, academic achievement, psychological processing, and approaches to instruction.

REFERENCES

2018 Annual Report to Congress on the Individuals With Disabilities Education Act. (2018). Retrieved from https://sites.ed.gov/idea/2018-annual-report-to-congress-on-the-individuals-with-disabilities-education-act/#Ages-6-12-Part-B

Hale, J., Alfonso, V., Berninger, V., Bracken, B., Christo, C., Clark, E., . . . Yalof, J. (2010). Critical issues in response-to-intervention, comprehensive evaluation, and specific learning disabilities identification and intervention: An expert white paper consensus. *Learning Disability Quarterly, 33*(3), 223–236.

IDEA (Individuals With Disabilities Education Act). (2004). *Section 300.307*. Retrieved from https://sites.ed.gov/idea/regs/b/d/300.307

IDEA (Individuals With Disabilities Education Act). (2004). *Section 300.308*. Retrieved from https://sites.ed.gov/idea/regs/b/d/300.308

IDEA (Individuals With Disabilities Education Act). (2004). *Section 300.309*. Retrieved from https://sites.ed.gov/idea/regs/b/d/300.309

IDEA (Individuals With Disabilities Education Act). (2004). *Section 300.310*. Retrieved from https://sites.ed.gov/idea/regs/b/d/300.310

IDEA (Individuals With Disabilities Education Act). (2004). *Section 300.311*. Retrieved from https://sites.ed.gov/idea/regs/b/d/300.311

IDEA (Individuals With Disabilities Education Act). (2004). *Section 300.8*. Retrieved from https://sites.ed.gov/idea/regs/b/a/300.8/c/10

Jennings, J., Caldwell, J., & Lerner, J. (2010). *Reading problems: Assessment and teaching strategies* (6th ed.). Boston, MA: Allyn & Bacon.

Maki, K., Burns, M., & Sullivan, A. (2018). School psychologists' confidence in learning disability identification decisions. *Learning Disability Quarterly, 41*(4), 243–256.

McGill, R., Styck, K., Palomares, R., & Hass, M. (2016). Critical issues in specific learning disability identification: What we need to know about the PSW Model. *Learning Disability Quarterly, 39*(3), 159–170.

Miciak, J., Fletcher, J. M., Stuebing, K. K., Vaughn, S., & Tolar, T. D. (2014). Patterns of cognitive strengths and weaknesses: Identification rates, agreement, and validity for learning disabilities identification. *School Psychology Quarterly, 29*(1), 21–37.

Phipps, L., & Beaujean, A. (2016). Review of the pattern of strengths and weaknesses approach in specific learning disability identification. *Research and Practice in the Schools, 4*(1), 18-28.

Polloway, E. A., Patton, J. R., Serna, L., & Bailey-Joseph, J. (2018). *Strategies for teaching learners with special needs* (11th ed.). New York, NY: Pearson Education.

Raymond, E. (2012). *Learners with mild disabilities: A characteristics approach* (4th ed.). Boston, MA: Pearson Education.

Reading Rockets. (n.d.). *Six syllable types*. Retrieved from https://www.readingrockets.org/article/six-syllable-types

Intellectual Disabilities

Mary A. Houser, EdD

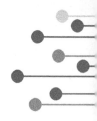

Learning Objectives

After completion of this chapter, you should be able to:

- Explain the three criteria required for an intellectual disability (ID) diagnosis.

- Discuss how an ID diagnosis is made and who makes the diagnosis.

- Recognize other areas of ID to be assessed, such as academics/areas of achievement, behavioral characteristics, social/emotional characteristics, and medical status.

- Discuss various instructional methods used when teaching students with ID: task analysis, class-wide peer tutoring, and direct instruction.

- Explain early intervention and the different domains that can be assessed for delays.

Key Terms

adaptive behavior (p. 205)	functional academics (p. 216)
Angelman syndrome (AS) (p. 215)	generalization (p. 229)
behavior rating scales (BRS) (p. 217)	global developmental delay (GDD) (p. 213)
class-wide peer tutoring (p. 227)	intellectual deficits (p. 203)
comorbidity (p. 220)	intellectual disabilities (IDs) (p. 202)
developmental delay (DD) (p. 212)	positive reinforcement (p. 229)
developmental milestones (p. 202)	Prader-Willi syndrome (PWS) (p. 215)
direct instruction (DI) (p. 228)	prompting (p. 229)
Down syndrome (DS) (p. 214)	task analysis (p. 227)
early intervention (EI) (p. 226)	unspecified intellectual disability (UID) (p. 213)
fragile X syndrome (FXS) (p. 214)	Williams syndrome (WS) (p. 215)

Introduction to the Chapter

Intellectual disabilities (IDs) are neurodevelopmental disorders characterized by significantly sub-average intellectual quotient (IQ) and deficits in adaptive behavior (AAIDD, 2018a). In the case of an ID, the neurological system has been negatively affected, resulting in problems with cognition, communication, behavior, and/or motor skills. IDs occur during the developmental period (i.e., before a child turns 18 years old), and their severity can range from mild to profound. IDs currently affect more than 3 million individuals and are chronic conditions requiring a medical diagnosis. Statistically speaking, more males than females each year are diagnosed with an ID. In the United States, African-American children are approximately twice as likely as other children to receive an ID diagnosis. Hispanic children are about one and a half times as likely to be diagnosed as white non-Hispanic children. Poverty is among the most consistent risk factors for developing an acquired ID.

Evaluating individuals for IDs did not begin until the second half of the twentieth century. In fact, it was not until the 1960s that newborns could even be assessed for developmental delays. *Haemophilus influenzae* type b (Hib), a bacterium that causes meningitis, was the leading cause of an intellectual disability until a vaccine was developed. In addition, prior to the 1970s, this disability population was often institutionalized (NIH RePORT, 2018) and could not receive the benefit of a public education as provided by P.L. 94-142. Another noteworthy advancement regarding IDs is that the term "intellectual disabilities" replaced "mental retardation" in 2010 as a result of legislation called Rosa's Law. This law came about as the result of a Maryland family seeking respect and acceptance for their daughter, who was intellectually disabled and being bullied. The family's desire was to abolish the derogatory terms "mental retardation" and "mentally retarded," and it effectively did so. As a result of legislation, these terms are no longer used in federal health, education, and labor policy due to their dehumanizing nature.

Individuals with developmental disabilities, such as an ID, possess several unique and identifiable characteristics that set them apart from their typically developing peers. The most distinguishable characteristic of an ID is that children with this diagnosis do not meet their developmental milestones as expected. Examples of failure to meet developmental milestones are rolling over, walking, or learning to talk later than most children. These differences are revealed when affected children undergo assessment, either at school or by a medical professional.

IDEA Definition of Intellectual Disability

According to IDEA (2004), intellectual disability "means significantly sub-average general intellectual functioning, existing concurrently [at the same time] with deficits in adaptive behavior and manifested during the developmental period, that adversely affects a child's educational performance" (20 U.S.C. § 300.8(c)(6)). This definition will be used as the basis for the chapter's definition of intellectual disability.

Although we will not be referring to this definition of ID, another widely accepted definition of ID comes from the American Association on Intellectual and Developmental Disabilities (AAIDD). The AAIDD is the world's oldest and largest organization of professionals serving individuals with IDs. The AAIDD (2018b) defines intellectual disability as "a disability characterized by significant limitations in both intellectual functioning and in adaptive behavior, which covers many everyday social and practical skills. This disability originates before the age of 18."

Diagnostic Criteria

In order to best understand students with intellectual disabilities, it is relevant to examine the various components of their diagnosis. When the diagnosis of an intellectual disability has been made, two particular areas have been assessed: intelligence and adaptive behavior skills. Understanding IQ and adaptive behavior will give the special educator a genuine idea of the challenges that individuals with this disability might possess.

Intelligence Quotient (IQ) and ID

As detailed previously, IQ is a measure of human intelligence. Individuals with an ID have IQs that fall in the low or sub-average range. This means that they must possess an IQ of about 70 or lower. An IQ score of 70 is two standard deviations below the mean, or what is considered to be average intelligence (average IQ being 100). The bell curve in Figure 7.1 depicts where an individual with an ID's intelligence falls as compared to those with average or above-average intelligence.

Why does having a low IQ matter? Having a sub-average IQ impacts an individual's cognitive functioning with respect to memory, generalization, metacognition, motivation, language, and academic skills (Bergeron & Floyd, 2006). There are specific difficulties associated with having a low IQ. Most noteworthy to educators, a low IQ impacts a child's ability to learn and be successful in school. Other challenges related to possessing a low IQ include problems with reasoning, problem solving, planning, abstract thinking, judgment, academic learning, and experiential learning (Reynolds, Zupanick, & Dombeck, 2013).

Intellectual deficits refer to problems with planning, academic learning, abstract thinking, reasoning, learning from experience, and problem solving. Historically speaking, the two greatest indicators of an ID have been a low IQ and significant deficits in adaptive behavior. Recently, however, there have been some changes to the DSM as to where the diagnostic emphasis should be placed. In the latest edition (DSM-5), there has been a movement away from using specific IQ scores as a diagnostic criterion (although two standard deviations below the mean is still the general rule), and more emphasis is now being placed on an individual's adaptive behavior deficits.

There are several appropriate assessments that can be used for assessing a student's IQ. The choice should depend on the age of the student and subtest

Figure 7.1 Bell Curve of IQs Associated With Intellectual Disabilities

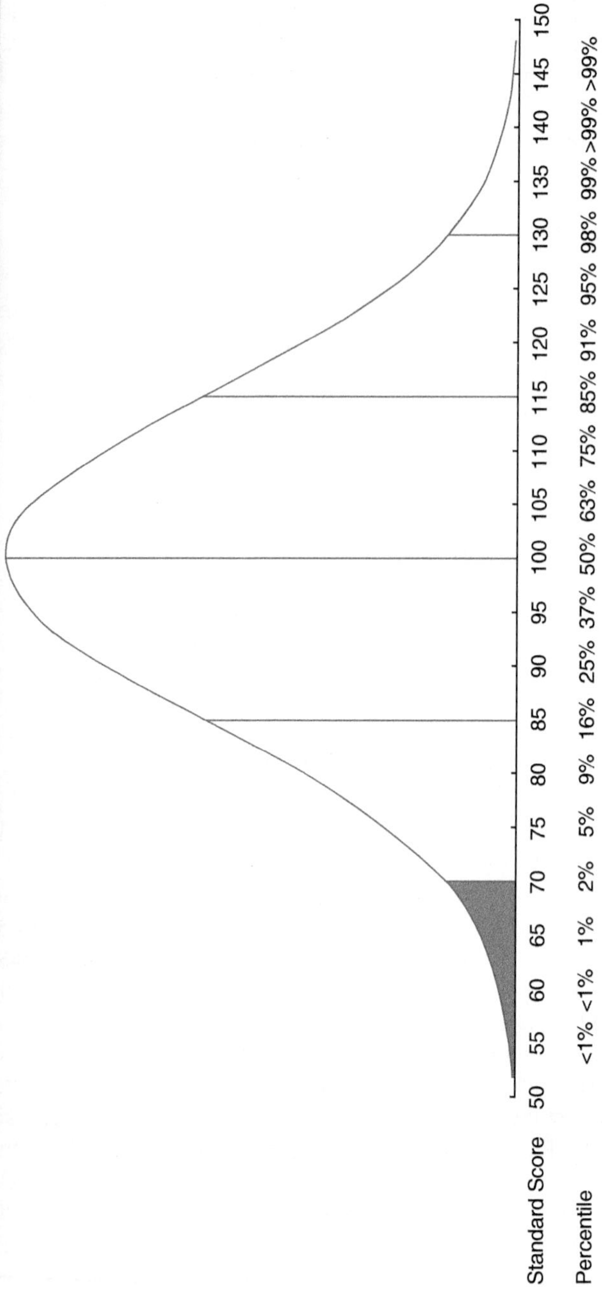

Standard Score	50	55	60	65	70	75	80	85	90	95	100	105	110	115	120	125	130	135	140	145	150
Percentile	<1%	<1%	1%	2%	5%	9%	16%	25%	37%	50%	63%	75%	85%	91%	95%	98%	99%	>99%	>99%		

preferences. For example, the WISC is an IQ test that is appropriate for children ages 6 to 16 years and examines verbal skills and spatial skills. The Bayley Scales of Infant Development, on the other hand, examine infant and toddler development from 1 to 42 months. This assessment examines mental abilities, motor abilities, and social and emotional behavior. The following tests are commonly used to measure intelligence when diagnosing for an intellectual disability (Reynolds et al., 2013).

- The Wechsler Intelligence Scale for Children (WISC)
- The Wechsler Preschool and Primary Scale of Intelligence (WPPSI)
- The Stanford-Binet Intelligence Test (SB)
- The Bayley Scales of Infant Development (BSID)

As previously stated, IQ tests are often administered by a school psychologist or clinical psychologist, depending on the state.

Adaptive Behavior

The other diagnostic criterion for possessing an intellectual disability is poor adaptive behavior skills. **Adaptive behavior** refers to conceptual, social, and practical skills needed for everyday living to be safe and socially responsible and to be able to live an independent life and interact with others. Adaptive behavior skills can be categorized into several domains. Table 7.1 details various types of adaptive behavior skills.

One way to better understand how adaptive behavior skills can impact an individual is to compare the adaptive skills demonstrated by a typically developing child to one with an intellectual disability. Table 7.2 compares the adaptive behavior skills of a typically developing 6-year-old child and the adaptive behavior skills of a 6-year-old child with an ID.

From the table, it is apparent that the 6-year-old child with an ID lacks several of the adaptive skills that he should have acquired by age 6 under normal circumstances. These adaptive behavior skill deficits will negatively impact his ability to function at a level that would be expected of someone his age, and he will require additional instruction in order to acquire such skills. To illustrate, under most circumstances, a typical child is able to toilet himself independently by the age of three. This allows the child to no longer wear diapers or require assistance from a caregiver during the school day. A 6-year-old child with an ID might not have yet mastered toilet training and will require help with this task during the school day.

To help determine a student with an ID's adaptive behavior skills, a behavioral checklist or rating scale can be administered to parents and/or teachers who work with the student on a regular basis and know him well. Most checklists are organized by domain and ask the reporter to indicate the degree to which a child can perform a specific behavior. For example, under the self-care domain, the checklist might ask whether the child is able to independently perform basic hygiene and

Table 7.1 Types of Adaptive Behavior Skills

Category	Definition/Explanation	Examples
Self-care skills	skills used to participate in everyday life. These are sometimes also referred to as activities of daily living (ADLs)	Examples include feeding, dressing, grooming, hygiene, and toileting
Communication skills	skills needed to express one's wants and needs	An example of a communication skill is using clear and intelligible speech when speaking
Social skills	skills needed to be competent in social situations	An example of a social skill is establishing and maintaining friendships
Academic skills-skills	skills such as functional math and language skills needed to live independently	Examples include following oral and written directions, telling time, and balancing a checkbook
Occupational skills	skills needed to perform a job	Examples of occupational skills include clerical skills such as word-processing or collating papers
Community living skills	skills needed to access the community	Examples of community living skills are using public transportation, shopping, eating at restaurants, and crossing the street
Leisure/recreation skills	skills that individuals participate in during their free time when they are not at school or working	Examples include going bowling, visiting the library, and taking a walk in the park

Torreno, S. (2012). *Special education students—what are adaptive skills?* Retrieved from https://www.brighthubeducation.com/special-ed-learning-disorders/73324-improving-adaptives-skills-in-students-with-intellectual-disabilities

Table 7.2 Adaptive Behavior Comparison

Typical 6-Year-Old	6-Year-Old With an Intellectual Disability
Bathes, dresses, feeds, and toilets independently	Requires another person's assistance with daily living skills
Communicates effectively with others in multi-word sentences	Communicates with others in single words or short phrases
Performs academically on a first-grade level across all academic areas	Performs academically at a preschool level or below across all academic areas
Maintains several friendships with other children in class and neighborhood	Has trouble making friends with peers
Maintains appropriate table manners when eating at a restaurant with family	Chews with mouth open and speaks too loudly when eating at a restaurant with family

grooming. Another behavioral checklist item might ask whether the student can budget money. The results of such checklists provide the teacher with an understanding of the daily living/adaptive skills that the student possesses and, consequently, what he needs to learn. Following are examples of appropriate checklists and rating scales to measure daily living/adaptive skills in individuals with IDs:

- The AAMR Adaptive Behavior Scale
- The Adaptive Behavior Inventory
- The Brigance Life Skills Inventory (LSI)
- The Functional Skills Inventory
- The Kaufman Functional Academic Skills Test (K-FAST)
- The Life Centered Career Education Knowledge and Performance Batteries
- The Responsibility and Independence Scale for Adolescents (RISA)
- The Scales of Independent Behavior
- The Street Survival Skills Questionnaire
- The Vineland Adaptive Behavior Scale
- The Woodcock-Johnson Scales of Independent Behavior (SIB)

Like various IQ tests, adaptive behavior instruments assess various competencies at different ages. For example, when assessing a child in infancy, one might examine sensorimotor development, communication, and interaction with others. As the child moves into adolescence, the focus would change to examining academic skills as they relate to daily living and social skills. As the adolescent reaches adulthood, the focus would turn to vocational and social responsibilities associated with maturity.

Age of Onset

As mentioned earlier, identification of low IQ and adaptive behavior skills for an ID diagnosis must occur during the developmental period. A person's developmental period is between the time of birth and age 18. Therefore, if challenges with IQ and adaptive skills do not present themselves within this time frame, a diagnosis of ID would not be given.

Intellectual Disability and Skill Deficit Areas

As a result of a sub-average IQ and poor adaptive behavior skills, individuals with IDs often demonstrate skill deficits across several domains. It will be important for you, as a special educator, to be aware of these deficits and how they will inform your instruction. These skill deficits are often those deficiencies that prove to be the most troublesome in accomplishing tasks.

As illustrated in Table 7.3, students with IDs demonstrate pervasive challenges with respect to all areas of development. These deficits have a significant impact on their ability to learn and the type of instruction they will need to be successful, as well as the setting in which they will receive their education.

Table 7.3 ID Skill Deficit Areas

Thinking and Reasoning

- Cause-and-effect relationships (e.g., failure to understand that being unkind to others will result in a lack of friends)
- Generalizing information to new places (e.g., being able to use a debit card in multiple situations with various card readers)
- Speech and language (e.g., reaching language milestones later than expected or not at all)
- Sentence structure and vocabulary skills (e.g., challenges with putting words together to make sentences)
- Language is very concrete (e.g., difficulty understanding idioms)
- Problems understanding complex instructions (e.g., understanding only simple or one-step directions)

Academic

- Academically behind their peers and gaps increase with age (e.g., being 10 years old yet performing on a first-grade level)
- Problems learning and applying basic skills (e.g., difficulty learning simple addition and using it to budget money)

Attention and Task Completion

- Short attention span (e.g., difficulties successfully completing tasks)
- Difficulty initiating tasks and staying on task (e.g., failure to independently start classwork and complete it without prompting)

Behavior and Emotional Issues

- Low self-confidence and self-efficacy (e.g., not joining a play group for fear that the children will not like you)
- Anxiety and worry (e.g., stress about being somewhere new or having new experiences)
- Depression or sadness (e.g., unhappiness due to stressful social interactions)

Social Skills

- Difficulty making and maintaining friendships (e.g., possessing few friends)
- Problems with understanding social cues and social rules (e.g., standing too close to others and not understanding one's personal space)
- Difficulty with dealing with large groups of unfamiliar people (e.g., being overwhelmed by crowds)

Adapted from Evely, M., & Ganim, Z. (2018). *Intellectual disability*. Retrieved from https://www.psych4schools.com.au/free-resources/intellectual-disability

1. What term was previously used to describe ID? What brought about this change in terminology?

2. Select any three of the listed skill deficits associated with an ID. Why would having these deficits be problematic in a classroom setting?

3. What are the diagnostic criteria for ID?

4. What is adaptive behavior? Provide three adaptive behavior skills needed in everyday life. Why is it important for someone to have good adaptive behavior skills?

5. What is age of onset? How does it apply to diagnosing an ID?

6. What recent change has occurred in the way that educators view the importance of an individual's IQ in the diagnostic process for ID?

How the Diagnosis Is Made/Who Makes the Diagnosis

Diagnosing an individual with an ID is a multifarious process. This means that one must consider several aspects of an individual's development in order to make a proper diagnosis. Screening is the first assessment performed to determine any developmental challenge. Screening for an ID, however, is more likely to occur for those individuals who are at risk of a mild ID than for those at risk of a moderate to severe/profound one. For those who are more severely affected, it is likely that the screening will be skipped and that professionals will move directly to a comprehensive diagnostic evaluation to confirm the diagnosis.

Similar to the other disability categories under IDEA, in order to determine whether a student should receive the diagnosis of ID, a team of professionals must complete a comprehensive diagnostic evaluation to determine whether the child meets the specified criteria. The following are the components of a comprehensive diagnostic evaluation for ID:

1. *Comprehensive medical exam.* This includes a medical history, vital signs, general appearance, heart exam, lung exam, head and neck exam, abdominal exam, neurological exam, dermatological exam, and an extremities exam. It can also include laboratory tests.

2. *Possible genetic and neurological testing.* If deemed necessary by a medical doctor, genetic and neurological testing can provide information regarding genetic conditions or the chance/likelihood of developing a genetic disorder as well as ruling out the presence of a neurological disorder.

3. *Social and familial history.* This provides relevant information about relatives, living situation, recreational activities, occupation, and sexual preferences.

4. *Educational history.* This provides critical information about the grade levels the child has completed, his educational placements, his academic performance, and any educational challenges or diagnoses.

5. *Psychological testing to assess intellectual functioning.* This is conducted by a psychologist to determine the child's IQ.

6. *Testing of adaptive functioning.* This provides information about how well the child is able to complete everyday tasks relevant to his age.

7. *Interviews with primary caregivers.* These provide valuable information about the child's home life, siblings, and relationships with immediate and extended family.

8. *Interviews with teachers.* These provide important information about the child's academic, behavioral, and social life at school.

9. *Social and behavioral observations of the child in natural environments.* These provide an authentic look at the child's behavior in familiar settings.

(adapted from Reynolds et al., 2013)

Classifying Intellectual Disability Severity

Once an individual has been diagnosed with an intellectual disability, he can then be assessed to determine the severity of his intellectual disability. This is the degree to which he is impacted by his disability and how the severity impacts his ability to function in everyday life. Table 7.4 indicates the various levels of ID severity, the approximate percent of individuals with a particular severity, the DSM-5 criteria for ID, and the AAIDD criteria for ID.

As seen in Table 7.4, the classifications of severity have been developed to best differentiate between the various functioning levels of ID. Although this is not an educational tool, this classification system helps inform special educators and other professionals about the student with an ID's current levels and needs, and it offers information to help them make educational placement decisions. For example, based on the information provided above, it might appear challenging to educate a student with a severe or profound ID in general education; however, educating an individual with a mild ID in this setting is often appropriate. In order to understand the classification system, it is necessary to examine each classification of ID, as they possess their own unique characteristics. They are as follows:

- Mild: Individuals in this ID range have an IQ between 50 and 69. This constitutes the majority of individuals with this disability (85% of ID

Table 7.4 Intellectual Disability Severity Classification

ID severity category	Percentage of individuals within ID severity category	DSM-5 criteria (according to their ability to perform daily skills)	AAIDD criteria (according to the intensity of support needed)
Mild	85%	Able to live independently with minimal support	Periodic assistance needed during transitions or uncertain times
Moderate	10%	Able to live independently with moderate levels of support (e.g., group homes)	Occasional assistance needed in daily living
Severe	3.5%	Needs daily assistance with personal care activities (e.g., hygiene) and safety supervision (e.g., navigating traffic)	Substantial assistance needed for daily living
Profound	1.5%	Needs 24-hour supervision (i.e., cannot be left alone)	Extensive assistance needed for every aspect of daily living

Adapted from American Psychiatric Association. (2013). *Diagnostic and statistical manual of mental disorders* (5th ed.). Arlington, VA: American Psychiatric Publishing.

population). They are usually able to live independently with a minimal amount of support. Such support is often needed during transitions or times of uncertainty.

- Moderate: Individuals in this ID range have an IQ between 36 and 49 (10% of ID population). With moderate levels of support, they can live independently in a group home or otherwise supervised environment. They require limited support in daily situations and possess basic communication skills.

- Severe: Individuals in this ID range have an IQ between 20 and 35 (3.5% of ID population). They require extensive daily assistance with self-care activities and safety supervision. They have limited communication and need extensive help in social situations.

- Profound: Individuals in this ID range have an IQ less than 20 (1.5% of ID population). They require 24-hour care or constant support for every aspect of their daily routines. They have significant delays in all areas of development.

It is relevant to mention that this information should be regarded only as a guideline, as there are a range of abilities within each classification.

Check Your Understanding 7.2

1. List the nine components of the comprehensive diagnostic evaluation for ID.

2. Select any three of the components of the comprehensive diagnostic evaluation for ID, and explain how each would provide valuable information to you as the special education teacher working with this student population.

3. Using the Intellectual Disability Severity Classification chart above, identify some similarities and differences between individuals with a moderate ID and those with a profound ID.

Other Areas to Be Assessed

In order to obtain a comprehensive understanding of ID, it is helpful for the special educator to be aware of some of the other reasons behind this diagnosis. What causes ID? What are some of the specific disabilities that fall under the ID category? Knowing the answers to these questions will help inform the special educator's instruction in the classroom.

Causes

To date, there are several known causes of ID. These are commonly classified according to the time relative to the child's birth in which they occurred. Such times are referred to as *prenatal* (before birth), *perinatal* (during birth or immediately after), and *postnatal* (after birth). It is important to note, however, that in the majority of cases, the cause of ID is unknown. Table 7.5 lists possible causes of ID, categorized by when they occurred in relation to the mother's pregnancy.

Developmental Delay (DD) and Related Syndromes

From an educational perspective, IDEA sets forth regulations to support young children with delayed development. As such, IDEA includes developmental delay (DD) as one of its disability categories under which children can receive special education services. According to IDEA (2004), developmental delay is defined as follows: "[F]or children from birth to age three (under IDEA Part C) and children from ages three through nine (under IDEA Part B), the term developmental delay, as defined by each State, means a delay in one or more of the following areas: physical development; cognitive development; communication; social or emotional development; or adaptive [behavioral] development" (IDEA Partnership, n.d., para. 4). It is also important, however, to understand how one arrives at a DD diagnosis. In order to do so, it is helpful to spend some time exploring the DSM-5.

Table 7.5 Causes of Intellectual Disabilities

Prenatal Causes of ID

- Down syndrome (Trisomy 21) - a genetic syndrome in which an individual has a full or partial extra copy of chromosome 21

- Fetal alcohol syndrome (FAS) – a preventable form of ID that is caused by the mother's consumption of alcohol during pregnancy, resulting in mild to moderate ID

- Fragile X syndrome (FXS) - a genetic syndrome resulting in several developmental problems such as cognitive impairment and learning disabilities

- Malnutrition – a condition that occurs when the mother does not get the adequate nutrition during her pregnancy and can result in an ID

- Phenylketonuria (PKU) – an inherited genetic disorder that increases the levels of a substance called phenylalanine in the blood, resulting in ID

- Prader-Willi syndrome (PWS) – a genetic disorder caused by a partial deletion of chromosome 15 (passed down by the father) that results in intellectual disabilities, behavior problems, and short height

- Toxoplasmosis - a disease that results from infection with the *Toxoplasma gondii* parasite, causing ID in pregnant mothers

Perinatal Causes of ID

- Birth injury (oxygen deprivation) – a lack of oxygen to the brain during the birth process

- Prematurity – when children born before full term risk developing an ID due to the brain's inability to completely mature. The earlier a child is born, the more at risk he is of developing an ID

Postnatal Causes of ID

- Brain injury – traumatic brain injury, resulting in either a closed-head trauma or an open-head trauma

- Encephalitis – inflammation of the brain, commonly caused by a viral infection

- Lead poisoning – high levels of lead (e.g., through ingesting lead paint) can have a negative impact on the brain

Newborns with physical abnormalities often need laboratory tests to determine possible metabolic and genetic disorders. In some cases, magnetic resonance imaging (MRI) can be used to look at brain structure. An electroencephalogram (EEG) can be used to determine possible seizure activity (Sulkes, 2018).

As previously indicated, the DSM-5 is a manual that delineates the diagnostic criteria for various recognized disorders.

In the most recent edition of the DSM (DSM-5), two new diagnoses have been added to the ID category: global developmental delay (GDD) and unspecified intellectual disability (UID). GDD is a diagnostic category introduced in the DSM-5 for children *under age 5* who are suspected of having an intellectual disability but are not yet able to be assessed, often due to being too young. This category refers to children who take longer to reach their developmental milestones than their typically developing peers. It should be noted that GDD is considered a temporary diagnosis and should only be used until a child receives a proper diagnosis. Ultimately, however, many children with a GDD diagnosis will go on to receive the diagnosis of intellectual disability. Diagnosis of a GDD is determined by the use of various tests, including genetic, molecular, and metabolic tests. Chromosome testing can also be used to determine genetic defects that contribute to a developmental delay. Testing for lead exposure and thyroid hormone levels also provides key information about the child's development (Okoye, 2018). UID is another new diagnostic category introduced in the DSM-5 that includes children *over age 5* who cannot be assessed due to specific impairments, such as a sensory dysfunction or significant behavior problems, that make the assessment process difficult. This is also considered a temporary diagnosis and should only be used until a child receives a proper diagnosis.

There are several syndromes associated with IDs. As a special education teacher, you will find it helpful to be aware of such syndromes and their common characteristics. The more common syndromes seen in schools today include fragile X syndrome, Down syndrome, Prader-Willi syndrome, Williams syndrome, and Angelman syndrome.

Fragile X syndrome (FXS) is currently the most common known cause of an inherited intellectual disability. This disorder in caused by a mutation in the X chromosome. Those born with fragile X syndrome experience a range of difficulties, including physical, behavioral, developmental, and emotional problems. More boys than girls are affected by fragile X syndrome. Some common characteristics of FXS include (National Fragile X Foundation, 2018):

Physical—large ears, long face, soft skin, large testicles (post-pubertal males)

Behavioral—social anxiety, hand-flapping, poor eye contact, sensory disorders, aggression

Cognitive—males typically demonstrate significant IDs; only about one third of females have a significant ID; mild or moderate learning disabilities

Other—friendly, excellent imitation skills, strong visual memory, good sense of humor

Down syndrome (DS) is the most common chromosomal condition. It is a genetic disorder that occurs when an individual has a partial or full extra copy of chromosome 21. DS is a lifelong condition resulting in intellectual and other developmental disabilities. DS varies in severity from mild to severe. The following are common physical characteristics associated with DS:

- Flattened face
- Small head
- Short neck

- Protruding tongue

- Upward slanting eye lids (palpebral fissures)

- Unusually shaped or small ears

- Poor muscle tone

- Broad, short hands with a single crease in the palm

- Relatively short fingers and small hands and feet

- Excessive flexibility

- Tiny white spots on the colored part (iris) of the eye, called Brushfield's spots

- Short height

(Mayo Clinic, 1998–2018, para. 5)

Prader-Willi syndrome (PWS) is a genetic disorder causing intellectual disabilities, caused by several types of mutation on chromosome 15. It is characterized by hypotonia, feeding problems, poor growth, and delayed development. A primary characteristic of PWS is an insatiable appetite, which can lead to diabetes (type 2) as well as obesity (NIH, 2018a).

Williams syndrome (WS) is a developmental disorder that results in a mild to moderate intellectual disability. It is caused by the deletion of genetic material from a specific region of chromosome 7 (NIH, 2018b). It is characterized by a small, upturned nose; long philtrum (upper lip length); wide mouth; full lips; small chin; and puffiness around the eyes (Williams Syndrome Association, 2018). Health problems such as cardiovascular disease, joint problems, and soft, loose skin are associated with WS.

Angelman syndrome (AS) is a neuro-genetic disorder resulting in developmental delays, seizures, lack of speech, and a friendly or excitable personality. Typically, AS is caused by problems with a gene located on chromosome 15.

Check Your Understanding 7.3

1. If you were a parent of a child suspected of having a global developmental delay (GDD), what would be your greatest concern? Why?

2. Discuss the similarities and differences between fragile X syndrome and Williams syndrome.

3. How might a child with Prader-Willi syndrome's insatiable appetite affect his family's ability to store their food at home and maintain regular family dining experiences?

Academics/Areas of Achievement

Generally speaking, students with intellectual disabilities do not perform on grade level in academic subjects as their typical peers do. This is true for even those diagnosed with a mild form of intellectual disability. One way that students with IDs reach their potential is through the implementation of quality intervention beginning as early as symptoms are present (often in the form of early intervention). The timeliness of this intervention will help ensure the greatest developmental gains, as under most circumstances the sooner a child with a suspected disability receives intervention, the better gains he will make. It is relevant to note, however, that even with high-quality programs and instruction, individuals with IDs will not attain normal intelligence or keep up with the academic progress of their typical peers.

Students with IDs can and often do develop basic literacy and functional math skills (Rosenberg, Westley, & Mc Leskey, 2013). **Functional academics** are an area that many educators focus on when educating this student population, particularly for those who are more significantly impacted by their IDs. Functional academics are academics that teach real-life skills to students. Examples of functional academics include how to count; keep a budget; use money wisely; maintain safety awareness in the community; obtain domestic skills, such as food preparation and cleaning; and how to purchase food at the grocery. Students who are more mildly affected by IDs will often participate in inclusive classrooms, learning the same curriculum as their typical peers, with appropriate special education services and support. They do tend to have some challenges in this setting, however. A common learning problem for students with IDs in inclusive educational settings is when the content of an academic subject becomes increasingly more difficult and requires the use of advanced skills, which they are often lacking.

One area of achievement that is particularly challenging for students with IDs is the development of oral language. Language delays possessed by students with IDs can significantly impact their reading ability, because this skill is needed across the curriculum. For example, a student must demonstrate oral language skills in his ELA class, his science class, and his social studies class in order to participate. Even if a child with an ID is able to read simple words, his ability to successfully comprehend what he is reading is often challenged. This is a primary reason why appropriate special education services and supports must be made available to all students with IDs when they are being educated in an inclusive placement.

Behavior

In addition to academic concerns, many children with IDs experience behavioral challenges. Such challenges can lead to difficulties in everyday life, making it hard to successfully perform daily tasks. The following are behavioral challenges associated with intellectual disabilities:

- *Sleep disorders.* The most common problems are night-walking, night-settling, and early waking. The prevalence rate of sleep disorders may be as high as 80% for those with IDs. Sleep disorders can lead to other issues, such as decreased alertness, mood changes, and cognitive changes.

- *Agitation.* This includes a wide range of behaviors where the child is restless and hyperactive. Examples are restlessness, fidgeting, pacing, racing thoughts, and fast talking. Agitation can trigger behavioral challenges, such as disruptive, uncooperative, and belligerent behavior. Individuals with IDs are more likely to have attention-deficit/hyperactivity disorder (ADHD).

- *Aggression.* This may include aggression toward others, aggression toward oneself, and destructive/disruptive behaviors. Examples are biting, kicking, hitting, breaking objects, and screaming. Common triggers of aggression in children with IDs are pain and an inability to comprehend something.

- *Self-injury (SIB).* This consists of repetitive and stereotypic behaviors with no intended function. Injury from such behaviors can occur to the head, neck, and hands and can cause potential harm, such as scars or damage to the eyes.

(Ageranioti-Bélanger et al., 2012)

It is paramount that we, as special educators, be able to accurately assess the behavioral needs of this disability population in order to best serve them. One way to determine an individual's behavioral needs is through completing a behavior rating scale. **Behavior rating scales (BRS)** are assessment tools that can provide valuable information. BRSs are quantitative tools that allow the observer to rank student behavior with respect to frequency, latency, duration, or other dimension. For example, you might have a student with an ID who frequently has tantrums. A BRS can be used to determine how frequently or for how long the student engages in this behavior. This type of information will be needed in order to select an appropriate intervention to reduce or eliminate this behavior of concern. Rating scales can be completed by a wide variety of individuals, such as parents, teachers, and therapists, and allow those who know the child well to better evaluate the student's problematic behavior. Once the significant behavior(s) of concern are identified, the IEP team can conduct a functional behavior assessment (FBA) to determine the function or purpose of the child's inappropriate behavior. Once the function(s) is determined, the IEP team can then generate a Positive Behavior Support Plan (PBSP) to help reduce or eliminate the problem behaviors (FBA and PBSP will be addressed in detail in Chapter 9). Here are some examples of behavior rating scales used to evaluate individuals with IDs:

- The Achenbach System of Empirically Based Assessment (ASEBA)
- The Behavior Assessment System for Children (BASC)

- The Conners 3rd Edition (Conners 3)

- The Conners Comprehensive Behavior Rating Scale (Conners CBRS)

- The Emotional Disturbance Decision Tree (EDDT)

Social/Emotional Characteristics

Students with IDs demonstrate deficits in social/emotional development. These deficits are, many times, due to their cognitive deficits.

It should be noted that although a child with an ID will not reach these milestones at the same rate as his typical peers, it is possible that he might reach some of them at a slower rate, depending on the severity of his disability.

Socially speaking, students with IDs often require direct instruction in social skills in order to make gains in this developmental area. Social-skill deficits can become more apparent during adolescence (Radley, Dart, Moore, Battaglia, & LaBrot, 2016). These deficits are often reflected in one or more of the following areas in individuals with IDs: the level of a child's social-interaction skills, the development and stability of peer relationships and friendships, and a child's ability to process social information. Children who fall in the mild to moderate range of ID receive more extensive social-skills training, such as conflict resolution and cooperative play (Sukhodolsky & Butter, 2007, p. 602). For those falling in the severe and profound ID range, social-skills training usually involves asking for help and making eye contact.

Children with IDs exhibit particular social-emotional difficulties. Some children will realize that they are not performing at the same level as their typical peers. Because of this, they may become anxious, withdrawn, or frustrated. Some children with IDs are also the subjects of bullying, both in the community and in school. This can lead to an increased risk of depression and even suicide (American Academy

Table 7.6 Age and Social/Emotional Milestones of Typically Developing Children

Age	Social/Emotional Milestone
2 months	Begins to smile at people
4 months	Smiles spontaneously, especially at people
6 months	Likes to play with others, especially parents
9 months	May be afraid of strangers
1 year	Cries when Mom or Dad leaves
18 months	Likes to hand things to others in play
2 years	Gets excited when with other children

Adapted from Centers for Disease Control and Prevention. (2017). *Developmental milestones.* Retrieved from https://www.cdc.gov/ncbddd/actearly/milestones/index.html

of Child and Adolescent Psychiatry, 2018). Students with IDs are also at risk of developing problem behaviors—such as aggression, self-injuring, disruptive, and self-stimulatory behaviors. These behaviors can serve many functions, such as to gain attention, to allow escape, and to secure tangible reinforcement (ASHA, n.d.).

Health and Medical Status

Another area that warrants discussion are medical concerns surrounding intellectual disabilities. It has been reported that individuals with intellectual disabilities have more health problems than the general population. This is compounded by the fact that this disability population can have difficulties expressing health issues they are experiencing, which means those problems sometimes go undiagnosed and untreated (May & Kennedy, 2010). Table 7.7 lists health problems associated with individuals with IDs.

Table 7.7 Health Problems Associated With Intellectual Disabilities

- Sensory problems – vision problems are common among individuals with IDs. Hearing impairments can affect as many as 25% of the ID population who are aged 50 and over. Oral health can also be problematic.

- Nutrition – individuals with IDs have less nutritional diets compared to typical peers. Those with severe and profound IDs are found to have higher rates of under-nutrition.

- Obesity – poor nutrition and lack of physical activity significantly impact the ID population. Obesity can lead to further health problems.

- Type 1 and type 2 diabetes – individuals with IDs are 3 to 4 times as likely to be diagnosed with diabetes. Type 1 is more commonly found in those with Down syndrome. Type 2 is often seen in younger individuals who lack an active lifestyle and have poor diets.

- Epilepsy – up to 44% of individuals with IDs can experience epilepsy.

- Cardiovascular disease – individuals with IDs are more prone to high blood pressure and coronary heart disease.

- Respiratory disease – individuals with IDs under 40 are more than twice as likely as the general population to die from respiratory disease (largely due to pneumonia).

- Sexual health – individuals with IDs have historically received opposition to sexuality and how to express their sexuality in a healthy and safe manner.

- Mental health – there is a significantly higher prevalence of mental health disorders for those with IDs. These can include affective disorders and anxiety disorders.

- Addictions – those with IDs have reported addictions to smoking, alcohol, and illicit drugs and/or prescribed medication.

Davis, R., Proulx, R., & van Schrojenstein Lantman–de Valk, H. (2013). Health issues for people with intellectual disabilities: The evidence base. In L. Taggart & W. Cousins (Eds.), *Health promotion for people with intellectual and developmental disabilities* (pp. 7–16). London, England: Open University Press. Retrieved from https://www.mheducation.co.uk/openup/chapters/9780335246946.pdf

Other reported medical problems for individuals with ID include motor deficits, allergies, otitis media, gastroesophageal reflux disease (GERD), dysmenorrhea, sleep disturbances, and constipation (May & Kennedy, 2010).

In some instances, a child with an ID might have another disability present in addition to his ID. This is referred to as comorbidity. Several comorbidities can occur with intellectual disabilities, such as bipolar disorder, autism spectrum disorder (ASD), stereotypic movement disorder, impulse-control disorders, major neurocognitive disorder, attention-deficit/hyperactivity disorder (ADHD), depressive disorders, anxiety disorders, aggression, and self-injury (Millcreek of Magee Treatment Center, 2018, para. 17).

Benefits Available to Those With IDs

As with any disability, diagnosis is a critical step in receiving proper treatment. Without a formal diagnosis, it is almost impossible to access resources that will benefit the individual with a disability. Each of the following benefits addresses a specific need that individuals with ID possess.

Special Education Services

As mentioned earlier, in order for a student to receive special education services under IDEA, he must be diagnosed with one of the 14 recognized disabilities, it must adversely affect his educational performance, and he must be viewed in need of specially designed instruction. In order for this child to learn and develop to his potential, special education services are warranted. Having special education services allows the student to obtain proper education placement, curricula, and teaching methodologies. It also allows for related services—such as transportation, speech-language therapy, and physical therapy, to name a few.

Home and Community-Based Waiver Services

Individuals with IDs might be eligible for certain home and community-based waiver services. These services provide opportunities for Medicaid beneficiaries to receive services in their own home or community rather than in institutions or other isolated settings. This can vary from state to state. For example, Pennsylvania offers individuals with ID a community-living waiver that includes services such as therapies, behavioral support, and respite, to name a few.

Social Security Administration Benefits and Medicaid

SSI is supplemental security income administered by Social Security. Different populations, such as individuals who are disabled, blind, or over 65, can receive monthly monetary benefits once they turn 18 years of age. This benefit is often received by students with ID who are still in the educational system until they turn 21 years of age. Those who qualify for SSI are often eligible to receive Medicaid. This is a medical program that benefits low-income individuals.

Check Your Understanding 7.4

What are three examples of services an individual with an ID can receive that will support both his learning and his adult living?

The following case study depicts a young girl with an ID and her upbringing and early school experiences. It examines environmental factors surrounding IDs and the impact they have on Casey's starting school for the first time.

Case Study 7.1: Casey Goes to First Grade

Casey is a 6-year-old girl who is beginning first grade at Pennsbury Elementary School. She is a shy child who likes dolls, chasing butterflies in the neighborhood park, and listening to music on her radio. Life has always been challenging for Casey and her family. To begin, Casey was born prematurely at 29 weeks gestation, and although she was able to come home from the hospital a few weeks after birth, her mother, Wilma, was unable to give her the attention and stimulation she needed as an infant. This has contributed to some of the developmental problems that Casey is experiencing.

Casey's family lives in a small urban apartment. Wilma is a single parent who works two jobs that take her away from her home and her children for the majority of the day. She leaves the house early in the morning, so a family friend has to get her school-age children on the bus and also babysit Casey and her sisters until Wilma gets home. During the day, Wilma works as a cashier at a local grocery store

until dinnertime and then catches the bus across town to her other job as a nurse's aide at a retirement facility. Because of her intense work schedule, Wilma has also had to rely on her older children to complete many of the household chores, such as preparing meals, doing the laundry, and bathing. Wilma has never been able to help her children with homework and has spent little time reading to them. She loves her children but has largely been absent from their daily lives due to her demanding work schedule and efforts to support the family. One example of Wilma's limited parenting was Casey's lack of stimulation as an infant. Casey spent a great deal of time lying in her crib, with only the sounds of her siblings playing to entertain her, because Wilma did not have the time to spend interacting with or nurturing her.

Although Wilma did not have much time to spend with her children, she did notice that Casey was learning to walk and talk later than her siblings. She reasoned that Casey would be okay and

(Continued)

eventually catch up to them. Casey never played with children other than her siblings, so no one ever commented to Wilma that Casey did not possess the same skills as other 6-year-old children. In addition, Casey only saw a pediatrician in emergency situations, due to a lack of health insurance, so her development was not regularly followed by a medical doctor.

In September, Casey went to school for the first time. The first day of school, Casey's neighbor put her on the school bus. It was exciting for Casey but a little scary too. She had not attended preschool like most of the other students in her class. In fact, in the state where Casey lives, students are not required to attend kindergarten, so her mother decided to wait until first grade to enroll her, thinking that this would give her extra time to catch up to the other students in her class. When Casey walked through the classroom doors, she was captivated by all the children and the colorful classroom decorations. There was even a guinea pig as the classroom pet! She was glad to be at school but knew very little about how to act or what she would be taught. Casey had no knowledge of appropriate classroom behavior. She did not know how to raise her hand to be called on, stay seated in her desk chair, or line up for lunch with her classmates. In fact, she did not have the prosocial behaviors that typical first-graders demonstrate, such as sharing, helping, and turn-taking with her peers. At recess time, many of the young girls would play together outside on the swings or jungle gym, but Casey did not know how to join the group and often played alone. This was hard for her, because she wanted to fit in and be part of the class.

Casey also significantly lagged behind her classmates with respect to academics. Because of their previous schooling, most of the students in her class were able to identify their letters and had letter-sound correspondence. Many of them were reading sight words and could write their names and some of their numbers. Casey did not have any of these skills. She had hardly ever colored, and she had never even used a pair of scissors. Her fine motor skills were significantly underdeveloped for a child her age. Not having these skills coming into first grade made participating in activities and discussions very difficult for Casey.

Mrs. Sheeran, Casey's teacher, noticed her difficulties right away. She carefully watched Casey the first week of school, making notes of all her academic, behavioral, and social weaknesses. Mrs. Sheeran then contacted Wilma and discussed her concerns. They spoke for over an hour about the problems that Casey was having at school. Mrs. Sheeran also contacted the school's pre-referral team to discuss the case and obtain suggestions about how to best work with Casey. After the meeting, Mrs. Sheeran worked diligently with Casey for several weeks using evidence-based practices the team had suggested that should have helped Casey make the necessary progress, but Casey continued to struggle. By the end of the second marking period, Mrs. Sheeran referred Casey for a comprehensive evaluation to determine whether she needed special education services.

After reviewing Casey's skill deficits and behaviors, and taking into consideration the time that Mrs. Sheeran had spent working with Casey on a one-on-one basis, the pre-referral team concluded that a comprehensive diagnostic evaluation was needed to determine the reason for Casey' s school challenges. The IEP team was composed of Mrs. Sheeran, a special education teacher, the school psychologist, an LEA representative, a speech-language pathologist, an occupational therapist, and an assistant principal.

Over the next two weeks, the IEP team conducted interviews with Casey's mother and aunt to gather more information about Casey. She was also observed in several settings, such as the classroom, the playground, and the lunchroom, by a speech-language pathologist and an occupational therapist. Wilma and Mrs. Sheeran both completed the Vineland-3, an adaptive rating measure. This gave a clear picture of how Casey was performing everyday skills. The school psychologist administered the WPPSI-IV to test Casey's intellectual functioning. Casey also had a complete physical exam.

Finally, the results of the comprehensive evaluation were complete, and Wilma and the IEP team met to discuss the findings and what would happen next for Casey. The results of the WPPSI-IV indicated that Casey had a full-scale IQ of 55. It reported that she had relative strengths in the area of Visual Spatial: block design and weaknesses in both Working Memory and Processing Speed. Her adaptive behavior composite on the Vineland-3 was 65. Casey's areas of relative strength were in Daily Living Skills: Personal as well as Socialization: Play and Leisure Time. Casey demonstrated significant weaknesses in both her gross and fine motor skills as determined by this measure. The IEP team also discussed the results of the various interviews and observations that had been conducted to support the IQ and adaptive behavior tests. Casey was diagnosed with a mild intellectual disability. Although Wilma was distraught when she heard the news, she was glad that the school was willing to help her. As the IEP team made suggestions about how to approach Casey's education, Wilma remembered that two of Casey's cousins also had intellectual disabilities but the family had never really discussed it.

Check Your Understanding 7.5

1. What signs of an intellectual disability does Casey demonstrate?

2. Do you think Casey not attending preschool and kindergarten contributed to her being behind her peers in first grade? Why or why not?

3. What environmental conditions might have contributed to Casey's ID?

4. Explain the steps Mrs. Sheeran took to help Casey when she realized that she was having problems in first grade.

5. What test of intellectual ability was performed? Adaptive behavior?

6. What were Casey's strengths as evidenced by the WPPSI-IV? The Vineland-3?

7. What were Casey's weaknesses as evidenced by the WIPPSI-IV? The Vineland-3?

Extension to Instruction

Having a solid understanding of how ID is diagnosed, as well as the various disabilities that comprise this disability category, allows special educators the ability to begin thinking about ways they can best teach students with IDs. This begins with early intervention services for young children with ID, all the way through the transition process that occurs after a student has completed his secondary program, when he might be looking for educational opportunities as an adult with a disability.

Evaluating Infants and Young Children

Evaluating a child's development begins before he is even born. When mothers are pregnant, obstetricians monitor the mother and the developing baby's health. Questions such as "Is the baby making sufficient growth?" "Is the mother's due date correct?" "Are there any signs of abnormalities?" are considered, to determine their health status. Evaluation also occurs at the time of birth. Medical professionals will complete assessments on the infant—such as Apgar scoring, birth weight, and head circumference, to name a few. As an infant continues to get older, pediatricians will track a child's development at his well-child visits to be sure that he is developing according to his developmental milestones. Such milestones give medical professionals an idea of whether a child is making expected growth and alert them to any problems in particular developmental domains. Developmental domains that are commonly assessed are social/emotional, language/communication, cognitive, and movement/physical development. Developmental milestones are indicated by a child's age, as in Table 7.8's example of a typically developing 2-month-old.

Table 7.8 indicates the behaviors that a typical 2-month-old infant would be expected to demonstrate. When a child does not meet one or more of his developmental milestones, this can raise concerns about his development, especially if a cause for the lag is unknown. The possible cause(s) of a developmental delay and whether it indicates the possible presence of a disability should be considered. For example, a child might not have reached a developmental milestone in the language/communication domain. If a child does not say his first word by the time he is 3 years old, this would raise concern. When trying to determine the cause of this language delay, the pediatrician might ask the parent whether the child had experienced any ear infections in his first year of life that could have caused a fluctuating hearing loss and impacted the child's ability to develop expressive speech. He might also question whether the child is living in a stimulating environment where he frequently hears spoken language and has appropriate social interaction.

Whatever the circumstances, if a child is not meeting his developmental milestones, early intervention might be warranted. In the case of a child with an ID, developmental milestones are commonly not met on time. To illustrate, a child with an ID will often not begin to sit, crawl, talk, or walk at the same time as his typically developing peers.

The following are examples of screening instruments and child assessment instruments that help determine whether early intervention is needed. Remember, screening instruments are used with large groups of children to help identify children who are experiencing problems and need a more in-depth evaluation. Child assessment instruments, on the other hand, determine what a child can do in relation to typical developmental expectations.

Table 7.8 Typical Development of a 2-Month-Old

Social/Emotional

- Begins to smile at people
- Can briefly calm himself (may bring hands to mouth and suck on hand)
- Tries to look at parent

Language/Communication

- Coos, makes gurgling sounds
- Turns head toward sounds

Cognitive (learning, thinking, problem solving)

- Pays attention to faces
- Begins to follow things with eyes and recognize people at a distance
- Begins to act bored (cries, fussy) if activity doesn't change

Movement/Physical Development

- Can hold head up and begins to push up when lying on tummy
- Makes smoother movements with arms and legs

Centers for Disease Control and Prevention. (2017). *Developmental milestones*. Retrieved from https://www.cdc.gov/ncbddd/actearly/milestones/index.html

Screening Instruments

- The Ages & Stages Questionnaire
- The Developmental Activities Screening Inventory

Child Assessment Instruments

- The Assessment, Evaluation, and Programming System for Infants and Children (AEPS)
- The Bayley Scales for Infant Development
- The Brigance Inventory of Early Development
- The Creative Curriculum Developmental Continuum for Infants and Toddlers
- The Early Learning Accomplishment Profile (Early-LAP/ELAP)
- The Infant Toddler Development Assessment (IDA)

- The Ounce Scale

- The Transdisciplinary Play-Based Assessment (TPBA)

(Florida Partnership for School Readiness, 2004)

The Importance of Early Intervention

The Infants and Toddlers With Disabilities Program (Part C of IDEA) was enacted to provide a means by which children ages birth to 3 receive appropriate services to enhance their development and reduce the chance of a developmental delay. **Early intervention (EI)** grew out of Part C of IDEA, providing programs and services to young children who were diagnosed with a developmental delay or a medical condition leading to a developmental delay. Conceptually, the idea of early intervention was to build interagency partnerships among state agencies that promote wellness in education, health, human services, and developmental disabilities.

As with most other disabilities, early intervention plays a critical role in the development and outcomes of individuals with IDs. This type of intervention is primarily geared toward helping young children gain the key skills that they are lacking. In addition to helping children succeed, early intervention provides valuable support to the parents, in the form of needed resources and support groups. Early intervention for IDs can begin as early as birth but should be implemented as soon as a child is identified for being at risk of a developmental delay. The benefits of early intervention are vast. They include improvement in health, language and communication development, and social/emotional development, all of which positively affect a child with an ID. Families of children with IDs also benefit from EI programs, as they are better able to support their child's special needs than if they wait until they are school-age to be served.

Inclusion

All children with disabilities who qualify for special education services, including those with IDs, must be placed in their least restrictive environment (LRE). When considering an appropriate placement for this student population, know that the general education classroom can serve as an appropriate and viable educational placement. This is particularly true if the child has a milder form of ID. With the use of child-specific special education supports and services, children with IDs can make adequate academic gains in a general education setting. In addition to the academic benefits of inclusion, children with IDs can benefit from the social experiences that can occur as a result of being educated with their typical peers. Being in a general education classroom allows students with IDs to see typical children model prosocial behaviors and interact with each other as well as with them.

One place where inclusion for students with IDs frequently occurs is at the preschool level, because preschool learning and activities tend to be more inclusive by nature. In addition, teachers are not concerned about state test scores with this age group. Following are some benefits of inclusion at the preschool level (Division for Early Childhood of the Council for Exceptional Children, 2007; Manual & Little, 2002):

- Children with and those without disabilities play together.
- Children with disabilities show higher rates of social interaction.
- Typically developing children have no negative consequences.
- Typically developing children have a greater appreciation and respect for individual differences.

Teaching Methodologies

Students with IDs benefit from specialized teaching methods. One commonly used method of teaching students with moderate to severe IDs adaptive skills is called a **task analysis**. A task analysis is a process by which everyday skills can be broken down into discrete steps and taught individually. For example, to teach people to wash their hands, one might use the steps (see Figure 7.2). It is important to note that each step in the process must be mastered before moving on to the next step.

Teaching a child with an ID how to wash his hands can take several days or even weeks, depending on the child's functional abilities. The use of visual aids to support task analyses is common. To illustrate, when teaching a student with an ID to wash his hands by using a task analysis, you might place above the sink a photo or a step-by-step illustration of someone washing his hands.

Figure 7.2   Task Analysis of Handwashing

1. turn on the water
2. put hands under the water
3. pump soap into palm of hand
4. rub hands back and forth
5. rinse hands
6. dry hands with towel

Teaching students with IDs in today's public schools is different than it was a few decades ago. As indicated above, students with IDs are now being included more frequently in the general education classroom. Inclusion of this student population requires the use of teaching methods that best support this type of learner. Class-wide peer tutoring, direct instruction, and use of various instructional techniques have been recognized as effective teaching methods. **Class-wide peer tutoring** occurs when students with IDs are paired with typical peers in the general education classroom. The typical peer will tutor, or act as a one-on-one helper, to the student with an ID when extra support is needed. This can occur in a wide range of academic classes. When paired with their typical peers, students with IDs tend to perform better academically. When determining how you will pair students, it is important to consider not only the intelligence of the student with an ID, but also the social skills and appropriate behavior that he will need to demonstrate in order for the partners to be successful.

Direct instruction (DI) is a long-standing preferred teaching method for students with developmental disabilities. DI consists of specialized lessons that teach skills in small increments, by way of clearly defined and prescribed tasks. The idea behind DI is to provide very clear instruction that can not only improve learning but also accelerate the rate of learning. Research indicates that students with IDs benefit from instruction that is direct and broken down into small increments.

As suggested by Table 7.9, this method of teaching students is positively based. When teachers are systematic in their teaching, this method of instruction can be successful for a variety of learners. In order to close the learning gap as efficiently as possible, students must be taught at a relatively accelerated rate. The precise nature of DI and the benefit of teacher-directed instruction are important when working with this student population.

Keeping in mind the key principles of DI, following are some suggested practices when teaching individuals with IDs:

1. *Teach one concept or activity component at a time.* Keep language and instruction as simple and direct as possible. For example, when teaching students how to use various kitchen tools, teach each tool independently, and check for mastery before moving on.

2. *Teach one step at a time, to help support memorization and sequencing.* Do not combine steps when teaching a concept, as this can lead to confusion and inability to retain important information.

3. *Teach students in small groups, or one-on-one, if possible.* Teaching students in smaller groups allows more time to problem solve and for students to ask questions and demonstrate their learning progress.

4. *Always provide multiple opportunities to practice skills, in a number of settings.* Students with developmental disabilities tend to have problems

Table 7.9 The Five Key Principles of DI
1. All children can learn.
2. All children can improve academically and in terms of self-image.
3. All teachers can succeed, if provided with adequate training and materials.
4. Low performers and disadvantaged learners must be taught at a faster rate than typically appears, if they are to catch up to their higher-performing peers.
5. All details of instruction must be controlled, to minimize the chance of students misinterpreting the information being taught and to maximize the reinforcing effect of instructions.

National Institute for Direct Instruction. (2015). *Basic philosophy of direct instruction*. Retrieved from https://www.nifdi.org/what-is-di/basic-philosophy

generalizing information. Generalization occurs when a student is able to demonstrate learned skills in various settings. The more opportunities a student with an ID has to practice a skill in several environments, the better he will become at using that skill.

5. *Use physical and verbal prompting to guide correct responses, and provide specific verbal praise to reinforce these responses.* Prompting has proven to be an effective method of instructing students with developmental disabilities. Prompting is a cue or instruction to encourage student to perform a specific behavior. Using positive reinforcement when a student has performed a desired activity, by way of either a primary or secondary reinforcer, has also proven to be a successful way to teach students with ID. Positive reinforcement might take the form of a special treat, extra play time, or high-fives.

(Project Ideal, 2013)

Postsecondary Transitions

Planning for what happens after a child with an ID turns 21 years of age is critical to his postsecondary school success. Educational services that supported a child with an ID that were once considered an entitlement when he was in school, become eligibility-based after his twenty-first year when he is no longer a student. This means that a child must prove that he meets eligibility requirements as mandated by a particular governing body, as opposed to automatically receiving them or being entitled to them through the school system. Secondary transition is required by IDEA to take place by the age of 16; however, many states begin transition services at the age of 14. "Age appropriate assessment is the all-important initial and ongoing component of transition planning" (Heward, 2017, p. 501). Areas that are included in transition planning are employment, postsecondary education/training, and independent/interdependent living (Freedman, Eisenman, Cowin, & Roy, 2018; Heward, 2017). "A combination of formal and informal assessment methods are used to determine the student's strengths, needs, preferences, and interests in current and future work, education, domestic, and social environments" (Heward, 2017, p. 501). Assessments that measure vocational and technical skills are often beneficial when planning for life after school.

Transition Assessments

The need to assess students with disabilities often continues into their adulthood. It is critical during the transition process (once a child turns 14 years of age) that professionals involved with transition planning have an accurate idea of the individual with an ID's skill set. For example, they must assess his adaptive behavior skills in a variety of contexts. In doing so, they will be better able to plan for the individual's future (e.g., home, work, and community involvement) once he graduates or completes his secondary education at age 21.

Since the 1980s, there has been a movement to assess the transition needs of students with disabilities. According to Clark (2005), transition assessments are defined as "a process of obtaining, organizing and using information to assist all individuals with disabilities of all ages and their families in making all critical transitions in those individuals' lives both successful and satisfying" (p. 9). The results of such assessments help in developing a plan for how the individual with an ID will proceed with adult living once he completes his K–12 education. In essence, they can help determine the amount of support that he will need when considering adult housing, whether he is a candidate for competitive employment, and whether he is able to care for his personal finances.

As such, there are various components of adult living that should be assessed for individuals with IDs. These include the following assessment domains:

- Functional academics

- Leisure and social skills

- Adaptive behavior

- Sensory needs

- Communication

- Physical mobility

- Medical and health

- Support skills/self-determination

- Special skills and interests

The different domains can be assessed through the use of standardized assessments, formal assessments, informal assessments, and person-centered planning. The following are examples of transition assessments that are currently used:

- The Transition Planning Inventory–Modified

- The Transition Behavior Scale

- The Enderle-Severson Transition Rating Scales

As stated, knowing a child with an ID's present levels of performance with respect to the transition domains helps the team best plan for his future. In addition, IDEA makes it clear that transition planning as a result of such assessments requires a collaborative process between school and home and should be outcome-oriented. This means that not only will several individuals—such as the student himself, his family, school personnel, and community services—be involved in this process, but also specific goals must be outlined for the student.

College Programs for Students With Intellectual Disabilities

Over the past decade or so, a relatively new concept of educating students with IDs at colleges and universities has emerged. The Higher Education Opportunity Act of 2008 (P.L. 110-315) has launched creative programs for students with disabilities, providing them opportunities to learn academic, career, and independent-living skills on college and university campuses (PACER, n.d.). Students select academic areas of interest and typically audit college courses—with the option of living on campus, for an inclusive college experience. Early research indicates that such programs are enabling individuals with IDs to develop necessary skills for more independent living.

Check Your Understanding 7.6

1. Why is it important that a child diagnosed with an ID receive early intervention?

2. Discuss the five key principles of direct instruction.

3. What is the purpose of transition assessments?

4. What are some possible postsecondary options for young adults diagnosed with IDs?

CHAPTER SUMMARY

In this chapter, we took a broad look at IDs and their diagnostic process. We reviewed the causes and various types of IDs: Down syndrome, fragile X syndrome, Williams syndrome, and others, and we highlighted new additions to this DSM-5 diagnosis. We discussed the diagnostic process and popular assessment tools that are used to make an ID diagnosis. We also looked at other issues relevant to school-age children with IDs, such as how this disability affects their ability to learn and be successful in school. Medical problems associated with IDs and transition to adulthood were highlighted, as was the importance of early intervention for children with IDs.

APPLY WHAT YOU HAVE LEARNED

1. Contact a school psychologist or a clinical psychologist who diagnoses children with IDs for an interview. Create a list of interview questions that reflect how a diagnosis is made and how this professional presents the assessment findings to the family of those being assessed.

2. Write an informational essay about how the results of the various assessments used for

diagnosis of IDs help inform teachers how to best serve this student population. Be specific and provide examples.

3. Select two of the syndromes associated with IDs (e.g., Down syndrome, Prader-Willi syndrome, fragile X syndrome). Create a fact sheet about these syndromes that includes the following information: definition of the

syndrome, cause, etiology, and effective teaching methods.

4. Visit an early intervention classroom for students with IDs in your school district or local area. Consider the instructional techniques for students with IDs that were discussed in this chapter, and explain how they are being implemented in this classroom. Write a two-page essay that discusses your observations.

REFERENCES

Ageranioti-Bélanger, S., Brunet, S., D'Anjou, G., Tellier, G., Boivin, J., & Gauthier, M. (2012). Behaviour disorders in children with an intellectual disability. *Paediatrics & Child Health, 17*(2): 84–88. doi: 10.1093/pch/17.2.84. Retrieved from https://www.ncbi.nlm.nih.gov/pmc/articles/PMC3299352

American Association on Intellectual and Developmental Disabilities. (2018a). *Definition of intellectual disability*. Retrieved from https://aaidd.org/intellectual-disability/definition

American Association on Intellectual and Developmental Disabilities. (2018b). *Frequently asked questions on intellectual disabilities*. Retrieved from https://aaidd.org/intellectual-disability/definition/faqs-on-intellectual-disability

American Academy of Child and Adolescent Psychiatry. (2018). *Intellectual disabilities*. Retrieved from https://www.aacap.org/AACAP/Families_and_Youth/Facts_for_Families/FFF-Guide/Children-with-an-Intellectual-Disability-023.aspx

American Psychiatric Association. (2013). *Diagnostic and statistical manual of mental disorders* (5th ed.). Arlington, VA: American Psychiatric Publishing.

American Speech-Language-Hearing Association (ASHA). (n.d.). *Intellectual disabilities*. Retrieved from https://www.asha.org/PRPSpecificTopic.aspx?folderid=8589942540&section=Assessment

Bergeron, R., & Floyd, R. (2006). Broad cognitive abilities of children with mental retardation: An analysis of group and individual profiles. *American Journal of Mental Retardation, 111*, 417–432.

Centers for Disease Control and Prevention. (2017). *Developmental milestones*. Retrieved from https://www.cdc.gov/ncbddd/actearly/milestones/index.html

Clark, G. (2005). *Quickbook of transition assessments*. Retrieved from https://www.ocali.org/up_doc/Quickbook_of_Transition_Assessment.pdf

Davis, R., Proulx, R., & van Schrojenstein Lantman–de Valk, H. (2013). Health issues for people with intellectual disabilities: The evidence base. In L. Taggart & W. Cousins (Eds.), *Health promotion for people with intellectual and developmental disabilities* (pp. 7–16). London, England: Open University Press. Retrieved from https://www.mheducation.co.uk/openup/chapters/9780335246946.pdf

Division for Early Childhood of the Council for Exceptional Children. (2007). *Promoting positive outcomes for children with disabilities. Recommendation for curriculum, assessment, and program evaluation*. Missoula, MT: Author.

Evely, M., & Ganim, Z. (2018). *Intellectual disability*. Retrieved from https://www.psych4schools.com.au/free-resources/intellectual-disability

Florida Partnership for School Readiness. (2004). *Birth to three screening and assessment resource guide.* Jacksonville, FL: University of North Florida.

Freedman, B., Eisenman, L, Cowin, C., & Roy, S. (2018). Postschool. In V. McGinley & M. Alexander (Eds.), *Parents and families of students with special needs: Collaborating across the age span* (pp. 246–275). Thousand Oaks, CA: SAGE.

Heward, W. (with Alber-Morgan, S., & Konrad, M.). (2017). *Exceptional children: An introduction to special education* (11th ed.). Boston, MA: Pearson Education.

IDEA Partnership. (n.d.). *Definitions of disability terms: Part B (ages 6 through 21).* Retrieved from http://www.ideapartnership.org/topics-database/idea-2004/idea-2004-part-b/1397-definitions-of-disability-terms.html

Individuals With Disabilities Education Act, 20 U.S.C. § 1400 (2018). *Intellectual disabilities.* Retrieved from https://sites.ed.gov/idea

May, M., & Kennedy, C. (2010). Health and problem behavior among people with intellectual disabilities. *Behavior Analysis in Practice, 3*(2), 4–12. Retrieved from https://www.ncbi.nlm.nih.gov/pmc/articles/PMC3004690

Manual, J., & Little, I. (2002). A model of inclusion. *Early Developments, 6,* 14–18.

Mayo Clinic. (1998–2018). *Down syndrome.* Retrieved from https://www.mayoclinic.org/diseases-conditions/down-syndrome/symptoms-causes/syc-20355977

Millcreek of Magee Treatment Center. (2018). *Causes and effects of intellectual developmental disorder.* Retrieved from http://www.millcreekofmagee.com/disorders/intellectual-disability/signs-causes-symptoms

National Fragile X Foundation. (2018). *Fragile X syndrome.* Retrieved from https://fragilex.org/learn

National Institute for Direct Instruction. (2015). *Basic philosophy of direct instruction.* Retrieved from https://www.nifdi.org/what-is-di/basic-philosophy

NIH RePORT (2018). *Intellectual and developmental disabilities.* Retrieved from https://report.nih.gov/nihfactsheets/ViewFactSheet.aspx?csid=100

National Institutes of Health. (2018a). *Prader-Willi syndrome.* Retrieved from https://ghr.nlm.nih.gov/condition/prader-willi-syndrome

National Institutes of Health. (2018b). *Williams syndrome.* Retrieved from https://ghr.nlm.nih.gov/condition/williams-syndrome#genes

Okoye, H. (2018). *Global developmental delay DSM-5 315.8 (F88).* Retrieved from https://www.theravive.com/therapedia/global-developmental-delay-dsm%C2%AD-5-315.8-(f88)

PACER. (n.d.). *Inclusive postsecondary education for students with intellectual disabilities.* Retrieved from https://www.pacer.org/transition/learning-center/postsecondary/college-options.asp

Project Ideal. (2013). *Intellectual disabilities.* Retrieved from http://www.projectidealonline.org/v/intellectual-disabilities

Radley, K., Dart, E., Moore, J., Battaglia, A., & LaBrot, Z. (2016). Promoting accurate variability of social skills in children with autism spectrum disorder. *Behavior Modification, 41*(1), 84–112.

Reynolds, T., & Zupanick, C. E., & Dombeck, M. (2013). *Diagnostic criteria for intellectual disabilities: DSM-5 criteria.* Gulf Bend MHMR Center. Retrieved from https://www.gulfbend.org/poc/view_doc.php?type=doc&id=10348&cn=5

Rosenberg, M. S., Westley, D. L., & Mc Leskey, J. (2013). *Primary characteristics of students with intellectual disabilities.* Retrieved from https://www.education.com/reference/article/characteristics-intellectual-disabilities

Sulkes, S. B. (2018). Intellectual disability. *Merck manual, consumer version.* Retrieved from https://

www.merckmanuals.com/home/children-s-health-issues/learning-and-developmental-disorders/intellectual-disability

Sukhodolsky, D. G., & Butter, E. M. (2007). Social skills training for children with intellectual disabilities. In J. W. Jacobson, J. A. Mulick, & J. Rojahn (Eds.), *Handbook of intellectual and developmental disabilities* (pp. 601–602). Issues on Clinical Child Psychology. Boston, MA: Springer.

Torreno, S. (2012). *Special education students—what are adaptive skills?* Retrieved from https://www.brighthubeducation.com/special-ed-learning-disorders/73324-improving-adaptives-skills-in-students-with-intellectual-disabilities

Williams Syndrome Association. (2018). *What is Williams syndrome?* Retrieved from https://williams-syndrome.org/what-is-williams-syndrome

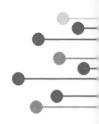

CHAPTER 8

Autism Spectrum Disorder (ASD)

Mary A. Houser, EdD

Learning Objectives

After completion of this chapter, you should be able to:

- Identify diagnostic criteria and related characteristics of ASD.

- Summarize the diagnostic process for ASD.

- Discuss other characteristics of ASDs: intelligence, academics, common learning characteristics, educational placements, severity levels, health and medical, and sensory assessments.

- Examine the impact of an ASD diagnosis on the family.

- Identify the various ways that an ASD diagnosis extends to instruction: early intervention, evidence-based practices, daily living/adaptive behavior domains, transition to postsecondary life, and social skills training.

Key Terms

Applied Behavior Analysis (ABA) (p. 254)	sensory processing difficulties (p. 249)
Asperger's syndrome (p. 236)	social cognition (p. 237)
augmentative and alternative communication (AAC) (p. 259)	social communication (p. 237)
autism spectrum disorder (ASD) (p. 236)	social reciprocity (p. 237)
autistic disorder (p. 236)	social skill deficits (p. 237)
early intervention (p. 254)	social skills training (p. 261)
nonverbal communication (p. 240)	Theory of Mind (p. 261)
pervasive developmental disorder not otherwise specified (PDD-NOS) (p. 236)	verbal communication (p. 240)
restricted and repetitive behaviors (RRBs) (p. 236)	

Introduction to the Chapter

Autism spectrum disorder (ASD) is a neurodevelopmental disorder character-ized by difficulties in communication, social challenges, and restricted and repet-itive behaviors (RRBs). In today's world, more and more children are coming to school with an ASD diagnosis. As of 2020, 1 in 59 students are being diagnosed with ASD, and both general education teachers and special education teachers are being called on to provide the best possible education for this student population. But what do we know about ASD? How are students diagnosed? What causes ASD? How do we educate our students with this disorder?

As special educators, we are particularly interested in what autistic behav-iors look like in the classroom. This can depend on the child and his severity of symptoms. A child with ASD may sit or play alone instead of joining in with his peers. He may make inappropriate sounds during class instruction or flap his hands when he gets excited. He may get frustrated and have a tantrum due to his language deficits and inability to express himself.

ASD is considered a spectrum disorder, which means that individuals with ASD can exhibit a wide range of symptoms and severity. To illustrate, there are individ-uals "on the spectrum" whose IQs range from average to superior, as well as those who have an intellectual disability. Nevertheless, both types of individuals will receive the same ASD diagnosis. Under the current DSM classification (DSM-5), ASD includes several conditions: autistic disorder, pervasive developmental disorder not otherwise specified (PDD-NOS), and Asperger's syndrome. This chapter provides an overview of this disorder, its diagnostic process, and how to proceed from an educational standpoint.

IDEA Definition of Autism

The following is the IDEA definition of autism:

> a developmental disability significantly affecting verbal and nonverbal com-munication and social interaction, generally evident before age three, that adversely affects a child's educational performance. (20 U.S.C. § 1400, 2004)

This definition will be used as the basis for the chapter's definition of autism.

Diagnostic Criteria and Related Characteristics

Historically, autism was not a common disorder. In fact, when the first prevalence studies were conducted in the United States and Europe in the 1960s and 1970s, roughly 2 to 4 individuals out of 10,000 were diagnosed with this disorder. Com-munication problems, social challenges, and RRBs are the three diagnostic criteria for ASD and are referred to as its core symptoms. Communication problems are a hallmark sign of those on the autism spectrum. Such problems take the form of expressive and/or receptive language delays, as well as problems with social communication. Some children with ASD will learn to speak in full sentences; some, in phrases and/or single words; others will remain nonverbal throughout their lifetimes. For higher-functioning individuals on the autism spectrum who develop language, they will continue to have difficulties with pragmatics, or the rules that govern the social use of language. Social skill deficits are another challenge that individuals with ASD experience. These are difficulties with social cognition and social reciprocity. Social skill deficits involve understanding what constitutes both social interactions and social relationships, as well as the turn-taking that occurs between people in a social situation. RRBs and interests are also considered diagnostic criteria for possessing ASD. These are behaviors children perform over and over again and that are not considered functional. Head banging, rocking, and hand-flapping are considered repetitive behaviors. Individuals with ASD also tend to have very limited interests. For example, a young child with ASD may like to play only certain games, watch only specific TV shows, or talk about only particular topics.

There are many different communicative, behavioral, and social characteristics associated with individuals with ASD. Each individual with ASD presents his own unique strengths and challenges, and no two individuals with ASD are exactly alike. Table 8.1 lists the various behaviors associated with ASD. It should be noted that not every individual with ASD will demonstrate all of these behaviors.

As stated, over the past several years there has been a significant increase in the number of individuals being diagnosed with ASD. What was once considered a low-incidence disability is now considered the fastest-growing developmental disability. More males than females are being diagnosed with this disorder. This surge in diagnosis is believed to be related to several factors: expanded diagnostic criteria, more awareness of the disorder, diagnosis at earlier ages, and the recognition that ASD is a lifelong condition (Matson & Kozlowski, 2011, p. 428). Because of the heightened prevalence of those being diagnosed with ASD, there has been a significant increase in the number of children with ASD receiving special education services in today's schools. More teachers are needed with specialized training in ASD to teach this student population. Additional related service personnel (e.g., speech-language pathologists, occupational therapists, physical therapists, and behavior specialists) are needed to address the particular speech-language, motor, behavioral, and everyday challenges related to being on the autism spectrum. This need for additional qualified school personnel has been difficult for many schools, at times, to meet.

Currently, genetics and environmental risk factors have been identified as the primary possible causes of ASD. The once-contemplated notion that the MMR immunization causes autism has been dispelled. Another myth from the 1950s that has been dismissed is that the mother of the child with autism was responsible for her child's condition because she behaved coldly and

Table 8.1   ASD Characteristics

- Not pointing at objects to show interest (for example, not pointing to an airplane flying over)

- Not looking at objects when another person points at those objects

- Trouble relating to others or not having an interest in other people at all

- Avoiding eye contact and wanting to be alone

- Difficulty understanding other people's feelings or difficulty talking about their own feelings

- Preferring not to be held or cuddled, or perhaps cuddling only when they want to

- Appearing to be unaware when people talk to them, but responding to other sounds

- High interest in people, but not knowing how to talk, play, or relate to them

- Repeating or echoing words or phrases said to them, or repeating words or phrases in place of normal language

- Difficulty expressing their needs using typical words or motions

- Not playing "pretend" games (for example, not pretending to "feed" a doll)

- Repeating actions over and over again

- Difficulty adapting when a routine changes

- Unusual reactions to the way things smell, taste, look, feel, or sound

- Losing skills they once had (for example, no longer saying words they used to)]

Centers for Disease Control and Prevention. (2018). *What is Autism Spectrum Disorder?* Retrieved from https://www.cdc.gov/ncbddd/autism/facts.html

indifferently toward him (i.e., "refrigerator mother"). So, what do we know to be true about the cause of ASD? First, ASD runs in families, and research has determined that changes in particular genes might increase the likelihood, but not be the cause, that a child will have autism. Such genes might be passed down from the parents to a child. Other genetic changes might develop spontaneously in the early prenatal stages of development (Autism Speaks, 2018). Research also suggests that environmental risk factors for ASD likely occur before and/or during the birth process. Like genetics, environmental factors have not been determined to cause autism; rather, it is thought that they contribute to the likelihood that an individual will develop autism. It has been revealed that advanced paternal age at the time of conception; prenatal exposure to air pollution, maternal obesity, or diabetes; oxygen deprivation to the baby's brain during birth; and prenatal exposure to pesticides might also be contributing factors. In addition, mercury exposure continues to be investigated as a possible contributing factor (NIEHS, 2018).

1. What are the three diagnostic criteria for ASD?

2. List any four characteristics of ASD, and explain why these might be challenging in a classroom setting.

3. To date, there is no known cause of ASD. Scientists indicate that there are two contributing factors. What are they? Provide an example of each.

How the Diagnosis Is Made/Who Makes the Diagnosis

Diagnosing a child with ASD can be challenging. It requires several professionals' input, and there is no simple way to diagnose it, such as a blood test or an X-ray or a scan. During an evaluation, there can be difficulties distinguishing ASD from other disorders, such as ADHD or a speech delay. Many children with more significant ASD can be reliably diagnosed by 3 years of age and sometimes younger, particularly if they demonstrate problems with language development. Children who are higher-functioning, or considered to be more able, may not be diagnosed until they are school-age or older. This is usually because their IQ and language development appear more typical, like that of their peers, making their differences somewhat less noticeable. Some parents are relieved to receive the ASD diagnosis, because they are finally able to pinpoint and give a name to the different issues that their child has been experiencing. Other parents might resist an ASD diagnosis and be unwilling to accept the presence of this disorder.

Parents/caregivers are typically the first ones to notice problems related to their child's development. Problems with a child's development can also be identified in school by educators and in daycares by childcare personnel. Regardless of who recognizes these developmental differences, an ASD screening should occur as soon as possible. Conducting a screening in a timely manner is essential, because if ASD is present, intervention should begin quickly in order to procure the best outcome.

Evaluative Methods and Steps in the Diagnostic Process

As with diagnosing other disorders, there are specific steps that must occur in order to arrive at an accurate diagnosis. The following is a description of the typical diagnostic process for a child who is being evaluated for ASD. It should be noted, however, that there might be variations in this process, depending on the child.

First, the parents or school personnel notice academic, language, behavioral, and/or social problems with a child and determine it is necessary for the child to be examined. The child visits his pediatrician. During his visit, the doctor will discuss the child's development with his parents. Parents often report issues related to their child's lack of language development, lagging social skills, or challenging or unusual behaviors. Parents' experiences and concerns play an important role in this screening process. In addition to speaking with parents, the pediatrician will use an ASD screening tool. The following are examples of screening instruments for ASD:

- The Ages and Stages Questionnaire (ASQ)
- The Asperger Syndrome Diagnostic Scale (ASDS)
- The Childhood Autism Rating Scale (CARS)
- The Modified Checklist for Autism in Toddlers (M-CHAT)
- The Screening Tool for Autism in Toddlers and Young Children (STAT)

As indicated, there are various screening tools available for identifying students with developmental difficulties. It is relevant to note, however, that screening tools for individuals with ASD differ from other assessment tools, in that assessors for ASD specifically look for difficulties related to the following when assessing for ASD: eye gaze, orienting to one's name, pointing to or showing objects of interest, pretend play, imitation, nonverbal communication, and language development (ASHA, n.d.). Such assessments attempt to determine deficits in both the child's **verbal communication** and his **nonverbal communication**. In addition to the screening tools mentioned, the pediatrician orders a hearing screening. A hearing screening is performed because if a child cannot properly hear, this can affect his speech, language, and communication as well as his social skills. Based on the parent interview, the pediatrician's observations, the hearing screening, and the results of the screening tool, the pediatrician may refer the child for a comprehensive diagnostic evaluation by a team of professionals who specialize in ASD.

Second, the child undergoes a comprehensive diagnostic evaluation performed by professionals in the field of ASD to determine an accurate diagnosis. This generally is a team of professionals including a developmental pediatrician, a child neurologist, a child psychiatrist or child psychologist, and a speech-language pathologist.

As you can see, there are several important professionals on the IEP team who contribute their areas of expertise to the diagnostic process (see Figure 8.2). Each professional brings his specialized knowledge about typical development and whether or not the child being evaluated possesses characteristics associated with ASD. To illustrate, a speech-language pathologist will look very carefully at the child's expressive and receptive language skills. She will also pay particular attention to the child's pragmatic skills and his ability to use social language effectively.

Table 8.2	Professionals Involved in Diagnosing ASD

- *Developmental pediatrician* – medical doctor whose training is similar to pediatricians but who has also completed additional subspecialty training in developmental-behavioral pediatrics.

- *Child neurologist* – medical doctor who specializes in the brain, spine, and nerves.

- *Child psychiatrist* – medical doctor who specializes in the treatment of mental, emotional, and behavioral disorders of childhood.

- *Child psychologist* – specialist in diagnosing and treating children with emotional, mental, and behavior disorders.

- *Speech-language pathologist* – therapist who diagnoses, assesses, and treats speech, language, and communication problems.

As with other the disabilities we have examined, it is important to break down the various parts of the comprehensive diagnostic evaluation for ASD by this team of professionals to obtain a clear picture of what this disorder comprises. These components give us a distinct idea of what goes into making an ASD diagnosis. The components of an ASD evaluation for diagnosis are given in Table 8.3.

Third, determination of the presence of an ASD diagnosis is conducted, with standardized tools that operationalize the DSM criteria. Clinical expertise with a review of the DSM-5 criteria must be used to interpret the results of the objective tests. There are a variety of diagnostic tools available to determine the presence of ASD. The following assessments are commonly used:

- The Autism Diagnostic Interview, Revised (ADI-R)

- The Autism Diagnostic Observation Schedule (ADOS)

- The Communication and Symbolic Behavior Scales (CSBS)

- The Childhood Autism Rating Scale (CARS)

- The Gilliam Autism Rating Scale (GARS)

Once the tests have been performed and scored by the team of professionals, they meet to discuss the findings, discuss a possible diagnosis, and make recommendations. Next, the parents/guardians are brought in for a meeting to discuss the findings of the comprehensive diagnostic evaluation and treatment recommendations are made.

Treatment recommendations are highly individualized, depending on the needs of the child with ASD. Together with the parents, the evaluation team will discuss the test results and make suggestions about an appropriate course of action with respect to the child's education and related therapies. Ultimately, it is the

Table 8.3 Components of an ASD Evaluation

1. Medical history – significant pre- and perinatal problems, medical issues, surgeries or hospitalizations, seizures, or ear infections

2. Developmental history – language, social, and motor milestones; history of any developmental regression; and current communication abilities

3. Behavioral history – current behavior; socialization; odd or stereotypical behaviors or play interests

4. Family history – family members who have or had ASD, language disorders, intellectual disabilities, learning disabilities, ADHD, depression, schizophrenia or other mental illnesses, obsessive-compulsive disorder, or genetic disorders

5. Physical examination – general examination, growth parameters including head circumference, neurological exam, skin examination, and search for dysmorphic features

6. Developmental and/or psychometric evaluation – assessment of functioning across all developmental domains. Tests (depending on child's age and abilities) that may be performed by a variety of specialists in an interdisciplinary team include:

7. Cognitive – measures intelligence or general mental ability. These can be either verbal or nonverbal. Which assessment is used typically depends on the language abilities of the individual being assessed. Examples of assessments are:

   - The Bayley Scales of Infant Development

   - The Mullen Scales of Early Learning

   - The Stanford-Binet Intelligence Scales

   - The Comprehensive Test of Nonverbal Intelligence (CTONI)

   - The Universal Nonverbal Intelligence Test (UNIT)

     Motor – measures gross motor and fine motor abilities. Examples of assessments are:

   - The Pediatric Evaluation of Disabilities Inventory (PEDI)

   - The School Function Assessment (SFA)

     Adaptive – measures social, conceptual, and practical skills used in everyday life. Adaptive functioning measures a child's social competence, self-help/independent living skills, and play skills. Examples of assessments are:

   - The Adaptive Behavior Assessment System

   - The Vineland Adaptive Behavior Scales

parents who decide what intervention(s) will take place. The team of professionals will also provide a list of appropriate resources to the parents so that they know whom to contact to begin receiving services. This generally begins with the child's local school district but also might include private providers who offer behavioral therapy, speech-language therapy, occupational therapy, or physical therapy, as well as support groups for both the parents and the siblings.

Test Administration and ASD

The test-administration process for children with ASD can be challenging. As high-lighted in Chapter 2, there can be environmental issues, such as sensory processing differences and challenging behaviors, that disrupt the assessment process by affecting the student's ability to accurately respond to test items. Common environmental distractions, such as fluorescent lights or visual distractions (e.g., busy posters) can affect how a child with ASD will perform on any given test. He might be hyper-sensitive to the humming that fluorescent ceiling lights create, making it hard to concentrate. A colorful poster might distract him from attending to the test admin-istrator. In addition, children with ASD often do not usually have the same desire to please the test administrator that typical children demonstrate, and building rapport between the test administrator and child is not always possible. Some children with ASD will have a tantrum when a demand is placed on them, making test administra-tion hard to complete. When assessing children with ASD, environmental supports and reinforcement strategies need to be implemented. Testing in a child-friendly setting with familiar family members present can sometimes increase the chance of successful assessment administration. Reinforcers such as preferred toys or treats to reward a child when he exhibits appropriate test behavior should also be considered.

Check Your Understanding 8.2

1. Who are the people in a child's life who typically notice ASD characteristics initially?

2. List three screening tools a pediatrician might use when examining a child for ASD.

3. Identify the professionals who participate in the comprehensive diagnostic evaluation for ASD. Describe their roles.

4. Summarize the challenges that can occur when assessing a child for ASD.

The Diagnostic and Statistical Manual of Mental Disorders (DSM)

In order for a child to receive an official diagnosis of autism spectrum disorder, his symptoms must align with the most current diagnostic criteria as defined in the DSM-5. The DSM, or Diagnostic and Statistical Manual of Mental Disorders, as discussed previously, is published by the American Psychiatric Association and defines and classifies mental disorders. It is important to note that the DSM refers to this group of disorders as one entity, or autism spectrum disorder. This is dif-ferent from the educational context, in which ASD is referred to as "autism" and is considered a disability category under IDEA. In 2013, when the DSM-5 was published, several significant changes were made to the autism diagnosis from the previous edition. They are as follows:

Autism spectrum disorder is a new DSM-5 name that reflects a scientific consensus that four previously separate disorders are actually a single condition with different levels of symptom severity in two core domains. ASD now encompasses the previous DSM-autistic disorder (autism), Asperger's disorder, childhood disintegrative disorder, and pervasive developmental disorder not otherwise specified. ASD is characterized by 1) deficits in social communication and social interaction and 2) restricted repetitive behaviors, interests, and activities (RRBs). Because both components are required for diagnosis of ASD, social communication disorder is diagnosed if no RRBs are present.

(American Psychiatric Association, 2013, p. 1)

Severity Levels for ASD

As part of the DSM-5 diagnostic criteria, categorization of severity levels for ASD has been created. This categorization helps educators best understand how significantly a student is impacted by his ASD. It makes decisions about educational placement easier and more accurate for school personnel. It should be noted that as a child receives intervention, his ASD designation can change.

Table 8.4 Levels of Autism Spectrum Disorder (ASD)	
Level 1: Requiring Support	Considered the least severe ASD designation
	Possesses social difficulties that require some support
	Demonstrates difficulty initiating conversations and responds inappropriately or loses interest too soon
	Demonstrates inflexible behaviors
	Possesses problems with environmental change
	Needs help with planning and organization
Level 2: Requiring Substantial Support	Needs more support than Level 1
	Possesses more significant social challenges than Level 1
	Struggles to communicate effectively even with support and is likely to respond inappropriately to others
	Demonstrates challenges with nonverbal communication
	Speaks in short sentences about limited interests
	Exhibits inflexibility that interferes with daily living
	Shows significant problems with environmental change
Level 3: Requiring Very Substantial Support	Considered the most severe ASD designation
	Shows severe verbal and nonverbal impairments
	Tends to avoid interactions with others
	Exhibits very inflexible and repetitive behaviors

Adapted from Kandola, A. (2019). *Levels of autism: Everything you need to know.* Retrieved from https://www.medical-newstoday.com/articles/325106.php

As mentioned in Table 8.4, this categorization helps educators make important decisions about students with ASD so that they can be successful at school. It is particularly helpful with understanding how students can be effectively placed in various educational settings. A child who is performing at Level 1 is considered to have the most abilities of the three categories. Although he has some social challenges, with proper support, an inclusive class is seemingly an appropriate placement for him. A child who is performing at Level 2 requires more support than a child at Level 1, and educators will have to consider how his language challenges, social problems, and behavioral difficulties will impact his success in the various educational settings. A child who is performing at Level 3 has significantly different needs than children performing at the other two levels. When making the decision about where a child performing at Level 3 should receive his education, educators must take into account all aspects of his disability and how the severity of his ASD will influence where he will make the most progress while at school.

Check Your Understanding 8.3

1. How does the severity of levels assist educators when making placement decisions about a student with ASD?

2. Identify two differences between a child identified in the Level-1 category and a child identified in the Level-2 category.

Other Areas to Be Assessed

In addition to assessing the communication, behavior, and social abilities of a child with ASD, it is also relevant to look at his intelligence and academic abilities to gain a better perspective of how to best educate him. Understanding both his intelligence and his academic abilities will not only inform you (as his teacher), where he is functioning from a cognitive viewpoint, but also indicate areas in which he excels or that he finds challenging.

Intelligence

Assessing the IQ of individuals with ASD can be complicated. Most IQ tests are language-based, which is a deficit area for individuals on the autism spectrum. Therefore, it can be tough to determine whether a student is able to both fully understand and respond to the items on this type of assessment. As indicated above under cognitive assessments, nonverbal IQ tests are sometimes considered for use.

Historically, the majority of individuals with ASD were believed to have some type of intellectual disability. Now, with improved diagnosis and early intervention services available, this statistic has changed considerably. Currently, roughly half of the individuals being diagnosed with ASD are considered to have average to above-average intelligence. This is determined by having an IQ score of roughly 90 or higher. Approximately one-quarter of individuals with ASD have been determined to fall in the "borderline range" of having an IQ between 71 and 85, and less than one-third actually had an intellectual disability (Sarris, 2015).

Academics/Areas of Achievement

The academic abilities of a child with ASD will largely depend on the severity of his ASD and the degree to which he is impacted by it. As mentioned, because ASD is a spectrum disorder, children will demonstrate a wide range of academic abilities. Areas of relative strength for individuals with ASD include strong math skills, good memories, and the ability to excel at auditory and visual tasks. Many children with ASD are also rule-governed and can show expertise in a specific area. In addition, children with ASD are reported to demonstrate strong creative skills in the visual arts and music.

Common Learning Characteristics

In order for special educators to be able to most effectively teach and work with this student population, it is pertinent to identify common learning characteristics that they may possess.

Table 8.5 shows the common learning characteristics of students with ASD that have been reported.

Table 8.5 Common Learning Characteristics of ASD

- Individuals with ASD often demonstrate exceptional rote memory skills; however, their working memory or the time it takes to process information, especially processing several pieces of information at one time, can be difficult for people with ASD.

- Many individuals with ASD are able to better process information when presented visually. They may benefit from pictures, modeling the behaviors of others, hands-on activities, and concrete examples.

- Unstructured time or extensive waiting can be difficult for many. Schedules or checklists can help ease the anxiety or confusion surrounding unstructured time. Educators may also consider having a box of wait time activities, such as books, toys, or sensory items.

- Individuals with ASD often have difficulty generalizing learned skills from one setting to another. Educators may need to teach skills across different settings, people, and activities.

- Organization of materials and activities can be problematic for individuals with ASD. Educators may need to teach individuals with ASD how to organize their materials for different classes, keep their lockers tidy, how to use an agenda, and gather materials for homework. Individuals with ASD typically perform unevenly within and across academic skill areas.

- Some individuals with ASD are high-achieving in all areas. Others have high word-recognition skills but poor comprehension. Others have high calculation skills but poor applied math problem skills. Others are low in all areas.

Pratt, C., Hopf, R., & Larriba-Quest, K. (2017). Characteristics of individuals with an autism spectrum disorder (ASD). *The Reporter, 21*(17). Retrieved from https://www.iidc.indiana.edu/pages/characteristics

Educational Placements and ASD

Some children with ASD will receive their education in the general education setting or an inclusive placement, while others will need more individualized instruction provided by a self-contained special education classroom, separate school, or residential facility. Where a child is functioning "on the spectrum" will contribute greatly to his particular educational placement.

IDEA states that all children with disabilities must be placed in their least restrictive environment. Because of the wide range of ability levels demonstrated by children with ASD, they can be served in various educational placements available to them through special education in their local school district or a private-school setting.

Figure 8.1 illustrates the possible educational placements for students with ASD. This continuum is the same continuum of educational placements that exists for all children receiving special education under IDEA. Several factors are considered when the IEP team decides upon an educational placement. To begin, the IEP team must consider how the child's disability affects different areas of achievement (math, English/language arts, reading, etc.) in which the child performs. It is impossible, due to the complex nature of this disorder, to say that all children with ASD will perform well or poorly in any academic area. For example, we know that reading comprehension is often a difficult skill for many children with ASD to excel in, because it is language-based. There are some children on the spectrum,

Figure 8.1 Continuum of Educational Placements for Students With ASD

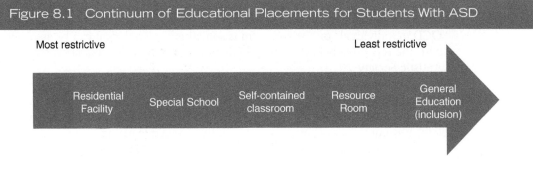

Most restrictive   Least restrictive

Residential Facility   Special School   Self-contained classroom   Resource Room   General Education (inclusion)

however, who will excel in their English/language arts classes and demonstrate high achievement at this skill. This reinforces the fact that children with ASD can vary significantly in their abilities and challenges. Other factors affecting educational placement for students with ASD include parent input and opportunities for social skills and language development. It is also relevant to note that most children receiving special education services will be educated in more than one educational placement during the school day, so as to adhere to the principle of least restrictive environment (LRE).

Health and Medical

There are potential medical issues associated with the diagnosis of ASD. Seizures tend to occur more frequently in children with ASD than in typically developing children. For those who develop seizures, they usually present after age 10. Seizures associated with ASD vary in type and might be focal or generalized. Children with ASD who seize will be administered an electroencephalogram (EEG), a diagnostic test measuring electrical activity in the brain, to confirm seizure activity (CAR, 2016). Gastrointestinal disorders also plague individuals with ASD. Children with ASD are 3.5 times more likely than their typical peers to suffer from chronic constipation or chronic diarrhea. Reasons for these GI issues are not completely understood, but some believe that they are due to toxins produced by abnormal gut bacteria. Gastroesophageal reflux disease and eosinophilic esophagitis can also affect children on the spectrum (Dave, 2017). In addition, individuals with ASD can experience sleep disturbances which can go unrecognized. Disturbances include both difficulty falling asleep and frequently waking during the night. These are challenging, because they can impact the child's ability to socially interact, his ability to do well in school, and the well-being of caregivers.

Mental health issues for individuals with ASD should be addressed, as they can sometimes be overlooked. Among the more common mental health challenges for this population are anxiety, depression, and obsessive-compulsive disorder (OCD). Research indicates that approximately 40% of individuals with ASD will experience anxiety. Anxiety symptoms cause excess stress and can subsequently lead to depression. Anxiety is believed to be due to biological brain differences in brain structure and function and social skill deficits. OCD is characterized by experiencing obsessions (thoughts) and compulsions (behaviors). Recognizing OCD in individuals on the spectrum is sometimes missed, as it can be associated with the repetitive behaviors already demonstrated by this population (National Autistic Society, 2018).

Another potential medical issue for those on the autism spectrum is the possibility of a comorbid condition. Common comorbidities to ASD include ADHD, Down syndrome, hearing impairments, dyslexia, dyspraxia, epilepsy, fetal anti-convulsant syndrome (FACS), hyperlexia, learning disabilities, social communication disorder, and visual impairment (National Autistic Society, n.d.) Many times, genetic testing is recommended to determine whether a genetic syndrome for individuals diagnosed with ASD is present. Approximately 20% of individuals with ASD also have a genetic disorder. Determining whether a genetic disorder is present can help explain some of the characteristics the child exhibits or will exhibit, as well as identify potential health concerns. Possible genetic syndromes associated with ASD include 22q deletion syndrome, Angelman syndrome, CHARGE, Cornelia de Lang syndrome, Down syndrome, Duchenne Muscular Dystrophy, fragile X, Prader-Willi syndrome, and Rett syndrome.

Sensory

Although not part of the diagnostic criteria for ASD, individuals on the autism spectrum often experience **sensory processing difficulties**. This means that they process sensory information differently than typical individuals. More precisely, children with this disorder often experience challenges with respect to the five senses: hearing, seeing, touching, tasting, and smelling. An example of a sensory challenge would be a child reacting adversely to a particular sound or taste. You might observe a child with ASD covering his ears because a particular sound bothers him or refusing to eat a particular food because he does not like the taste or smell of it. Another child with ASD might not like being touched and refuse to allow his parent/caregiver to hug him. These are all examples of processing sensory stimuli differently than would be expected. Children with ASD can exhibit both hyposensitivity and hypersensitivity to sensory stimuli. If a child experiences hyposensitivity, he experiences less than normal sensitivity to sensory stimuli. To illustrate, a child with a hyposensitivity to cold might feel comfortable walking outside in the snow in his bare feet. Conversely, another student with ASD might experience greater than normal sensitivity. He might be hypersensitive to the feeling of a particular fabric against his skin, making it difficult to wear clothes made of that particular material. These clothes might feel rough or scratchy to the point of irritation. The effects of difficulties processing sensory information can result in behavior challenges, such as meltdowns, tantrums, or withdrawal.

A sensory evaluation can be conducted by an occupational therapist, who can help resolve or minimize some of these sensory issues. The following are some of the sensory assessments that might be conducted on a child with ASD, depending on his age.

- The Infant/Toddler Sensory Profile (ITSP) is a "judgment based" questionnaire to be completed by an infant or toddler's parent or caregiver in order to best understand a child's sensory processing skills. This tool is designed for children up to 36 months.

- The Sensory Profile is used to determine a child's sensory processing abilities in his everyday activities. It can be administered to children ages 3 to 10.

- The Sensory Processing Measure (SPM) is a rating scale designed to give a thorough look at a child's sensory processing abilities and challenges both at home and at school. It is available for 5-to-12-year-old children; however, a version is available for younger children (the SMP-P). It includes seven areas: visual, auditory, tactile, proprioceptive, vestibular sensory systems, praxis, and social participation.

- The Sensory Rating Scale for Infants and Young Children (SRS) is a rating scale designed to be completed by parents for children up to 3 who are at risk of sensory challenges.

Check Your Understanding 8.5

1. Where do students with ASD receive their education (educational placement)?

2. Summarize the medical issues that individuals with ASD might experience.

3. What does it mean to have sensory processing difficulties? List three sensory assessments.

The Impact of an ASD Diagnosis on the Family

Much like other disabilities, the impact of an ASD diagnosis can have widespread effects on a child's family. Special educators need to be aware that parents can exhibit a variety of reactions when receiving the diagnosis that their child has ASD. Some parents are upset, scared, or bewildered, while others feel a sense of relief that they can attach a diagnosis to the problems that their child has been demonstrating. There are some salient points of note regarding receiving this diagnosis. When a diagnosis of ASD is made, all members of the family are affected. This includes parents, siblings, grandparents, aunts and uncles, and other extended family members. It is often a very stressful and difficult time for parents. Some family and friends might not be accepting of the diagnosis and be in disbelief that the child has ASD, or they might suggest that he will simply "grow out of it." This can be a source of additional confusion and tension for the parents and family.

Because of the significant impact that receiving an ASD diagnosis can have on the family, it has been correlated to the six stages of grief model. The six stages of grief model depicts the various stages that people go through when someone close to them has died (see Figure 8.2). In the case of receiving an ASD diagnosis, the loss is not a literal one, but parents may feel as though their dreams and aspirations for their child have perished. It is important to mention that not all parents will experience the six stages of grief, as they might be more accepting of an ASD diagnosis.

Figure 8.2 The Six Stages of Grief Model

Fear ➡ Anger ➡ Denial ➡ Bargaining or Guilt ➡ Acceptance ➡ Resolve to Overcome

Romaniec, M. (n.d.). *After the autism diagnosis: Staying connected as a couple.* Retrieved from https://tacanow.org/family-resources/after-the-autism-diagnosis-staying-connected-as-a-couple

1. The first stage of grief is *fear*. Parents might be fearful when they receive a diagnosis of ASD, for several reasons. Often they know little about the disorder and feel overwhelmed by the news. They might be unsure of how to go about finding appropriate services or resources for their child. The financial implications can also be worrisome, because medication and therapies to improve autistic symptoms may be expensive if they lack medical insurance.

2. The second stage of grief is *anger*. During this stage, parents might become angry that they have received this diagnosis. They question, "Why did this happen to us? or state things like "We did not do anything to deserve this."

3. The third stage of grief is *denial.* During this stage, parents might wonder whether the diagnosis is accurate or simply deny that the diagnosis could be possible. Sometimes parents will seek a second opinion from another medical professional.

4. The fourth stage of grief is *bargaining or guilt*. During this stage, parents blame themselves for something that they must have done to cause the ASD. For example, a mother might blame herself for not taking proper care of herself during her pregnancy. The parents might try to bargain by reasoning *If we do x, y, and z, our child will be okay.*

5. The fifth stage of grief is *acceptance*. By the time parents reach this stage, they are now able to accept the diagnosis that their child has ASD. They have come to terms with the reality that it is a lifelong disability and are no longer questioning or denying its existence.

6. The sixth stage of grief is the *resolve to overcome*. During the sixth stage, the parents accept that their child has ASD and are ready to move forward, beginning with appropriate education and/or therapies to best support their child's development.

Not all parents will experience the six stages in the same way. Some parents will not successfully move through all six stages of grief and will remain or get "stuck" in any one stage for an extended or indefinite period of time. In addition, other issues can arise after the final stage of grief. Examples include adjusting parental expectations, worrying about the siblings of their child with ASD, tending to their marriage, and maintaining a social life in the presence of this new diagnosis. On a positive note, recent research has indicated that families are now showing increased benefits from having a child with ASD. Siblings of children with ASD, for example, are growing up to be better-adjusted adults, and greater family cohesiveness is evident (Harris, 2020).

Check Your Understanding 8.6

1. Imagine you have a brother or a sister who has just been diagnosed with ASD. What would your reaction be? What concerns might you have?

2. If you knew that a family had just received the diagnosis of ASD, how could you support them in finding appropriate resources for their child?

The following case study depicts what a family going through the diagnostic process for ASD might encounter. It showcases a 2-year-old child and the steps his parents go through in attempting to determine the cause of his developmental differences.

Case Study 8.1: Joey

Joey is a 2-year-old boy who lives with his mother, father, and two older sisters. The family resides on Long Island, NY, about an hour outside of Manhattan. The father, Sam, is a computer engineer for a large software company and commutes into NYC daily for work. Louise, Joey's mother, is a teacher at a local elementary school. Recently, Louise has expressed concern to Sam that Joey appears to be developing differently than his sisters. One evening, Louise sat down with Sam to discuss her concerns. She stated that Joey's language development was slow. She told Sam that, by age 2, Joey should be able to put two words together when he talks, yet all he seems to do is to label a few familiar objects. Because she is an elementary school teacher, Louise knows that this is not typical language development. Sam agreed that their daughters were easily putting words together—for example, saying "I want more" and "Daddy, come here"—by this age. Sam commented that he had seen Joey lining up his toy trains each morning when he was getting ready for work. He said that he had tried to get him to play with his trains by rolling them across the table and making "choo choo" sounds, but Joey wanted no part of his father's play attempts and would throw a tantrum when his father interfered with him lining them up. Louise mentioned that she had seen Joey flashing toys back and forth in front of his face as he looked at them out of the corner of his eyes the other day. She also told Sam that she was most concerned about Joey's lack of interest in the other children at church on Sundays when the couple leaves him in the nursery. The next day Louise called Joey's pediatrician to make an appointment to discuss their concerns about him.

The following week, Louise took Joey to see Dr. Davidson. Dr. Davidson has been the family pediatrician since Joey's sisters were born. He has seen the girls grow up, tracking their development at their well-child visits and seeing them for minor illnesses. Today's visit went a bit differently from other appointments with the girls. The appointment began with Dr. Davidson asking Louise why she wanted Joey examined, since it was not yet time for his regular check-up. Louise stated that she and Sam had concerns about Joey. Louise discussed his language development, difficult behaviors, and lack of interest in other children. Dr. Davidson listened carefully to Louise and asked several follow-up questions. After discussing Joey with her at length and observing his behavior in the examining room, Dr. Davidson interviewed Louise using the M-CHAT. Following are examples of the questions from the assessment:

If you point at something across the room, does your child look at it?

Does your child play pretend or make-believe?

Dr. Davidson scored the M-CHAT and told Louise that Sam scored a 10, indicating that he was at high risk of ASD and that he would like to refer Joey to a developmental pediatrician for a comprehensive assessment. Dr. Davidson gave Louise the name of a board-certified developmental pediatrician and suggested that she make an appointment with him to evaluate Joey for ASD.

When Louise got home, she was distraught. She sat down with Sam after dinner to discuss their visit to Dr. Davidson's office. Both Louise and Sam were overwhelmed with the prospect of Sam being on the autism spectrum. Neither of them had any family members who had autism, and they knew very little about the disorder. That night, Louise spent the evening researching ASD online. There was so much information it was difficult for her to discern how it applied to Joey and his potential diagnosis. In the morning, she scheduled an appointment with Dr. Peters, the developmental pediatrician. The first available appointment was in several weeks' time, due to the large number of children needing to be evaluated at the clinic. This would also require a trip into NYC for the evaluation. The wait was difficult.

Over the weeks, the parents grew anxious. They watched Joey closely but saw few changes in him.

Finally, the day arrived, and Louise and Sam took Joey to his appointment. The appointment was to last a few hours, and they were worried that Joey would not be able to tolerate being in an examination room for this length of time without having a meltdown. Prior to the appointment, Louise and Sam had completed an extensive questionnaire for Dr. Peters that addressed Joey's language, social interaction, and behavior. This questionnaire played a major role in the conversations they had with the doctor that day.

Dr. Peters performed a full exam of Joey and recommended to his parents that he receive a comprehensive diagnostic evaluation by a team of professionals to determine whether he had ASD. This would include several individuals who would assess various aspects of his development. He explained to them that Joey would be evaluated by several professionals who specialize in the diagnosis and treatment of ASD. He spoke about the different types of developmental tests they would perform and characteristics they would be looking for to explain his symptoms. Louise and Sam agreed that this was a smart idea. Dr. Peters gave them the contact information for the person who schedules these evaluations at the hospital. Both parents agreed they would call the next day to set up the evaluation.

When Louise called to schedule a comprehensive diagnostic evaluation the next day, she was told that, due to the large number of children being evaluated for ASD, they would have to wait three months before Joey could be assessed. When Sam got home from work that evening, Louise expressed her frustration at not being able to secure a timely appointment for his evaluation. She told Sam that she felt like all they were doing was waiting to get the answers that they needed. Sam reassured her that the time between now and Joey's appointment would move quickly and they would finally get the answers that they needed to help Joey.

1. What screening tool was used by Dr. Davidson?

2. Discuss Louise and Sam's reaction to the possibility of Joey's having ASD. What would your reaction have been if you had a child going through this process?

3. What unusual behaviors did Joey demonstrate that concerned his parents?

4. How do you think Louise and Sam felt when Dr. Peters suggested they get a comprehensive diagnostic evaluation for ASD for Joey? Explain.

Extension to Instruction

It is through the diagnostic process that educators are able to get a clear picture of the abilities and challenges of a child with ASD. Information provided from a variety of assessments informs educators about the best course of action for the child. If a child demonstrates good achievement in a particular area, educators should capitalize on that ability, giving the child ample opportunities for continued growth. If, however, the child demonstrates academic, behavioral, or social problems, intervention should begin as soon as possible.

The Importance of Early Intervention

Significant research has shown that students who receive a diagnosis of ASD should begin receiving early intervention services as soon as possible. Early intervention consists of therapy and support services that children up to age 3 receive aimed at minimizing the effects of the disability. Early intervention for children with ASD typically includes speech and language therapy, Applied Behavior Analysis (ABA), physical therapy, and occupational therapy, to name a few. Several special education professionals can contribute to a student's early intervention program. Frequently, a child with ASD will begin a behavioral program as part of his early intervention. As indicated above, ABA is an umbrella term that refers to specific behavioral principles that are applied to improve a variety of problem behaviors. ABA has also been referred to as the "science of human behavior." A common ABA technique used to teach young children with ASD is known as discrete trial training (DTT). In DTT, the student is taught skills or concepts that are broken down into small steps and then reinforced for his correct responses or prompted with the correct response. A speech-language therapist or SLP will also work with a young student who has delayed expressive and/or receptive language skills, either one-on-one or in a small group setting, in both pull-out and push-in models. An occupational therapist (OT) might also work with this student on everyday skills such as brushing teeth, toileting, or getting dressed. The OT might also work on sensory issues that a young child with ASD is likely to experience. In some cases, a physical therapist (PT) is needed to work on issues related to movement dysfunction and physical function.

Receiving appropriate early intervention services provides children with ASD the opportunity to maximize their potential. More specifically, it has proven to increase IQ, language ability, and social interaction and has positive long-term effects. If a student is suspected of having ASD, optimally services should begin when symptoms first become apparent—in other words, before an official diagnosis is made. Early intervention for students with ASD should be intensive and developmental in nature. In other words, the child should receive several hours of daily therapy (25 per week is recommended), and the therapy should be focused on helping the child grow and learn. Typical early intervention curricula are language-based and focus on catching the student up so that he is more on grade level with his peers and to reduce his deficit areas. They may be used at school, in a clinic, or in the home. The student-to-teacher ratio is very low for students with ASD, to ensure a proper amount of support and learning occurs. Because early intervention is covered under Part C of IDEA, there is no cost to the parents.

Check Your Understanding 8.8

1. What is early intervention? Why is it critical that students with ASD receive appropriate early intervention?

2. What is Applied Behavior Analysis (ABA)? What is a common ABA technique for teaching skills to students with ASD?

3. Name some other related service personnel who might participate in early intervention services.

Evidence-Based Practices (EBPs)

After a child with ASD receives early intervention services, he will enter the regular system school and become part of the K–12 student population. Because of a surge in ASD diagnoses over the past decade, there has been increased speculation as to how to best educate students with ASD once they are in school. While some methods have proven to be highly effective, others are considered "fads" and should be avoided. Evidence-based practices (EBPs) are those practices, methods, or techniques that are derived from educational research or metrics of school, teacher, and student performance. They have been tested and proven advantageous.

Figure 8.3   Selected Behavioral-Based Strategies

Selected Behavioral-Based Strategies					
Prompting	Reinforce-ment	Task anal-ysis	Discrete trial training DTT Pivotal response training PRT	Computer-aided instruction CAI	Picture exchange communication system PECS

Adapted from National Professional Development Center on Autism Spectrum Disorder. (2013). *Evidence-based practices*. Retrieved from http://autismpdc.fpg.unc.edu/content/briefs

Selected behavioral-based strategies that are currently commonly used when teaching students with ASD are shown in Figure 8.3. All of these are EBPs.

- *Prompting* involves giving the child a hint or cue in order to get him to perform a desired behavior.

Example: A therapist might use a physical prompt to get a child to touch a particular object in order to discriminate between it and another object.

- *Reinforcement* involves providing a stimulus that will increase the probability of a particular response. Reinforcement can be either positive or negative.

Example: Praise and rewards are given to students who perform well on a test, so that in the future they will want to do well on a test again.

- *Task analysis* is the process of breaking down complex tasks into small steps in order to achieve a desired action/goal.

Example: A teacher might use a task analysis to teach a child how to brush his teeth (step by step).

- *Discrete trial training (DTT)* is an intervention strategy that is highly structured and typically conducted one-on-one, where tasks are broken down into small increments. There are four basic components of a discrete trial: the discriminative stimulus, the child's response, a consequence, and the inter-trial interval.

Example: A child with ASD can be taught how to identify shapes and colors through discrete trial training.

- *Pivotal response training (PRT)* is a naturalistic form of applied behavior analysis used as an early intervention method for children with ASD.

Example: A therapist follows the lead of a young child's play interests by engaging in the same activities.

- *Computer-aided instruction (CAI)* relies on computer technology to assist in both teaching and learning.

Example: A child with ASD plays computer games on his laptop that reinforce his understanding of pronouns.

- *Picture exchange communication system (PECS)* is an augmentative and alternative communication system for students, designed to teach speech. This method is a form of modified behavior analysis that focuses on "early nonverbal communication training" (Vicker, 2020.

Example: A nonverbal child with ASD uses his PECS board to communicate his wants and needs.

Check Your Understanding 8.9

1. Which of the behavioral-based strategies would you use if you wanted to teach a child with ASD how to communicate? Why?

2. As a child yourself, how were you reinforced by your parents/guardians for doing a particularly good job at something? Explain.

3. Do you think that using a task analysis would be a good method to teach a child with ASD how to get dressed? Why or why not?

4. Give an example of how you could prompt to someone to get out of bed in the morning if they were unwilling.

In addition to the instructional techniques that special educators use with a child on the autism spectrum, they must also consider the behavioral support strategies that will assist them in their learning process due to the behavioral differences they possess. Figure 8.4 lists positive behavior support strategies that are commonly used when teaching students with ASD. All of these are considered EBPs.

Figure 8.4 Selected Positive Behavioral Support Strategies

Selected Positive Behavioral Support Strategies							
Differential reinforcement	Extinc-tion	Functional behavior assessment (FBA)	Response interruption/ redirection	Self-management	Social story	Video modeling	Visual supports

Adapted from National Professional Development Center on Autism Spectrum Disorder. (2013). *Evidence-based practices*. Retrieved from http://autismpdc.fpg.unc.edu/content/briefs

- *Differential reinforcement* is a process in which an appropriate behavior is reinforced in the presence of one stimulus while not reinforcing an inappropriate behavior in the midst of another stimulus.

Example: A teacher praises the student who raises his hand to speak while ignoring the student who shouts out a response.

- *Extinction* involves weakening of a conditioned response, causing a behavior to decrease or disappear.

Example: A child with ASD throws a tantrum to get attention from his teacher. His teacher ignores this behavior until eventually he eventually stops his tantrum.

- *Functional behavior assessment (FBA)* is the process by which information is gathered to determine the function (purpose) of a child's inappropriate behavior(s).

Example: An FBA is conducted on a child with ASD who has a tantrum each day before reading class, to determine why his tantrums are occurring.

- *Response interruption/redirection* is a behavioral procedure used to treat stereotypic or repetitive behaviors that are typically maintained by sensory consequences. This takes the form of a prompt, comment, or distractor.

Example: A therapist redirects a student who is engaging in hand-flapping behavior by prompting him to touch a stimulus.

- *Self-management* consists of teaching students with ASD to manage their own emotions and resulting behaviors so that they are socially appropriate.

Example: A student with ASD keeps track of his own behavior during the school day on a data sheet that he keeps with him.

- *Social story* refers to a simple story or narrative that is written in clear, understandable language with appropriate visual aids meant to help a child with ASD learn a particular skill/concept or prepare him for an anticipated event.

Example: A teacher reads a social story to her students with ASD about what to do when there is a fire drill at school.

- *Video modeling* means, for purposes of instructing children with ASD, using videos that model appropriate behaviors.

Example: A child with ASD is shown a video that models how to engage in conversational turn-taking with his friends.

- *Visual supports* are photographs, pictures, labels, or text that help an individual with ASD better understand or learn a concept.

Example: Visual supports found in an autism support classroom include pictures of the children taped on the back of their chairs so that they can identify their proper seat. They also include picture schedules that tell the children what they are doing in class each day.

Check Your Understanding 8.10

1. Would a functional behavior assessment (FBA) be an appropriate tool to determine why a student with ASD cannot stay seated during class time? Why or why not?

2. Give an example of how you could teach a child with ASD a desired behavior through video modeling.

3. What visual supports would you use in your room if you had a class of children with ASD? How would these visual supports assist in student learning?

Daily Living/Adaptive Behavior Domains

Similar to students with intellectual disabilities, some students with ASD will benefit from a curriculum that addresses daily living skills as a central component. While some students with ASD will be educated in the general education classroom via inclusive models, others will need to learn a curriculum that assists them in their daily living and focuses on functional academics. This includes learning skills such as self-care, community living, occupational skills, and social skills. (Refer to Chapter 7 for details on ADL skills.)

Augmentative and Alternative Communication (AAC) for Students With ASD

Because many students on the autism spectrum possess significant speech, language, and communication issues, it is pertinent to discuss the benefits of augmentative and alternative communication. AAC helps individuals who might otherwise not be able to communicate. More specifically, AAC is a communication method that supplements or replaces an individual's natural language. Not all students with ASD will require AAC to successfully communicate, and others on the autism spectrum will use AAC as a catalyst or support to further develop their existing language skills. There are also some students with ASD, those who are nonverbal, who will use it exclusively as their personal voice. There are several types of AAC systems, and an SLP can help determine the best choice of AAC device for the student. Some students on the autism spectrum will manage well with low-tech devices, such as the picture exchange communication system (PECS), while others with more significant needs will benefit from high-tech devices, such as a Tobii Dynavox. In other words, finding the perfect AAC match for an individual on the autism spectrum is a very personal process.

Transition to Postsecondary Life

Now that we have looked at the diagnosis and eligibility process, as well as at different academic and behavior interventions for students with ASD, it is relevant to consider what life will be like for them once they exit the school system at the end of their 21st year. Considerable consideration should be given to postsecondary life for students on the autism spectrum. Postsecondary choices include attending college, vocational training, the workforce, or a sheltered work environment. Planning between the IEP members, parents, and child is necessary for a successful transition and begins early in the high-school years. Once a child turns 14, he is invited to attend and participate in his IEP transition meeting. The following are options available to individuals with ASD once they graduate with a high-school diploma or receive a certificate of attendance at the end of their postsecondary experience:

- *College.* Some students with ASD will attend two-year or four-year colleges and study any number of academic majors. Currently there are programs within higher education that are designed to support individuals with ASD with respect to both academics and social skills.

- *Vocational training and the workforce.* Some students with ASD will receive vocational training while they are in high school. Vocational training provides individuals with specific skill sets so that they are able to secure a job upon completing school at age 21. Examples of vocational training for individuals with ASD are office/clerical work, janitorial work, and restaurant jobs. Job coaches might be used to support these individuals, as needed.

- *A sheltered work environment.* Some students with ASD will work in a "sheltered" environment. This is a work setting under which special supervision is provided to the individual with a disability. It provides safety and protection to those who are more significantly impacted by a disorder.

In addition to schooling and employment, it will also be important to consider the type of living arrangement that will best fit the adult with ASD. Some adults on the autism spectrum can live independently, others will require some support, and yet others will require 24-hour care. All of these factors should be considered during transition planning.

The Importance of Social Skills Training

One critical component of the education of any child with ASD—no matter how slightly or severely he is affected by his disorder—is social skills training. Nearly all students with ASD have problems with social interaction, and this is an area that must be directly addressed in order to make significant gains with family, peers, and those they come in contact with each day. As mentioned earlier on, social skill deficits are part of the diagnostic criteria for ASD. Possessing adequate social skills is necessary for any individual to live a successful, productive life. One particular social skill deficit that individuals with ASD possess is joint attention (ASHA, n.d.). Joint attention refers to a shared focus between two or more individuals on a particular object or event. In typical development, this skill is acquired between the ages of 6 months and 18 months. Joint attention can occur in the form of an eye gaze, a gesture, or a verbalization. Another social challenge that those with ASD can experience relates to Theory of Mind. Theory of Mind involves the ability to differentiate one's own feelings from the feelings of others; it typically develops around age 4. To illustrate the problem, a child with ASD might not understand the mental state of his mother who is crying because she has tripped and fallen and hurt herself. Understanding why his mother is crying is critical to their social relationship. It is important that the child show his mother that he is concerned that she has been hurt. Children with ASD can be effectively taught to improve their social skills through various EBPs discussed earlier in this chapter, such as by the use of social stories or video modeling. Many times, the speech-language pathologist or classroom special education teacher at a child's school will focus on social skills training, as will the classroom teacher.

Following are examples of evidence-based social skills curricula:

- PATHS: Promoting Alternative THinking Strategies (K–6)
- Social Skills Intervention Guide (K–12)
- Skillstreaming the Elementary School Child (2–6)

Check Your Understanding 8.11

1. Identify the postsecondary schooling options available to individuals with ASD once they complete school.

2. Should children with ASD receive social skills training? Why or why not?

3. Define the concept of Theory of Mind.

CHAPTER SUMMARY

This chapter examined screening, evaluating, and diagnosing an individual with ASD from the point of recognizing a difference in the child by his parents or school personnel through the comprehensive diagnostic evaluation. It focused on how a diagnosis is made and the key professionals involved in determining the presence of this disability. It also addressed the six stages of grief that parents might experience when receiving an ASD diagnosis. Special attention was given to the importance of early intervention, as well as medical and sensory concerns surrounding ASD. This chapter provided an explanation of how an ASD diagnosis is extended to instruction, considering placement options and employing evidence-based instruction. Several key assessments during the diagnostic process were revealed and explained. Social skills training for individuals with ASD was highlighted.

APPLY WHAT YOU HAVE LEARNED

1. Write a five-minute reflection explaining the diagnostic criteria for ASD.

2. Conduct research on the ADOS and the ADI-R. Provide a detailed description of these assessments, and provide reasons why you believe they are popular diagnostic tools.

3. With your groupmates, generate a list of ideas to help accommodate a testing environment for students with ASD with respect to their sensory processing difficulties.

4. Should a child who is considered to have a Level-2 or Level-3 ASD classification be educated alongside his typical peers in the general education setting? Why or why not?

REFERENCES

American Psychiatric Association. (2013). *Highlights of changes from DSM-IV-TR to DSM V*. Retrieved from https://webcache.googleusercontent.com/search?q=cache:ZDGL1nozhbIJ:https://www.psychiatry.org/File%2520Library/Psychiatrists/Practice/DSM/APA_DSM_Changes_from_DSM-IV-TR_-to_DSM-5.pdf+&cd=5&hl=en&ct=clnk&gl=us

American Psychiatric Association. (2013). *Diagnostic and statistical manual of mental disorders* (5th ed.). Washington, DC: Author.

American Speech-Language-Hearing Association. (n.d.). *Autism spectrum disorder: Signs and symptoms*. Retrieved from https://www.asha.org/PRPSpecificTopic.aspx?folderid=8589935303&section=Signs_and_Symptoms

Autism Interactive Network. (2015). *Measuring intelligence in autism*. Retrieved from https://https://iancommunity.org/ssc/measuring-iq-autism

Autism Speaks. (2009, November 29). *Early intervention for toddlers with autism highly effective, study finds*. Retrieved from https://www.autismspeaks.org/science-news/early-intervention-toddlers-autism-highly-effective-study-finds

Autism Speaks. (2018). *What causes autism?* Retrieved from https://www.autismspeaks.org/what -autism/learn-more-autism/what-causes-autism

Center for Autism Research. (2016). *Seizures and autism spectrum disorder*. Retrieved from https://www.carautismroadmap.org/seizures

Centers for Disease Control and Prevention. (2015). *Developmental disability*. Retrieved from https://www.cdc.gov/ncbddd/developmentaldis-abilities/index.html

Centers for Disease Control and Prevention. (2018). *What is Autism Spectrum Disorder?* Retrieved from https://www.cdc.gov/ncbddd/autism/facts.html

Columbia Regional Program. (2016). *Columbia Regional Program: ASD transition toolkit*. Retrieved from https://www.crporegon.org/Page/285#How%20 do%20I%20determine%20appropriate%20postsec-ondary%20independent%20living%20goal(s)%20 with%20my%20student(s)%20with%20ASD?

Dave, M. (2017). *Gastrointestinal disorders in children with autism*. Retrieved from https://childrensgimd. com/gastrointestinal-disorders-children-autism

Harris, S. (2020). *Siblings*. Retrieved from http:// www.autism-society.org/living-with-autism/ autism-and-your-family/siblings

Individuals with Disabilities Education Act, 20 U.S.C. § 1400 (2004).

Kandola, A. (2019). *Levels of autism: Everything you need to know*. Retrieved from https://www .medicalnewstoday.com/articles/325106.php

Matson, J. L., & Kozlowski, A. M. (2011). The increasing prevalence of autism spectrum disorders. *Research in Autism Spectrum Disorders, 5*(1), 418–425.

National Institute of Mental Health. (2018). *Autism spectrum disorder*. Retrieved from https://www .nimh.nih.gov/health/topics/autism-spectrum-disorders-asd/index.shtml

National Professional Development Center on Autism Spectrum Disorder. (2013). *Evidence-based practices*. Retrieved from http://autismpdc.fpg .unc.edu/content/briefs

National Institute of Neurological Disorders and Stroke. (2017). *What is autism spectrum disorder?* Retrieved from https://www.ninds.nih.gov/Dis-orders/Patient-Caregiver-Education/Fact-Sheets/ Autism-Spectrum-Disorder-Fact-Sheet#3082_1

National Institute of Environmental Health Sciences. (2018). *Autism*. Retrieved from https:// www.niehs.nih.gov/health/topics/conditions/ autism/index.cfm

National Autistic Society. (n.d). *Related conditions*. Retrieved from: http://www.autism.org.uk/about/ what-is/related-conditions.aspx#

National Autistic Society. (2018). *Mental health and autism*. Retrieved from http://www.autism .org.uk/about/what-is/related-conditions.aspx

Pratt, C., Hopf, R., & Larriba-Quest, K. (2017). Characteristics of individuals with an autism spectrum disorder (ASD). *The Reporter, 21*(17). Retrieved from https://www.iidc.indiana.edu/ pages/characteristics

Romaniec, M. (n.d.). *After the autism diagno-sis: Staying connected as a couple*. Retrieved from https://tacanow.org/family-resources/after-the-autism-diagnosis-staying-connected-as-a-couple

Sarris, M. (2015, October 20). *Measuring intelli-gence in autism*. Retrieved from https://iancommu-nity.org/ssc/measuring-iq-autism

Vicker, B. (2020). *What is the picture exchange communication system or PECS?* Retrieved from https://www.iidc.indiana.edu/irca/articles/what-is-the-picture-exchange-communication-system-or-pecs.html

Wick, N. (2010, December 1). *IQ scores fail to predict academic achievement in children with autism* [University of Washington news release]. Retrieved from http://www.washington.edu/ news/2010/12/01/iq-scores-fail-to-predict-academic-performance-in-children-with-autism

CHAPTER 9

Speech or Language Impairment

Vicki A. McGinley, PhD

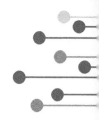

Learning Objectives

After completion of this chapter, you should be able to:

- Define speech or language impairments according to IDEA.

- Understand the difference between speech and language services offered as related services or as a primary disability served under IDEA.

- Describe the causes of speech or language impairments.

- Describe characteristics of children with speech or language impairments.

- Explain how speech and language disorders are evaluated and identified.

- Identify assessment tools used by speech-language pathologists.

Key Terms

aphasia (p. 273)	language (p. 268)
articulation (p. 269)	language impairment (p. 269)
childhood apraxia (p. 273)	morphemes (p. 268)
communication (p. 267)	morphology (p. 268)
congenital (p. 271)	phonemes (p. 268)
content (p. 268)	phonological awareness (p. 268)
expressive language (p. 268)	phonology (p. 268)
form (p. 268)	pragmatics (p. 268)

(Continued)

Introduction to the Chapter

This chapter provides information on those students identified with speech or language impairments, a very diverse group, and one that is considered to be a higher-incidence population. According to the National Institute on Deafness and Other Communication Disorders (2016), 5% of children in first grade have a speech disorder, and 6% of children in the primary grades have a language disorder not caused by a physical or sensory disability, with males more likely than females to have speech or language impairments. The Individuals With Disabilities Education Act (IDEA) definition below refers to those children who are evaluated as having a primary disability of speech or language impairment. As such, this chapter will focus on those children whose primary disability is speech or language impairment. However, it should be noted that many children receive speech and languages services as a related service according to their individualized education programs (IEPs).

The purpose of this chapter will be to define speech or language impairment and discuss the characteristics of this population and how they are evaluated and identified for services, as well as make an extension to instruction.

IDEA Definition of Speech or Language Impairment

[Speech or language impairment] . . . means a communication disorder such as stuttering, impaired articulation, language impairment, or a voice impairment that adversely affects a child's education performance.

(IDEA, 20 U.S.C. § 1401 (2004), 20 C.F. R. § 300.8(c)(11))

Diagnostic Criteria and Related Characteristics

As was previously mentioned, the focus of this chapter is on children with speech or language impairments (SLI) who do not evidence language problems as a result of other disabilities, such as autism, intellectual disabilities, or hearing impairments. However, it is important to note that many children with other conditions also have difficulties with speech and language and require remediation in this area.

For children with a primary speech and language deficit, the acquisition of language often does not keep pace with the child's chronologically aged peers in certain ways, and, a great deal of the time, this difference cannot be tied to a specific condition or disability. Although IDEA's category is speech or language impairment, terms such as "language delay," "language impairment," "specific language impairment," "early language delay," and "specific expressive language delay" may all be used among professionals to refer to children who have difficulty learning and communicating with language.

As was noted in Chapter 4, it is important to understand the concepts of language difference, language delay, and language disorder and to know that these terms are not synonymous with one another. This chapter will place emphasis on children with a language disorder. This chapter will not address children whose primary language is not English, because they have a language difference, not a language disorder. A language delay, in contrast, is often much more difficult to distinguish from a language disorder. At an early age, it is often difficult to determine whether children have a language delay that they may outgrow or whether they have an underlying language disorder. Language is typically nearly fully developed by the time children reach school age, and, as such, a speech or language impairment may not be diagnosed until after children are 4 years old, to account for the fact that many children often outgrow their early language delays (Schwartz, 2012).

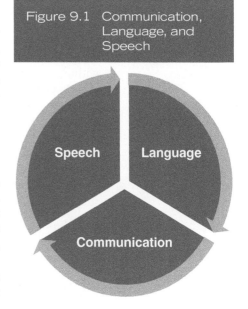

Figure 9.1 Communication, Language, and Speech

Communication, Language, and Speech

Prior to addressing characteristics, causes, evaluation, and identification of speech and language impairments, it is important to develop an understanding of the terms "communication," "language," and "speech" (see Figure 9.1). While they are often used synonymously, they have very different meanings.

Communication is the exchange of information among participants that requires a message to be sent from at least one person to another who receives the message (Zebron, Mhute, & Musingafi, 2015). The receiver must comprehend the message and complete the dyadic exchange with a return message of some kind, either verbal or nonverbal, indicating an understanding. Thus, communication may be a verbal or nonverbal exchange, and it doesn't necessarily require language or speech.

Language, a tool that is used for communication, requires a shared symbol system that is governed by complex rules that all participants must understand in order to be effective communicators. Language is culturally relevant, meaning that children aren't born with a particular language; they learn it based on their cultural surroundings. Similar to communication, the symbol systems associated with language can be either verbal (e.g., any spoken language) or nonverbal (e.g., American Sign Language). Recall from Chapter 4 that language can either be expressive or receptive. The sender of the message produces the language and exhibits expressive language, while the receiver of the message is the participant that comprehends the message and thus uses receptive language. Examples of skills in expressive language are the ability to retrieve and state words from memory, name objects, ask questions, speak to someone in a conversation, and write. Receptive language skills include the ability to follow instructions and to understand communication. For children with speech or language impairments, the most noticeable challenge lies in expressive language; however, receptive language may be equally challenging. Recall from Chapter 4 that language can be separated into three main components: form, content, and use and further subdivided into five elements of language (phonology, morphology, syntax, semantics, and pragmatics) (Bloom & Lahey, 1978). The following is a brief overview of the components and elements of language. Refer back to Chapter 4 for a comprehensive explanation.

- Phonology is the study of the sound structure and sound patterns within a language; it relates to the phonemes, syllables, and prosodic aspects of speech. It is important that a child develop phonological awareness (see Chapter 5 for specific examples of phonological awareness), or the ability to think about and manipulate sounds and syllables in words, as well as to separate a word's structure from its meaning. Thus, syllable segmentation and word manipulations, or the ability to deconstruct or construct words by deleting and adding sounds/syllables are needed skills (Gillon, 2004) for the child to be successful in this area.

- Morphology is the study of morphemes, or the smallest unit of language that has meaning.

- Syntax is the study of the grammatical structure and rules for forming language. Children need to understand the rule systems of constructing sentences, such as negatives (e.g., "There are no oranges left"), compound sentences (e.g., "I went to the store and I bought a gallon of milk"), and complex sentences (e.g., "If it rains tomorrow, we won't go to the park"), as well as different sentence types:

- ○ Declarative (e.g., "The sun is orange").

- ○ Interrogative (e.g., "How are you today?")

- ○ Imperative (e.g., "Sit down for dinner.")

- ○ Exclamatory (e.g., "I'm going on vacation tomorrow!")

- **Semantics** is the study of the meaning of words, phrases, sentences, and vocabulary.

- **Pragmatics** is the study of the social use or function of our language. It involves communicative functions or intentions—such as greeting, responding, naming, informing, commenting, and using humor and figurative language.

Speech relates to the production of speech sounds. For the most part, all the sounds (phonemes) needed to produce language will be developed in typically developing children by the time they start school, and they will be entering school with a rich vocabulary and multiple uses for expressing language. However, if there are deficits, such as difficulties with the physical and motor mechanisms needed to produce language, the child may not develop speech in a typical way. In the area of speech, sounds are produced by four separate physiological processes:

- Respiration

- Phonation, which produces sound in the larynx

- Resonations, which shapes the sounds

- Articulation, which forms the specific speech sounds

The use of one's oral structure produces sounds in which one's breath is expelled from the lungs and forced through the larynx (also called the voice box), which controls the amount of air causing the vocal cords to vibrate to produce the sounds combined that form language. The lips, jaw, tongue, teeth, and palate then provide the fine tuning of speech (Shames & Anderson, 2006).

Speech or Language Impairments in Relation to the Elements of Language

A language impairment impacts the way in which language is developed. A language impairment may impact the rate at which an individual develops language, the sequence in which language is learned and produced by the child, and/or any of the five elements of language (one or more elements may be impacted). A speech impairment is a disorder that affects the articulation of speech sounds, fluency, or voice.

The five elements of language are grouped by the language functions they serve. These functions are form, which is defined by two structural components, the sound (phonology) and the grammar system (morphology and syntax); content (semantics); and use (pragmatics) (Bloom & Lahey, 1978). These functions help us further understand speech or language impairments:

- impairments in *form* will indicate difficulty in learning the rules of sounds, syllables, prosodic aspects of words, grammatical endings, and/ or sentence types;

- errors in *content* will indicate delays in semantic development; and

- impairments in *use* indicate challenges in the area of pragmatic language.

(Newman & McGregor, 2006)

For children with speech or language impairments, the *form* of language poses challenges; specifically it is noted that there is great difficulty with the grammar of verbs (e.g., tense and agreement), the understanding of morphemes, and the development of more complex sentences, such as conjoined and embedded sentences.

In the area of *content* (semantics), children must understand that words can have multiple meanings (Nippold, 2007) that support the understanding of language (e.g., metaphors, idioms, humor). Children with speech or language impairments will tend to have smaller vocabularies and have challenges with word retrieval. They will often need more exposure to learning vocabulary. They may also have difficulty gleaning the meaning of a word within text (McGregor, 2009).

Impairment in the area of *use* (pragmatics) may hinder participation in the social or functional aspects of communication (Norbury, 2014). Although the *use* of language may not be as large a challenge for children with speech or language impairment as *form* and *content*, it can still pose a challenge for students with speech and language impairments, specifically in tasks such as making requests, making comments, and adjusting a message to ensure that the appropriate amount and type of information is conveyed to a listener. A child's social skill acquisition and competence may be impacted in this regard. For example, taking turns in conversations and initiating a topic of conversation are areas that may be challenging for children with speech or language impairments.

Overall, it is important to examine proficiency with the five elements of language as a means of truly understanding the scope of the speech or language impairment that a student has.

1. Give an example of how form, content, and use may be impacted for a child with a speech or language impairment.

2. Discuss the difference between expressive and receptive language, and describe how each area may be impacted for a child with a speech or language impairment.

3. What is the difference between communication, language, and speech? Why is it important to understand this in relation to understanding children with a speech or language impairment?

Causes and Types of Speech and Language Impairment

Genetics/Biological/Medical

Speech or language impairments may be congenital, or disorders present at birth, such as cleft lip and/or palate, which is a relatively common birth defect that impacts a child's speech.

Stuttering is a speech impairment that impacts fluency. It is thought to be neurogenetic (signal abnormalities between the brain and nerves, or muscles are not functioning properly) and/or psychogenic (originating from the part of the brain that governs speech). Stuttering is often very noticeable, as the child will use sound repetitions, prolong sounds in words, or have unanticipated stoppages. Children may also exhibit struggling body movements as a means of trying to speak (Wolk & LaSalle, 2015). Box 9.1 is an example of a speech-language pathologist's evaluation of a child who stutters (adapted from work by Erica Anne Pirolli, MS CCC-SLP, Speech Language Pathologist).

Box 9.1 Evaluation of Stuttering by a Speech-Language Pathologist

Stuttering Severity Instrument–4 (SSI-4)

The Stuttering Severity Instrument–4 (SSI-4) assesses the areas of fluency through speaking and reading tasks. The student is given a score based on the frequency and duration of stuttering moments and physical concomitants present. Kaitlyn received an overall score of 16, placing her in the 25th to 40th percentiles, indicating a mild fluency disorder. Kaitlyn's detailed performance is as follows:

(Continued)

(Continued)

Frequency

(Task scores range from 2 to 9, based on percentage of disfluencies)

	%SS (percentage of disfluencies)	Task Score
Reading Task	3.6	5
Speaking Task	8.9	7
Average %SS on all tasks	6.25	-N/A-
Total Frequency Score		12

Duration

(Scaled scores range from 2 to 9, based on average length of disfluencies)

Average length of 3 longest stuttering events	Scaled Score
Fleeting (< 0.5 sec)	2
Total Duration Score	2

Physical Concomitants

(Based on a psychometric scale, where 0 is not present and 5 is severe)

Distracting sounds (e.g., noisy breathing, clicking sounds)	0
Facial grimaces (e.g., jaw jerking, tongue protruding)	0
Head movements (e.g., excessive eye blinking, poor eye contact)	2
Movements of the extremities (e.g., foot- tapping, hand-tapping)	0
Total Physical Concomitant Score	2

Total Score = 16   Percentile = 25–40   Severity = mild

Naturalness

(Based on a psychometric scale, where 1 is highly natural-sounding speech and 9 is highly unnatural-sounding speech)

Speech naturalness	3

Kaitlyn's dysfluencies were characterized primarily by whole-word and phrasal repetitions and interjections (e.g., "uh, um"). Part-word repetitions were occasionally noted, particularly in the reading task. These repetitions were often repeated once (e.g., "and—and"), with a maximum repetition of two times (e.g., "and then—and then—and then"). These repetitions were fleeting and, on average, did not last longer than 0.5 seconds. Kaitlyn demonstrated excessive eye blinking while talking; however, this does not distract the listener from the content of the message.

Kaitlyn's overall speech is considered natural-sounding, with the exception of a slight soft-spoken quality with mild dysfluencies. It should be noted that Kaitlyn's dysfluencies increase in frequency when providing a speaking sample in Spanish. These dysfluencies were also characterized by interjections and whole-word, phrasal, and part-word repetitions. Kaitlyn reports that she is not bothered by her "bumpy speech." Overall, Kaitlyn's performance on this test indicates a mild fluency disorder.

Some researchers have proposed a neurological basis for language impairments, stemming from central nervous system dysfunction. Scans have shown differences between the brains of children who are typically developing and the brains of children with speech or language impairment during auditory processing tasks (Ullman & Pierpont, 2005). They note that there appear to be abnormalities in the frontal cortex, specifically Broca's area, and the basal ganglia. Additionally, there have been studies on how children with a speech or language impairment process information, indicating that there may be processing limitations, such as reduction in the speed at which information may be taken in and held in short- and long-term memory (Wareing, Fisk, Murphy, & Montgomery, 2005).

Other childhood disorders that result in language impairments are childhood apraxia, which is the inability to execute a learned movement, and aphasia, which results from damage to the language center of the brain. The most common cause of this is stroke and or brain injury (ASHA, 2007).

Chronic ear infections have also been noted as a cause that may impact a child's development of speech and language (Racanello & McCabe, 2010), as ear infections may result in a level of hearing loss that hinders the child's ability to hear the sounds of language.

Environmental

Some of the environmental causes that exist for other disabilities also exist for children with a speech or language impairment. For example, brain injury, abuse and neglect, and not having appropriate language models present in one's environment can impact a child's communication, language, and speech development. Poverty is often thought to be a leading cause of disability, as a lack of nutrition and malnourishment may negatively impact a child's brain and physical development (Perkins, Finegood, & Swain, 2013). Additionally, parental and family factors, such as a parent's level of education, will impact a child's language abilities due to such things as access to a language model, as well as stress within the family system. To illustrate, Barton's 2004 study revealed that 3-year-old children coming from professional families had vocabularies that were as large as those of parents who were on welfare. Additionally, family history of literacy and/or communication problems, as well as birth order, particularly later birth, indicates a greater risk of speech and language impairments (Choudhury & Benasich, 2003).

How the Diagnosis Is Made/Who Makes the Diagnosis

After thinking about the criteria, characteristics, and causes that are associated with speech and language impairments, we will now turn our attention to thinking about how a diagnosis is made and who makes the diagnosis.

In the area of Speech or language impairment, the parent(s), teacher(s) and student will be involved with the speech-language pathologist in completing the evaluation. The speech-language pathologist will play a key role in the evaluation, assessment, and intervention of this population of students, and teachers often will provide input on student performance and work toward helping achieve the goals that have been placed within the child's IEP. Communication, language, and speech will all be assessed. Depending on the outcome of the evaluation, a determination of eligibility will be made. If the child is deemed eligible for special education services, an IEP will be developed.

The speech-language pathologist will use both formal and informal assessment techniques—such as norm-referenced assessments; interviews of the teacher(s), the parent(s), and the student; developmental scales; observation of the child in the home and school settings; and language samples. The following are examples of information that could be gained from interviews and observations:

- "Joseph currently attends one speech-language therapy session per week in a small group for 30 minutes each session. Therapy focuses on increasing social skills and flexibility of thinking."

- "Joseph has made good progress in initiating topics with his peers and clinician in the speech room, as well as asking connected questions to show interest in another person's topic. He still struggles in areas such as taking another person's point of view, drawing conclusions and making inferences regarding a person's behavior or words (e.g., say one thing, mean a different thing), and applying these skills to the classroom setting. Strategies that have been successful in addressing these goals include direct instruction, modeling, and role-playing."

- "Joseph's teacher reported that these skills negatively impact his performance in the classroom. Joseph struggles with taking the perspective of characters in books, making inferences, and understanding motives. He also struggles in thinking flexibly when writing (e.g., embellishing true events)."

Examples of two types of norm-referenced assessments (Clinical Evaluation of Language Fundamentals–5 and the Comprehensive Assessment of Spoken Language) used by a certified speech-language pathologist are included in Box 9.2 (adapted from work by Erica Anne Pirolli, MS CCC-SLP, Speech Language Pathologist).

Box 9.2 Examples of Two Formal Evaluation Tools Used by a Speech-Language Pathologist

The Clinical Evaluation of Language Fundamentals–Fifth Edition (CELF-5) (Ages 9 and above)

The Clinical Evaluation of Language Fundamentals–Fifth Edition (CELF-5) assesses the areas of word meanings (semantics), word and sentence structure (morphology and syntax), and the recall and retrieval of oral language. Julie's core language score of 78 fell within borderline limits. Specific subtest scores were as follows:

Subtest	Raw Score	Scaled Score	Percentile Rank	Interpretation
Receptive Language				
Understanding Spoken Paragraphs	12	9	37	Average
Semantic Relationships	6	5	5	Low
Expressive Language				
Formulated Sentences	38	7	16	Borderline
Recalling Sentences	40	5	5	Low
Core & Index Scores	Raw Score	Standard Score	Percentile Rank	Interpretation
Core Language Score	26	78	7	Borderline

(Continued)

(Continued)

Individual subtests have a mean scaled score of 10, with a standard deviation of 3; average scores range from 8 to 12.

Core and index scores have a mean standard score of 100, with a standard deviation of 15; average scores range from 86 to 114.

Receptive Language

The Semantic Relationships Subtest

This subtest assesses the ability to interpret comparative, passive, spatial, and temporal relationships presented in spoken sentences. The student listens to a sentence and then draws a conclusion, answering from visually provided multiple choices. For example, the student listens to "Dan is taller than Jeff, and Lee is taller than both of them. Dan is . . ." The student then selects the answers "shorter than Lee" and "not the shortest." Julie received a scaled score of 5 on this subtest, equivalent to the 5th percentile. This indicates a low ability to interpret semantic relationships when compared to her peers.

Understanding Spoken Paragraphs Subtest

This subtest assesses the ability to attend to and comprehend the content of spoken paragraphs. The student listens to a paragraph read by the examiner and answers six to eight literal and inferential orally presented questions about the paragraph. A total of three paragraphs are presented in this manner. Julie's scaled score of 9 on this subtest indicates average listening comprehension skills when compared to her peers.

Expressive Language

The Formulated Sentences Subtest

This subtest assesses formulation of simple, compound, and complex sentences. The child is given a target word accompanied by a pictured stimulus and asked to use it in a sentence. For example, given the word "book" and a picture of students reading in a library, the student may say "The girl is reading a book." Julie's sentences were characterized by accurate semantic use but morphosyntactic errors (e.g., verb tense). She received a scaled score of 7 on this subtest, equivalent to the 16th percentile. This indicates borderline average morphosyntactic skills when compared to her peers.

The Recalling Sentences Subtest

This subtest assesses the ability to recall and repeat sentences of increasing length and complexity. Syntax and auditory memory skills primarily affect performance. Julie received a scaled score of 5 on this subtest, equivalent to the 5th percentile. This indicates low auditory memory and morphosyntactic skills when compared to her peers.

The Comprehensive Assessment of Spoken Language (CASL)

The CASL is an individually and orally administered, research-based, theory-driven oral language assessment battery for ages 3 through 21. Fifteen tests measure language-processing skills—comprehension, expression, and retrieval—in four language-structure categories: Lexical/Semantic, Syntactic, Supralinguistic, and Pragmatic. Based on Julie's performance on the CELF-5, only the tests required for the syntactic composite score were administered. Julie's performance was as follows, with detailed information below.

Individual Test	Raw Score	Standard Score	Percentile Rank	Interpretation
Syntax Construction	36	76	5th	Low
Grammatical Morphemes	15	66	1st	Very low
Grammaticality Judgment	56	83	13th	Borderline
Composite Scores	Sum of Standard Scores	Standard Score	Percentile Rank	Interpretation
Syntactic	225	74	4	Low

All scores have a mean standard score of 100, with a standard deviation of 15; average scores range from 86 to 114.

Syntactic Tests: Knowledge and Use of Grammar (Morphology and Syntax)

Syntax Construction (Grammatically Correct Oral Expression of Phrases and Sentences)

Examiner reads the stimulus item while the student looks at a picture. The student must respond in a way that is semantically and grammatically appropriate. "Here the boy is standing." (picture of a boy standing) "Here the boy is . . ." (picture of a boy sitting). Julie's standard score of 76 on this test, equivalent to the 5th percentile, indicates low morphosyntactic skills.

Grammatical Morphemes (Knowledge and Expression of Grammatical Analogies)

The examiner reads one set of words that demonstrates an analogy, and then reads the first word or phrase of a second pair. The student must then complete the analogy. "*Skate* is to *skated* as *talk* is to . . ."

Additional prompting and repetition of demonstration items was required to orient Julie to the analogy format of the test. After several repetitions, she was able to accurately respond to the demonstration items. Julie received a standard score of 66 on this test, equivalent to the 1st percentile. This indicates very low skills in this area.

(Continued)

Grammaticality Judgment (Judgment of and Ability to Correct Sentence Grammar)

The examiner reads a sentence, and the student has to determine whether it is grammatically correct. If it is incorrect, the student then has to correct the sentence using only one word. "The boy are happy. Does that sound right?" If the student says no, then he or she must make it sound right using only one word (e.g., "The boy *is* happy" or "The *boys* are happy"). Julie typically accurately identified sentences as correct/incorrect and was able to fix the incorrect sentences until she reached her ceiling. She received a standard score of 83 on this test, equivalent to the 13th percentile. This indicates borderline average receptive and expressive morphosyntactic abilities.

Assessment of Speech Sounds, Articulation, and Phonological Disorders

In the area of **speech**, problems may be related to a child's physical structure. However, a holistic evaluation will rule out hearing problems, as well as include an oral-facial examination, speech sound inventories, conversational sampling, and error pattern analysis.

An oral-facial examination may note such things as poor oral hygiene, enlarged tonsils, structural deviations of the teeth, or drooling (Schwartz, 2012). In this area, a speech-language pathologist will also note such things as the child's ability to move his or her tongue, blow, and purse his or her lips. Speech challenges may impact the child's voice in terms of loudness, quality, resonance, or richness; articulation, or the accurate production of sounds; and/or fluency, speaking without hesitation.

The speech inventory will primarily examine consonants and consonant blends, as most vowels are mastered early. Since consonants can appear at the initial, middle, and final positions of words, the speech inventory will address all sounds in different positions in words. Speech sound inventories generally include a set of pictures that targets a sound in a specific position. The child must name the pictures. In addition, speech-language pathologists will assess words within the context of sentences, recognizing that speech sounds are influenced by sounds and words that both proceed and follow. Speech inventories are usually audio or videotaped for further phonetic analysis. An example of an outcome in the area of voice from the speech-language pathologist's evaluation on the child noted above in Box 9.1 is presented in Box 9.3 (adapted from work by Erica Anne Pirolli, MS CCC-SLP, Speech Language Pathologist).

It is true that many very young children exhibit articulation disorders, including omissions, substitutions, or additions of sounds in words; however, it is those children for whom it lasts beyond the developmentally appropriate age that further

Box 9.3 Evaluation Result Related to Articulation/Fluency/Voice

Articulation at the time of this evaluation was characterized by dentalized productions of /s, z/, an anteriorly distorted "sh" sound, a substitution of "sh" for "j," and an /f, d/ substitution for voiceless and voiced "th," respectively. The substitutions could be due to the influence of a second language at home. An oral mechanism evaluation indicated an anterior overbite. Julie was stimulable for accurate productions of the /s, z/ sounds given verbal and visual cues to model. Through informal observation, voice quality was judged to be normal, and no dysfluencies were noted at the time of this evaluation.

assessment is needed. Of note is that an articulation disorder can negatively affect a child's ability to spell accurately. If the child is substituting sounds, sometimes he or she may have difficulty hearing the difference between the sounds (e.g., the difference between /key/ and /tea/).

In addition to those assessment techniques outlined above, the speech-language pathologist may use both standardized tests and informal methods of assessment in all areas. A widely used instrument used to assess articulation is the Goldman-Fristoe Test of Articulation. In this test, the speech-language pathologist asks students to complete sentences and/or name pictures to see if the child has any omissions, substitutions, and/or distortions of sounds.

The speech-language pathologist gains useful information for intervention by using conversational speech sampling, an important form of evaluation that is conducted via play for very young children or through the reading of passages for older children. It is often beneficial to record the samples through audio or video for further analysis. Speech will be transcribed, and the analysis will include the use of the International Phonetic Alphabet to examine speech sound errors. This type of analysis extends beyond a speech sound analysis, as many children may be able to produce sounds in single-word tasks but have difficulty producing sounds in context (Schwartz, 2012).

Assessment of Language

To assess language, informal assessments such as interviews with family members (to better understand the child's language and obtain an understanding of family history) and data collected via play, conversation, and narration can be used to assess aspects of both receptive and expressive language, including the comprehension of sentences and discourse (e.g., narratives), word retrieval, use of grammar, and the ability to process and produce language.

Language samples are a good means of analyzing many of the elements of language—such as determining any phonological errors that exist; measuring mean length of utterance (MLU) to analyze syntax; completing an NDW (number of different words) analysis, which helps examine word diversity and vocabulary; and evaluating pragmatics (Kuder, 2013). It is often best to record (either audio or video) language samples to allow for a more thorough evaluation (Kuder, 2013). In addition to informal assessments, the following are some of the most widely used norm-referenced assessments for assessing language:

- The Test of Language Development–Primary (TOLD-P) (Newcomer & Hammill): This test assesses picture vocabulary, relational vocabulary, oral vocabulary, grammatic understanding, sentence imitation, and grammatic completion

- The Expressive Vocabulary Test (EVT) (Williams)

- The Comprehensive Assessment of Spoken Language (CASL) (Carrow-Woolfold) (as used above in Box 9.2)

- The Test of Adolescent and Adult Language–5 (TOAL-4) (Hammill, Brown, Larsen, & Wiederhold)

Since they are norm-referenced assessments, they allow for a comparison to same-aged peers. Since language is one of the four developmental domains that describe child development, a child's language can also be compared to typical language development according to language development scales.

Assessment of pragmatics, which looks at language used in social contexts can be assessed both formally and informally. A popular test used in this area is the Test of Pragmatic Language (TOPL; Phelps-Terasaki & Phelps-Gunn), which requires the child to view pictures and describe the intent of the interaction that may be occurring within the picture. An example of testing in the area of pragmatic skills is shown in Box 9.4 (Adapted from work by Erica Anne Pirolli, MS CCC-SLP, Speech Language Pathologist).

Box 9.4 Results of an Evaluation of Pragmatics by a Speech-Language Pathologist

The Social Language Development Test–Elementary is a diagnostic test of social language skills, including nonverbal communication. It examines a student's ability to take the perspective of someone else, in order to make correct inferences, negotiate conflicts with peers, be flexible in interpreting situations, and support friends diplomatically. This test was administered to address concerns regarding John's social skills and pragmatic language skills. His scores are below, followed by detailed information.

		Raw Score	Standard Score	Percentile Rank	Interpretation
Making Inferences	Task a	5	89	23rd	Average
	Task b	6	82	11th	Low average
	Total	11	84	14th	Low average
Interpersonal Negotiation	Task a	18	81	11th	Low average
	Task b	13	86	18th	Average
	Task c	6	73	4th	Below average
	Total	37	77	6th	Below average
Multiple Interpretations		2	74	4th	Below average
Supporting Peers		26	96	41st	Average
Total Test		76	80	9th	Below average

Subtest and total scores on this test have a mean of 100 and a standard deviation of 15; average scores range from 85 to 115.

The Making Inferences Subtest

This subtest assesses how the student makes inferences about what a person is thinking, based on nonverbal and context clues and prior knowledge. During this task, the student is shown a picture of a live-action person with a thought bubble coming from his or her head. The student is asked to complete two tasks—one answering "What is this person thinking?" and the other answering "What do you see that tells you what s/he's thinking?" On the first task, the student must respond with a direct quote in first person (e.g., "I have so much work to do" vs. "He has so much work to do"). On the second task, the student must identify specific, relevant visual cues in the picture that match his or her response (e.g., "She is smiling" vs. "She looks happy").

John's performance on the first task was characterized by indirect quotes (e.g., "She's lonely"), difficulty drawing conclusions (e.g., "I found my car keys" rather than someone just acquiring their license), or literal interpretations (e.g., "He needs to rub something off his face"). John received a scaled score of 89 on this task, falling within the average range. His performance

(Continued)

(Continued)

on the second task was typically characterized by unspecific information (e.g., "Because of his facial expression," "Because she's hiding"). John received a scaled score of 82 on this task, falling within the low average range. Overall, John's standard score of 84 on this subtest indicated a low average ability to make inferences based on visual information and prior knowledge and experiences.

The Interpersonal Negotiation Subtest

This subtest assesses the student's ability to solve conflicts with peers through the skills of defining a problem, taking someone's perspective, and considering consequences of various resolutions. In this subtest, the student is orally presented with a situation (e.g., "You want to see a new pirate movie. Your friend wants to see a Disney cartoon that you have seen before"), and is asked to complete three tasks: (a) "What is the problem?" (b) "What could you do?" and (c) "Why would that be a good thing to do?" To receive full credit, the student's answer must (a) state the problem using a mutual perspective (e.g., "We both want different things"), (b) present a solution indicative of a mutual decision and dialogue (e.g., "We could agree to . . ." or "We could talk it over"), and (c) provide a justification that includes a reason to stay friends long-term (e.g., "We would stay friends" or "Friendship is more important than . . .").

John demonstrated difficulty on this subtest. His answers to task (a) typically included both perspectives, but not a mutual perspective (e.g., "I want X and he wants Y," rather than "We both want different things"). He received a score of 81 on this task, falling within the low average range.

In task (b), he typically presented a solution that satisfied one party without including dialogue (e.g., "I could go get a drink than we could go to the mummies [sic]"). He received a score of 86 on this task, falling within the low average range.

In task (c), John's justification typically indicated satisfaction for one party rather than pleasing both (e.g., "Because I don't wanna miss the fun"). John also did not include the importance of friendship in his answers. He received a score of 73 on this task, falling within the below average range.

Overall, John's performance on this subtest indicated an overall below-average ability to negotiate wants and needs while considering consequences and others' perspectives.

The Multiple Interpretations Subtest

This subtest assesses a student's ability to be a "flexible thinker." In this subtest, the student is presented with a picture of a live-action person and a brief oral description of his or her character (e.g., "This boy is hiking with the group ahead of him") and is asked to make two distinct interpretations about the picture. John demonstrated difficulty on this subtest. Often his interpretations were very similar (e.g., "I did something bad" and "I did something wrong") or irrelevant (e.g., "It might be a bouncy house" regarding a picture with a girl covering her eyes). His standard score of 74 on this subtest indicated a below-average ability to think flexibly in order to make two distinct interpretations about the same situation.

The Supporting Peers Subtest

The subtest assesses a student's ability to inhibit truthful but blunt responses and provide responses that support or please a friend. In this subtest, the student is orally presented with a situation (e.g., "Your friend asks you how you like her haircut. You don't like it. What do you say?") and asked to respond in a way that would be supportive. The student's responses are rated based on level of support (1 = little to no support; 4 = high support).

John performed well on this subtest; his responses typically indicated a high level of support with no indication of his true feelings, particularly on common occurrences (e.g., A bad haircut, what do you say? "It's beautiful"). Occasionally, John's responses were hurtful, particularly on questions regarding uncommon situations (e.g., "A friend wets a sleeping bag, what do you say? "Mom! He wet the sleeping bag!"). His score of 96 fell within average limits, indicating a relative strength in an ability to support his peers. Specifically, his performance on this subtest indicates a positive ability to learn appropriate responses based on real-life experiences.

Once the assessment is complete, the multidisciplinary team will examine the information specifically related to speech and language to determine eligibility. Eligibility will be considered if:

1. given the student's age, the student has a significant delay or difference in speech or language that would be considered a speech or language impairment;

2. the student's speech or language impairment adversely affects educational performance; and

3. the student would benefit from special education services.

Check Your Understanding 9.2

1. What is the role of the speech-language pathologist in the evaluation of children with a speech or language impairment? What areas of focus will he assess?

2. Following the evaluation, what needs to be considered for a child to receive special education services?

Other Characteristics

Intelligence/Academic Areas of Achievement

Children with a speech or language impairment may have varying levels of intelligence and cognitive abilities; further, they may be gifted learners, or they may struggle with academics and learning. However, due to the fact that language and cognition go hand in hand, many children with a speech or language impairment may struggle to learn, since language is how we communicate, understand, and explore (Apel & Henbest, 2016). Language is how the child is expected to produce in the school setting through both verbal and written means. Vocabulary and comprehension are expected to increase, and all written communication is to become more complex as the child progresses through the grades.

Students with a speech or language impairment may have challenges in academics—specifically in the areas of reading and writing—and may also have difficulty in other areas, due to language comprehension difficulties (e.g., following directions in math). Research focusing on reading has shown that children with a speech or language impairment are at a higher risk of difficulties in reading (Reed, 2012), as they may have difficulties sounding out words and challenges with fluency that impact their reading comprehension. Further, some math programs/curricula are highly language-dependent and can result in children having greater difficulties in math as a result of their language impairment.

Behavior and Social/Emotional Characteristics

Research has shown that children who have challenges with communication may exhibit frustration and inappropriate behaviors (either externalizing or internalizing) and may develop a tendency to isolate themselves, due to not getting their needs and wants met and/or not being able to keep up socially with peers (Carr & Durand, 1985). This may result in the child being considered as a child with a behavioral problem, and at the extreme end, a child with an Emotional Disturbance (Benner, Ralston, & Feuerborn, 2012) (see Chapter 10).

Many children with a speech or language impairment may have difficulties socially interacting with peers and emotionally with self-esteem as a result of their speech and language difficulties. Additionally, many children with problems in this area may be the target of bullying and negative opinions related to their struggles with fluency, mispronunciations, and difficulties with conversations. Children with these difficulties may choose to not communicate very much, if at all, leading to social isolation (Lee, Gibbon, & Spivey, 2016).

Case Study 9.1: Extension to Instruction

According to Polloway, Miller, and Smith (2012), for children to be successful communicators, they must develop phonological awareness, understand the connection between speech and print, be able to exhibit both narrative and non-narrative discourse, and reflect upon as well as synthesize language.

In the school setting, the child may receive either individualized or small-group instruction outside of the classroom, and/or the speech-language pathologist may serve as a consultant and team member within the classroom. Each of these approaches could be advantageous for the child; however, regardless of which approach is used, all team members must be aware of goals being worked on and ways in which they can incorporate the goals and interventions throughout the day to support the child's education. Attainment of goal areas in spontaneous communication will mean success (Bernstein & Teigerman-Farber, 2009). Depending on the child's needs, he or she may receive articulation therapy, intensive instruction in phonics, work in language and literacy skills, and instruction in the social aspects of communication. The mode of instruction may include the following (Shriberg & Kwiatkowski, 1982):

- Soliciting targeted goal responses from the child

- Using training stimuli to elicit goal responses

- Incorporating antecedent instructional events with feedback

- Sequencing instruction and motivation

Interventions aimed at expanding the child's communication, such as extending beyond the child's utterance, embedding a new comment with the child's prior utterance, modeling, and scaffolding, are all communicative techniques used by speech-language pathologists and teachers to enhance communication (Bernstein & Teigerman-Farber, 2009).

Assistive Technology

Assistive technology may play a large part in supporting instruction in each of these areas but specifically for language and literacy instruction (see Table 9.1). If literacy becomes the area of focus, specifically in the later grades, the speech-language pathologist will likely collaborate with general and special education teachers to address such things as phonemic awareness, sequencing, and comprehension, as well as syntax and semantics in writing and oral communication.

Assistive technology including computer hardware and software, tablets, and smartphones for children with a speech or language impairment can support both practice and production of language. For example, software such as Dragon Dictation uses voice recognition through which students can speak and see their words to compose. Children with more severe language disorders may require a speech-generating device (SGD) that the speech-language pathologist can program to meet their educational, personal, or functional needs.

Table 9.1 Assistive Technology to Enhance Language and Literacy

Technology	Description	Citation/Source
Software		
Fast ForWord	Phonemic awareness and skills	www.scilearn.com
Earobics	Phonemic awareness and skills	www.earobics.com
Simon S.I.O. (Sounds It Out)	Uses an onset/rime or word-families approach and provides clear visual presentations	www.donjohnston.com
Lexia	Phonemic awareness and skill development	www.lexialearning.com
Classroom Suite 4	Phonemic awareness and skills	www.intellitools.com
Read Naturally Software Edition	Fluency practice	www.readnaturally.com
Reading Assistant	Feedback on misread words	www.scilearn.com
Raz-Kids.com	Reading books	www.raz-kids.com
Start-to-Finish Library	Reading books	learningtools.donjohnston.com/product/start-to-finish
Storyline Online	Provides reading models	www.storylineonline.net
e-Texts		
Project Gutenberg		www.gutenberg.org
Accessible Book Collections		www.accessiblebookcollections.org

Check Your Understanding 9.3

1. What are some characteristics of children with a speech or language impairment? How do they manifest in the classroom?

2. Describe three evaluation techniques that could be used to assess speech and language performance.

3. In which settings may speech and language services take place? What role may the teacher play in those services?

Case Study 9.2: Sabrina

At 5 years of age, Sabrina was referred by her kindergarten teacher for evaluation—although Sabrina's family could understand most of her speech, primarily it was assumed due to context; her expressive language was only understood by others approximately 40% of the time. She was making mistakes on speech sounds that should have been secured by now, such as /k/, /g/, and /f/, as well as making substitutions—/p/ for /f/, /t/ for /k/, and /d/ for /g/. This was occurring in all words spoken. An evaluation was done that included evaluating Sabrina's oral structure, which revealed an articulation disorder that impacted her ability to make particular sounds. The speech-language pathologist began to intervene on these early developing sounds by modeling and using a tactile approach (e.g., touching of lips and mouth). He also used games that required Sabrina to use her sounds in conversation.

Currently, at age 7, Sabrina continues to struggle; however, what is most noticeable now is her below-age-level grammar mistakes (e.g., dropping the "is" verb, misproducing past tenses of verbs, especially irregular verbs like "go" and "went"). She also struggles with syntax order, expressing her thoughts, word retrieval, and organization. The speech-language pathologist provides an hour of services a week. Due to the severity of Sabrina's disability, 1:1 direct services are provided, as well as consultation with the classroom teacher. Drill and practice work are done with grammar, as well as within conversation.

Check Your Understanding 9.4

1. Why do you think the family could "understand" Sabrina, but those outside of her family could not?

2. Looking at the goals the speech-language pathologist is working on with Sabrina, what do you think would be recommended to be carried out in the classroom? What could the kindergarten teacher have done, and what could the present teacher do?

CHAPTER SUMMARY

This focus of this chapter was to explain the definition, diagnostic criteria, eligibility, and needs of children with a speech or language impairment. Several sample reports were included, to demonstrate the complex procedures and analyses that are involved in the diagnostic and eligibility process associated with speech and language impairment. Additionally, we covered the role of the multidisciplinary team, with specific emphasis on the role of the speech-language pathologist, which is critical in evaluation and intervention to support this very diverse group of students.

APPLY WHAT YOU HAVE LEARNED

1. Discuss the assessment process for identifying speech disorders as compared to language disorders. How might you assess the elements of language differently when evaluating for speech as compared to language disorders?

2. How might you assess for expressive language? Receptive language? Research and identify some strategies a classroom teacher might use to address areas of need in each.

3. Select a technological tool to research from Table 9.1. What have you learned about this tool? How would this tool help a child with a speech or language Impairment? How might it be incorporated into the classroom?

REFERENCES

American Speech-Language-Hearing Association (ASHA). (2007). Childhood apraxia of speech [Position Statement]. Retrieved from www.asha.org/policy

Apel, K., & Henbest, V. S. (2016). Affix meaning knowledge in first through third grade students. *Language, Speech and Hearing Services in Schools, 47*(2), 148–156.

Barton, P. (2004). Why does the gap persist? *Educational Leadership, 62*(3), 8–13. Retrieved from http://www.ascd.org/publications/educational-leadership/nov04/vol62/num03/Why-Does-the-Gap-Persist%C2%A2.aspx

Benner, G. J., Ralston, N. C., & Feuerborn, L. (2012). The effect of the Language for Thinking Program on the cognitive processing and social adjustment of students with emotional and behavioral disorders. *Preventing School Failure, 56*(1), 47–54.

Bernstein, D. K., & Teigerman-Farber, E. (2009). *Language and communication disorders in children* (6th ed.). Boston, MA: Pearson Education/Allyn and Bacon Publishers.

Bloom, L., & Lahey, M. (1978). *Language development and language disorders.* New York, NY: Wiley.

Carr, E. G., & Durand, M. (1985). Reducing behavior problems through functional communication training. *Journal of Applied Behavior Analysis, 18*(2), 111–126.

Centers for Disease Control and Prevention. (2016, February). *National estimates for 21 selected major birth defects, 2004–2006.* Atlanta, GA: National Center for Birth Defects and Developmental Disabilities. Retrieved from http://www.cdc.gov/ncbddd/birthdefects/data.html

Choudhury, N., & Benasich, A. A. (2003). A family aggregation study. The influence of family history and other risk factors on language development. *Journal of Speech, Language and Hearing Research, 46,* 261–272.

Gillon, G. T. (2004). *Phonological awareness: From research to practice.* New York, NY: Guilford Press.

Kuder, S. J. (2013). *Teaching students with language and communication disabilities* (4th ed.). Boston, MA: Pearson.

Lee, A. L., Gibbon, F. E., & Spivey, K. (2016). Children's attitudes toward peers with unintelligible speech associated with cleft lip and/or palate. *The Cleft Palate-Craniofacial Journal, 54*(3), 262–268.

McGregor, K. K. (2009). Semantics in child language disorders. In R. G. Schwartz (Ed.), *Handbook of child language disorders* (pp. 365–387). New York, NY: Psychology Press.

Montgomery, J. (2005). Effects of input rate and age on the real-time language processing of children with specific language impairment. *International Journal of Language and Communication Disorders, 1*, 177–178.

National Institute on Deafness and Other Communication Disorders (NIDCD). (2016, April). *Quick statistics about voice, speech, language.* Bethesda, MD: National Institutes of Health. Retrieved from https://www.nidcd.nih.gov/health/statistics/quick-statistics-voice-speech-language

Newman, R. M., & McGregor, K. K. (2016). Teachers and laypersons discern quality differences between narratives produced by children with or without SLI. *Journal of Speech, Language, and Hearing, 49*(5), 1022–1036.

Nippold, M. A. (2007). *Later language development: School-age children, adolescents, and young adults* (3rd ed.). Austin, TX: PRO-ED.

Norbury, C. F. (2014). Practitioner review: Social (pragmatic) communication disorder: Conceptualization, evidence and clinical implication. *Journal of Childhood Psychology and Psychiatry, 55*(3), 204–216.

Perkins, S. C., Finegood, E. D., & Swain, J. E. (2013). Poverty and language development: Roles of parenting and stress. *Innovations in Clinical Neuroscience, 10*(4), 10–19.

Polloway, E. A., Miller, L., & Smith, T. E. C. (2012). *Language instruction for students with disabilities* (4th ed.). Denver, CO: Love Publishing.

Racanello, A., & McCabe, P. C. (2010). Role of otitis media in hearing loss and language deficits. In P. C. McCabe & S. R. Shaw (Eds.), *Pediatric disorders: Current topics and interventions for educators* (pp. 29–31). Thousand Oaks, CA: Corwin.

Reed, V. A. (2012). *An introduction to children with language disorders* (4th ed.). Upper Saddle River, NJ: Pearson.

Schwartz, H. D. (2012). *A primer on communication and communicative disorders.* Upper Saddle River, NJ: Pearson.

Shames, G. H., & Anderson, N. B. (2006). *Human communication disorders: An introduction* (7th ed.). Boston, MA: Allyn & Bacon.

Shriberg, L., & Kwiatkowski, J. (1982). Phonological disorders II: A conceptual framework for management. *Journal of Speech and Hearing Disorders, 47*, 242–256.

Ullman, M., & Pierpont, E. (2005). Specific language impairment is not specific to language: The procedural deficit hypothesis. *Cortex, 41*(3), 399–433.

Wareing, M., Fisk, J. E., Murphy, P., & Montgomery, C. (2004). Verbal working memory deficits in current and previous users of MDMA. *Human Psychopharmacology, 19*, 225–234. doi:10.1002/hup.586

Wolk, L., & LaSalle, L. R. (2015). Phonological complexity in school-aged children who stutter and exhibit a language disorder. *Journal of Fluency Disorders, 43*, 40–53.

Zebron, S., Mhute, I., & Musingafi, M. C. C. (2015). Classroom challenges: Working with pupils with communication disorders. *Journal of Education and Practice, 6*(9), 18–22.

Emotional Disturbance

Vicki A. McGinley, PhD

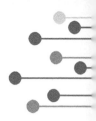

Learning Objectives

After completion of this chapter, you should be able to:

- Define emotional disturbance (ED).

- List the various types of EDs and discuss their distinguishing features.

- Explore the different assessments used to make an ED diagnosis.

- Explain how children with ED are identified for eligibility for special education.

- Discuss why a Functional Behavior Assessment (FBA) is an effective diagnostic tool when assessing problematic behaviors associated with ED.

- Examine a positive behavior support plan (PBSP) and identify its different components.

Key Terms

anxiety disorder (p. 295)	manifestation determination (p. 305)
conduct disorder (p. 295)	mood disorder (p. 295)
eating disorder (p. 296)	personality disorder (p. 296)
externalized behaviors (p. 297)	positive behavior support plan (PBSP) (p. 306)
Functional Behavior Assessment (FBA) (p. 304)	psychotic disorder (p. 296)
internalized behaviors (p. 297)	

Introduction to the Chapter

This chapter provides information about students who are identified with emotional disturbance (ED). A student with ED might exhibit an inability to build or maintain interpersonal relationships, exhibit inappropriate types of behavior, display unhappiness or depression, or develop physical symptoms or fears to such a marked degree that they have a negative impact on his education and require special education services.

EDs may be the result of physiological causes or heredity, and some research suggests that biochemical abnormalities and temperament also play a part. For example, children who have been exposed in utero to maternal alcohol or drugs are more likely than other children to develop ED. There are also a number of factors in a child's life that can impact social, psychological, and emotional development resulting in ED. These include different forms of trauma, such as abuse and neglect; poor living conditions (e.g., living in poverty, which can expose a child to environmental toxins); and living with any form of oppression (e.g., racism). In the past, research on disordered behaviors indicated they can stem from learned behaviors that may come from such activities as viewing violence, watching violence on television, playing video games that are violent, and listening to violent music, as these activities may desensitize a child. This is particularly true if these activities are coupled with any of the risk factors identified above (American Academy of Pediatrics, 2009). There is also strong evidence that both biological and psychosocial factors play a role, as some children have a predisposition to developing a disorder.

To date, students with ED compose the fourth-largest disability category of children served in K–12 classrooms (Oswald, Best, Coutinho, & Nagle, 2003). Similar to other disabilities discussed in this text, it is necessary that evaluations conducted on students with ED be accurate and non-biased (e.g., reduce possible cultural and ethnic factors associated with the testing) to reduce overrepresentation and issues of disproportionality. It is also relevant to make a distinction between students who have emotional disturbance and those who have been identified as being socially maladjusted, as the latter have been excluded from this IDEA disability category. To illustrate, there are notable differences in school behaviors, attitudes, and relationships between children who are eligible for special education under the category of ED and those excluded children considered socially maladjusted. Table 10.1 depicts the differences between these two.

Having ED impacts social, emotional, and behavioral domains. Because of the complexity of this IDEA category, it is important that the child's multidisciplinary team (MDT) be composed of individuals who will best support the child. Parents, teachers, school social workers, school counselors, and community-based psychologists can all play a vital role in supporting a child with ED. Additionally, a pediatrician and/or psychiatrist may be employed by the child's family to prescribe medication and monitor the student's progress in an effort to support his education, and life, in general.

Table 10.1	Differences Between Emotional Disturbance and Social Maladjustment	
Indicator	**Emotional Disturbance**	**Social Maladjustment**
Behavior(s)	May exhibit either internalizing or externalizing behaviors, such as hurting self and others; noncompliance with authority; needy or avoids seeking help; tense; fearful	Noncompliant with authority; rejects support; mostly exhibits externalizing behaviors; hurts others
School Impact	School is challenging—does better with structure; truant due to emotional and psychosomatic issues; achievement may be uneven and may be impacted by anxiety, depression, or emotions	Dislike for school except for social purposes; breaks rules and structure; chooses to miss school; achievement influenced by the above
Relationships	Difficulty making and keeping friends; may be perceived as odd; poorly developed social skills	May have a peer group that is delinquent, tough, "perceived as cool"; well-tuned to social cues

Adapted from Wayne County Regional Educational Services Agency. (2004). *Social maladjustment: A guide to differential diagnosis and educational options*. Retrieved from http://mosi.mysdhc.org/teacher/0119silverman/Social%20 Maladjustment.pdf

Children with ED may be referred to by many different titles in the school setting. Examples of the various terms associated with ED are "behavior disordered," "emotionally impaired," and "seriously emotionally disturbed." These names exist despite the fact that the correct educational label designated by IDEA is "emotional disturbance."

IDEA Definition of Emotional Disturbance

(i). Emotional disturbance means a condition exhibiting one or more of the following characteristics over a long period of time and to a marked degree that adversely affects a child's educational performance:

a. An inability to learn that cannot be explained by intellectual, sensory, or health factors.

b. An inability to build or maintain satisfactory interpersonal relationships with peers and teachers.

c. Inappropriate types of behavior or feelings under normal circumstances.

    d. A general pervasive mood of unhappiness or depression.

    e. A tendency to develop physical symptoms or fears associated with personal or school problems.

(ii). Emotional disturbance includes schizophrenia. The term does not apply to children who are socially maladjusted, unless it is determined that they have an emotional disturbance under paragraph (c)(4)(i) of this section.

(IDEA, 20 U.S.C. § 1401 (2004), 20 C.F.R. § 300.8(c)(4))

This definition will be used as the basis for the chapter's definition of emotional disturbance.

Diagnostic Criteria and Related Characteristics

Although mental disorders have been studied and treated throughout our history, it was not until recently that children exhibiting emotional and behavioral problems were reported in the research and subsequently considered for diagnosis, classification, and intervention. The first classification of individuals with ED began in 1893, when the World Health Organization (WHO) developed a system to classify diseases and illnesses, referred to as the International Statistical Classification of Diseases (ICD). This document eventually included a section on mental disorders (Shorter, 2013).

In 1921, the American Psychiatric Association (APA) developed the first edition of the American Medical Association's Standard Classified Nomenclature of Disease. This system was designed for diagnosing persons with severe psychiatric and neurological disorders. In the late 19th and early 20th centuries, other professional organizations worked to classify populations they were seeing with psychological and personality disorders, such as veterans returning from war. (APA, n.d.)

In 1952, the APA developed a variant of the ICD with the first publication of the DSM, containing diagnostic categories for clinical use. Since that time, professionals involved in the mental health field have worked to update and amend the DSM over the years. These revisions require extensive work in validating the diagnostic criteria for research and clinical work, as well as adding and deleting disorders. The final version to date, the DSM-5, was published in 2013 (Shorter, 2013).

Within the DSM-5's classification system, there are a number of conditions, referred to as mental disorders, that are not explicitly stated in IDEA. Students with mental disorders, however, may be served under the category of emotional disturbance if their disability rises to the level where their educational performance is impacted. Other children with ED may not require special education and related services and may be effectively served under Section 504 of the Rehabilitation Act of 1973. These students would likely benefit from accommodations, such as preferential seating, frequently reviewing rules and expectations, consistent routines, and minimal transitions throughout the day, in order to be successful (see Chapter 1 for more information on the Section 504 Agreement Plan).

Types of Disorders

When discussing EDs, it is important to highlight some of the more prevalent mental disorders. These include anxiety disorders, mood disorders, conduct disorders, personality disorders, eating disorders, and psychotic disorders.

Anxiety Disorders

The DSM-5 describes anxiety disorders as disorders that share the features of excessive fear and anxiety (American Psychiatric Association, 2013). "Fear" is defined as the emotional response to a real or perceived threat, and "anxiety" is defined as the anticipation of a future threat. Anxiety disorders occur more frequently in females (2:1 ratio) than males, and each is diagnosed only when the symptoms are not attributed to the psychological effects of substances and/or medications, or another medical condition not explained by another mental disorder. Physical symptoms include restlessness, feeling "keyed up" or on edge, being easily fatigued, difficulty concentrating, irritability, and sleep disturbance (American Psychiatric Association, 2013).

Mood Disorders

Mood disorders are another type of ED that are exhibited by children in schools today. These include disorders such as depression and bipolar disorder. The federal definition of emotional disturbance in IDEA defines depression as a "pervasive mood of unhappiness or depression" (IDEA, 1997). Common features of these disorders include disruptive mood dysregulation disorder, major depressive disorder, and persistent depressive disorder (dysthymia). When individuals possess a mood disorder, they may feel sad, empty, or irritable, and these feelings might be accompanied by somatic and cognitive changes that significantly affect functioning. Mood disorders can lead to distracted students, oppositional behavior, missed class time, social withdrawal, substance abuse, suicidal risk, and suicide itself.

Conduct Disorders

Conduct disorders are a severe type of ED. The DSM-5 defines conduct disorders as a "repetitive and persistent pattern of behavior in which the basic rights of others or social norms are violated" (APA, 2013, p. 469) manifested by a lack of remorse or guilt, exhibiting lack of empathy, and violating the rights of others. Conduct disorders in the classroom can lead to a child consistently breaking rules, as well as inflicting harm on others.

Personality Disorders

Personality disorders are a type of ED that make obtaining positive social relationships with peers and others difficult for children who possess them. Characteristics associated with a personality disorder usually become recognizable during adolescence or early adult life when the child is experiencing other challenges with adolescence. By definition, a "personality disorder is an enduring pattern of inner experience and behavior that deviates markedly from the expectations of the individual's culture, is pervasive and inflexible, has an onset in adolescence or early childhood, is stable over time, and leads to distress or impairment (APA, 2013, p.645). The DSM-5 includes a number of personality disorders. Though each possesses its own distinct characteristics, they have similar characteristics (APA, 2013).

Eating Disorders

Eating disorders are a group of EDs characterized by behaviors associated with eating that are related to thoughts and emotions. There are three eating disorders that are commonly present in today's schools: anorexia nervosa, bulimia nervosa, and binge-eating disorder. Individuals with anorexia nervosa severely limit or restrict their food, resulting in extreme weight loss and even death. Those with bulimia nervosa frequently eat large quantities of food and then vomit, use diuretics, or overexercise to purge themselves of what they have eaten. Individuals with a binge-eating disorder engage in behaviors similar to those with bulimia nervosa, yet they do not purge, exercise excessively, or fast after they have consumed large quantities of food (NIMH, 2016).

Psychotic Disorders

Psychotic disorders are considered serious illnesses affecting one's mind. There are several different types of psychotic disorders, including schizophrenia, psychotic disorder, schizotypal personality disorder, and delusional disorder. Each of these disorders is a severe mental disorder that results in abnormal thinking and perceptions, making it possible for an individual to lose touch with reality (MedlinePlus, 2019). Similar to students with conduct disorders, students with psychotic disorders have difficulty making and maintaining friendships.

Check Your Understanding 10.1

1. Based on what you have read in this section, do you believe that professionals in educational settings should have access to information from the community mental health facilities? Why or why not?

2. Select two of the disorders outlined above (anxiety disorder, conduct disorder, personality disorder, etc.), and discuss why the characteristics associated with these disorders would be problematic in a classroom setting.

Behavioral Manifestations

In the field of behavior, in order to more effectively classify challenging behaviors, professionals categorize behavior into two distinct groups: externalized behaviors and internalized behaviors. These two categories are shaped by environmental and biological factors. On the whole, males tend to exhibit more externalizing behaviors, and females tend to demonstrate ones that are internalizing in nature (Trout, Nordness, Pierce, & Epstein, 2003).

Externalized Behavior

Externalized behaviors are hard-to-miss behaviors such as loud, disruptive, and often annoying and potentially aggressive behaviors. They are more overt and directed outward at, or toward, someone or something else. Students who show these behaviors tend to lack self-control and find challenges in interactions with other students and adults. Examples of externalized behavior are being easily angered, verbal and physical aggression, acting out, lack of self-control, hyperactivity and impulsivity, noncompliance, tantrums, stealing, lying, and cheating. Students with extreme externalized behaviors may be educated in segregated classes or schools, due to their severe nature. Children demonstrating externalized behaviors tend to be more frequently referred for a comprehensive diagnostic evaluation, as these children's difficult behaviors stand out and can be more problematic in the school setting.

Internalized Behavior

On the other end of the spectrum, children who exhibit internalized behaviors seem introverted and may have problems that include worrying, fears, social withdrawal, sad affect, depression, headaches, dizziness, and other somatic complaints. Internalized behaviors are the opposite of acting out; they are directed inward (Gage, 2013). Special educators need to be particularly attentive to students suspected of having an internalized behavior, because such behaviors are not as easy to notice in the classroom as are externalized ones.

How the Diagnosis Is Made/Who Makes the Diagnosis

Although the DSM-5 has limited relevance to the evaluation and identification of children in the educational setting, it is used extensively in diagnosing and classifying children with mental disorders in the community. It is not uncommon for teachers to be unaware of a child's diagnosis made by an outside mental health professional, as it is not customarily expressed on the student's IEP, or even in the child's school records. In most cases, it is left to the child's parent or guardian to provide outside information (regarding evaluations, medication doses, etc.) to the school.

A child can be evaluated for ED either at school or in the community. Outside of the school setting, a psychologist, clinical licensed social worker, and/or psychiatrist working with the child will conduct observations of the child, examine and review the child's existing assessment information starting with any physical complaints, rule out alternatives, use his clinical judgment to decide a tentative classification, and then confirm it with diagnostic criteria from the DSM-5. Although a school psychologist may use the psychiatric diagnosis for confirmation of ED, a comprehensive diagnostic evaluation by the child's multidisciplinary team must be performed.

At school, when the child's problem behaviors occur over an extended period of time and are severe in nature, a child will be referred for a comprehensive diagnostic evaluation, where the emphasis of the evaluation will be on the emotional, behavioral, and social areas of concern. While teachers do not bear the responsibility of diagnosing students with ED, they do have the responsibility to refer students for an evaluation if they suspect that a student may qualify for special education. Once a student has been referred to the MDT for testing, several assessments will take place to determine the presence of a disability. Parents can be valuable members of the MDT during the assessment process, because they can provide key information about the student's behaviors at home and in the community that may be similar or different to those behaviors being exhibited in school. A comprehensive diagnostic evaluation for ED includes, at a minimum, the following:

1. A developmental history

2. Assessments of emotional and behavioral functioning

3. Assessment of academic achievement

4. Assessment of intellectual functioning

5. Medical information (if under the care of a professional, such as a psychiatrist)

Other areas of suspected delay that may also be assessed include speech, language, and communication, as well as adaptive behavior skills. As part of the comprehensive diagnostic evaluation, several assessments may be used. Table 10.2 details some assessments that might be included in the diagnostic process for ED.

Table 10.2 Assessments/Checklist for Identification of Emotional Disturbance		
Name of Assessment	Author(s)	Purpose of the Assessment
The Minnesota Multiphasic Personality Inventory	Butcher, Dahlstrom, Graham, Tellegen, & Kraemmer	Assesses personality traits and psychopathology using true/false questions
The Personality Inventory for Children	Wirt, Lachar, Seat, & Broen	The Personality Inventory for Children is an objective multidimensional test of child behavior, emotional and cognitive status. It consists of 275 items to be completed by the child's parent or other rater who knows the child well.
The Rorschach Ink Blot Test	Rorschach	Examines personality characteristics and emotional functioning. This test is often employed in diagnosing underlying thought disorders and differentiating psychotic from non-psychotic features.
The Children's Apperception Test	Bellak	A projective personality test used to assess individual variations in children's responses to standardized stimuli presented in the form of pictures of animals in common social situations. It takes 20–45 minutes to administer.
The Piers-Harris Children's Self-Concept Scale	Piers & Harris	Provides an overall view of an individual's self-perception. Areas measured include popularity, physical appearance, anxiety, intellectual and school status, behavioral adjustment, happiness and satisfaction. There are 60 test items.
The Child Behavior Checklist	Achenbach	A parent-report questionnaire on which the child is rated on various behavioral and emotional problems. It is used for evaluating maladaptive behavioral and emotional problems in preschool subjects aged 2 to 3 or in subjects between the ages of 4 and 18. It assesses internalizing and externalizing behaviors.
The Behavioral and Emotional Rating Scale	Epstein & Sharma	Gathers information on interpersonal strengths, family involvement, intrapersonal strength, school functioning, and affective strength.
The Behavior Assessment System for Children	Reynolds & Kamphaus	A test that looks for things like hyperactivity, aggression, and conduct problems. It also looks for anxiety, depression, attention and learning problems, and the lack of certain essential skills.

(Continued)

Table 10.2 (Continued)

The Social Emotional Dimension Scale	Hutton & Roberts	A rating scale for teachers, counselors, and psychologists to screen students ages 5-1/2 through 18-1/2 who are at risk of conduct disorders, behavior problems, or emotional disturbance. It assesses physical/fear reaction, depression reaction, avoidance or peer interaction, avoidance of teacher interaction, aggressive interaction, and inappropriate behaviors.
The Behavior Evaluation Scale	McCarney & Arthaud	Aids in diagnosis, placement, and planning for children with ED. It consists of 54 items (school) and 52 items (home), each associated with one of the five characteristics of the definition of behavioral disorders/emotional disturbance included in IDEA.
The Scales for Assessing Emotional Disturbance	Epstein & Cullinan	A norm-referenced instrument that teachers complete that references each dimensions of the IDEA definition.
The Behavior Rating Profile	Brown & Hammill	Evaluates students' behavior in home and school through various perspectives, including parents, teachers, peers, and the students themselves. It contains three scales: Student Rating Scales (home, school, and peer), Parent Rating Scales, and Teacher Rating Scales. In addition, a sociogram to be completed by peers is included.

Once the comprehensive diagnostic evaluation has been completed, the decision as to whether the child will be eligible for special education services under the category of ED is determined by responses to the following questions:

1. Does the child have one or more of the characteristics in the IDEA definition of ED?

2. Does the child's behavioral characteristics adversely affect his or her educational performance?

3. Can social maladjustment be eliminated as the sole cause of the child's behavioral problems?

4. Will the child benefit from specially designed instruction?

Other Characteristics

In addition to the main characteristics described above that are the reason a child will be classified with emotional disturbance, there are other characteristics that must be considered for evaluation, assessment, and intervention to best serve the child in the school setting.

Intelligence and Academics/Areas of Achievement

Students with ED typically fall into the average to low-average range of intelligence. As a result, they tend to be low performers in school, because, in addition to possessing moderate IQs, they are challenged with behavioral difficulties that add to their difficulties with regard to academic achievement. Several factors can contribute to lower achievement demonstrated by this student population, such as distractions in class, truancy, or time out of class for disciplinary reasons. The ability to achieve becomes increasingly challenging for students with ED, as the demands placed on students increases as they advance through the grade levels and more academic, social, and independent skills are required at each level. Without proactive and consistent behavioral monitoring and appropriate intervention, students with ED will continue to fall further behind their typical peers.

Social Characteristics

One of the most prevalent issues a child with ED faces is in the area of social skills and social competence. One specific social difficulty might be problems with peer relationships. Students with ED may not have very many, if any, friends. Children with more externalized behaviors tend to associate with younger children, whom they can boss around, or children who have similar types of behavioral problems. When surrounded with students who behave similarly, they may find their own behavior rewarded with positive responses. For children with more internalized behaviors, social withdrawal may be desired by these students, or it may be the result of a lack of social skills and social competence.

Health and Medical Status

Children with ED may not always experience physical health problems that are outside of the norm, but they can be prone to health issues due to past trauma, poverty, and the side effects of medicine. If a student with ED has experienced some type of trauma (e.g., physical abuse), it can directly impact his or her overall health and require medical attention. Similarly, if a child with ED is the product of an impoverished environment, he or she may not have been properly fed or cared for, resulting in a myriad of potential health issues. Although medications to treat the symptoms of ED can be very effective, they only last only as long as the individual takes the medicine prescribed. Typically, medications are paired with behavioral interventions to obtain the best results. For example, a specific medication may greatly reduce the symptoms of ED, but the addition of behavioral therapy can teach the individual self-management skills and coping strategies (Jensen, 2005).

Case Study 10.1: Emily Smith, a 10-Year-Old Child With Emotional Disturbance

Emily is withdrawn. She does not speak in class to the teacher or her peers. When she is "forced" to speak, no one can hear her and she makes intermittent eye contact. When in group work, she will not contribute, and at lunch and recess, she remains alone and isolated. The teacher has tried to pair her with more "sensitive, accepting" children, but she will not address them directly either.

Her attendance at school has been mediocre at best, and her grandmother, who is her primary guardian, has been notified on numerous occasions about attendance. She has indicated that "Emily is afraid of everything" and it sometimes is very hard to get her to leave the house.

There is a past history of abuse and neglect by Emily's biological parents, and, as a result, primary guardianship was granted to Emily's grandmother when Emily was 5 years old. Emily has half-siblings, but they have been placed in foster care, and Emily really does not know them or have any contact with them. The grandmother reports that she tries to get Emily to her psychologist at the community mental health provider, but Emily's refusals, lack of money to get across town on public transportation, and the grandmother's poor health at times have affected the ability to get her to sessions. Despite this, the grandmother believes that when Emily does get there, she seems to be better for a while. There has been no communication between the community mental health provider and the school. Up to this date, Emily has done fair in school, and, as she is

quiet and "no problem," she has not been referred for evaluation.

Although the school counselor has been supportive to the teacher and Emily to date this school year, the teacher has asked for an evaluation by the school psychologist and the behavioral consultant to help in formulating interventions in the classroom directly.

For the evaluation, a number of formal and informal assessments have been performed. The school psychologist implemented the Social Emotional Dimension Scale (SEDS-2). The teacher and behavioral consultant have taken data on social behaviors, as well as evaluated Emily using the Behavior Assessment System for Children (BASC-2) and the Behavioral Evaluation Scale (BES-2). They have asked the grandmother to fill out the Child Behavior Checklist. In addition, Emily's academic achievement was assessed in full. All scales indicated that Emily is a child with emotional disturbance, as she is at risk of fear reaction, depression, avoidance of interactions, and disturbed thinking.

As a result of the updated evaluation, Emily was referred for special education services as a child with emotional disturbance. She will receive an IEP with focus in the social/emotional area. The school counselor, with consent from the grandmother, is reaching out to the community mental health providers to obtain records and to coordinate services and interventions.

1. Emily is a 10-year-old girl who is being evaluated for special education services in school at this time. Do you believe she should have been evaluated prior to her fourth-grade year? Why or why not?

2. Community mental health providers must adhere to the laws of confidentiality as schools do. In your opinion, do you believe collaboration should always take place between community mental health providers and the school? Why or why not? If so, in what specific instances? What about for Emily?

3. What kind of supports do you believe Emily's family should receive? Who can help and how?

4. What behavioral interventions do you think could help Emily in the classroom? Provide a rationale for your choices.

Extension to Instruction

When considering how to best educate students with ED, educators are constantly looking for new and improved strategies that will help them be successful. Students with ED want and need to be successful in school, and the more teachers use evidence-based strategies to aid in their success, the better the chances are that students with ED will be successful. According to Vaughn, Bos, and Schumm (2007), the top strategies for working with children with emotional and behavioral challenges can be organized into a collection of major techniques:

1. *Maintaining an organized physical environment.* Students with ED tend to behave more appropriately and be more productive in orderly classrooms.

2. *Establishing positive relationships.* Students with ED thrive when teachers and peers work to create friendly, productive relationships with them.

3. *Changing behavior through a positive behavior support plan.* Students with ED benefit from a structured plan to increase positive behaviors and decrease inappropriate behaviors.

4. *Resolving conflicts and promoting self-control.* Students with ED are more successful when teachers work to help them settle disputes and learn to take control of their own actions.

5. *Adapting instruction.* Students with ED may need certain accommodations and/or modifications in the classroom setting to maximize their academic, social, and behavioral potential.

Behavioral Interventions

The behavioral model of intervention assumes that the behaviors of students are products of what they have learned from others and what is reinforcing their behavior. In the past, professionals only accounted for observable behaviors of children, and the behavioral model of intervention continues to address those behaviors that can be observed and measured. However, more frequently professionals are noting that less observable behaviors, such as emotions and cognitive behaviors—to include perceived threats, fears, and so on (Carlson, Pliszka, & Swanson, 1999)—play a role in children's behaviors and are being addressed through cognitive-behavioral interventions. Such interventions include reframing, self-talk, and mindfulness techniques. These interventions have been noted to support children who have experienced trauma as well. IDEA does not address children who are at risk of or who have experienced trauma, and although trauma may be difficult to assess, we know that children with disabilities are at risk of bullying and various forms of abuse. Best practices in trauma-informed education, such as the incorporation of social and emotional skills in the curriculum, mindfulness activities, teaching self-regulation skills, and cognitive-behavioral interventions, must be incorporated into the classroom routine (McGinley, Salako, & Dubov, 2018). All teachers must be trauma-informed and sensitive providers, as trauma impacts the child behaviorally and emotionally, resulting in such things as lack of self-control and faulty thinking that impact the ability to function, such as by inducing self-blame.

Many behavioral programs in schools are designed to help students with ED rely on operant-conditioning techniques of reinforcement and punishment. These interventions work to support the child in making the connection between the behavior and the consequence, so that positive behaviors will result in reinforcers that the child will work for, and when a child exhibits a negative behavior, something positive may be removed, such as recess, or something negative may be added, such as time out.

These interventions are implemented to decrease problem behaviors including aggression, social withdrawal, and lack of following directions and rules, among many other aberrant behaviors, and also used to increase appropriate replacement behaviors. Praise, attention, and some social reinforcers can be highly effective when it comes to maintaining and increasing desirable behaviors, as well. As discussed in Chapter 8, students with behavioral challenges, such as those with ASD, benefit from highly structured, evidence-based methods of managing difficult behaviors. More specifically, applied behavior analysis (ABA techniques)—such as positive reinforcement, negative reinforcement, prompting and fading, task analysis, and teaching a student to generalize knowledge and skills from one setting to the other—will result in positive gains.

One commonly used and particularly effective way of assessing student behavior is to determine its root cause by conducting a **Functional Behavior Assessment (FBA)**. FBAs are regularly conducted in schools to assess behaviors demonstrated by students that are not easily managed by conventional classroom-management techniques. When a child exhibits more significant behaviors, the first step in reducing or eliminating the inappropriate behavior is to determine its function, or reason for occurring. There are several possible functions of behavior, including attention, escape, obtaining a tangible item, automatic (or self-stimulatory), and medical reasons, to name a few. Once the function(s) of the inappropriate behavior has been identified, a replacement behavior (aka more desirable behavior serving the same function as the inappropriate behavior) can be taught and reinforced to replace the inappropriate behavior. An FBA can be done prior to the identification of any disability, but it is also done with children who exhibit behaviors that warrant such an assessment, such as those who have been diagnosed with ED. FBAs can also be performed when a child needs to be removed from his or her educational placement due to extreme behaviors that have been demonstrated. In this case, the student will go through the process of a manifestation determination. The manifestation determination process follows the mandatory removal of a child into an interim alternative education setting (IAES) for up to 45 days while a full evaluation of the behavioral episode is performed and a decision is made as to whether the behavior was a manifestation of the child's disability.

During the FBA process, the special education teacher will observe the student by taking data on the inappropriate behavior(s) as well as conducting interviews of others who know and work with this student to learn more about his or her troubling behavior. One critical type of behavioral data that will be collected is referred to as A-B-C data (A: antecedent, B: behavior, C: consequence). This data-collection process records the behavioral sequence (or behavior chain) demonstrated by the child and others in his environment. Figure 10.1 is an example of what an A-B-C form might look like.

As you can see, this behavioral-data form records the date, time, and events that occur right before the inappropriate behavior (antecedent), the inappropriate behavior itself (behavior), events that occur right after the inappropriate behavior

Figure 10.1 Sample Antecedent-Behavior-Consequence Form					
Date	Time	Antecedent	Observable Behavior	Consequence	Possible Function
12/11	1:05p	Teacher prompts student to transition to Science class	Student throws his books	Teacher asks student to pick up his books	Escape
12/11	2:09p	Teacher prompts student to get off of the computer	Student stays seated at computer and continues with game	Teacher's aide turns computer off	Escape

(consequence), and the possible function(s) of this undesirable behavior. Knowing the function(s) of a student's inappropriate behavior helps educators develop appropriate interventions that will work to remedy the problems that the student is demonstrating.

Once the FBA has been conducted, the MDT will create a positive behavior support plan (PBSP) for the student (see Appendix A). This plan is the direct result of the information gathered (a hypothesized function(s)) about the student's inappropriate behavior from the FBA. This plan will detail the process for decreasing inappropriate behaviors, increasing replacement behaviors, and rewarding the student for meeting expectations. Progress-monitoring data must be taken frequently to ensure that selected behavioral interventions are working, and, if they are not, the MDT must meet to discuss the plan and revise it where necessary. A collaborative team approach is necessary in implementing such a plan with fidelity.

Cognitive-Behavioral Interventions

Cognitive-behavioral interventions are based on the notion that behavior arises from faulty cognitions that precipitate extreme emotions and behaviors. With cognitive-behavioral interventions, the emphasis is on changing the child's dysfunctional thinking and behavior. Language, metacognition (thinking about thinking), and reflection play a huge role in the use of cognitive-behavioral interventions. Skills that are taught address students' interpersonal problem solving skills, emotion awareness, identifying their own triggers, and faulty thinking in general. An example of a curriculum that addresses all of the above is rational emotive behavior therapy (REBT), developed by Albert Ellis in 1980 (Ellis & Bernard, 2006). In addition, supporting the student's own self-regulation of behaviors is key, and self-monitoring may play a large role in this. Students with ED may also benefit from using self-monitoring checklists that allow them to check off desired behaviors they have exhibited, and goals accomplished, such as work completed and behavioral goals they have met. Teachers can assist students by monitoring their work environment and making sure that materials, equipment, and personal items are well-maintained, neatly arranged and presented in a predictable way, creating an organized and structured atmosphere (Vaughn et al., 2007).

Social Skills Interventions

As mentioned, most students with ED have problems demonstrating good social skills. There are a number of social skills curricula available that support the development of social skills and social competence in the classroom. Some examples are Superflex: A Superhero Social Thinking Curriculum (Madrigal & Garcia Winner, 2008) and Skillstreaming the Elementary School Child (McGinnis & Goldstein, 1997). Research has revealed mixed reports on the effectiveness of such programs, however. In addition to those curricula mentioned, modeling of socially appropriate behaviors, coupled with teacher prompts, are also noted in the literature as having some success with children (Odom & DeKlyen, 1986). Social coaching, which includes verbal discussion and role play, has also been met with some success (Oden & Asher, 1977; Ladd, 1981).

Academic Interventions

All too often, academic interventions are overlooked as the focus for children with ED due to the attention being paid to their challenging behaviors. A very specialized, structured method of instruction is often recommended for students with EDs. Assessing the skills that need to be taught, as well as addressing the environment in which they are taught, is also critical to the academic success of students with EDs. Curriculum-based assessments and direct instruction, as well as differentiated and strategic instruction, will be important to implement for these children.

Check Your Understanding 10.3

1. What is an FBA? Why is this an important assessment tool when determining why a student is behaving inappropriately?

2. What is the purpose of a PBSP? How is the plan connected to an FBA?

3. What can be said about the social skills of most children with ED? How can this be helped?

CHAPTER SUMMARY

In this chapter, we examined emotional disturbance as a disability category covered under IDEA. We discussed concepts related to its diagnostic process and highlighted selected assessments used to make an ED diagnosis. The various types of EDs were presented and described. Attention was given to the differences between a diagnosis made in a private setting versus a child being evaluated for ED at school. Functional Behavior Assessment (FBA) and positive behavior support plans (PBSPs) were explained as highly effective methods of serving students with ED in today's schools. Behavioral and cognitive-behavioral interventions were explored.

APPLY WHAT YOU HAVE LEARNED

1. Select one of the six emotional disorders discussed (anxiety disorders, mood disorders, conduct disorders, personality disorders, eating disorders, psychotic disorders). Write a 2-to-3-page summary of this disorder. In addition, consider if you had a child with

that particular diagnosis in your classroom. What academic and behavioral supports might you need to provide him or her in order to be successful? Why?

2. Select a sociological variable that can play a part in the cause of a child being labeled with ED (e.g., poverty, trauma, racism) to research. What are some things that have you researched that are currently being done to support children who are impacted? Describe them, and provide examples.

3. Visit the PBIS website: https://www.pbis. org. Create a list of Tier 1, Tier 2, and Tier 3 interventions that could be useful when teaching students with ED. Provide a rationale for your selections.

Appendix A
Positive Behavior Support Plan

Student Name: John Smith   Date of Plan: 10-31-2016

Team Signatures and Position:

Stephanie Buckley, ELA Teacher

Sally Jones, Math Teacher

Alice Moran, School Counselor

Brian Wright, Principal

Joseph Renn, Learning Support Teacher

Paula Rollen, Emotional Support Teacher

Assessment Summary

Antecedents to the Behavior of Concern	Behavior of Concern	Consequences Maintaining the Behavior of Concern	Perceived Function of the Behavior of Concern
Identify what happens *before* the behavior of concern: Independent Work: morning work, math, word study, writing	Describe the behavior using measurable, observable terms: John will slam books/chairs.	Identify what happens after the behavior of concern: - leaving the classroom - gains attention from teacher - gains attention from students	To gain escape from a nonpreferred activity To avoid, escape, or postpone

Identify educational (skill) deficits (s) related to the behavior of concern: (Academic skill deficits, communication and/ or social skill deficits. Sensory processing skill deficits)

_____

_____

Refer for further assessment: (Check here and describe plan for assessment if skill deficits have not previously been assessed and identified)

Describe: Assessment Plan

_____

_____

_____

X Educational deficits addressed in the other areas of IEP: (Check here if deficits have previously been assessed and identified and describe how they are being addressed in the IEP)

Describe: Areas of IEP address the identified skill deficit(s) __The student has a 504 for

ADHD

_____

Student Name: _____

V. Goals and Objectives- Include, as appropriate, academic and functional goals. Use as many copies of this pas as needed to plan appropriately. Specially designed instruction may be listed with each goal/ objective or listed in Section VI.

Short term learning outcomes are required for students who are gifted. The short term learning outcomes related to the student's gifted program may be listed under Goals or Short Term Objectives.

MEASURABLE ANNUAL GOAL Include: Condition, Name, Behavior, and Criteria	Describe HOW The student's progress toward meeting this goal will be measured	Describe WHEN Periodic reports on progress will be provided to parents	Report of Progress
John will reduce slamming books/chairs from 5 occurrences to 1 occurrence, through direct social skill instruction. The data will be collected with frequency recording, in Math and ELA for 3 consecutive observations.	Weekly observations of target behavior over 15-minute frequency recording.	District quarterly report card intervals: 11-1-2016; 2-13-2016; 4-2-2016; 6-7-2016 Daily comments on behavior made on behavior management sheet.	Stars will be awarded daily based on observations for the target behavior for each designated period. Daily teacher comments written on the behavior management sheet to be sent home for parent signature and return.

Through direct social skill instruction, when given an assignment for completion; John will complete 50% of classroom assignments within the allotted time on 3 out of 5 observed opportunities with a baseline of 25% task completion.	Weekly observations of target behavior over 10-minute frequency recording.	District quarterly report card intervals: 11-1-2016; 2-13-2016; 4-2-2016; 6-7-2016 Daily comments on behavior made on behavior management sheet.	Stars will be awarded daily based on observations for the target behavior for each designated period. Daily teacher comments written on the behavior management sheet to be sent home for parent signature and return.

SHORT TERM OBJECTIVES- Required for students with disabilities who take alternate assessments aligned to alternate achievement standards (i.e., PASA).

Short term objectives/ benchmarks

John will reduce slamming books/chairs from 5 occurrences to 4 occurrences during a 15-minute observation for 3 consecutive observations by 12-24-2016. Then reduce from 4 occurrences over a 15-minute observation to 3 occurrences for 3 consecutive observations by 1-24-2016. Reduce from 3 occurrences over a 15-minute observation to 2 occurrences for 3 consecutive observations by 2-24-2016. Reduce from 2 occurrences over a 15-minute observation to 1 occurrence for 3 consecutive observations by 3-24-2016.

John will finish classroom assignments within the allotted time on 3 out of 5 observed opportunities from a baseline of 25%. John will complete 34% of classroom assignments within the allotted period on 3 out of 5 opportunities by 1-16-2016. He will complete 39% of classroom assignments within the allotted period on 3 out of 5 opportunities by 2-16-2016. He will complete 44% of classroom assignments within the allotted period on 3 out of 5 opportunities by 3-16-2016 and he will complete 50% of classroom assignments within the allotted period on 3 out of 5 opportunities by 4-16-2016.

Task analysis of Social Skills instruction for gaining the teacher's attention by raising his hand and asking to escape. Acquisition of task analysis chain 1-16-2016, proficiency of task analysis chain 2-16-2016, maintenance of task analysis chain 3-16-2016, generalization of task analysis chain 4-16-2016.

Program Modifications and Specially Designed Instruction For The Positive Behavior Support Plan:

A Antecedent (prevention) Strategies:

Outline strategies to assist in preventing the behavior of concern from occurring and to increase the occurrence of the replacement behavior. This may include description of environmental adjustments to type of content or instruction presented to the student.

- Student will have preferential seating (he will sit next to students who will not encourage off task behaviors).

- Student will have a printed schedule on his desk

- Teacher will have a written agenda for each subject being taught and will be displayed for all students.

- At the first of every month, the students will be retaught the schoolwide rules and revisit our schoolwide positive behavior interventions and supports (GYRO).

- The teacher will have the students create signs and posters with pictures and icons associated with each rule. These signs and posters will be posted in key places.

- John will participate in a behavior management point system, the teacher will remind John before the start of an assignment. The teacher will make sure John fully understands the assignment and what he was asked to do.

- John will give himself a star for each subject that he starts his work promptly. If John has two stars, the paraprofessional will take a brain break in the hallway (Hacky Sack). The teacher will review contract after math and science/social studies in the morning. She will also review the contract after writing and reading workshop in the afternoon.

- The teacher will use graphic organizers and chunking when applicable.

- The teacher will use proximity control.

- Social Skill Instruction- forward chaining- **Step 1**- Listen to instructions given **Step 2**- Review instructions presented on promethean board **Step 3**- Start independent work **Step 4**- recognize when he needs a brake **Step 5**- Raise Hand **Step 6** Tell adult that a break is needed

- **Step 4, 5, and 6 will be taught, modeled, and practiced through explicit instruction.**

- John will participate in the Emotional Support group during his lunch period every Friday. In this group, the teacher will teach and practice to recognize when a break is needed and appropriate behaviors to escape.

B Replacement Behavior:

Identify the behavior that will be taught to the student as a replacement to the behavior of concern. The replacement behavior should efficiently achieve the same function as the behavior of concern. Include the plan for instruction including prompts, and systematic adjustment of the behavior requirement over time (based on data).

When given an assignment for completion, John will utilize his coping strategies to complete classroom assignments within the allotted time, in 3 out of 5 observed opportunities. Through direct social skill instruction, John will reduce slamming books/chairs from 5 occurrences to 1 occurrence, data will be collected with frequency recording, in Math and ELA for 3 consecutive observations.

C Consequence (reinforcement) for when the student performs the replacement behavior:

Describe specific procedures for providing reinforcement when the student performs the replacement behavior, so that the replacement behavior will be effective and evident for the student in achieving the same function. Reinforcement should increase the likelihood that the student will continue or increase the replacement behavior. Also, include a plan for systematically thinning the reinforcement schedule over time (based on data).

John will be able to escape the classroom with the paraprofessional on a fixed response duration reinforcement schedule. During the acquisition stage of learning, John will earn a star on his behavior management sheet for every 10 minutes he has not slammed is books/chair and is on task during independent work. His goal being, staying on task and not slamming books/chairs 50% of the time for 3 consecutive stars earned. After 3 consecutive stars earned, the fixed duration would increase by 3 minutes, and so on until John is working for 25 minute intervals for 3 consecutive stars earned. To achieve thinning, the reinforcement schedule will use the variable response duration of 25 minutes for 3 consecutive stars earned. The variable response duration will increase by 3 minutes for every 3 consecutive stars earned until John demonstrates the replacement behaviors over a 45-minute class period.

When John earns 50% for completing assignment during the allotted period he can earn tickets to pick from the treasure box every Friday. For every star, he earns on his behavior management sheet, he receives one ticket. After 3 consecutive days with 50% or more, John can choose 15-minute computer time or lunch with the teachers with two friends. After 5 consecutive days with 50% or more, John can choose to paint a ceiling tile or have a 15-minute recess with two friends.

Special Education/ Related Services/ Supplementary Aids and Services/ Program Modifications – Include, as appropriate, for nonacademic and extracurricular services and activities.

A. PROGRAM MODIFICATIONS AND SPECIALLY- DESIGNED INSTRUCTION (SDI)

- SDI may be listed with each goal or as part of the table below
- Include supplementary aids and services as appropriate
- For a student who has a disability and is gifted, SDI also should include adaptations, accommodations, or modifications to the general education curriculum, as appropriate for a student with a disability

Modifications and SDI	Location	Frequency	Projected Beginning Date	Anticipated Duration
Behavioral Management Plan	Math and ELA	Daily	12-24-2016	12-24-2017
Social Skills	Emotional Support	Weekly	12-24-2016	12-24-2017
Response duration reinforcement schedule	Math and ELA	Daily	12-24-2016	12-24-2017

B. RELATED SERVICES- List the services that the student needs in order to benefit from his/ her special education program

Service	Location	Frequency	Projected Beginning Date	Anticipated Duration

SUPPORTS FOR SCHOOL PERSONNEL- List the staff to receive the supports and the supports needed to implement the student's IEP

School Personnel to Receive Support	Support	Location	Frequency	Projected Beginning Date	Anticipated Duration
ELA and Math Teachers	Training on diffusion techniques and behavioral management plan	Classroom	Quarterly	12-24-2016	12-24-2017
Paraprofessionals	Training on diffusion techniques and behavioral management plan	Classroom	Quarterly	12-24-2016	12-24-2017

REFERENCES

American Academy of Pediatrics. (2009). Media violence. *Pediatrics, 124*, 1495–1503. doi:10.1542/peds.2009-2146

American Psychiatric Association. (n.d.). *DSM history.* Retrieved from https://www.psychiatry.org/psychiatrists/practice/dsm/history-of-the-dsm

American Psychiatric Association. (2013). *Diagnostic and statistical manual of mental disorders* (5th ed.). Arlington, VA: American Psychiatric Publishing.

Brown, L., & Hammill, D. (1990). *The Behavior Rating Profile.* Austin, TX: PRO-ED.

Butcher, J. N., Graham, J. R., Ben-Porath, Y. S., Tellegen, A., & Dahlstrom, W. G. (2001). *Minnesota Multiphasic Personality Inventory–2 (MMPI-2): Manual for administration and scoring* (Rev. ed.). Minneapolis, MN: University of Minnesota Press.

Barbosa-Leiker, C., Fleming, S., Hollins Martin, C. J., & Martin, C. R. (2015). Psychometric properties of the Birth Satisfaction Scale–Revised (BSS-R) for US mothers. *Journal of Reproductive and Infant Psychology, 33*(5), 504–511. doi: 10.1080/02646838.2015.1024211

Carlson, C. L., Pliszka, S. R., & Swanson, J. M. (1999). *ADHD with comorbid disorders: Clinical assessment and management.* New York, NY: Guilford Press.

Ellis, A., & Bernard, M. E. (Eds.). (2006). *Rational emotive behavioral approaches to childhood disorders.* New York, NY: Springer.

Epstein, M. H., & Cullinan, D. (2010). *Scales for Assessing Emotional Disturbance* (2nd ed.). Austin, TX: PRO-ED.

Gage, N. A. (2013). Characteristics of students with emotional disturbance manifesting internalizing behaviors: A latent class analysis. *Education and Treatment of Children*, West Virginia University Press, *36*(4), 127–145.

Hutton, J. B., & Roberts, T. G. (2004). *Social Emotional Dimension Scale* (2nd ed.) (SEDS-2). Austin, TX: PRO-ED.

Individuals With Disabilities Education Act Amendments of 1997 [IDEA]. (1997). Retrieved from https://www.congress.gov/105/plaws/publ17/PLAW-105publ17.pdf

Jensen, M. M. (2005). *Introduction to emotional and behavioral disorders: Recognizing and managing problems in the classroom.* Upper Saddle River, NJ: Pearson Education.

Ladd, G. W. (1981). Effectiveness of a social learning method for enhancing children's social interaction and peer acceptance. *Child Development, 52*(1), 171–178.

Madrigal, S., & Garcia Winner, M. (2008). *Superflex: A superhero social thinking curriculum.* San Jose, CA: Think Social Publishing.

McCarney, S. B., & Arthaud, T. J. (2014). *Behavior Evaluation Scale* (4th ed.) (BES-4). Columbia, MO: Hawthorne.

McGinley, V. A., Salako, O. O., & Dubov, J. (2018). Trauma: How educators can support children and their families. In K. Norris & S. Collier (Eds.), *Social justice and parent partnerships in multicultural education contexts* (pp. 162–186). Hershey, PA: IGI Global.

McGinnis, E., & Goldstein, A. P. (1997). *Skillstreaming the elementary school child: New strategies and perspectives for teaching prosocial skills.* Champaign, IL: Research Press.

MedlinePlus. (2019). *Psychotic disorders.* Retrieved from https://medlineplus.gov/psychoticdisorders.html

National Institute of Mental Health. (2016). *Eating disorders.* Retrieved from https://www.nimh.nih.gov/health/topics/eating-disorders/index.shtml

Oden, S., & Asher, S. (1977). Coaching children in social skills for friendship making. *Child Development, 48,* 496–506.

Odom, S. I., & DeKlyen, M. (1986). Social Withdrawal in childhood. Unpublished manuscript, Department of Special Education, Vanderbilt University, Nashville, TN.

Oswald, D. P., Best, A. M., Coutinho, M. J., & Nagle, H. A. (2003). Trends in the special education identification rates of boys and girls: A call for research and change. *Exceptionality, 11*(4), 223–237. doi: 10.1207/S15327035EX1104_3

Piers, E. V., Shemmassian, S. K., Herzberg, D. S., & Harris, D. B. (2018). *Piers-Harris Self-Concept Scale* (3rd ed.). Lutz, FL: PariConnect.

Reynolds, C. R., & Kamphaus, R. W. (2015). *Behavior Assessment System for Children* (3rd ed.). Bloomington, MN: Pearson.

Shorter, E. (2013). The history of DSM. In J. Paris & J. Phillips (Eds.), *Making the DSM-5: Concepts and controversies* (pp. 3–20). New York, NY: Springer.

Trout, A. L., Nordness, P. D., Pierce, C. D., & Epstein, M. H. (2003). Research on the academic status of children with emotional and behavioral disorders: A review of the literature from 1961 to 2000. *Journal of Emotional and Behavioral Disorders, 11*(4), 198–210.

Vaughn, S., Bos, C. S., & Schumm, J. S. (2007). *Teaching students who are exceptional, diverse, and at risk in the general education classroom* (4th ed.). Boston, MA: Pearson Education.

World Health Organization. (n.d.). WHO Family of International Classifications (WHO-FIC). Archived from the original on 22 December 2013. Retrieved March 14, 2014, from http://www.who.int/classifications/en

Medically Diagnosed Disabilities

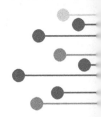

CHAPTER 11

Attention-Deficit/ Hyperactivity Disorder (ADHD)

Tara S. Guerriero, PhD

Learning Objectives

After the completion of this chapter, you should be able to:

- Define Other Health Impairment according to IDEA.

- Identify the general criteria for ADHD.

- Identify the specific criteria for the following: ADHD–Predominantly Inattentive Type, ADHD– Predominantly Hyperactive-Impulsive Type, and ADHD–Combined Type.

- Describe the factors that should be evaluated as part of the process used to diagnose ADHD.

- Indicate who is able to make a diagnosis of ADHD.

- Analyze the complexities associated with diagnosing ADHD.

Key Terms

attention-deficit/hyperactivity disorder (ADHD) (p. 322)
    predominantly inattentive type
    predominantly hyperactive-impulsive type
    combined type
	inattention (p. 324)

comorbid (p. 323)	other health impairment (p. 323)
hyperactivity (p. 324)	partial remission (p. 326)
impulsivity (p. 324)	

Introduction to the Chapter

Attention-deficit/hyperactivity disorder (ADHD) is a disorder that impacts many children and adults, often causing difficulties with everyday functioning in multiple settings, including home, school, and work. Since the focus of this textbook is on assessment as it relates to the educational system and IDEA, this chapter will focus primarily on ADHD during childhood and adolescence.

ADHD is considered to be one of the most common neurodevelopmental disorders of childhood (CDC, 2018c), occurring in about 11% of school-age children (CHADD, 2017).

Types of ADHD

ADHD is classified into three types; students with ADHD will often exhibit very different characteristics, depending on the type of ADHD with which they have been diagnosed.

Predominantly Inattentive

Individuals with this type of presentation exhibit symptoms of inattention, such as difficulties with attention to detail and organization, as well as being easily distracted and forgetful (CDC, 2018c).

Predominantly Hyperactive-Impulsive

Those with this type of presentation demonstrate symptoms of hyperactivity and impulsivity, such as excessive movement (e.g., running, climbing), fidgeting, and talking, as well as interrupting others' conversations and difficulties waiting for their turn (CDC, 2018c).

Combined

Individuals who present with the combined type show symptoms associated with inattention, hyperactivity, and impulsivity (CDC, 2018c).

IDEA Definition of Other Health Impairment

In considering eligibility criteria according to IDEA, ADHD is unlike some of the other common childhood disorders (e.g., autism, specific learning disabilities, intellectual disabilities) in that it is not represented by its own disability category under IDEA. Instead, students who are diagnosed with ADHD may receive services under the category of other health impairment if they meet the eligibility criteria and show evidence of need for special education services. They may also receive services under other disability categories (e.g., specific learning disabilities, autism) if they present with a comorbid, or co-occurring, condition. A diagnosis of ADHD is typically thought to be evidence that a student may have a disability that substantially limits one or more major life activity, unless there is evidence to the contrary (U.S. Department of Education, Office of Civil Rights, 2016). Therefore, it is the responsibility of the school's evaluation team to determine whether the student meets eligibility criteria under IDEA and whether he or she needs special education services in order to obtain an appropriate education.

> Other health impairment means having limited strength, vitality, or alertness, including a heightened alertness to environmental stimuli, that results in limited alertness with respect to the educational environment, that—
>
> (i). Is due to chronic or acute health problems such as asthma, attention deficit disorder or attention deficit hyperactivity disorder, diabetes, epilepsy, a heart condition, hemophilia, lead poisoning, leukemia, nephritis, rheumatic fever, sickle cell anemia, and Tourette syndrome; and
>
> (ii). Adversely affects a child's educational performance.
>
> (IDEA, 2004, § 300.8(c)(9))

Diagnostic Criteria

In examining the diagnostic criteria, you will likely notice that ADHD is a disorder in which the behavioral characteristics that a student demonstrates and the actual diagnostic criteria used to diagnose the disorder are consistent with one another. As you learn about the diagnostic criteria for ADHD, think about those children whom you know with ADHD and consider which diagnostic criteria seem in keeping with patterns that you notice in their behavior.

According to the fifth edition of the Diagnostic and Statistical Manual of Mental Disorders (DSM-5) (APA, 2013) and the National Institute of Mental Health (2019), a child may have ADHD if he or she demonstrates the following:

1. A consistent pattern of behavior (inattention, hyperactivity-impulsivity, or both) that is not developmentally appropriate for the child and that interferes with development and/or functioning (e.g., social, academic)

2. Six or more symptoms (five or more if 17 years or older) of inattention or hyperactive-impulsive behavior (or six of both inattention and hyperactivity-impulsivity) that are chronic and long-lasting (a minimum of six months)

The following signs and symptoms are associated with inattention and hyperactive-impulsive behavior (APA, 2013; NIMH, 2019):

- ○ **Inattention** "means a person wanders off task, lacks persistence, has difficulty sustaining focus, and is disorganized; and these problems are not due to defiance or lack of comprehension" (NIMH, 2019, p. 1). Figure 11.1 is a list of inattentive symptoms.

- ○ *Hyperactive-impulsive behavior*: **Hyperactivity** "means a person seems to move about constantly, including in situations in which it is not appropriate; or excessively fidgets, taps, or talks" (NIMH, 2019, p. 1). **Impulsivity** "means a person makes hasty actions that occur in the moment without first thinking about them and that may have a high potential for harm, or a desire for immediate rewards or inability to delay gratification" (NIMH, 2019, p. 1). Figure 11.2 is a list of hyperactive and impulsive symptoms.

In addition to examining patterns of behavior to see whether they are consistent with the signs of inattention, hyperactivity, and impulsivity, the following conditions are also considered in the diagnosis of ADHD (APA, 2013; NIMH, 2019):

1. There is evidence that symptoms are/were present before the age of 12.

2. The symptoms are manifested or present in two or more settings (e.g., school, home, extracurricular activities).

3. There is evidence that the inattentive and/or hyperactive-impulsive behavior diminishes or impairs the child's functioning (e.g., socially, academically, at work).

Figure 11.1 Symptoms of Inattention

Inattention:
Individuals with inattentive patterns might demonstrate difficulties with the following:

attending to details

maintaining attention for long periods of time in a variety of different types of activities

listening when someone is speaking to them

following directions

organization and task completion

participating in or finding enjoyment in activities that require sustained thought

locating belongings

not being distracted by unrelated thoughts or activity

remembering

Figure 11.2 Symptoms of Hyperactivity and Impulsivity

Hyperactivity: Individuals with hyperactive patterns might demonstrate difficulties with the following:	**Impulsivity:** Individuals with impulsive patterns might demonstrate difficulties with the following:
staying still in their seats (may fidget or move around)	not shouting out an answer to a question prematurely
staying seated when it is expected to do so	waiting for their turn
not running around when it isn't appropriate	not intruding in on others' conversations or activities
playing in a controlled and quite manner	
not being constantly in motion	
not talking incessantly	

4. The symptoms are not resulting from another medical or psychiatric disorder (e.g., schizophrenia) or mental disorder (e.g., mood disorder, anxiety disorder).

5. Symptoms aren't "solely a manifestation of oppositional behavior, defiance, hostility, or failure to understand tasks or instructions" (APA, 2013, Diagnostic Criteria A.1 para. 2).

In addition, the DSM-5 (APA, 2013) indicates that the following should also be specified when diagnosing ADHD:

1. *Type of presentation.* The type of presentation that the student demonstrates should be identified as part of the diagnosis:
   - a predominantly inattentive presentation (meeting criteria for inattention);
   - a predominantly hyperactive-impulsive presentation (meeting criteria for hyperactivity/impulsivity); or
   - a combined presentation (meeting criteria for inattention and hyperactivity/impulsivity).

2. *Level of severity.* One of the following levels of severity should be indicated based on the symptoms that the student exhibits:
   - *Mild:* "Few, if any, symptoms in excess of those required to make the diagnosis are present, and symptoms result in no more than minor impairments in social or occupational functioning" (APA, 2013, Diagnostic Criteria, Mild).
   - *Moderate:* "Symptoms or functional impairment between 'mild' and 'severe' are present" (APA, 2013, Diagnostic Criteria, Moderate).

Severe: "Many symptoms in excess of those required to make the diagnosis, or several symptoms that are particularly severe, are present, or the symptoms result in marked impairment in social or occupational functioning" (APA, 2013, Diagnostic Criteria, Severe).

3. *Whether the disorder is in partial remission.* If a child has previously met the criteria for ADHD, but currently (for the past six months) demonstrates fewer than six symptoms, and continues to demonstrate impaired functioning, he or she can be considered to have ADHD that is in **partial remission** (APA, 2013).

Check Your Understanding 11.1

1. List three symptoms of each of the following: inattention, hyperactivity, and impulsivity.

2. Why is it important for a student to show six or more symptoms of inattention or hyperactivity-impulsivity to be diagnosed with ADHD?

3. Explain why you think the criteria state that the symptoms must be present for six months or more in order to be diagnosed with ADHD.

4. What is the importance of observing symptoms in two or more settings?

How the Diagnosis Is Made

While the criteria for diagnosing ADHD may seem straightforward, the process of diagnosing ADHD is actually quite complex. There isn't a particular test that can be used to diagnose ADHD; rather, it should be a multistep process. The following are often completed as part of the diagnostic process, as a means of both determining the presence of ADHD and ruling out other conditions as possible causes of the child's symptoms (CDC, 2018c; CHADD, 2019):

- A full medical exam

- Checklists or behavior rating scales for evaluating ADHD symptoms and the developmental appropriateness of those behaviors

  The Child Behavior Checklist (CBCL), the Behavior Assessment System for Children (BASC), and the Conners Comprehensive Behavior Rating Scales (CBRS) are all examples of instruments that can be used in the process of diagnosing ADHD. These assessments are often completed by parents, teachers, and/or other adults who interact with the child on a regular basis (e.g., leader of an extracurricular activity) to better understand the child's behavior in different settings.

- A history of the child, typically provided by parents, teachers, and the child (as appropriate)

- A clinical assessment of the child's developmental level, as well as the child's functioning in areas of academics and social/emotional status

The Centers for Disease Control and Prevention (2018a) indicate that the following guidelines are recommended for the diagnosis/evaluation of ADHD according to the American Academy of Pediatrics (AAP):

- If a child between the ages of 4 and 18 exhibits symptoms of inattention, hyperactivity, and/or impulsivity, the primary care clinician should initiate an evaluation for ADHD. In thinking about this guideline, the following may be considered:

  - Hyperactive behavior may be evident earlier than the age of 4, but it is difficult to distinguish between typical and atypical behavior before that age (APA, 2013).

  - It is important to make sure that the symptoms that a child is displaying are not developmentally typical. There are several criteria of inattention, hyperactivity, and impulsivity that would be developmentally appropriate at certain age levels. For example, a child who is 4 years old may have difficulty following rules that require him or her to sit still without fidgeting, but that may be due to developmental patterns, as opposed to ADHD.

  - Further, if a child has another condition that impacts his or her developmental level (e.g., intellectual disability, autism spectrum disorder), there needs to be evidence that the child's behavior deviates from his or her current developmental level, which may not be consistent with his or her age level.

- In diagnosing ADHD, the primary care clinician should adhere to the criteria that have been established by the DSM-5 (see criteria above).

- Information provided by several different sources (e.g., parents/guardians, teachers, and/or other caretakers; coaches) would be beneficial in accurately evaluating a student for ADHD.

- There should be evidence that the symptoms exist in more than one setting (home, school, extracurricular activity, etc.). It is important to ensure that the child is not behaving in a particular way in just one setting, because that may indicate that the behavior is a function of the environment as opposed to being characteristic of the child.

- It is also important to rule out other possible causes of the symptoms that the student exhibits; ADHD can have symptoms similar to those of other types of medical or psychological disorders. It is important to be certain that the correct diagnosis is obtained.

- When determining whether a child has ADHD, it is also important to consider whether the child has a comorbid condition—such as an emotional or behavioral disorder (e.g., depression, anxiety, conduct disorder), a learning disability, or a medical condition (e.g., sleep apnea).

- ADHD should be considered a chronic condition, and those with ADHD should be considered to have special health-care needs.

It is important to note that if these procedures aren't followed, then underdiagnosis, overdiagnosis, or misdiagnosis may be likely to occur. Manos, Giuliano, and Geyer (2017) indicated that "guidelines for diagnosing ADHD are still not rigorously applied, contributing to misdiagnosis. For example, in a study of 50 pediatric practices, only half of clinicians said they followed diagnostic guidelines to determine symptom criteria from at least 2 sources and across 2 settings, yet nearly all (93%) reported immediately prescribing medications for treatment" (Manos, Giuliano, & Geyer, 2017, p. 874).

Check Your Understanding 11.2

ADHD could be easier or more difficult to recognize, depending on the child's specific symptoms, in combination with his or her age and the setting in which the behaviors are observed. Think about what you have learned about the diagnostic criteria and the process for diagnosing ADHD while completing the following exercise:

Without referring back to the previously stated symptoms and criteria for ADHD, look at the following criteria and put a check next to the six criteria that you think would be the most obvious to (1) a parent and (2) a teacher:

Criteria

- ☐ Constantly in motion

- ☐ Difficulties with organization and task completion

- ☐ Loses belongings

- ☐ shouts out answers to questions prematurely

- ☐ easily distracted by unrelated thoughts or activity

- ☐ Forgetful

- ☐ talks incessantly

- ☐ runs around when it isn't appropriate

- ☐ difficulties staying in seat or staying still in seat (fidgets or moves around)

- ☐ difficulties listening when someone is speaking to them

- ☐ difficulties waiting for turn

- ☐ difficulties participating in or finding enjoyment in activities that require sustained thought

Now, look back at the criteria for the predominantly inattentive type as compared to the predominantly hyperactive-impulsive type of ADHD, and answer the following questions:

1. Which symptoms did you check most often: inattentive symptoms or hyperactive-impulsive symptoms?

2. If you noticed a pattern, why do you think that pattern emerged?

3. Are some patterns of behavior more evident than others? If so, how might that impact the diagnosis of ADHD?

4. Would your responses have differed based on the age of the child? For example, what might you think if the child was 6? 16?

5. Would the setting (e.g., classroom, home, extracurricular activity) in which the behaviors were taking place have changed any of your responses? For example, imagine that these behaviors are occurring during an extracurricular activity, such as sports practice. Which behaviors do you think would be the most noticeable to the coach?

The following are some examples of how these factors may play a role in determining whether a child has ADHD:

- Consider the impact of behavior in the following settings: a classroom setting, the home environment, and an extracurricular activity, such as a sports team.
  - Would inattentive behaviors be more evident in any of these settings?
  - Would hyperactive-impulsive behaviors be more evident in any of these settings?

- How likely is it that the symptoms of ADHD will be evident in each of these settings?

It is possible that in a classroom setting, it may be much more apparent that a student is demonstrating hyperactive-impulsive behaviors as compared to inattentive behaviors, because hyperactive-impulsive behaviors may seem to be in greater contrast with typical classroom rules and procedures. If this is the case, is it also possible that children with hyperactive-impulsive behaviors may be much more likely to be identified as having difficulties in the classroom and, subsequently, may be more likely to be evaluated and diagnosed? Would this then mean that students who present with the inattentive type might be less likely to be identified in the classroom setting and, thus, may not be evaluated and diagnosed when they do in fact have the disorder? Feldman and Reiff (2014) suggested that this may be the case. More boys than girls are diagnosed with ADHD, and girls tend to be more likely than boys to demonstrate inattentive symptoms (APA, 2013; NIMH, 2019). If inattention were more readily seen in the classroom, would it still be the case that more boys than girls are diagnosed with ADHD? There may be no definitive answers to any of these questions, but it is important that, as a teacher, you recognize and attempt to identify all symptoms of ADHD (i.e., inattentive, hyperactive, and impulsive), even if they are not disruptive in the classroom. Remember, it isn't the teacher's job to diagnose ADHD, but it is important for the teacher to be able to provide insight into student behaviors in order to contribute to the diagnostic process.

Let's switch the setting now to an extracurricular activity, such as soccer practice. In this setting, it is possible that hyperactive-impulsive behaviors may not be as evident, since the activity itself requires a lot of physical

(Continued)

(Continued)

movement; whereas inattention may be evident if it appears that the child isn't focusing on the practice. Would that result in the opposite finding as was described in the classroom setting? If so, would it be as evident that the child is exhibiting hyperactive-impulsive behaviors in that setting?

In looking at these two scenarios (behavior in the classroom setting and behavior in soccer practice), it becomes apparent how potentially complex the process of diagnosing ADHD is. One of the reasons why it is so important to see symptoms in more than one setting is because it has to be shown that the behavior is specific to the child, not to the environment. Therefore, it is important to really examine behavioral patterns that a child exhibits across several settings, to make sure that there is a true pattern of behavior and that it isn't simply situational. Consider now the possible differences that might be seen with different age ranges.

- Would inattentive behaviors be more evident in a particular age range than in another age range?

- Would hyperactive-impulsive behaviors be more evident in a particular age range than in another age range?

The DSM-5 (APA, 2013) and the National Institute of Mental Health (2019) indicate that certain types of behaviors may be more prevalent at particular ages:

- During the preschool years, hyperactive behavior tends to be the most common.

- During the elementary-school years, inattentive behaviors become more noticeable and often more impairing than they were during earlier years.

- During the adolescent years, more overt motor-based signs of hyperactivity (e.g., running climbing) that were common during the elementary years tend to become less common. Instead, adolescents may be more likely to fidget, to feel restlessness and impatience, and to demonstrate impulsivity and inattention.

The purpose of this activity is to really make you think about how complex the diagnostic process for ADHD could be, because there are so many different factors that could contribute to a child's behavior. Overall, great efforts must be made to make an accurate diagnosis, so as to ensure that appropriate steps can be taken to manage the condition; thus the purpose of our next section is defining who is qualified to make the diagnosis.

Who Makes the Diagnosis

ADHD is not a disorder that is typically diagnosed in an educational setting; rather, it is diagnosed "by a mental health professional like a psychologist or psychiatrist, or by a primary care provider, like a pediatrician" (CDC, 2018b, para. 2). Other types of professionals who are qualified to diagnose ADHD include "clinical social workers, nurse practitioners, neurologists, psychiatrists and pediatricians" (CHADD, 2019, para. 2). However, it is important to note that some states and school districts do allow trained school psychologists to evaluate a student for ADHD (Schutte et al., 2017). While the actual diagnosis may or may not be made in a school setting, the role of the school in conducting a comprehensive evaluation is essential in order to determine whether the student is eligible for services under IDEA. As with any disability or disorder, in order to qualify for special education services, a student with ADHD would need to both meet eligibility criteria for a category of disability and demonstrate a need for specially designed instruction.

The school's multidisciplinary team will determine whether the student is eligible for special education services under IDEA, based on disability criteria and evidence that the student needs special education services; however, determining eligibility for services is not the same as diagnosing a medically diagnosed disability, such as ADHD.

Concluding Thoughts on How the Diagnosis Is Made and Who Makes the Diagnosis

The diagnostic process associated with ADHD is often more complex than it may seem. There are many different considerations that should be made before making a diagnosis. Professionals who are trained to identify ADHD must be the ones to diagnose ADHD. Input from many different sources (e.g., parent, teacher, caretaker) will assist them in the procedure, but ultimately the diagnosis is made by them. The school's multidisciplinary team may evaluate a student to determine whether he or she is eligible for services; however, in many states they will not typically be making a diagnosis.

Check Your Understanding 11.3

1. What is the difference between making a diagnosis of ADHD and determining eligibility for special education services?

2. How can differences in setting or age impact behavioral characteristics associated with ADHD?

Other Characteristics

While the main characteristics associated with ADHD relate to behavior, there are other characteristics that may need to be considered for students with ADHD, including intelligence, academic achievement, social and emotional status, and health and medical status.

Intelligence

In Chapter 4, intelligence was described as an individual's level of mental capacity or potential for learning that is unique to that individual and the way in which his or her mind works. As has been previously discussed for other disabilities, it is important to obtain an accurate picture of a student's intelligence level when considering ADHD. The attentional demands involved in taking an intelligence test may reduce the child's ability to demonstrate his or her true IQ. Further, when taking IQ tests, impulsive behavior, such as answering a question before it is finished being asked or the tendency to give an impulsive response instead of a well-thought out response, may reduce the accuracy of responses. Additionally, there is evidence that students with ADHD have deficits in executive functioning (Holmes et al., 2010), which may impact their performance on measures of intelligence. In general, students with ADHD can have a wide range of intelligence; however, it is important to ensure that it is measured accurately and, subsequently, is a true reflection of the child's capabilities.

Academic Achievement

Students with ADHD may have reduced academic performance, depending on their ADHD symptoms. When examining academic performance, it is important to determine whether the underlying difficulties are caused by symptoms of ADHD (i.e., inattention, hyperactivity, and/or impulsivity) or whether there is another underlying condition (e.g., a learning disability) that is causing academic problems. Pham (2016) indicated that inattention can impact reading comprehension and fluency and, subsequently, impact academic achievement. Further, Berninger et al. (2017) indicated that individuals with ADHD often have co-occurring handwriting and written-language deficits that may impact academic achievement. If ADHD symptoms lead to underperformance, it would stand to reason that a reduction of those behaviors may improve the student's ability to perform. However, if the student falls behind because of the symptoms, he or she may develop academic deficits that may increase over time and that may not improve with a reduction of symptoms.

Social/Emotional Status

Students with ADHD often have difficulties socially and emotionally that may impact their peer relationships, family relationships, and relationships with teachers and health-care providers. They may experience social rejection, conflict with peers, reduced peer relationships, and teasing. Additionally, people may interpret their behaviors as lazy, irresponsible, or uncooperative. They may also be at increased risk of developing comorbid conditions that impact their emotional state, such as conduct disorder, depression, and anxiety disorders (APA, 2013; Feldman & Reiff, 2014; Lawrence, Estrada, & McCormick, 2017).

Health and Medical Status

ADHD is considered to be a health-related medical condition, and it should be treated as such. When a child is diagnosed with ADHD, it is important that the condition be continuously monitored by a pediatrician. It is also important to rule out any other medical conditions when evaluating a child for ADHD. The following medical concerns may impact those with ADHD (APA, 2013; Leahy, 2018; Shemmassian & Lee, 2016):

- Those with ADHD may be more likely to sustain injuries than those without ADHD.

- Those with ADHD may have more car accidents and driving violations than those without ADHD.

- Those with ADHD may be more likely to engage in substance abuse.

- There might be a greater likelihood of obesity in those with ADHD.

- There might be a greater prevalence of teenage pregnancy in those with ADHD.

Many individuals with ADHD take stimulant and/or nonstimulant medications to reduce their symptoms of ADHD. As with any medication, there are often many side effects that could impact a child's health. Medications impact everyone differently, and it is important to find the right medication and determine the proper dosage for each individual (NIMH, 2019). If dosage is not monitored or if an individual changes the prescribed dose, there may be many negative implications. It is also important to think about the age of the child before deciding whether to prescribe medication (CDC, 2018a), as medications may have a different impact on children of different ages.

Case Studies, Treatment, and Extension to Instruction

The following case studies will highlight two siblings with different types of ADHD; John has the predominantly hyperactive-impulsive type, and Jennifer has the combined type. Following the discussion of the background and diagnosis associated with each case study, a discussion of treatment and an extension to instruction will be highlighted for each.

Case Study 11.1: John

John is a 15-year-old boy who is currently finishing ninth grade and was diagnosed with ADHD–predominantly hyperactive-impulsive type when he was 7 years old.

Background and Diagnostic Evaluation

John lives with his biological mother and father as well as his sister, Jennifer, who is three years younger than he. When John was 7 years old and in the first grade, his parents talked to his pediatrician during a routine well-child visit about concerning behaviors that they were seeing at home: He talked over others (often yelling at them), constantly fidgeted or played with things, often threw objects at inappropriate times, hit his parents and sister, was constantly running or jumping, and had a really difficult time sitting still. The doctor asked when they had first noticed these behaviors, and they indicated that he had been showing these behaviors since he was a toddler, but that they had been getting progressively more noticeable. The pediatrician decided to evaluate John for ADHD. As part of the evaluation, his doctor completed a medical exam, conducted an interview with his parents to learn more about his behavioral, social, and educational backgrounds, and asked his parents and teacher to complete a behavior rating scale. The results of the evaluations helped John's doctor to rule out medical difficulties and other psychological conditions that may cause these types of behaviors and ultimately diagnose him with ADHD–predominantly hyperactive-impulsive type. His diagnosis was fairly straightforward, as he showed many hyperactive behaviors and was very impulsive; it was also clear that he was consistently exhibiting these behaviors both in school and at home.

During second grade and the beginning of third grade, John's parents started noticing more and more that he was having difficulties socially and that he seemed really unhappy at school. His friends weren't really playing with him anymore, and they were starting to make fun of him. He was also starting to fall behind in school. By the middle of the school year, John's parents decided to share their concerns with the school and requested an evaluation for special education, as a result of his ADHD. Following a comprehensive evaluation, it was determined that he qualified for special education services under the disability category of Other Health Impairment.

Treatment and Extension to Instruction

Following the evaluation, the IEP team determined that John would be included in the general education classroom for most of the school day, with the exception of 2.5 hours per week, when he would receive one-on-one behavior therapy from a special education teacher as well as social skills training in a group setting. John also started receiving private services from a behavior therapist to help him in controlling his hyperactive and impulsive behaviors. Additionally, when he was 9, he began taking a stimulant medication for his disorder. He continued taking medication and receiving services both at school and privately through middle school. The combination of the medical and behavioral therapy had proven to be highly beneficial for him. He learned metacognitive strategies that helped him control his impulsive and hyperactive behaviors by thinking through the potential consequences before acting. For example, instead of throwing a pencil in the classroom, he learned to think about what would happen if he did throw his pencil and, instead, to tell himself to put the pencil down. As another example, instead of talking over others (or yelling) while they were talking, he would purposefully wait until his conversational partner(s) had stopped talking for at least three seconds before joining in the conversation. At the end of eighth grade, both he and his parents decided that he had developed the coping skills necessary for him to be successful in high school. With input from their pediatrician, teachers, and behavioral therapist, they made the decision to take him off of medication during the summer before he started ninth grade and continue with special education services during his ninth-grade year. He transitioned well into ninth grade and is finishing his ninth-grade year with much success.

Case Study 11.2: Jennifer

Jennifer is a 12-year-old girl who is currently in seventh grade and has recently been diagnosed with ADHD–combined type. She is currently receiving accommodations through a Section 504 service agreement and is showing progress as a result of her newly implemented service agreement.

Behavioral and Educational Background

Jennifer lives with her biological mother and father as well as her brother, John, who is three years older than she. When Jennifer was young, she was considered a "shy" child, and her parents described her as often being "in a world of her own." They noticed that she didn't seem to be listening when they would talk with her. She also had a lot of difficulties keeping her room organized and often lost her belongings. When playing, she frequently switched activities or toys very quickly. She also had a habit of snapping her fingers while she was playing. As she became older, her parents noticed that she was starting to seem less "shy" and would often jump into other people's conversations or interrupt while they were talking. For example, when they were at the dinner table, talking about their day, she would often jump into the story and say something that was unrelated. Her brother had a very boisterous personality, so her parents assumed that she was seeking attention.

Throughout her elementary-school years, Jennifer was generally successful in school and was typically described by her teachers as polite and well-behaved. Her second-grade teacher noted that she often stood up during class instead of sitting in her seat, but she seemed to be learning and was so well-behaved in other ways that the teacher didn't focus on it. Her third-grade teacher described her as well-mannered and a joy to have in class. However, that same teacher noted that she was having a lot of difficulties paying attention during class. She seemed to have difficulty remembering to write down her homework in her assignment notebook, and she often forgot to bring in her completed homework. The teacher noted that Jennifer often looked out the window or had a "blank" look on her face when the teacher

(Continued)

was talking. Additionally, her desk was always a mess. As Jennifer got older, her teachers noted similar behavior. Her fifth-grade teacher reported that she often shouted out answers in class without raising her hand or waiting to be called on. She also tapped her pencil and bounced her leg a lot during class. When asked to stop, she said that it helped her think about what she was learning. During her sixth-grade year, Jennifer began to show much more difficulty with school. She struggled when changing classrooms and often failed to get to each class on time; she often forgot her materials in her locker or at home; and she had difficulties keeping her binders and notebooks organized. During the sixth-grade parent-teacher conference, her team of teachers said that her disorganization, forgetfulness, and lack of attention in the classroom were really hindering her academic progress. The teaching team and Jennifer's parents worked out an organizational system that included a checklist that would be signed by each teacher and the parents. This seemed to help, and Jennifer showed improvement in her organizational skills and her ability to turn in her homework.

Diagnostic Procedure and Findings

During her sixth-grade physical, Jennifer's mother mentioned to the pediatrician the difficulties Jennifer was having in school, and the doctor indicated that perhaps Jennifer should be tested for ADHD. Jennifer's mother replied that she didn't think Jennifer had ADHD, because her brother John had it and his symptoms didn't resemble Jennifer's behavior at all. They talked about the different subtypes of ADHD, and Jennifer's mother realized that Jennifer did demonstrate many of the signs associated with the inattentive type. Jennifer's

parents, soccer coach, and sixth-grade teachers completed a rating scale, and their responses were fairly consistent. Jennifer presented with multiple symptoms from each of the three categories associated with ADHD (inattention, hyperactivity, and impulsivity) and was subsequently diagnosed with ADHD–combined type. Jennifer's parents met with the sixth-grade teachers and guidance counselor to discuss the diagnosis and determine how to move forward with Jennifer's education. They decided to complete a comprehensive evaluation to see whether she was eligible for special education services as a result of her ADHD. The comprehensive evaluation showed that she was performing well academically, that her behavior really wasn't interfering with school, and that she was socially getting along well with her peers. Her most prominent difficulties were related to organization. The team determined that she was not eligible for special education services, because there didn't appear to be a need that required specially designed instruction or a modification to her education. Instead, they determined that she should receive accommodations under a Section 504 service agreement. The school developed a Section 504 service agreement with input from the parents that included various accommodations, such as keeping an extra set of books at home, receiving additional time for getting to each class, using checklists for organization, being encouraged to ask for clarification regarding directions, being provided a weekly schedule of assignments, and being allowed the use of a stress ball during class. These accommodations have proven to be beneficial for Jennifer, and, through discussions with the pediatrician, Jennifer and her parents have decided not to seek treatment through medication but continue to monitor her progress with the accommodations that are in place.

1. List three different types of treatment/services that John received.

2. Why did he decide to discontinue ADHD medication before he started ninth grade?

3. Describe the differences between John and Jennifer in school that led to John receiving special education services and Jennifer receiving accommodations through a Section 504 service agreement. Why did Jennifer not receive special education services?

4. Why did John and Jennifer's parents recognize John's ADHD symptoms earlier than they did Jennifer's?

CHAPTER SUMMARY

ADHD is a common neurodevelopmental disorder that impacts many children, adolescents, and adults. It is classified into three subtypes (i.e., predominantly hyperactive-impulsive, predominantly inattentive, and combined), which differ according to the symptoms (inattention, hyperactivity, and/or impulsivity) that an individual exhibits. Guidelines for diagnostic criteria must be demonstrated before an individual can be diagnosed with ADHD. It is important that trained professionals (e.g., pediatricians) adhere to a comprehensive process when diagnosing ADHD, to ensure that an accurate diagnosis is made.

APPLY WHAT YOU HAVE LEARNED

1. Create a list of behaviors that might be demonstrated by an individual with ADHD. Develop a survey that would allow you to survey your classmates about whether they consider these behaviors examples of inattentive, hyperactive, or impulsive symptoms.

2. Think about an individual whom you know with ADHD, and make a list of the characteristics that you see with that individual. Be sure to think about behavior, intelligence, academic achievement, social/emotional status, and health and medical status. Relate those characteristics to the symptoms associated with the three types of ADHD. Do you see any correlations between the characteristics and the criteria for diagnosis?

REFERENCES

American Psychiatric Association (APA). (2013). Section II: Neurodevelopmental disorders: attention-deficit/hyperactivity disorder. In *Diagnostic and statistical manual of mental disorders* (5th ed.). Arlington, VA: Author. Retrieved from https://dsm-psychiatryonline-org.proxy-wcupa.klnpa.org/doi/book/10.1176/appi.books.9780890425596

Berninger, V., Abbott, R., Cook, C., Nagy, W., Cirino, P., & Willcutt, E. (2017). Relationships of attention and executive functions to oral language, reading, and writing skills and systems in middle childhood and early adolescence. *Journal of Learning Disabilities, 50*(4), 434–449.

Centers for Disease Control and Prevention (CDC). (2018a). *ADHD treatment recommendations.* Retrieved from https://www.cdc.gov/ncbddd/adhd/guidelines.html

Centers for Disease Control and Prevention (CDC). (2018b). *Symptoms and diagnosis of ADHD.* Retrieved from https://www.cdc.gov/ncbddd/adhd/diagnosis.html

Centers for Disease Control and Prevention (CDC). (2018c). *What is ADHD?* Retrieved from https://www.cdc.gov/ncbddd/adhd/facts.html

Centers for Disease Control and Prevention (CDC). (2019). *ADHD in the classroom: Helping children succeed in school.* Retrieved from https://www.cdc.gov/ncbddd/adhd/school- success.html

Children and Adults With Attention-Deficit/Hyperactivity Disorder (CHADD). (2017). *About ADHD.* Retrieved from https://chadd.org/wp-content/uploads/2018/03/aboutADHD.pdf

Children and Adults With Attention-Deficit/Hyperactivity Disorder (CHADD). (2019). *Diagnosing ADHD.* Retrieved from https://chadd.org/about-adhd/diagnosing-adhd

Feldman, H., & Reiff, M. (2014). Attention deficit–hyperactivity disorder in children and adolescents. *The New England Journal of Medicine, 370*(9), 838–846.

Holmes, J., Gathercole, S., Place, M., Alloway, T., Elliott, J., & Hilton, K. (2010). The diagnostic utility of executive function assessments in the identification of ADHD in children. *Child and Adolescent Mental Health, 15*(1), 37–43.

IDEA (Individuals With Disabilities Education Act). (2004). *Section 300.8(c)(9).* Retrieved from https://sites.ed.gov/idea/regs/b/a/300.8/c/9

Lawrence, K., Estrada, R., & Mccormick, J. (2017). Teachers' experiences with and perceptions of students with attention deficit/hyperactivity disorder. *Journal of Pediatric Nursing, 36,* 141–148.

Leahy, L. (2018). Diagnosis and treatment of ADHD in children vs adults: What nurses should know. *Archives of Psychiatric Nursing, 32*(6), 890–895.

Manos, M., Giuliano, K., & Geyer, E. (2017). ADHD: Overdiagnosed and overtreated, or misdiagnosed and mistreated? *Cleveland Clinic Journal of Medicine, 84*(11), 873–880.

National Institute of Mental Health. (2019). *Attention-deficit/hyperactivity disorder.* Retrieved December 17, 2019, from https://www.nimh.nih.gov/health/topics/attention-deficit- hyperactivity-disorder-adhd/index.shtml

National Institute of Mental Health. (n.d.). *Attention-deficit/hyperactivity disorder (ADHD): The basics.* Retrieved July 9, 2019 from https://www.nimh.nih.gov/health/publications/attention-deficit-hyperactivity-disorder-adhd-the-basics/qf-16-3572_153275.pdf

Pham, A. (2016). Differentiating behavioral ratings of inattention, impulsivity, and hyperactivity in children: Effects on reading achievement. *Journal of Attention Disorders, 20*(8), 674–683.

Schutte, K., Piselli, K., Schmitt, A., Miglioretti, M., Lorenzi-Quigley, L., Tiberi, A., & Krohner, N. (2017). Identification of ADHD and autism spectrum disorder: Responsibilities of school psychologists. *Communique, 46*(1), 4.

Shemmassian, S., & Lee, S. (2016). Predictive utility of four methods of incorporating parent and teacher symptom ratings of ADHD for longitudinal outcomes. *Journal of Clinical Child and Adolescent Psychology: The Official Journal for the Society of Clinical Child and Adolescent Psychology, American Psychological Association, Division 53, 45*(2), 176–187.

U.S. Department of Education, Office for Civil Rights. (2016, July). *Students With ADHD and Section 504: A resource guide*. Washington, DC: Author. Retrieved from https://www2.ed.gov/about/offices/list/ocr/letters/colleague-201607-504-adhd.pdf

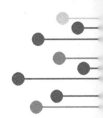

Sensory Impairments (Including Visual Impairment, Hearing Impairment, Deafness, and Deaf-Blindness)

Vicki A. McGinley, PhD

Learning Objectives

After completion of this chapter, you should be able to:

- define Sensory Impairments to include Hearing Impairment, Deafness, Visual Impairment, and Deaf-Blindness as outlined in the Individuals with Disabilities Education Act.

- identify the causes and characteristics of children with Sensory Impairments.

- explain how children with Sensory Impairments are diagnosed/identified.

- identify some educational considerations for children with Sensory Impairments.

Key Terms

acquired or adventitious (p. 344)	deafness (p. 343)
amblyopia (p. 358)	functional vision (p. 359)
authentic assessment (p. 370)	glaucoma (p. 358)
blindness (p. 357)	hearing impairment (p. 343)
conductive (p. 345)	learning media (p. 359)
congenital (p. 344)	legal blindness (p. 359)
congenital cataracts (p. 358)	low vision (p. 357)

(Continued)

(Continued)

mixed (p. 345)	sensorineural (p. 345)
orientation and mobility (O&M) (p. 368)	sensory information for learning (p. 359)
post-lingual (p. 344)	total communication approach (p. 370)
prelingual (p. 344)	visual acuity (p. 359)
retinitis pigmentosa (p. 358)	visual awareness distance (p. 359)
retinoblastoma (p. 358)	visual field (p. 359)
retinopathy (p. 358)	visual impairment (p. 357)

Introduction to the Chapter

This chapter provides information on disabilities that fall under the inability to receive information adequately through the various sensory systems. For children with sensory impairments, specifically those with deafness and hearing impairments and/or blindness and visual impairments, there is a long history of services in our country. Although, in recent years, advancement in research and subsequent interventions (specifically in the area of technology) for the populations of children with sensory impairments—as well as where many of these children are served in the educational system—have changed, many educational strategies for helping children with sensory impairments have been in use for decades.

This chapter is organized by discussion of each of the identified sensory impairments separately. The first section addresses hearing impairment and deafness.

Hearing Impairment and Deafness

The Centers for Disease Control and Prevention (2019) report that approximately 14.9% of school-age children have some degree of hearing loss, and 5 out of every 1,000 have a significant hearing loss. This includes both children who have a hearing impairment and/or deafness and those who have hearing loss in one ear only (unilateral hearing loss). This sensory impairment is considered a low-incidence disability, with approximately 2% of school-age children served under the Individuals With Disabilities Education Act (IDEA) and thus receiving an individualized education program (IEP).

IDEA Definitions

[Hearing impairment] means an impairment in hearing, whether permanent or fluctuating, that adversely affects a child's education performance but that is not included under the definition of deafness in this section.

(IDEA, 20 U.S.C. § 1401 (2004), 20 C.F.R. § 300.8(c)(5))

[Deafness] means a hearing impairment that is so severe that the child is impaired in processing linguistic information through hearing, with or without amplification [and] that adversely affects a child's education performance.

(IDEA, 20 U.S.C § 1401 (2004), 20 C.F.R. § 300.8(c)(3))

History of Educational Strategies

To fully explain present-day assessment of children who are identified as having a hearing impairment and/or deafness, it is important that we outline some of the history of their education leading up to the present.

In the United States, Thomas Hopkins Gallaudet opened the first residential school in 1817 for children specifically with deafness, named the American Asylum for the Education of the Deaf and Dumb (now the America School for the Deaf), in Hartford, Connecticut (Winzer, 1993). This remote school became the standard model as regarded education of children with hearing impairments. At the same time, debate and controversy swirled over how to educate these children, specifically whether to instruct them in the use of sign language rather than oral language. Many educators believed that if children signed, they would not learn to speak, which was considered the preferred method of communication. Proponents of oral language prevailed, and this paradigm profoundly influenced education for years to come. Needless to say, this frustrated many teachers and children who could not optimally, if at all, learn to use speech as their primary mode of communication and, thus, wound up with no formal means of communication.

Then, in the 1950s, following a rubella epidemic in the United States, an increasing number of children became deaf. As a result, more local schools needed to provide education for the hearing impaired, and although hearing impairments were considered a low-incidence disability, both the educational placement and instruction of children with hearing impairments began to change with the combination of American Sign Language (ASL) and the oral language approach (Higgins & Lieberman, 2016). Presently, many children in the Deaf community are users of ASL and, thus, will choose to, at times, segregate themselves into the Deaf community and culture with other users of ASL. This is now a choice rather than a societal force.

Besides rubella, there are a number of causes of hearing impairment and deafness. The next section addresses some of those causes.

Causes

The causes of hearing loss are generally categorized as occurring either before or after birth, as both the timing and the severity of loss impact a child's communication and language skills, as well as cognition. A congenital hearing loss, which is present at birth, occurs prelingually, prior to speech and language development, and an acquired or adventitious hearing loss occurs post-lingually, after speech and language have developed. The longer a child has normal hearing, the greater the chance he or she will reach typical developmental milestones concerning language and communication.

For children who are deaf and/or hearing-impaired, nearly half of all hearing losses have a genetic cause (CDC, 2016). However, other causes of hearing loss (those that are not hereditary) include the following:

Prelingual

- Infections, including rubella and herpes simplex virus
- Premature birth
- Severe jaundice in the neonatal period
- Anoxia (lack of oxygen) to the child before, during, or immediately after birth
- Toxemia during pregnancy
- Fetal alcohol syndrome
- Physical malformation of the ear structures

Post-Lingual

Post-lingual causes of hearing loss are usually the result of an injury or disease and include:

- Ear infections (otitis media)
- Head injuries
- Childhood diseases including measles, chicken pox, mumps, and influenza
- Encephalitis
- Loud noises
- Use of certain medicines

(WHO, 2020)

1. What are some causes of hearing impairment and deafness?

2. How does the loss of hearing prelingually differ from the loss of hearing post-lingually? What impact does that have on the child?

How the Diagnosis Is Made/Who Makes the Diagnosis

It is the goal to identify a hearing loss early enough, even in infancy, so that early intervention, specifically in the area of communication and language, can begin for the child. With recent advances in technology, children can be identified earlier; however, according to the Center for Deaf and Hard of Hearing Education (2010), prior to 2000 the average age of identification was 2.5 years of age, which still presents great challenges to a child's language development.

Diagnosis of a hearing loss is always performed by a medical practitioner—usually a general practitioner, an audiologist, an otolaryngologist, or an audiovestibular physician. Many school districts require universal screening for hearing loss as early detection, so that intervention will minimize the negative impact to the child's language, communication, and educational development. However, as indicated above, a firm diagnosis of hearing loss will be done by a specialized doctor. Measuring the degree of loss is the initial step and an important one, as the quantity and quality of sound that children are able to process will determine whether further testing (e.g., MRI, CT scan, speech-to-noise test) is needed. With an older child, initial testing will be done by measuring sound in decibels (dB), or volume, and hertz (Hz), or frequency (pitch or tone) of sound. The more frequent the sound waves, the higher the pitch and the higher the hertz number. The higher the level of decibel not heard by the child, the more significant the hearing loss. Hearing loss is categorized by type, severity, and configuration, may exist in only one ear (unilateral) or in both ears (bilateral), and can be temporary or permanent and sudden or progressive. Table 12.1 shows the classifications of hearing loss by sound.

It will be important to identify what the child can hear (residual hearing), as well as what the child cannot hear. The doctor will start with a case history, and then examine the outer and middle ear using an optical instrument. She will then proceed to a test of auditory functions, such as using a tuning fork, which can provide a quick indication of hearing loss. There are three main types of hearing loss: conductive, sensorineural, and mixed, or a combination of these two. Conductive hearing loss is when sound does not reach the inner ear (the cochlea), sometimes due to external ear canal malformation or to dysfunction of the eardrum or the bones in the middle ear. Scar tissue as a result of ear infections may

Table 12.1 Classification of Hearing Loss

Hearing Level (decibels, dB)	Examples	Description
1–15 dB	Whispering, breathing	Normal hearing
16–40 dB	Rustling, muffled speech	Mild hearing loss
41–70 dB	Noise in background, party, conversations, loss of directionality of sound	Moderate hearing loss
71–90 dB	Old-fashioned telephone ring	Severe hearing loss
91 dB and above	Loud rock music	Profound hearing loss

Adapted from Friend, M. (2019). *Special education: Contemporary perspectives for school professionals* (5th ed.). New York, NY: Pearson.

cause eardrum dysfunction. **Sensorineural** hearing loss is caused by dysfunction of the inner ear (the cochlea) or the nerve that transmits the impulse from the cochlea to the brain. **Mixed** hearing loss may be caused, for example, by chronic ear infections, which may cause a defective eardrum, middle-ear damage, or both. (RightDiagnosis.com, n.d.)

In the school setting, the multidisciplinary team (MDT) will consider medical results, but also must assess all suspected areas of disability—specifically, those areas potentially impacted by the hearing loss of the child. For example, academic achievement may have been impacted, and, thus, a full psychological evaluation with achievement tests will help determine at what level the child is functioning. In addition to the parent(s), important MDT members will likely include a speech-language pathologist, a certified hearing impairment teacher, and the classroom teacher of record. Depending on the child's mode of communication, a sign-language interpreter may be involved to support adaptations and modifications needed for the child to access his education. If all the information indicates that the child's disability impacts his education, he will be provided with specially designed instruction (SDI) and related services.

Check Your Understanding 12.2

1. Which multidisciplinary team members are part of the MDT for a child with hearing impairment/deafness? Why do you believe each member is important? What do you think are their roles in the assessment process?

2. How does level/severity of hearing loss impact the child's education? In what ways?

Assessment

Cognitive/intelligence evaluations *are not required*, as the absence of hearing does not cause a cognitive delay or reduce intelligence. However, since a lack of exposure to language can impact a child's cognitive development, developmental and academic evaluations will be necessary. Assessment must occur in the child's preferred mode of communication—either verbal, sign, or written—and/or with the use of technologies. Assessments for a child's initial evaluations, and subsequent reevaluations, include the following:

- Assessment of academic achievement
- Evaluation of functional skills or adaptive behavior across various environments and in multiple forms
- Social and developmental history
- Reports from the audiologist, otologist, or otolaryngologist
- Any other educational evaluations (e.g., cognition, motor, sensory) necessary to inform the MDT

In addition to the team members noted above, the MDT conducting the evaluation may include the following members:

- The audiologist
- A teacher of the deaf and hard of hearing, a deaf educator (if needed), and/or an American Sign Language Specialist (if needed)
- An occupational therapist, physical therapist, and speech-language pathologist (if needed)
- A school psychologist
- A social worker
- The child's teacher of record
- The child's parents

Parents, being critical team members, will provide information on child development to include hearing screening results; medical, social, and developmental history; the preferred mode of communication in the home; the child's strengths/areas of need; educational history; adaptive behaviors; and other pertinent information.

Assessment will include addressing the child's preferred mode of communication (to include signed, spoken, and/or written language), as well as testing by a speech-language pathologist and hearing impairment consultant to include phonology, voice quality, intelligibility of speech, grammar, semantics, pragmatics, and cognitive academic language proficiency (CALP). Assessment results will tell whether the child may benefit from amplification or other assistive technologies and whether the child will benefit from sign language or a combination of support. An example of an evaluation for a child with a potential hearing loss can be found in Box 12.1.

Box 12.1   Sample Hearing Assessment

Functional Hearing Evaluation

NAME:	James Paige
DATE OF BIRTH:	4/19/2011
AGE:	7.0
SCHOOL:	Stoney Brook Elementary
GRADE:	1
EVAL. DATE(s):	5/2/18 & 5/16/18
EVALUATOR:	Jill Christopher

Reason For Referral

James was referred for a functional hearing evaluation to determine James's eligibility for itinerant hearing support services.

Background Information

James was born prematurely. He has a medical history of ear infections and has a history of PE tubes. Mrs. Paige reported that James passed his newborn hearing screening; however, they began to suspect he was having difficulty hearing when he was approaching school age. She reported he asked for the volume to be turned up when watching television or when on his iPad. He also said, "What?" often when someone was speaking to him. There is no medical history for hearing loss in the family.

Audiological Information

James received an audiological assessment at East General Hospital on March 19, 2018. He was tested by Melinda Fletcher, Au.D., CCC-A. James was referred for audiology by his pediatrician after he failed his hearing screening at school. Test results show right ear consistent with normal hearing from 500 to 1,000 Hz dropping to mild conductive from 2,000 to 8,000 Hz. The left ear is consistent with mild to moderate conductive hearing loss. It was recommended that James be seen again in three months for an audiological reevaluation. It was also recommended that the family consider scheduling a visit for a hearing aid evaluation. The educational team should also be alerted to hearing difficulty and consider strategic classroom seating and request a trial with an FM system in school.

Amplification

At the time of the evaluation, James was not wearing amplification; however, the family is planning to move forward with having James fit for bilateral hearing aids with an integrated digital modulation (DM) system. An appointment is scheduled later in May.

Auditory Functioning

James's auditory word identification skills were assessed using the CID Phonetically Balanced Word Lists. James was asked to repeat unrelated one-syllable words, with the following results:

Modality	Distance	Background Noise	Score
Auditory-alone	3 feet	Quiet	94%
Auditory-alone	12 feet	Quiet	88%
Auditory-alone	12 feet	Moderate	76%
Auditory-visual	12 feet	Moderate	80%

James was also evaluated with the CID Sentence List. He was asked to repeat unrelated sentences. The following results were obtained:

Modality	Distance	Background Noise	Score
Auditory-alone	3 feet	Quiet	100%
Auditory-alone	12 feet	Quiet	92%
Auditory-alone	12 feet	Moderate	78%
Auditory-visual	12 feet	Moderate	85%

James was also evaluated with an ear-level (right ear) FM system during the session, using the CID Phonetically Balanced Word Lists. The following results were obtained:

(Continued)

(Continued)

Modality	Distance	Background Noise	Score
Auditory-alone	12 feet	Quiet	96%
Auditory-alone	12 feet	Moderate	92%
Auditory-visual	12 feet	Moderate	96%

Although James performed well when in quiet and with visual access, his scores decreased when the visual aids were removed and when background noise was present. Children with typical hearing average 93–97% accuracy in a standard level of background noise (around 50 dB HL with a +5 dB S/N). It is necessary to achieve functional listening scores in the 90%+ range in order for children with hearing loss to "compete" with their typically hearing peers.

It should be noted that James's performance was 76% for single words and sentences under the most difficult listening conditions of distance, background noise, and audition-alone. His score obtained while using the FM system under this same condition improved to 92%.

James was also presented with the Word Identification Picture Inventory (WIPI). He is presented with six phonetically similar–sounding words and corresponding pictures. One word was said, and he had to point to the correct picture (e.g., glass/grass/cap/rat/bat/cat). This activity was presented auditorily in quiet, within 3 feet of the test administrator. He scored 100% on this test.

James was presented with the Wepman Auditory Discrimination Test. This test asks the student to identify 40 word pairs as the same (e.g., man-man) or different (e.g., hat-pat). The test was presented in quiet, and James was seated within 3 feet of the administrator. The first half was presented auditorily (no visual cues). James scored 75%. The second half was presented with visual cues. James was noted to watch the speaker's face while this additional cue was provided. He scored 90% on this test.

The Listening Comprehension Test–2 was administered to evaluate James's strengths and weaknesses in specific listening skill areas related to classroom listening situations. This test assesses the student's performance of skills such as summarizing and sequencing information, participating in classroom discussions, following directions, understanding the main idea, attending to the details of a message, understanding language concepts, problem solving and predicting, and listening for meaning. It also requires auditory memory skills to retain information from the passage and then answer questions. It was administered in a quiet environment, with the examiner seated in close proximity and directly across from James. On this instrument, a standard score that falls between 85 and 115 is within normal age expectations, with a score of 100 being the exact average.

The following information lists the subtest, followed by the standard score and percentile rank:

Main Idea:	118/88
Details:	98/44
Reasoning:	102/54
Vocabulary:	110/74

| Understanding Messages: | 80/9 |
| Total Test: | 101/52 |

James's Listening Comprehension Test–2 standard scores and percentiles ranged from below average to above average. His total test score fell in the average range. James demonstrated the ability to comprehend auditory information for determining the main idea. His strong performance on the Main Idea portion of the test proves he is able to use details from the passage to identify the big picture. Although he used the various details to conclude the main idea, he had greater difficulty in recalling specific information about the details that were presented. When James was unable to recall the details that were being probed, he used his prior knowledge to try to answer the questions. James's score of 102 in the Reasoning portion of the test demonstrates his ability to answer inferential questions and questions requiring him to draw conclusions. These skills are all critical for his academic achievement in all subject areas. James had the most difficulty on the Understanding Messages portion of the test. In this section, short, concise passages are read aloud that are common school-related announcements and directions given in the classroom. There are not a lot of details in the prompts, so students do not have as much opportunity to figure out missed or misheard information. James exhibited similar difficulties with accurately following directions during the observation in his classroom.

During the evaluation, James was very pleasant and cooperative, and he frequently initiated conversation. He sat quietly and demonstrated appropriate eye contact. His speech was intelligible.

Classroom Observation

James was observed in his first-grade classroom on May 16, 2018. There were 16 students present in the class. Ms. Dempsey was seated in a chair in front of the children, who were sitting on the carpet. The group was finishing their morning meeting as the observation began. James was seated at the corner of the rug, approximately 8 feet from the teacher. The students were directed to go to their desks for some seat work.

James returned to his seat, which is located at the front of the classroom with good visual access to the teacher, the smartboard, and his peers. One student was chosen to "roll the word die" on the smartboard while the rest of the class read aloud the word that showed up on the board. James did not participate during this activity. The students were instructed to get out their whiteboards. James hesitated and did not follow the instruction immediately until he noticed his peers taking out their whiteboards, at which point he did the same. The class completed a word-building activity on their whiteboards. James raised his hand to participate in two out of eight opportunities.

The students read along and, at times, choral read a story from the anthology. Although it was not a significant amount of time, James was noted to have greater difficulty than his peers with sitting during this activity. He was observed shifting, possibly for comfort, as well as squatting, rocking, and stepping on his hands and fingers during the reading. His attention varied between the book and the teacher.

When the activity was finished, the students were directed to return to the rug with their word-family books. The students were directed to get into groups of three. James followed directions independently. While working on the activity with his group, he was observed looking around at other

(Continued)

groups rather than engaging in the discussion with his group. The background noise increased during this activity, as there were multiple groups working together while seated in close proximity to one another on the carpet.

Classroom Functioning

James's teacher, Ms. Dempsey, was given the SIFTER (Screening Instrument for Targeting Educational Risk) to complete. This form looks at needs for academics, attention, communication, class participation, and school behavior. Scores falling within both PASS and MARGINAL range occur within the broad range of normal performance. Any student who receives a score of FAIL in any area should be considered for educational accommodations.

James scored within the PASS range in the areas of Academics, Communication, and School Behavior. He scored within the FAIL range for Class Participation and Attention.

Ms. Dempsey shared that James is progressing in his academics but does not often participate in class discussions without prompting. James benefits from prompting and reminders to follow directions and/or stay on task. She also observes that James has a difficult time focusing while working in a small group.

Summary

Educational Strengths:

1. Pleasant and cooperative
2. Interested in communicating
3. Utilizes good communication skills

Educational Needs:

1. James needs to demonstrate strategies to compensate for the effects of his hearing loss and to express his hearing-related needs.
2. The school staff needs to develop strategies and environmental modifications to compensate for the effects of James's hearing loss.
3. An itinerant hearing support teacher needs to be available to the school staff, to be a resource regarding James's hearing loss and implications for his education.

Recommendations

1. Based on the results of this evaluation, and also the Hearing Itinerant Service Rubric, it is recommended that James be considered an eligible student for specially designed instruction for students who are deaf or hard of hearing.
2. James presently utilizes an auditory-oral communication mode, and he should continue to use speech, audition, and speechreading as his primary means of communication.

3. The results of this evaluation indicate that James will benefit from the following specially designed instruction items:

– James should be seated near the speaker and away from background noise.

– Allow for flexible seating.

– If/when a DM system is being worn, it should be used for all direct instruction, including individual and small/large group.

– Passing of the DM transmitter to the speaker.

– The teacher should repeat other students' comments and questions, especially if they are at a distance from James, if there is background noise, or if they have a quiet voice.

– The teacher should check for understanding, especially when presenting new material or when there is background noise.

– The teacher should repeat and/or *rephrase* information if James is unsure of what he has heard.

– A hearing support teacher will instruct James on coping strategies, as well as provide opportunity to practice his self-advocacy skills.

Adapted from Jill Christopher, MEd., LSLS Cert. AVEd., CED

As a result of the evaluation, the MDT will gain valuable information related to the child's sensory-related characteristics. Those characteristics are described below.

Sensory-Related Considerations/Characteristics

For evaluation, assessment and intervention, sensory (as well as other) characteristics must be considered, as they will impact how the MDT evaluates the child, how assessments are carried out, and ultimately the success of intervention. Following are some related considerations and characteristics of note.

Communication

A child with deafness and/or a hearing impairment's level of communication will be dependent on a number things, such as whether the child's parents are hearing or deaf, the level of communicative interactions that occur throughout the child's day and with what communicative partners, when the hearing impairment or deafness occurred, and the life experiences the child is exposed to for learning. For example, if a child's parents are deaf, and sign language is the primary mode of communication, speech and language used in the classroom may not be used by the child. Additionally, limited life experiences that occur as a result of hearing impairment or deafness, such as exploring one's environment fully, will impact the child's vocabulary, sentence structure, and idiomatic expressions and, thus, the child's academic achievement. (Packer, 2018)

Cognitive/Academic Skills

Research has indicated that cognitive skills of children who are deaf and/or hearing-impaired generally lag behind their typical peers; however, of note is that a hearing loss in and of itself should impose no limitations on cognitive skills (Maller & Braden, 1993). However, the absence of early communication may impact a child's academic achievement, as language is central to communicating what we learn. Thus, areas that require significant language and communication skills, such as reading and writing, may be impacted (Easterbrooks et al., 2015). All academic areas may be impacted. For example, in the area of mathematics, Hrastinski and Wilbur (2016) reported that students who are deaf and/or hearing-impaired may achieve on grade level or higher than their typical peers, but generally they will score lower due to difficulty with mathematical language and mathematical symbols. Children with hearing impairments and deafness will be involved in all testing, such as state and local assessments, with accommodations if needed.

Social/Emotional/Behavioral Characteristics

Because social and emotional characteristics are impacted by interactions, children who are deaf and/or hearing-impaired may be challenged in both of these areas due to lack of communication and interactions with others. Both knowledge of pragmatic communication (functions or reasons why we communicate) and development of a descriptive vocabulary of feelings may be affected. This may result in isolation from friends, family, and community members. Socialization is of particular concern. Since their socialization will be curtailed, children who are deaf and/or hearing-impaired may not understand why certain behaviors are necessary and others inappropriate.

Safety/Mobility

Sounds such as shouts, a vehicle approaching, a fire alarm, and a dog barking often serve to warn us of danger. As a result, parents of nonhearing children may inadvertently curtail a child's development due to safety concerns. Also, of note, children with hearing impairments and/or deafness may need extra support around victimization, specifically bullying and abuse prevention. However, in a lot of environments, technology—specifically, alert systems—have helped to support users by means of visual as well as tactile notification, through such technology as vibrators on mobile devices. Additionally, all materials for children with hearing impairments and/or deafness will need to be in print. Organizations such as the National Association of the Deaf can support and advocate where needed. For example, according to the NAD (n.d.), as a result of the Americans With Disabilities Act, all transportation systems (airline, train, bus, subway, etc.) require audible information accessible in visual (text) format.

Assessment in the area of mobility is needed, as a child with hearing impairment and/or deafness may have challenges related to visual-perceptual motor skills as a result of vestibular damage that impacts the child's equilibrium, body awareness, and visual-motor functioning. The evaluation will be conducted by an occupational and/or physical therapist (Center for Deaf and Hard of Hearing Education, 2010), as well as a teacher of the hearing-impaired.

Check Your Understanding 12.3

1. What are some causes of deafness and/or hearing impairment prelingually and post-lingually? Which do you believe results in more severity of language and communication impairment for the child? Why?

2. What are some characteristics of a child with hearing impairment and/or deafness? Which areas are impacted?

Extension to Instruction

There are a number of ways in which we educate students who are deaf and/or hearing-impaired; however, the greatest benefit will be from visual teaching strategies. Written or printed text used in many ways, such as through the provision of captioning interpretation to facilitate access to information, and the use of a TTY device (telecommunication device for the deaf) will support many children. Additionally, the development of sign language, lipreading, and a wide array of assistive technologies play a large role in educating children with hearing impairment and deafness. One important assistive technology is FM (frequency modulation), a wireless assistive device that allows teachers to talk into a microphone that transmits a signal directly to a deaf or hearing-impaired child's hearing aid.

In addition, mobile devices (e.g., smartphones and tablets) to include the texting feature have helped immensely.

Many children benefit from speech-language pathology services, as well as from a certified hearing impairment teacher consultant who works with classroom teachers to support access to the child's IEP and curriculum. In the area of assistive technology, in addition to the FM device to amplify speech, hearing aids work to improve the hearing and speech comprehension of children with hearing loss. However, of note is that for some children, particularly adolescents, the aesthetic factor may be an issue and, thus, result in refusal to use such a device. The selection of technologies needs to be child-centered. Other assistive technology devices include the following:

- Telecommunications devices for the deaf (TDD)
- Real-time text technologies
- Videophones and video conferencing (for sign-language use)
- Signaling transmitters
- Amplification devices
- Closed captioning

Although not an educational intervention, some children have benefited from the medical intervention of receiving a cochlear implant, which is an electronic device that restores the ability to hear sounds and thus understand speech. This device is for those children who would not benefit from hearing aids. It is a surgically implanted receiver and simulator of sounds. (American Cochlear Implant Alliance, n.d.)

Check Your Understanding 12.4

1. What are some technologies that may support a child with deafness and/or hearing impairment?

2. What types of support do you think a classroom teacher will need in order to support a child with deafness and/or hearing impairment?

Visual Impairment and Blindness

This sensory impairment, like hearing impairments and deafness, is considered a low-incidence disability, with estimates being in the 0.5% range of the general population for children with this disability (U.S. Department of Education, 2015).

IDEA Definition

Visual Impairment including Blindness is impairment in vision that, even with correction, adversely affects a child's educational performance. The term includes both partial sight and Blindness.

(IDEA, 20 U.S.C. § 1401 (2004), 20 C.F. R. § 300.8(c)(13))

History of Educational Strategies

Just like hearing impairments and deafness, the education of children with visual impairment and blindness has a long history, beginning in France in the mid-19th century. The first school in the United States, the New England Asylum for the Blind (now Perkins School), was established in Chicago, known best for its work with students with deaf-blindness, such as Helen Keller. A significant historical event occurred in the 1950s, when there was a dramatic increase in children with visual impairments due to retrolental fibroplasia (RLF), now referred to as retinopathy of prematurity (ROP), which is the abnormal development of retinal blood vessels resulting in proliferation of fibrous tissue immediately behind the lens of the eye and potentially leading to visual impairment or blindness (Appelbaum, 1952). According to the National Eye Institute (2019), it affected many premature babies due to the excessive administration of oxygen.

Following this event in history, the higher number of children with blindness and/or visual impairments gave rise to educational programs being offered in local schools (U.S. Department of Education, 2015).

Severity

For children with visual impairments, visual loss ranges from mild to severe. For children with low vision (having some vision), some tasks may be difficult, requiring environmental modifications, technology, and some compensatory strategies. They may need large print, but they may also learn to read Braille and use both tactile and auditory strategies. Children who have blindness may have no vision at all, or they may have only some light perception. Almost all tasks will be performed through the tactile or auditory senses. Braille is used for reading and writing; orientation and mobility instruction will support a child's mobility skills; and a variety of strategies for performing different tasks may or may not include assistive technologies.

Depending on when the visual impairment or blindness occurs—that is, whether it is congenital (at birth) or adventitious—will impact a child's functioning and education. Children who are blind from birth will need early intervention immediately, to support them in accessing the environment though all other senses.

Causes

As noted above, for a child with visual impairment or blindness, abilities in many areas may be impacted, and, thus, how we educate the child will be impacted. Causes of visual impairment and blindness may happen before birth and very early on in a child's life or at any point in the child's developmental years, thus requiring interventions that may be different for a child who had sight and then lost it. Below are some of the more prevalent causes of visual impairment and blindness.

Prenatal

One of the most common causes of visual impairment and blindness is the result of chromosomal and genetic disorders, as well as retinopathy, a diabetes complication caused by damage to the blood vessels of the light-sensitive tissue at the back of the eye (retina). Prenatal retinopathy is mainly caused by babies being born premature and being placed in high-oxygen environments. Other prenatal causes of visual impairment are glaucoma (causing damage to the optic nerve, which carries visual information form the eye to the brain) and congenital cataracts. Rubella, if it is contracted by the mother during pregnancy, may also cause blindness. Inherited conditions, such as retinitis pigmentosa, which is a hereditary disease characterized by black pigmentation and gradual degeneration of the retina, are sometimes to blame (Boyd, 2019).

An environmental cause of visual impairment in pregnancy is maternal substance abuse, which may impact the visual pathways in the brain.

In rare instances, a child may be born without eyes.

Postnatal

Injuries to the brain as a result of seizure disorders and traumatic brain injuries, as well as retinoblastoma (cancer starting in the retina), are two causes of visual impairment and blindness that occur postnatally. Additionally, strabismus (misaligned or crossed eyes) is a common cause of amblyopia (reduced vision in one eye caused by lack of use of that eye in early childhood).

In certain instances, irregularities in children's visual pathways in the brain may impact their ability to function visually, resulting in what is known as cerebral visual impairment (CVI). Causes may be prenatal, such as chromosomal or genetic abnormalities, or postnatal, due to traumatic brain injury (Hall Lueck & Dutton, 2015).

Check Your Understanding 12.5

1. What are some causes of low vision and/or blindness?

2. What is the difference between low vision and blindness, and what impact will each have for the child?

How the Diagnosis Is Made/Who Makes the Diagnosis

Just as with hearing impairment and deafness, the MDT will use the clinical information from a doctor, specifically the level and severity of the visual loss. A healthcare specialist, such as an ophthalmologist, an optometrist, or a pediatrician, will examine the child. Additionally, most school-age children will be required to have a vision screening, at minimum, using tests that are used to diagnose visual acuity and visual impairment, including the Snellen test. This may be followed by more extensive examinations that assess the external and internal structure of the eyes. A tonometry test, which measures pressure inside the eyes, may be used to test for glaucoma. More specialized tests, such as Ocular Motility Assessment, the visually evoked potential (VEP), an electroretinogram (ERG), and an electro-oculogram (EOG), are sometimes prescribed to determine whether the signals from the eye are traveling adequately to the brain. (Mandal, 2019)

Clinical measures will include **visual acuity**, the clarity or sharpness of vision, and **visual field**, the range in which objects can be seen centrally or peripherally. **Legal blindness** refers to the condition in which central visual acuity is 20/200 or less in the better eye with corrective lenses or central visual acuity is more than 20/200 if a visual-field defect exists so that the field is 20 degrees or less in each eye (Koestler, 2004).

Although the school may have access to all clinical information—particularly following information from an ophthalmologist or an optometrist—essentially, the school will assess all areas of suspected disability, focusing on visual impairment and how it impacts the child's academic achievement and his or her participation in school activities. A visual impairment specialist, which is a certified teacher, will be involved in the assessment and will determine whether the visual impairment is such that it adversely affects the child's educational performance. The visual impairment specialist will be involved in assessing **functional vision**; **learning media**, to assess what learning and literacy media will be used for the child to facilitate learning; **visual awareness distance**; and the child's overall ability to use **sensory information for learning** (McLinden & McCall, 2016).

Assessment

Just as for children with hearing impairments and deafness, all areas of suspected disability for children with low vision and blindness must be assessed. However, cognitive evaluations are also not required, as the absence of vision does not cause a cognitive delay. However, since a potential lack of exploring one's environment and the learning of abstract concepts may impact a child's cognitive development, developmental and academic evaluations will be necessary.

As described above, a teacher of the visually impaired will assess the following as part of the overall functional vision assessment: functional vision, learning media, visual awareness distance, and sensory information for learning as part of the learning media assessment (Ponchillia et al., 2007).

According to Koenig and Holbrook (1995), the learning media assessment obtains information on students by examining how the student gathers information from sensory channels, the types of learning media he or she uses, and the literacy media he or she will use for reading and writing. The sensory information assessment will look at the child's primary and secondary sensory channels for learning, such as use of visual, tactile, and auditory channels (Levack, 1991).

Overall assessments for a child's initial evaluations, and subsequent reevaluations, include the following:

- Assessment of academic achievement

- Evaluation of functional skills or adaptive behavior across various environments and in multiple forms

- Social and developmental history

- Reports from the audiologist, ophthalmologist, optometrist, low vision specialist

- Any other educational evaluations (e.g., cognition, motor), all medical information, and sensory abilities or information necessary to inform the MDT

Thus, the MDT conducting the evaluation may include the following members:

- The ophthalmologist, optometrist, pediatrician, or other specialist

- A teacher of visually impaired students

- An occupational therapist, a physical therapist, and an orientation and mobility specialist

- A school psychologist

- The child's teacher of record

- The child's parents

Parents, being critical team members, will provide information on child development to include vision screening results; medical, social, and developmental history; the preferred mode of communication in the home; the child's strengths; areas of need; educational history; adaptive behaviors; and other pertinent information. A sample vision evaluation appears in Box 12.2.

As a result of the evaluation, the MDT will gain valuable information related to the child's sensory-related characteristics. Those characteristics are described below.

Sensory-Related Considerations/Characteristics

According to Holbrook and Koenig (2000), overall, visual abilities that will be impacted as a result of visual impairment and/or blindness include:

- optical abilities, such as attending to objects, shifting gaze, and focus and tracking;

Box 12.2 Sample Vision Evaluation

Functional Vision Evaluation

NAME: Shaquie Jones

DATE OF BIRTH: 8/16/04

SCHOOL: Allen High School

DISTRICT: East Moreland

AGE: 15

GRADE: 9th

EVALUATOR: Paula Rollins

DATE OF ASSESSMENT: 8/10/10; 8/12/19

DATE OF REPORT: 8/21/19

Purpose of Evaluation

A functional vision evaluation was requested for Shaquie by her school in order to assess how Shaquie uses vision for everyday tasks at school that accommodates her cultural background, linguistic status, and/or disability determining the need for vision support services.

Assessments

- Parent Interview
- Student Interview
- Teacher Input (obtained from most current IEP)
- Review of Records
- Observations of Student
- Assessment of Visual Characteristics
- Learning Media Assessment (**abridged)
- Lighthouse Near Vision Acuity Measure
- Distance Vision Screening

Background Information

Shaquie is a 15-year-old student currently attending The Allen High School's virtual setting. Shaquie receives education in the virtual setting with assigned certified teachers via web mail and live/guided

(Continued)

(Continued)

instruction. Background information obtained from her most current IEP dated February 7, 2019, identifies Shaquie as legally blind, with visual difficulties and visual perceptual difficulties, having a white cane, and receiving support from a CTVI (certified teacher of the visually impaired) for 60 minutes a month. It is noted here that information summarized on the IEP pertaining to functional vision assessment is more than two years old and no longer relevant.

Shaquie receives full-time learning support. Shaquie's current IEP reflects the following accommodations related to her decreased visual functioning ability: large-print texts, visual breaks, enlarged keyboard, larger computer screen, and PowerPoints provided ahead of time whenever available.

Information from current medical report available to the evaluator from a qualified ophthalmologist at the time of the assessment (Dr. Nelson, Wills Eye Ophthalmology): Shaquie is a student with bilateral Optic Nerve Hypoplasia and visual-field deficits. She is severely farsighted. At her last office visit, in December 2018, alternative learning media (Braille) was discussed with both Shaquie and her mother.

PARENT AND STUDENT INTERVIEW

An in-person interview took place between the evaluator, Shaquie, and Shaquie's mother, Mrs. Wynita Jones, on August 12, 2019, before observation and assessment of visual characteristics took place.

Parent Input

Mrs. Wynita Jones reports that Shaquie is diabetic—the nerves in the back of her eyes are damaged due to her diabetes. She also is identified as autistic, has adrenal deficits, and has hypothyroidism. Shaquie sees doctors at Children's Hospital for the following: endocrinology, neurology, cardiology, and sleep disorders. Shaquie is prescribed two types of insulin.

Mrs. Jones reports that Shaquie cannot see at night or dusk and often trips and falls. Shaquie cannot cross streets or navigate the environment independently, and she is sensitive to bright lights, both environmental and artificial. At Shaquie's last eye-doctor appointment (December 2018), Dr. Smith informed both Shaquie and Mrs. Jones that instruction in Braille and alternative media for learning should begin to be considered due to the severity of Shaquie's medically documented visual impairment, her visual-field deficits, and the instability of her visual conditions.

Mrs. Jones reports Shaquie brings things extremely close to her face for viewing, even with her prescriptive lenses on, which she always wears. Shaquie cannot see her schoolwork and needs her mother to read it to her to complete it. Shaquie requires extremely large print to see (> 24-point font). Shaquie will cover her eyes to allow time for lighting adjustments. Shaquie cannot see her food and requires assistance completing activities of daily living, such as cleaning shampoo out of her hair, matching her clothes, and making simple foods. Shaquie is incapable of independently accessing or taking her medicines.

Student Input

Shaquie did not know the name of her visual impairment, but said, in general, it is just hard to see. She stated she cannot walk independently outside at any time of day or inside at night. She cannot see well enough to complete most activities of daily living, and her mother has to ensure all the soap is out of her hair after washing. She cannot operate a microwave or make simple foods and is unable to give herself her required medicines independently.

Shaquie accesses her schoolwork by having her mother read it to her or by making the fonts exceptionally large on her desktop. Shaquie's teachers sometimes provide her with enlarged print, but often the print quality and clarity is compromised as a result of enlarging material this way. Shaquie has had no introductions or instruction on any low-vision devices besides a page magnifier given to her more than five years ago, when she was a student at St. Catherine's School. Shaquie cannot see material presented during an active class.

Shaquie cannot read menus at restaurants, cannot read labels or tags, cannot see items with any clarity when shopping, will play on her phone using a very large font, will play large-sized board games, and can walk her dogs because dogs are on a leash and they lead her (otherwise, she would not be able to participate in the walking of her dogs).

Both Shaquie and her mother would like her to begin learning Braille and for Shaquie to receive instruction in the use of low-vision devices and assistive technology for students who are blind or visually impaired.

Teacher Questionnaire

All teacher input listed as part of Shaquie's current IEP indicates that Shaquie demonstrates no adverse behaviors, participates in live classes, and has minimal difficulty completing her work. Her teachers have noticed a decrease in completion of assignments since December 2018. All teachers feel current SDI is meeting Shaquie's needs. Shaquie requires enlargements of all materials as reported.

Shaquie wore her prescription lenses throughout this assessment.

Present Level Of Visual Functioning

Testing Environment

Shaquie was assessed by the evaluator in the lobby and at an outside table in a school setting.

Appearance of Eyes

Shaquie's eyes appeared normal, with no obvious signs of scaling, redness, crusting, or tearing.

Visual Reflexes

A consistent blink and response to visual threat response was present during evaluation.

Alignment/Muscle Balance

Right eye appears misaligned at times, with a slight inward turn toward the nose.

Visual Compensation

Throughout evaluation, evaluator looked for any typical behaviors often demonstrated by students when they are compensating due to decreased ability in functional vision. These include covering or

(Continued)

closing of one eye; head tilt; thrusting head forward to see; attempting to "brush away" a blur; rubbing or blinking eyes often; flapping hand in front of eyes; looking away when reaching; squinting or frowning when viewing; avoiding near tasks; holding materials for view either too close or too far away; touching to recognize; eye pressing; rocking behaviors; banging or hitting head; staring at lights; lack of eye contact.

Shaquie demonstrated the following compensatory behaviors during the evaluation process:

- Head tilt
- Thrusting head forward to see
- Squinting
- Avoidance of near tasks
- Holding materials too close when viewing
- Lack of eye contact

Light Sensitivity and Preference

Shaquie demonstrated an extreme sensitivity to light, both environmental (sunlight) and artificial (fluorescent lighting, glare from a computer screen). Sensitivity to lighting conditions was present throughout assessment. When evaluator and Shaquie moved from indoors to outside, from dim lighting to bright sunshine, Shaquie could not see outside. Shaquie requires three to five minutes for her eyes to adjust properly to changes in light.

Ocular Pursuit and Fixation

Shaquie's ability to visually locate and track objects was tested using a mini flashlight with a red overlay in near distance. In near distances, Shaquie could track and visually locate the red flashlight. Light was presented to her in the environment at distances of 13 to 6 inches, 6 to 12 inches, 18 inches to 3 feet, 3 feet to 8 feet, and 8 feet to 12 feet. Shaquie could not visually locate or track at distances closer than 3 feet. When asked to visually locate objects requested in the environment, Shaquie could do so if objects requested had high-contrast markings on them for added visibility, such as a white marking for a car on a black environmental surface.

Color Preference

Throughout assessment, Shaquie demonstrated color preference for highly saturated, bright colors, due to their visibility. Shaquie preferred bold line writing paper consisting of bold black lines on either white or yellow paper. Shaquie visually identified the following colors: white, black, gray, orange, blue, green, red, pink, purple, red, yellow, and brown, and all the slight variations both lighter and darker of the listed colors when presented color targets that were at least 1 inch in size and presentation had no visual clutter or complexity to compete with the requested color. When assessed using color plates of The Color Vision Test, Shaquie could not complete or identify colors, objects, or numbers in 18 of 18 color slides presented.

Visual Latency

Throughout assessment, there were signs of visual latency or visual delay when completing activities.

Visual Field Preference

Observations by listed evaluator: Shaquie appears to have viewing preference from midline of her visual field. Shaquie has documented visual-field deficits, which were present to the evaluator throughout evaluation testing.

Visual Complexity

Shaquie could not complete a visually cluttered hidden-picture activity. Visual targets were less than 1 inch in size, and text was black on white paper, 8 inches by 11 inches. When given a large-print version of the same activity, where targets presented were approximately 2 inches in size, Shaquie was still unable to complete the activity.

Distance Viewing

Shaquie was tested with distance acuity measures at distances of 3 feet, 3 to 8 feet, and 8 to 20 feet. At a 3-foot distance, Shaquie could name presented LEA Symbols. Shaquie could not complete at the greater distances listed.

Visual Scanning (Visual Search in Systematic Pattern)

In near distance, Shaquie experienced great difficulty with a large-print word find, and she could not complete the activity.

Distance scanning in the environment, tested at distances of 18 inches up to 10 feet and greater, utilizing top, middle, and lower visual planes: success when requested targets were approximately 3 feet or larger with bright colors and no background complexity competing.

Contrast Sensitivity

Shaquie prefers and provided evaluator a legible writing sample on bold line writing paper, with white background. Shaquie could not see the lines on regular blue lined writing paper.

Visual Shift of Gaze

Observable insufficiencies

Visual Responsiveness

- Light perception—deficiency
- Light projection—deficiency
- Shadow/form—deficit
- Direction of motion—deficit

(Continued)

(Continued)

Convergence

Shaquie demonstrated convergence insufficiency when tested.

In addition, Shaquie cannot safely navigate her home environment, both indoors and outside. Surface changes, inclines, and lighting are factors in her ability to move in her environments. She needs to walk with sighted guide assistance. She cannot complete many activities of daily living with independence.

Printed Media

Shaquie was evaluated on her ability to see and read the following examples of printed media:

- Recipe books
- A ticket from a sporting event
- A menu
- A newspaper
- Cards
- Game pieces
- Passages from a novel (*The Client*, in paperback)

Media assessed ranged from 6-point font to 24-point font, from excellent print quality to poor print quality, and from glossy paper surfaces to matte and dull paper surfaces.

Throughout testing of printed media, Shaquie could not see or read each example correctly, and she held all media presented (regardless of font size, print quality, or color of letters) at midline from her face, 18 inches from center, moving all examples closer for viewing (next to the nose on her face). Shaquie requires enlargement of materials and specialized font to read.

SUMMARY

Based on the testing results of the functional vision assessment, the printed media assessment, information gathered from Shaquie and her mother, and the clinical judgment of the evaluator, it is merited that Shaquie receive education-based direct vision services from a teacher of the visually impaired at this time. Shaquie demonstrated an observed inability to complete activities that are required to be independently successful both in school and in home settings. It is the opinion of the evaluator that this difficulty is not adequately addressed by already established IEP goals in the areas of vision support or SDI required of a student demonstrating such diminished functional vision and of transition age. Shaquie should be regarded as functionally blind, based on medical documentation of established diagnosis and on her degree of visual-field deficits.

The following are recommended at this time:

1. Braille instruction from a CTVI
2. Vocational rehabilitation teaching from a CTVI to address deficits in Shaquie's ability to participate in independent activities of daily living, such as giving herself her own insulin or dressing herself

3. Orientation and mobility instruction to include cane technique and independent travel

4. Access to and instruction on proper use of technology (low- and high-tech) available to students who are blind and visually impaired for trial by student, to include bold line writing paper, magnification device, and monocular

5. Access to audible information presented during live instructional sessions.

6. Enlarged copies of any material presented as printed media (**It is noted here that this will not replace Shaquie's need for high-contrast presentation or magnification.)

7. Referral to Bureau of Blindness and Visual Services
Adapted from Paula Rollins, Certified Teacher of Students with Visual Impairments and Blindness. Sayegh Pediatric Therapy Services

- visual-motor skills, such as pointing, reaching, and locating objects;

- visual discrimination skills, such as recognizing family, people, and objects and identifying shapes, drawings, and pictures;

- visual sequencing, such as following a pattern and arranging pictures to tell a story;

- visual memory and imagery, such as remembering a location and describing its details; and

- drawing and figure-ground perception.

Cognitive/Achievement

For children with visual impairment and blindness, cognitive abilities may be impacted in a number of different ways. For example, the range and variety of experiences, as well as interaction with one's environment, to include a social environment, is certainly impacted by one's vision. Since many things we learn are abstract, such as the color of the sky, and/or cannot be experienced tactically, these children are at a disadvantage in their learning. Although children with visual impairments are a heterogeneous group with a wide range of intellect and achievement, generally they may lag behind their peers. Academic areas such as reading and writing are difficult specifically in learning new vocabulary (Swenson, 1999). Since literacy is the cornerstone of all learning, selection of tools and interventions to support attainment of literacy skills is critical. For students who are blind, Braille will be taught by the teachers of the visually impaired, which will support reading and writing skills. However, research in the use of Braille indicates that the rate of reading tends to be half of print reading rates, and, thus, children may need additional strategies for learning (Ely et al., 2006); thus, support and accommodations will be needed for these children through their IEPs.

Social and Emotional/Behavioral

Since much of our social and behavioral skills are learned though observation of others, many students with visual impairments and blindness may demonstrate what are considered to be socially inappropriate behaviors (Ozkubat & Ozdemir, 2014), such as stereotypic behaviors (repeated behaviors) that include such behaviors as eye pressing, finger flicking, rocking, and twirling (Desrochers, Oshlag, & Kennelly, 2014). According to Levack (1991), "without careful intervention the child may become withdrawn, self-centered, limited in mobility and over dependent on others" (p. 194). Social skills including greetings, nonverbal communication, and gestures, as well as technological social skills such as the use of Facebook and other social media sites, may be hindered by a visual impairment. Since children with visual impairments and blindness may be more isolated, they may be less social in general and more immature in their behaviors.

Mobility/Safety

Children with visual impairments and/or blindness will be impacted both in gross and fine motor skills. To learn to interact with our environments, we must locate objects and people. We must grasp items and explore them. From the very beginnings of the disability, interventions in this area of orientation and mobility will be needed. As such, a specialized, certified teacher in **orientation and mobility** (O&M) will be assigned. An O&M specialist supports those with visual impairments and blindness to become more independent in safe travel. This is done in the child's environment. The goal is to teach the child how to travel alone, potentially only using a cane for help. Supporting the child with how to communicate and use the senses that are not affected by vision is important, as the child must learn to rely heavily on his or her sense of touch or hearing. (Dee S., 2019)

For some children who are blind, a Seeing Eye dog will serve as an assistance animal. Such animals are trained to support the child around obstacles. Training is extensive and may occur when the child is older, as the child does the directing and thus may have had the mobility training outlined above.

Extension to Instruction

Whether in inclusive or more segregated settings, students with visual impairments will be supported by teachers of the visually impaired, who will work with them on Braille reading and writing; use of low-vision aids, such as magnifiers; concept development; tactual skills; keyboarding; slate and stylus; abacus; use of computers and other assistive technology devices; visual efficiency skills; and listening skills. In addition, some children will receive support in activities of daily living (personal communication, Paula Rollins, June 2, 2019). These teachers will consult with the MDT on the unique educational needs of children with visual impairments and blindness, to include recommendations for the physical environment, such as with regard to seating and lighting. They will work with teachers to coordinate all aspects of the child's curriculum—to include ordering Braille, large print, recorded books, and other materials—and provide the MDT (along with students and parents) information regarding the Accessible Instructional Materials Library (AIM).

In addition to the core curriculum, IEP goals may include social skills instruction, direct instruction in academic areas, orientation and mobility to help with travel, spatial awareness, safety, and direction, as well as independent living skills. Self-determination and compensatory skills may be a part of the specialized curriculum. In addition, assistive technologies, outlined below, will play a huge part in the education of children who are blind, as well as some with visual impairments.

In addition to direct instruction in Braille, assistive technologies, both low- and high-tech devices, will provide the most important tools to support learning. Magnifiers for children with low vision will support access to print material. Recorded books (see, e.g., www.learningally.org) will support learning and can be obtained in a number of ways. For example, Bookshare (www.bookshare.org), the world's largest online library, will provide accessible reading materials that include recorded books, magazines, and newspapers that can be downloaded and accessed through text-to-speech software on computers and mobile devices. Other useful technology includes screen-reading devices, many of which can now be accessed on all computers and mobile devices. For children with low vision, all print can be enlarged on most mobile devices.

Deaf-Blindness

When we hear about children with deaf-blindness, we may think of a complete absence of hearing and sight; however, this population, too, is very diverse in the extent of their useful vision and/or hearing. It is true that some may be totally deaf and totally blind, and many will have additional disabilities (see Chapter 13). The age of onset will determine the child's needs. Because this population experiences some level of both hearing and visual loss, and the combined loss of both vision and hearing can cause delays and deficits in all areas, the members of the MDT that are typically needed for the effective delivery of educational programs will include the parents, teachers of the deaf and visually impaired, psychologists, school counselors, occupational therapists, physical therapists, and speech therapists. Children with deaf-blindness will always require specially designed instruction to meet their unique needs (Lynn Aylward, Farmer, & MacDonald, 2007).

IDEA Definition

[Deaf-blindness] means concomitant hearing and Visual Impairments, the combination of which causes such severe communication and other developmental and educational needs that they cannot be accommodated in special education programs solely for children with deafness or children with Blindness.

(34 CFR 300.8(c)(2))

Causes

In the early 1960s, there was an increase of children who developed additional disabilities as a result of the rubella outbreak of the previous decade; many children were born with deaf-blindness (Hatlen, 2000). Some students may have been born with a congenital infection (e.g., cytomegalovirus, a kind of herpes-type virus) and have a profound cognitive disability, cerebral palsy, seizure disorder, severe sensorineural hearing loss, and visual impairment. Both groups of students would meet the definition of deaf-blindness (Lynn Aylward, Farmer, & MacDonald, 2007). In addition, medical interventions that have kept younger premature infants alive has increased survival rate but have left children with multiple disabilities. Many of the causes already outlined above for the other sensory impairments are the same for children with deaf-blindness. However, Usher's syndrome, in which children are born deaf and lose vision as they get older, is specific to children with deaf-blindness.

Diagnosis/Assessment/Characteristics

Diagnosis of this population will be similar to what was outlined for children with hearing and visual impairments. However, according to Rowland (2009), assessment of a student with deaf-blindness will require a lot of planning and coordination with the MDT. Assessment of a child with deaf-blindness will take more time overall. Rowland (2009) offers some tips to support assessment, including identifying questions to guide information about the child's needs, observation in multiple environments, and treating the overall assessment as one of inquiry; essentially, completing an **authentic assessment.**

This authentic assessment requires a strong and inclusive team approach, and all the health-care providers, as well as all team members outlined above, for children with this sensory impairment will typically be involved, as no one professional can address all the needs for the child's senses, learning styles, physical abilities, and technologies that are critical for the child to learn.

An assessment that is contextually bound will help uncover the best ways to approach the child to interact and to communicate, as well as the most appropriate mode of doing so.

Extension to Instruction

More than likely, a **total communication approach** will be used, as communication may occur in a number of different ways. The layperson may know of finger spelling through the work of Helen Keller and her teacher Anne Sullivan Macy. However, just as outlined above for students with other sensory impairments, students with deaf-blindness may use and/or need to be taught the following (Huebner, Prickett, Welch, & Joffee, 1995):

- Speech
- Touch cues (communication prompts that are made on a child's body)
- Object cues (communication prompts that are made with objects that touch the child's body or are presented visibly)
- Gestures
- Print on palm (writing on a person's palm with the index finger)
- Braille
- Large print
- Sign language
- Finger spelling (shapes that symbolize alphabet letters that can be read visibly or through touch)
- Augmentative communication systems
- Amplification systems
- Other low- and/or high-tech devices

The development of communication skills is the highest priority for children with deaf-blindness. Other areas of great need and focus are mobility, as this will be a means for the child to obtain information; the teaching of functional activities, such as daily living skills; and functional communication and academics.

In the classroom, there may be concerns related to the safety of the child with deaf-blindness. For this reason, working with students with deaf-blindness will require a carefully designed environment, as well as specially designed instruction throughout the day. Incidental teaching will not be an option, so direct instruction will typically occur in all areas. Concepts, mental imagery, attachment, sense of self, motivation, preventing learned helplessness, and overcoming isolation are all areas of priority for children with deaf-blindness (Huebner et al., 1995).

Touch will be important, and the student will often need to "recognize" the teacher by touch and, possibly, even by smell. Therefore, it is helpful if the teacher consistently (and intentionally) wears the same deodorant or uses the same hand soap. An alert system to support the child in communicating will be necessary. This might take the form of a tactile box the child can go to when he or she needs help, or a mid-level technology, such as a switch device that makes noise to alert the teacher. Lighting, large print, physical arrangement of the environment to include some type of markers, and technology to include alert systems must be integrated throughout the classroom. Emergency procedures will need to be developed, implemented, and practiced (Huebner et al., 1995).

Check Your Understanding 12.6

1. Why are children with deaf-blindness unique in terms of assessment? What is the best approach to assessment? Why?

2. What MDT members will be involved in the education of children with deaf-blindness? Why? What function do you think they will serve in assessment and intervention?

CHAPTER SUMMARY

This chapter provided an overview of children identified with sensory impairments (hearing impairments, deafness, visual impairments, and deaf-blindness), including how they are diagnosed and identified for services. It discussed characteristics that may impact their education. Additionally, educational considerations and interventions were presented.

APPLY WHAT YOU HAVE LEARNED

1. Research one cause of sensory impairment (it does not have to be one that was mentioned in the chapter). Present your work as a training tool for other professionals (e.g., in the form of a slideshow presentation or an infographic poster).

2. Research a technology that would be useful in the classroom for a child with a sensory impairment. Outline the training you would need as a teacher to use this technology successfully in your classroom.

Appendix A

Functional Vision Evaluation for a Child With More Severe Disabilities

(adapted from work by P. Rollins, 2018)

Student's Name: Chloe	DOB: 5/21/2008
Sex: F	School: William Smith ES
Grade: 2	TVI Evaluator: Paula Jones
Date of Evaluation: December 7, 2018	

Background/Medical Information

Current Services/Therapies Student Receives: Chloe receives SLP, OT, PT, vision, and music therapy, all in the home setting.

Other Medical Diagnosis: History of prematurity, born at 23 weeks weighing 1 lb., 1 oz. Chloe stayed in neonatal ICU for six months and suffered many complications as a result of her prematurity, including grade IV intraventricular hemorrhage (grades 3 and 4 indicate more severe bleeding) with periventricular leukomalacia (death of small areas of brain tissue around ventricles; creates "holes" in brain). She is identified as having Dandy Walker malformation (affects brain development, particularly cerebellum, which is the part of the brain that coordinates movement), as well as hydrocephalus for which she was *not* shunted; however, she is considered to no longer have hydrocephalus. Chloe wears glasses for nearsightedness and is right-eye dominant, with little to no vision present in her left eye. **Most children with stage 3–5 ROP develop some form of serious eye damage.

Chloe has a seizure disorder that is treated with Onfi (clobazam). Her seizures are classified as partial/complex. Chloe was diagnosed with CVI through The Children's Hospital. Chloe is considered legally blind, her peripheral field is impacted by scar tissue, and her CVI also impacts her functional vision.

Chloe was evaluated on February 21, 2017, by Dr. Christine Smith at Westend Pediatric Program using the CVI Range Assessment, which is used to determine the degree of visual impairment for children with a CVI diagnosis. The CVI range is considered a reliable and valid instrument of assessment. The assessment is based on information gathered from interview, observation, and direct assessment.

Chloe was reassessed by Paula Jones, CTVI, using the CVI Range Assessment. The assessment determines the degree of visual impairment using a 0 to 10 scale, with 0 representing little to no visual functioning and 10 representing near-typical visual functioning. Based on this evaluation (December 7, 2018), Chloe is at the end of Phase II CVI with a score of 5.5 to above 6. This level of CVI suggests the use of vision in functional routines. Suggestions for adaptations will be provided in the following summary, to encourage and allow use of functional vision across the natural routines of the day.

Color Preference

The CVI characteristic of color is one where individuals with CVI show increased attention on targets of a particular color. Parent has indicated that Chloe responds best visually to brightly colored, highly saturated colors. I found this to be true during the evaluation. Color serves as a visual anchor and should be used during instructional and therapeutic sessions to draw and hold Chloe's attention. Color can also be used to highlight and outline the salient features of objects, images, or the environment. **Use of black and white materials is contraindicated for individuals with CVI in favor of color.

Need For Movement

Children with CVI tend to have an unusual response to movement. They may be captivated by moving targets and will often show increased visual attention to targets that have movement or light. Chloe preferred moving targets (e.g., a Slinky, a rolling car) for viewing, but movement was not necessary for visual attention and response to activity, as well as to locate presented objects (e.g., blocks, figurines). However, if Chloe demonstrates latency, or light gazing, it may be helpful to pair targets during instruction and daily routines with movement.

Visual Latency

The CVI characteristic of visual latency is one in which there is a delayed response between the time a target is presented and the time the child first visually attends to it. Parent feels that Chloe does not demonstrate large amounts of visual latency, and I found this to be true during the assessment. Rather, latency was varied and usually fluctuated no more when Chloe was presented with targets that held little to no interest for her, but mother could verbally redirect her to engage. Parent reported that visual latency increases for Chloe during times when she is fatigued (bedtime, illness) or is overstimulated (new environments). During period of latency, adults should refrain from speaking or touching, so as not to interrupt Chloe's visual processing.

Visual-Field Preferences

Chloe's responses are associated with her ocular impairment. Chloe appears to view best in her right central field in near to intermediate distance, but if she is interested in the presented target, Chloe will turn her head to the left to align her right eye to view. Materials presented should be presented to Chloe at midline, slightly to left, for visual access. Avoid presentations in lower and peripheral fields.

Difficulties With Visual Complexity

Children with CVI often have difficulty visually recognizing an object. It is important to present targets against a plain viewing array (background). This helps eliminate extraneous information in favor of the desired visual target. Children with CVI often have difficulty integrating vision with other sensory information. Chloe is able to visually attend in the presence of low-level background noise. Chloe can establish brief eye contact. Adults should be aware of the complexity of the color patterns of their clothing, the environmental space where teaching or therapy is taking place, and the level of noise.

Light Gazing and Non-Purposeful Gaze

Children with CVI often spend prolonged periods gazing at primary light sources. Chloe did not close her eyes when illuminated targets (red, white, blue, green) were presented to her at eye level. This indicates light may be important for her. Parent also indicated to evaluator that an APH light box is often used during instructional and therapeutic sessions. The use of a light box, tablet device, or other backlit systems aids the support and development of detail vision and fine motor skills.

Difficulty With Distance Viewing

Many children with CVI gaze at objects in close range. Their ability to locate targets at a greater distance is impacted by complexity of array—the further away an object is, the more likely it is to fall into the background array. Chloe best views materials presented within 1 to 2 feet, but she was successful viewing materials at distances of 3 feet during assessment. Parent indicates that if object presented is a favored object, distance is not an issue within 3–5 feet in the home.

Atypical Visual Reflexes

Chloe blinked consistently to both blink to touch and visual threat in three trials during evaluation. This is an improvement over previous assessment data. This is not used for intervention purposes during instruction.

DIFFICULTY WITH VISUAL NOVELTY

Children with CVI tend to show increased visual attention on targets they have previously viewed. Parent feels, and Chloe demonstrated, that she now has minimal difficulty when asked to view new objects.

Absence Of Visually Guided Reach

Children with CVI tend to show a distinct pattern of look and reach. They tend to look at the target, look away, and then reach for it without looking. Chloe demonstrates this characteristic of CVI, but parent reports, and CTVI did observe during the assessment, that Chloe only does this intermittently, not 100% of the time.

Summary and Recommendations

1. Chloe is a student with medically documented CVI, and direct supportive services from a certified teacher of the visually impaired are recommended at this time.

2. Frequency of vision services: 60 minutes weekly, to include both direct instruction and consultation with parents and other team members, and up to 120 minutes monthly for adaptations of materials for instruction as needed for Chloe's ability to visually access her curriculum materials as a student with CVI.

3. Use of a light box

4. Use of a tablet device

5. Use of materials with vibrant, highly saturated colors

6. Pair objects with movement when necessary.

7. Present objects at a distance no greater than 1–2 feet for viewing, in preferred visual field of view (midline to slightly left).

8. Allow additional time for visual processing.

9. Reduce visual complexity when presenting objects.

10. Reduce background noise, minimize complex arrays, and limit sensory overload when asking Chloe to visually attend during instructional periods.

Discussion Questions

1. Identify an area that the teacher assessed from the assessment above. What were the findings? How will the findings impact instruction in the classroom?

2. Look to the Summary of Recommendations provided. How would you address these in the classroom? What support do you feel you would need from the visual impairment teacher?

3. What least restrictive environment do you believe Chloe would have her needs best met in? Do you have enough information to make that decision? If not, what information would you need?

Appendix B

Assistive Technology Solutions for Students
With Visual Impairments

Low-Tech

Low-tech tools are relatively inexpensive and do not require batteries or an AC adapter.

Activities of Daily Living:	Mobility:	Writing:
• Adapted padlock (key or words) • Braille clothing labels • Finger guard (cutting) • Pocket money Brailler • Braille measuring spoons/cups • Adapted plate (sectioned, suctioned, etc.) • Low-vision black/white cutting board • Tactual dots for reference points • Magnifying mirror • Check-writing guide Learner & Studying: • Wikki Stix • Work-play tray Computer Access: • Keyboard skin for teaching tactile keyboarding	• Canes • Cane tips • Cane strap Reading: • Reading stand • Hands-free bookstand • Line guide • Line guide with highlighter • Acetate overlay • Drawer liner (place under Braille) • Textured paper • Clear labels (Brailleable) • Graphic art tape P.E., Leisure, & Play: • Braille games • Alerting tape	• High-contrast keyboard stickers • Braille keyboard stickers • Slate & stylus • Low-vision gel pens • Low-vision felt-tip pen • Soft leaded pencil • Bold line paper • Raised line paper • Off-white paper • Large paper • Writing guide • Signature guide Math: • Braille low-vision ruler • Tactile tape measure • Tactile dice • Graphing paper (bold line or raised line) • Large print/Braille protractor

Medium-Tech

Medium-tech tools are still relatively inexpensive but may require batteries or an AC adapter.

Activities of Daily Living:	Visual Aids:	Auditory Access:
• Adapted watch (large print, Braille, talking) • Liquid level indicator • Talking digital thermometer • Talking kitchen scale • Large-number phone **Writing:** • Large-print keyboard • Bluetooth keyboard • Tactile graphics board **Computer Access:** • IntelliTactiles overlay	• Bar magnifier • Dome magnifier • Lighted dome magnifier • Handheld magnifier • Monocular or binocular • Pocket magnifiers • Stand magnifier **Math Access:** • Scientific talking calculator • Abacus • Tactile graphics (maps, graphs, charts, geometric figures) **Reading:** • Braille labeler • Califone CardMaster	• Digital voice recorder • Audiobook player • Sound-minimizing headphones • Recordable labels **P.E., Leisure, & Play:** • Auditory puzzles • Beeper • Beeper ball • Bell balls • Portable sound source **Learner & Studying:** • Talking dictionary • Large-print clock **Environmental Control:** • Task lighting (daylight, OTT)

High-Tech

High-tech tools are generally more expensive, typically are more sophisticated, and require batteries and/or an AC adapter.

Computer Access:	Reading:	Writing:
• Voice-recognition software	• Portable electronic magnifier	• QWERTY or 6-key input note-taker
• Screen magnifier	• Tactile graphics maker	• Braillewriter
• Screen-magnification software	• Thermoform machine	• Braille translation software
• Screen-reading software	• Video magnifier	• Braille embosser
Environmental Control:	• Video magnifier with OCR	Social Studies/Science:
• Power Select (APH)	• Refreshable Braille display	• Video microscope
	Math Access:	Visual Aids:
	• Graphing calculator software	• Light box

REFERENCES

American Cochlear Implant Alliance. (n.d.). *What is a cochlear implant?* Retrieved from https://www.acialliance.org/page/CochlearImplant

Appelbaum, A. (1952). Rentrolental fibroplasia: Blindness in infants of low weight at birth. *California Medicine, 77*(4), 259–265.

Boyd, K. (2019). *What is retinitis pigmentosa?* Retrieved July 1, 2019, from https://www.aao.org/eye-health/diseases/what-is-retinitis-pigmentosa

Centers for Disease Control and Prevention. (2019). *Data and statistics about hearing loss in children.* Retrieved from https://www.cdc.gov/ncbddd/hearingloss/data.html

Centers for Disease Control and Prevention. (2016). Retrieved on June 29, 2019. https://www.cdc.gov/

Center for Deaf and Hard of Hearing Education. (2010). *ISDH: CDHHE home.* Retrieved June 29, 2019, from https://www.in.gov/isdh/25883.htm

Dee S. (2019). *What does an orientation and mobility specialist do?* Retrieved July 1, 2019, from http://www.wisegeek.net/what-does-an-orientation-and-mobility-specialist-do.htm

Desrochers, M. N., Oshlag, R., & Kennelly, A. M. (2014). Using background music to reduce problem behavior during assessment with an adolescent who is blind with multiple disabilities. *Journal of Visual Impairment & Blindness, 108*(1), 61–65.

Easterbrooks, S. R., Lederberg, A. R., Antia, S., Schick, B., Kushalnagar, P., Webb, M., . . . McDonald Connor, C. (2015). Reading among diverse DHH learners: What, how, and for whom? *American Annals of the Deaf, 159*(5), 419–432.

Ely, R., Emerson, R. W., Maggiore, T., Rothberg, M., O'Connell, T., & Hudson, L. (2006). Increased content knowledge of students with visual impairments as a result of extended descriptions. *Journal of Special Education Technology, 21*(3), 31–43. https://doi.org/10.1177/016264340602100304

Friend, M. (2019). *Special education: Contemporary perspectives for school professionals* (5th ed.). New York, NY: Pearson.

Hall Lueck, A., and Dutton, G. N. (2015). *Vision and the brain: Understanding cerebral visual impairment in children.* New York, NY: AFB Press.

Hatlen, P. (2000). Historical perspectives. In M. C. Holbrook & A. J. Koenig (Eds.), *Foundations of education, volume 1: History and theory of teaching children and youths with visual impairments* (2nd ed.) (pp. 1–54). New York, NY: AFB Press.

Higgins, M., & Lieberman, A. M. (2016). Deaf students as a linguistic and cultural minority: Shifting perspectives and implications for teaching and learning. *Journal of Education, 196*(1), 1–17.

Holbrook, M. C., & Koenig, A. J. (Eds.). (2000). *Foundations of education, volume 1: History and theory of teaching children and youths with visual impairments* (2nd ed.) (pp. 1–54). New York, NY: AFB Press.

Hrastinski, I., & Wilbur, R. B. (2016). Academic achievement of deaf and hard-of-hearing students in an ASL/English bilingual program. *Journal of Deaf Studies and Deaf Education, 21*(2), 156–170, https://doi.org/10.1093/deafed/env072

Huebner, K. M., Prickett, J. G., Welch, T. R., & Joffee, E. (Eds.). (1995). *Hand in hand: Essentials of communication and orientation and mobility for your students who are deaf-blind* (Vol. 1.). New York, NY: AFB Press.

Koenig, A. J., & Holbrook, M. C. (1995). *Learning media assessment of students with visual impairments: A resource guide for teachers* (2nd ed.). Austin: Texas School for the Blind and Visually Impaired.

Koestler, F. A. (2004). *The unseen minority: A social history of blindness in the United States.* New York, NY: AFB Press.

Levack, N. (1991). *Low vision: A resource guide with adaptations for students with visual impairments.* Austin: Texas School for the Blind and Visually Impaired.

Lynn Aylward, M., Farmer, W., & MacDonald, M. (2007, July). *Minister's review of services for students with special needs: Review committee report and recommendations.* Retrieved from https://www.ednet .ns.ca/docs/review-committee-report-e.pdf

Maller, S. J., & Braden, J. P. (1993). The construct and criterion-related validity of the WISC-III with deaf adolescents. *Journal of Psychoeducational Assessment, 11,* 105–113.

Mandal, A. (2019, June 4). *Diagnosis of visual impairment.* News-Medical. Retrieved July 11, 2019, from https://www.news-medical.net/health/ Diagnosis-of-visual-impairment.aspx

McClinden, M., & McCall, S. (2016). *Learning through touch: Supporting children with visual impairment and additional difficulties.* New York, NY: Routledge.

National Association of the Deaf. (n.d.). *Transportation and travel.* https://www.nad.org/resources/ transportation-and-travel/

National Eye Institute. (2019). *Retinopathy of prematurity.* Retrieved from https://www .nei.nih.gov/learn-about-eye-health/eye-conditions-and-diseases/retinopathy-prematurity

Ozkubat, U., & Ozdemir, S. (2014). A comparison of social skills in Turkish children with visual impairments, children with intellectual impairments and typically developing children.

International Journal of Inclusive Education, 18(5), 500–514. doi:10.1080/13603116.2013.789088

Packer, L. (2018). *How hearing loss affects school performance.* Retrieved June 25, 2019, from https://www.healthyhearing.com/report/52433- How-hearing-loss-affects-school-performance

Ponchillia, P. E., Mackenzie, N., Long, R. G., Denton-Smith, P., Hicks, T. L., & Miley, P. (2007). Finding a target with an accessible global positioning system. *Journal of Visual Impairment & Blindness, 101*(8), 479–488. https://doi .org/10.1177/0145482X0710100804

Rowland, C. (Ed.). (2009). *Assessing communication and learning in young children who are deaf-blind or who have multiple disabilities.* Portland, OR: Oregon Institute on Disability and Development. Retrieved from https://www.designtolearn .com/uploaded/pdf/DeafBlindAssessmentGuide .pdf

RightDiagnosis.com. (n.d.). *Deafness assessment questionnaire.* Retrieved July 6, 2019, from https:// www.rightdiagnosis.com/symptoms/deafness/ questions.htm

Swenson, A. M. (1999). *Beginning with Braille: Firsthand experiences with a balanced approach to literacy.* New York, NY: AFB Press.

U.S. Department of Education. (2015). https:// www.ed.gov/

World Health Organization. (2020, March 1). *Deafness and hearing loss.* Retrieved from https:// www.who.int/news-room/fact-sheets/detail/ deafness-and-hearing-loss

Winzer, M. A. (1993). *The history of special education: From isolation to integration.* Washington, DC: Gallaudet University Press.

CHAPTER 13

Health-Related Disabilities (Including Other Health Impairments, Orthopedic Impairment, Traumatic Brain Injury, and Multiple Disabilities)

Mary A. Houser, EdD

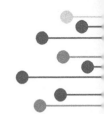

Learning Objectives

After completion of this chapter, you should be able to:

- Summarize common disorders under Other Health Impairments (OHI): Diabetes Mellitus, Tourette syndrome, leukemia, epilepsy, and asthma.

- Discuss the common types of orthopedic impairments prevalent in today's schools: cerebral palsy, spina bifida, and muscular dystrophy.

- Distinguish between the different types of Traumatic Brain Injuries (TBI): open head and closed head

- Summarize the IDEA category: Multiple Disabilities

Key Terms

acute (p. 385)	leukemia (p. 388)
asthma (p. 389)	muscular dystrophy (p. 395)
cerebral palsy (CP) (p. 393)	spina bifida (p. 393)
chronic (p. 385)	traumatic brain injury (TBI) (p. 397)
diabetes mellitus (p. 385)	Tourette syndrome (TS) (p. 386)
epilepsy (p. 388)	

Introduction to the Chapter

Health-related disabilities are another subgroup served under IDEA that stems from challenges existing within the body's various systems (e.g., circulatory, respiratory, immunological, neurological). Sometimes students will have a disability affecting one system and sometimes it can affect several systems. Health-related disabilities can be congenital or acquired and can vary in both their severity and their impact on the individual. Students with health-related disabilities may need to take medication during the school day or require the assistance of a nurse while at school. The degree of specialized attention they will need throughout the school day will depend on the nature and severity of their disability. For example, a student with an orthopedic disability might need assistance with mobility around the classroom, whereas a student who requires catheterization would need assistance changing his catheter throughout the day. Some students may be frequently absent from school due to doctor visits or hospitalizations.

We will discuss several common health-related disabilities and their symptoms, causes, diagnostic processes, and educational considerations that are relevant to special education professionals. The health-related IDEA disability categories that will be addressed in this chapter include other health impairment (OHI), orthopedic impairment (OI), traumatic brain injury (TBI), and multiple disabilities. Let's start with other health impairments (OHI).

Other Health Impairments

There are several health-related conditions that can affect a child's ability to attend and learn at school. Students whose health-related conditions negatively impact their educational performance will often be eligible for special education services under the category other health impairment (OHI).

IDEA Definition

Other health impairment means having limited strength, vitality, or alertness, including a heightened alertness to environmental stimuli, that results in limited alertness with respect to the educational environment, that—

(i). Is due to chronic or acute health problems such as asthma, attention deficit disorder or attention deficit hyperactivity disorder, diabetes, epilepsy, a heart condition, hemophilia, lead poisoning, leukemia, nephritis, rheumatic fever, sickle cell anemia, and Tourette syndrome; and

(ii). Adversely affects a child's educational performance.

(§ 300.8(c)(9))

This definition will be used as the basis for the chapter's definition of other health impairments.

Common Types

Conditions commonly served under the OHI category include diabetes, cancer, HIV, Tourette syndrome, epilepsy, ADHD, asthma, hemophilia, sickle-cell anemia, lead poisoning, rheumatic fever, heart condition, leukemia, and nephritis. This chapter will focus on some of the most common conditions under OHI seen in today's schools (with the exception of ADHD, as it has its own chapter): diabetes, Tourette syndrome, leukemia, epilepsy, and asthma.

In order to best understand conditions under other health impairment (OHI), it is important to distinguish between the two categories that comprise this disability group: chronic and acute. Although these terms were previously discussed at the beginning of this text, a special educator must also understand them within the context of the medical field. In medicine, the term **chronic** refers to those conditions that last more than three months. **Acute** conditions, however, are sudden and typically run a short course: less than three months. Several of the conditions discussed in this chapter are considered to be chronic conditions.

Diabetes Mellitus

Diabetes mellitus is a chronic disease in which one's blood glucose (blood sugar) is too high. This is due to inadequate insulin production or the body's cells' inability to respond properly to insulin or both. There are several adverse effects of diabetes, including heart failure, blindness, amputations, stroke, and kidney failure. There are two types of diabetes: type 1 and type 2. Type 2 diabetes is a more common form of diabetes.

Symptoms There are a number of symptoms indicative of diabetes. Individuals with diabetes might experience the symptons listed in Table 13.1.

Causes The causes of diabetes should be examined according to their specific type. In type 1 diabetes, the precise cause is unknown, although environmental factors and genetic factors are believed to be causal factors. In type 1, the immune system attacks and destroys insulin-producing cells that are located in the pancreas. As a result, the body has little to no insulin. Sugar builds up in the bloodstream instead of being transported into the cells. In type 2 diabetes (and prediabetes), cells become resistant to the action of insulin and the pancreas is unable to make

Table 13.1 Diabetes Symptoms
• Excessive hunger
• Excessive thirst
• Frequent urination
• Weight loss
• Difficulty with healing cuts/bruises
• Blurry vision
• Tingling/numbness
• Dry skin

insulin to overcome this. Similar to type 1, instead of it moving into the cells where it would be used for energy, the sugar builds up in the bloodstream (Mayo Clinic, 2018c).

Diagnosis A medical diagnosis is required for diabetes. Diabetes can be diagnosed by simple and routine blood tests (see Table 13.2) in a medical clinic but is frequently discovered during a workup in the emergency department when the patient presents for what seems to be a non-related symptom or illness, such as nausea and/or vomiting, frequent urination, or fatigue.

Table 13.2 Diabetes Tests
1. *A1C* – a commonly used blood test that can be used to test for both types of diabetes (type 1 and type 2) as well as how well people are managing their diabetes.
2. *Fasting plasma glucose (FPG)* – frequently used for screening diabetes. This test assesses blood sugar level after a person has fasted for 8 hours.
3. *Oral glucose tolerance test (OGTT)* – can be used for both screening and diagnosing diabetes. This is used to measure a person's response to sugar, otherwise known as glucose.
4. *Random plasma glucose test* – a test used to diagnose diabetes in which the doctor will check a patient's blood sugar. In this test, no regard is given to the last time the patient ate.

Tourette Syndrome (TS)

Tourette syndrome (TS) is a neurological disorder. Individuals with TS have repetitive movements or produce unwanted sounds or tics that can be challenging to control. TS is considered the most serious of the tic disorders. It is more commonly found in boys than girls. It also tends to affect younger children, but can continue throughout one's lifetime. TS has a high comorbidity with attention-deficit/hyperactivity disorder (ADHD), obsessive-compulsive disorder (OCD), and major depression.

Symptoms Tics are classified as simple or complex. A simple tic involves only one muscle group or body part. For example, an eye-blink is considered a simple tic. A complex tic can be a combination of several simple tics or a series of movements that involve several muscle groups. An example of a complex tic would be facial grimacing. The two most common tics are vocal tics and motor tics. Table 13.3 provides specific examples of vocal tics and motor tics.

Sensory tics and phantom tics are less common types of tics. Sensory tics may be experienced when a child experiences a sensory reaction (such as warmth or coldness) felt in the eyes, throat, and shoulders. A phantom tic is an out-of-body

Table 13.3 Vocal Tics and Motor Tics

Vocal tics	Motor tics (movement-based)
Throat clearing	Eye blinking
Tongue clicking	Jumping
Yelping	Squatting
Sniffing	Head jerking
Blurting out offensive words	Finger flexing
Uttering random words or phrases	Smelling objects frequently
Grunting	Touching objects frequently
Barking	Obscene gestures
	Self-injurious behaviors: hitting or biting oneself hopping

Mayo Clinic. (2018g). *Tourette Syndrome: Symptoms and causes.* Retrieved from https://www.mayoclinic.org/diseases-conditions/tourette-syndrome/symptoms-causes/syc-20350465

variation of a sensory tic in which the person feels a sensation in other people or objects. People with phantom tics experience temporary relief from the tic by touching or scratching the object involved (Encyclopedia of Children's Health, n.d., para. 15).

Causes The precise cause of TS is unknown. Tic disorders may sometimes develop after infections (e.g., strep throat) caused by a group of bacteria. Some speculate that tics develop when antibodies in the child's blood produced in response to the bacteria cross-react with proteins in the blood tissue. Neuroimaging studies have shown that tic disorders are related to abnormal levels of neurotransmitters known as dopamine, serotonin, and cyclic AMP in certain parts of the brain (Encyclopedia of Children's Health, n.d., para. 15).

Diagnosis TS requires a medical diagnosis. Diagnosing TS necessitates an evaluation of an individual's history and symptoms. Criteria for evaluation may include the following:

- Both motor tics and vocal tics are present, although not necessarily at the same time.

- Tics occur several times a day, nearly every day or intermittently, for more than a year.

- Tics begin before age 18.

- Tics aren't caused by medications, other substances, or another medical condition.

- Tics must change over time in location, frequency, type, complexity, or severity.

(Mayo Clinic, 2018f, para. 2)

Leukemia

Leukemia is a cancer affecting bone marrow. If someone has leukemia, his or her body makes too many white blood cells. Leukemia is the most common cancer affecting children and teens. It can be either acute or chronic. There are four distinct types of leukemia (see Table 13.4).

Of these four different types, the most common type of leukemia is acute lymphocytic leukemia (ALL).

Symptoms Symptoms of leukemia can vary but may include chronic fatigue, weight loss, having poor blood clotting, nausea, flu-like symptoms, and bone pain (Felman, 2017, para. 5).

Causes When the DNA of a single cell in bone marrow becomes damaged, leukemia can result. This is referred to as a mutation and alters the cells' ability to form and function properly. In addition, cells that arise from the initial cell will also have mutated DNA. It is not known what causes the initial damage to the DNA. There are certain risk factors associated with developing leukemia. These include exposure to very high doses of radiation; exposure to the chemical benzene; exposure to chemotherapy drugs; having certain genetic disorders (e.g. Down syndrome); and having the Philadelphia chromosome (Ph) (Cleveland Clinic, 2019).

Diagnosis Leukemia requires a medical diagnosis. When making the diagnosis, the medical provider will conduct a physical exam in which he or she looks for the physical signs of leukemia, such as unusual bruising or pale skin. He or she will also conduct blood tests to determine whether there are abnormal levels of red or white blood cells as well as platelets. In addition, a bone-marrow biopsy will be conducted.

Table 13.4 Types of Leukemia
1. Acute myeloid leukemia (AML)
2. Chronic myeloid leukemia (CML)
3. Acute lymphocytic leukemia (ALL)
4. Chronic lymphocytic leukemia (CLL)

Epilepsy

Epilepsy is a term used to describe a brain disorder that causes seizures. Epilepsy is also referred to as a seizure disorder. It is not a result of an underlying condition. There are two types of seizures: generalized and focal. Generalized seizures occur when both sides of the brain are affected. Focal (or partial) seizures occur when only one side of the brain is affected. There are four types of epilepsy: generalized epilepsy, focal epilepsy, generalized and focal epilepsy, and unknown if generalized or focal epilepsy.

Symptoms The primary symptom of epilepsy is seizures. Other symptoms associated with epilepsy include fainting, fatigue, rhythmic muscle contractions, muscle spasms, auras, temporary confusion, and staring blankly.

Causes Epilepsy can be caused by different underlying conditions. An individual might seize because of a genetic tendency that is passed down from one or both parents. He or she may have a genetic tendency (not inherited) that is a new change in his or her genes. He or she may have a structural change in the brain (e.g., the brain does not develop properly), brain injury, or infection (Epilepsy Society, 2016, para. 1). A febrile seizure is a seizure associated with a fever in children between the ages of 5 months and 5 years old. These types of seizures are not serious, frequently require no laboratory evaluation, and don't necessarily mean the child will grow up to have a seizure disorder. Other causes of epilepsy include stroke, brain tumor, traumatic brain injury (TBI), and central nervous system infection (Centers for Disease Control and Prevention, 2019). In many cases, the cause of epilepsy is unknown.

Diagnosis Epilepsy requires a medical diagnosis. If a child experiences a seizure caused by epilepsy, a doctor will follow these three steps to provide the correct diagnosis:

1. Determine the type of seizure that occurred.

2. Based on the type of seizure, determine the type of epilepsy.

3. Decide whether the patient has a specific epilepsy syndrome as well.

Additionally, the medical doctor will ask questions related to the seizure and might run tests such as an electroencephalogram (EEG) to examine the patient's brainwaves (Lava, 2017) and an MRI of the brain.

Asthma

Asthma is a chronic lung disease in which inflammation or swelling causes a narrowing of the airways, making it difficult to breathe. It can be a serious and life-threatening disease; although currently there is no cure, individuals are able to manage it so that they are able to live a normal life (American Lung Association, 2019).

Symptoms Some symptoms of asthma include shortness of breath, chest tightness or pain, trouble sleeping, coughing, wheezing, a whistling or wheezing sound when exhaling, and coughing (Mayo Clinic, 2018a).

Causes There are several possible causes or "triggers" for asthma. Examples include respiratory infections, smoke, physical activities, pollen, cold air, sulfites and preservatives, stress, and gastroesophageal reflux disease (GERD).

Diagnosis Asthma requires a medical diagnosis. The medical professional will conduct a physical exam and ask the patient whether he or she experiences the various signs of asthma, take the patient's medical history, and conduct lung-function tests such as the spirometry test and the exhaled nitric oxide test. The spirometry test is a breathing test that measures how much and how fast a person can blow air out of his or her lungs. The exhaled nitric oxide test requires the patient to breathe into a tube connected to a machine that measures the amount of nitric oxide in the patient's breath. The medical professional might also conduct a chest X-ray. (WebMD, 2019)

Educational Considerations

OHI is a broad category under IDEA. As a result, it is difficult to make general statements about the educational needs of each child with a different health impairment. There are some generalities that can be discussed, however. First, under IDEA, it is the educational right of all children with disabilities to be educated in their least restrictive environment to the greatest extent appropriate. This holds true for this student population as well. Many children with OHI are considered medically fragile and cannot attend school without proper support services in place. Another consideration is that children with OHI might experience frequent absences from school, and, at times, these can be lengthy. During these extended absences, the school system is responsible for continued special education and related services. Furthermore, classroom teachers must be properly trained in how to handle medical emergencies (NASET, 2019). Classroom accommodations—such as specially designed desks, standing tables, or wedges—will be needed for certain children to enable them to fully participate in classroom activities. Technology can also play a beneficial role with respect to aiding in their communication, in the form of augmentative and alternative communication (AAC).

The following case study is about a young boy who undergoes a diabetes diagnosis and his family's journey.

1. As a special educator, which of the medical conditions discussed would you find the most challenging when instructing a student? Why?

2. All the medical conditions above require a medical diagnosis. As a special education teacher, what can you do to ensure that you are knowledgeable about the different disorders that your students bring to the classroom?

3. Do you know anyone with any of the medical conditions listed above? If so, how has it affected them in their daily lives? Do you think this carries over to their school experience? Why or why not?

Case Study 13.1: Diagnosing Jamal

Jamal is a kindergarten student at Willingboro Elementary School. He is a kind boy who enjoys superheroes and playing tag football with his neighborhood friends. His favorite subject in school is English/language arts. Jamal lives at home with his younger sister and his two parents. Recently, Jamal has not been feeling well. He has been complaining to his parents, Akeem and Aliya, about being thirsty and has been making several trips to the bathroom throughout the school day. Jamal also told his parents the he has felt more tired than usual, and, although he has been receiving adequate nutrition, he has been unusually hungry. This concerns Akeem and Aliya, because they have noticed that he has also been losing weight. They decide to take him to see his pediatrician for an examination to determine the reason behind these new symptoms.

Dr. Lindgren has a small medical practice in the town where Jamal lives. He is also a family friend of Akeem and Aliya's. Akeem and Aliya tell him about how Jamal has been feeling recently, and he listens carefully to their concerns about Jamal. He reviews Jamal's medical history with them and gives Jamal a complete medical exam. After the examination, Dr. Lindgren tells them that he wants to conduct some tests to determine whether Jamal's pancreas is producing enough insulin. Jamal has a urinalysis, a random blood sugar test, an A1C test, and a fasting blood sugar test.

When Dr. Lindgren receives the test results back from the lab, they indicate that Jamal's body is not producing insulin, a hormone that controls blood-sugar levels. As a result, he diagnoses Jamal with type 1 diabetes. Dr. Lindgren informs Jamal's parents that type 1 diabetes is caused by an autoimmune reaction where the body attacks itself and destroys the cells in the pancreas that make insulin. He indicates that they will have to learn how to manage his condition medically through the use of insulin and proper diet and that his diabetes could also affect how he is performing at school. Dr. Lindgren recommends that they meet with a diabetes specialist and a nutritionist to help them learn how to manage this new condition.

A few days after his appointment, Aliya calls Jamal's school teacher, Mrs. Parker, to inform her

(Continued)

(Continued)

that he was recently diagnosed with diabetes and that he will need to begin taking his insulin shots during the school day. Mrs. Parker states that she has noticed Jamal having some problems learning in the past few weeks. She says that he has been processing information slower than his peers and that his attention is hard to maintain. She mentions that some children who have conditions such as diabetes, HIV, and epilepsy receive special education services under the IDEA category of other health impairment. Mrs. Parker proposes that Jamal's parents come in for a meeting to discuss Jamal's situation and to determine whether a referral to special education is warranted.

Check Your Understanding 13.2

1. What symptoms of diabetes was Jamal demonstrating at school before his visit to Dr. Lindgren?

2. What tests did Dr. Lindgren administer, and what did he suspect might be the reason for Jamal's not feeling well?

3. Mrs. Parker mentioned that Jamal was experiencing some learning problems in school recently. Do you think these were related to his diabetes diagnosis? Why or why not?

4. If you were Jamal's parents, how would you feel about the possibility of his receiving special education services for a health-related condition? Explain.

Orthopedic Impairment

Orthopedic impairments (OI), sometimes referred to as physical disabilities, are another disability category under IDEA through which children can receive special education services.

IDEA Definition

[Orthopedic impairment] means a severe orthopedic impairment that adversely affects a child's educational performance. The term includes impairments caused by a congenital anomaly, impairments caused by disease (e.g., poliomyelitis, bone tuberculosis), and impairments from other causes (e.g. cerebral palsy, amputations, and fractures or burns that cause contractures).

$$(\S\ 300.8(c)(8))$$

This definition will be used as the basis for the chapter's definition of orthopedic impairment.

Common Types

The most common physical disabilities seen in today's schools are cerebral palsy, spina bifida, and muscular dystrophy.

Cerebral Palsy

Cerebral palsy (CP) is a type of OI that inhibits the brain's ability to send messages to the body. It affects the person's ability to move as well as to maintain balance and posture and sometimes speak clearly. CP ranges from mild to severe and can be accompanied by a cognitive impairment. The most common type of CP is spastic cerebral palsy. Other types of CP include dyskinetic, ataxic, and mixed cerebral palsy.

Symptoms There are many symptoms associated with CP. These are demonstrated in the areas of movement and coordination, as well as neurological problems. The potential symptoms of this disability are listed in Table 13.5.

Causes CP is caused by damage to a developing brain or by abnormal development of the brain. In the case of brain damage, this can occur before, during, or within a month after a child's birth. It can also occur during the first year of life while the child's brain is still developing. The majority of CP is congenitally acquired, meaning the child is born with the disorder. German measles (rubella) and cytomegalovirus (CMV) during pregnancy are also causes of cerebral palsy.

Diagnosis CP requires a medical diagnosis. During a developmental screening, children are briefly assessed for specific developmental delays, such as those involving motor and movement. If a pediatrician is concerned about the results of a child's screening, he or she will make referrals for developmental and medical evaluations. The type of CP a child has typically correlates to when the child is diagnosed. For example, if the child has a moderate to severe form of CP, he or she will generally be diagnosed by age 2. If the child has a milder form of CP, the child might not be diagnosed until he or she is between 3 and 5 years of age.

Spina Bifida

Spina bifida is a type of neural-tube defect that affects the brain, spine, and spinal cord. Spina bifida occurs when the neural tube does not close all the way in

Table 13.5 Cerebral Palsy Symptoms

- Variations in muscle tone, such as being either too stiff or too floppy
- Stiff muscles and exaggerated reflexes (spasticity)
- Stiff muscles with normal reflexes (rigidity)
- Lack of muscle coordination (ataxia)
- Tremors or involuntary movements
- Slow, writhing movements (athetosis)
- Delays in reaching motor skills milestones, such as pushing up on arms, sitting up alone or crawling
- Favoring one side of the body, such as reaching with only one hand or dragging a leg while crawling
- Difficulty walking, such as walking on toes, a crouched gait, a scissors-like gait with knees crossing, a wide gait or an asymmetrical gait
- Excessive drooling or problems with swallowing
- Difficulty with sucking or eating
- Delays in speech development or difficulty speaking
- Difficulty with precise motions, such as picking up a crayon or spoon
- Seizures
- Difficulty with vision and hearing
- Intellectual disabilities
- Abnormal touch or pain perceptions
- Oral diseases
- Mental health (psychiatric) conditions
- Urinary incontinence

Mayo Clinic. (2018b). *Cerebral palsy—symptoms and causes*. Retrieved from https://www.mayoclinic.org/diseases-conditions/cerebral-palsy/symptoms-causes/syc-20353999

utero, resulting in the spinal cord not forming and closing as it should. This leads to exposure of the spinal column. As a result, there can be damage to the spinal cord and the nerves. The most common types of spina bifida include spina bifida occulta, meningocele, and myelomeningocele (the most serious type). Spina bifida can result in physical disabilities and intellectual disabilities.

Symptoms Symptoms of spina bifida depend on its type and severity (see Table 13.6).

Causes The exact causes of spina bifida are unknown. Spina bifida is most likely caused by genetic, environmental, and nutritional factors or a combination of all three. Lack of folate, plant proteins, iron, magnesium, and niacin before conception

Table 13.6 Types and Symptoms of Spina Bifida

Spina bifida occulta

- Most often no signs or symptoms
- Physical signs above the newborn's spinal defect, such as a tuft of hair on newborn's skin or a birthmark, may be present

Meningocele

- Membranes surrounding the spinal cord may emerge through an opening in the vertebrae that forms a sac filled with fluid

Myelomeningocele

- Spinal canal is open along several vertebrae in the lower or middle back
- Membranes of the spinal cord and nerves protrude at birth, creating a sac
- Tissues and nerves are exposed

Mayo Clinic. (2018e). *Spina Bifida—symptoms and causes.* Retrieved from https://www.mayoc linic.org/diseases-conditions/spina-bifida/symptoms-causes/syc-20377860

may be associated with an increased risk of a neural-tube defect. There is a slight risk if one child is born with spina bifida that future siblings will also have it. Last, certain medications (e.g., valproate) that have been used to treat bipolar disorder and epilepsy have resulted in an increased risk of such congenital disorders (Brazier, 2018).

Diagnosis Spina bifida requires a medical diagnosis. Spina bifida can be detected by a routine ultrasound scan during pregnancy. There is also a blood test called maternal serum alpha-fetoprotein (MSAFP) that determines unusually high levels of AFP, which can be indicative of a neural-tube defect. This is checked during the second trimester of the mother's pregnancy. If the AFP levels are high, additional tests will be run. This can include an ultrasound and perhaps an amniocentesis. In some milder cases, spina bifida is determined postnatally based on skin abnormalities or the structure of the back. This is confirmed with an X-ray.

Muscular Dystrophy

Muscular dystrophy is a group of genetic diseases characterized by progressive weakness and breakdown of the skeletal muscles affecting movement. In some cases, muscular dystrophy is seen in childhood; other times, it may not appear until an individual becomes middle-aged or older. There are more than 30 kinds of muscular dystrophy. The most common type is Duchenne muscular dystrophy. This type affects almost exclusively boys and is characterized by muscles becoming weaker and weaker over time until an individual's entire body is affected. Most individuals with muscular dystrophy will lose their ability to walk and will require a wheelchair.

Symptoms Symptoms include trouble walking, loss of reflexes, difficulty standing up, poor posture, bone thinning, scoliosis, mild intellectual impairment, breathing difficulties, swallowing problems, and lung and heart weakness (Martel, 2017, para. 6). Individuals with a family history of muscular dystrophy are at an increased risk of developing the disease as well as passing it down to their children.

Causes Muscular dystrophy runs in families and often develops after an individual inherits a faulty gene from one or both parents. It is caused by mutations in genes that are responsible for healthy muscle structure and function. Each type of muscular dystrophy is linked to a distinct genetic mutation.

Diagnosis Muscular dystrophy requires a medical diagnosis. As with most other disorders, a medical doctor will complete a physical examination and a medical history on the patient. The doctor might then recommend any of the following tests (see Table 13.7):

Table 13.7   Muscular Dystrophy Tests
1. Enzyme tests
2. Electromyography
3. Genetic testing
4. Muscle biopsy
5. Heart-monitoring (electrocardiography and echocardiogram)
6. Lung-monitoring tests

Mayo Clinic. (2018d). *Muscular Dystrophy—diagnosis and treatment*. Retrieved from https://www.mayoclinic.org/diseases-conditions/muscular-dystrophy/diagnosis-treatment/drc-20375394

Educational Considerations

Students with orthopedic impairments will need physical accommodations in the classroom and have physical challenges that require special attention. Special education teachers will need to strategically plan the physical arrangements of their classrooms so that the child with an OI is able to easily navigate and access all parts of the classroom. This can be challenging, because many students with orthopedic impairments will be educated in inclusive classrooms. Inclusive classrooms have a larger number of students than separate special education classrooms, which often limits space. In crowded conditions, it may be more difficult to create the needed accommodations. In addition, a child with an OI might require special furniture to accommodate his or her physical disability. This must also be part of the classroom planning process. Children who are not placed in an inclusive setting will still require physical accommodations; in addition, they will require modified curricula or lesson plans to address other educational needs they are experiencing. No matter the functioning level of children with orthopedic impairments, it is important that their teachers and their schoolwork include them with their typical peers as often as possible and encourage them to participate in extracurricular activities.

Check Your Understanding 13.3

1. Select any one of the OIs discussed. As a special education teacher, what can you do to ensure that a child with that particular disability will reach his educational potential? What steps will you take to get him there?

2. A child with CP can demonstrate various symptoms of this disorder. Select any three symptoms listed above, and discuss the direct impact they will have on a child's educational performance. Be specific.

3. Discuss the diagnostic process of being identified with spina bifida.

Traumatic Brain Injury

Traumatic brain injury (TBI) occurs when there is a sudden blow to the head, causing damage to the brain. It results in a complex injury with various symptoms and disabilities. TBI is one of the more recent disability categories added to IDEA (the other being autism).

IDEA Definition

[Traumatic brain injury] means an acquired injury to the brain caused by an external physical force, resulting in total or partial functional disability or psychosocial impairment, or both, that *adversely affects* a child's educational performance. The term applies to open or closed head injuries resulting in impairments in one or more areas, such as cognition; language; memory; attention; reasoning; abstract thinking; judgment; problem-solving; sensory, perceptual, and motor abilities; psychosocial behavior; physical functions; information processing; and speech.

The term does not apply to brain injuries that are congenital or degenerative, or to brain injuries induced by birth trauma.

(§ 300.8(c)(12))

This definition will be used as the basis for the chapter's definition of traumatic brain injury.

Symptoms

There are several potential symptoms of TBI, and symptoms can range from mild to severe. They include vomiting, lethargy, headache, confusion, paralysis, coma, lack of consciousness, dilated pupils, and vision changes (American Association of Neurological Surgeons, 2018, para. 4). In addition to physical symptoms, cognitive impairments (e.g., attention deficits, long-term and short-term memory problems, disorganization) can significantly impact how students with TBI learn. From a social perspective, the special educator will need to be mindful of the possibility of mood swings, depression, and/or anxiety, as well as restlessness and a potential lack of motivation. Again, these characteristics often impact a child with a TBI's education.

Causes

There are different kinds of injury associated with TBI. These include open-head injury (in which an object penetrates the skull), closed-head injury (e.g., sports injury, car accident), deceleration injuries, chemical/toxic, hypoxia, tumors, infections, and stroke (Traumatic Brain Injury.com, n.d.b).

Diagnosis

A TBI requires a medical diagnosis. Because TBI is a result of an injury, it is commonly assessed in the emergency room. If the TBI is moderate to severe in nature, many times the diagnosis is self-evident. In the event that the TBI coincides with a life-threatening injury, a closed-head injury can be missed. Cardiac and pulmonary function are assessed first, followed by an exam of the entire body and then a neurological exam. Brain-imaging tests with a CAT scan, MRI, SPECT, or PET scan can provide important information. A cognitive evaluation will be performed with neuropsychological testing. Additional evaluations by speech-language therapists, physical therapists, and occupational therapists may be conducted (Traumatic Brain Injury.com, n.d.a).

The following case study portrays a high-school student who endures a TBI as a result of a skateboarding accident.

Case Study 13.2: Hunter's Skateboarding Accident

Hunter is a 16-year-old junior in high school. He attends a local Catholic high school and has many friends. Hunter is a good student and participates mostly in honors classes. Since middle school, Hunter has been involved in extracurricular activities such as basketball, forensics, and the Spanish club. His favorite activity, however, is skateboarding. There is a skate park near his home, and he and his neighborhood friends meet there and ride their skateboards on the weekends.

One Saturday morning, Hunter called his friends and told them that he would meet them at the skate park as soon as he was done with his chores. On Saturdays, he was expected to cut the grass and help his dad with small projects around the house. This weekend, Hunter was in a particular hurry to get to the skate park. He had had a long week at school, with several tests and projects due, and he needed to expend some energy riding his skateboard and enjoying his friends' company. Quickly, he grabbed the lawn mower and dutifully started cutting the grass. He was done in no time and then went looking for his dad to see whether there was anything else he could help out with. Luckily for him, his father had to work this Saturday, leaving Hunter free to do as he pleased for the rest of the day.

Excited to get to the skate park, Hunter grabbed his skateboard and ran out of the house. It was only a five-minute walk to the park. When he arrived, his two best friends, Jack and Bryan, were waiting for him. Hunter grabbed his board and eagerly started off to show his friends some new tricks he had learned. Just as he hopped on his board, Hunter realized that he had left his helmet at home. For a moment, he thought about running back home to grab it, but he was so happy to be with his friends that he blew it off. Jack and Bryan reminded him to wear a helmet, but he skated off without it anyway. He always wore his helmet, and not having it on this one time would not matter, he thought.

Hunter glided across the terrain warming up and laughing with his friends. It felt good to be outside and free from the demands of school. After a few minutes, he headed over to the half-pipe ramp where he could do his jumps and other maneuvers. Jack and Bryan skated over too, wanting to take turns showing off their tricks. Hunter hopped on

the ramp and skated back and forth on the curved structure, gathering speed as he went. After a few turns, he had enough momentum to reach the top, where he would release from the structure on his board and turn around in an attempt to land his board and continue skating. He skated up the ramp and successfully launched. He twisted his board for the return but was unable to land his jump. Hunter came crashing down onto the ramp, hitting his head first on the ramp, followed by the rest of his body. Jack and Bryan ran over to him, realizing that this was a serious accident. Hunter was unconscious at first and unable to move due to a broken shoulder and arm. Quickly, Jack and Bryan called Hunter's mother and told her what had happened. She called 9-1-1. Within minutes, both Hunter's mother and an ambulance arrived at the skate park. The EMTs evaluated Hunter, lifted him onto a stretcher, and took him to the local hospital.

At the hospital, Hunter was met by several doctors, who examined him, asked questions about the accident, and ran diagnostic tests and performed a neurological exam. The neurological exam included a study of his eye movements and reactions, as well as his ability to whistle, smile, and clench his teeth. His hearing was also tested, and he was asked to perform hand and arm movements to evaluate his coordination and position. A CT scan was used to assess his head injury. He had several broken bones, but more serious than that was a severe concussion that he received as a result of his fall. It would be a long recovery for Hunter, and although he would go home from the hospital in a few days, he would spend several weeks at home recovering.

Hunter returned to school about five weeks after his injury. He was still having problems thinking clearly, concentrating, and remembering information. Clearly, this accident had lasting effects on his brain. It was evident that he would not be able to keep up academically in his previous classes and that

(Continued)

(Continued)

his educational placement needed to be reevaluated. After seeing him struggle, Hunter's mother spoke with his doctors and then his school about having a psychoeducational evaluation to determine how his accident had impacted his ability to learn and function in school. Hunter was evaluated through the local school district and was identified as having a traumatic brain injury (TBI) and subsequently eligible for special education services due to the adverse effect it had on his educational performance. This meant that he would have to leave his Catholic school, because they did not provide special education services, and attend a local public high school. This was additionally difficult for him, as it meant leaving his friends and teachers with whom he was close.

Check Your Understanding 13.4

1. Describe Hunter's educational performance prior to his skateboarding accident. What type of classes did he attend? What type of student was he?

2. What happened to Hunter at the skate park? What would have prevented this from occurring?

3. What tests were used to diagnose Hunter's condition?

4. How did the skateboard accident impact Hunter's ability to learn? Educational placement?

Educational Considerations

Although traumatic brain injury (TBI) is considered to be at high incidence, education professionals are still somewhat unaware of the effects that childhood head injury can cause. Children who have experienced a TBI are often improperly classified as have learning disabilities, emotional disturbance, or an intellectual impairment (Project Ideal, 2018).

The effects of TBI, like many disabilities served under IDEA, will vary from child to child, because each child's TBI will have occurred in its own unique manner and will have resulted in different damage to his or her functioning capabilities. The special education teacher will have to be aware of and plan for the adverse effects that a child with a TBI might experience.

The aspects of potential damage caused by TBI and areas that will need careful consideration in educational planning and teaching processes are listed in Table 13.8.

Table 13.8 Areas Impacted by a TBI

Cognitive Skills

- Thinking and processing difficulties
- Memory problems (short-term and long-term)
- Attention
- Executive function

Speech and Language

- Speech changes due to muscle and nerve damage
- Oral language problems
- Reading, spelling, and writing problems
- Social communication problems

Physical Difficulties

- Possible paralysis
- Headaches
- Fatigue

Emotional and Behavioral Considerations

- Emotional reactivity
- Emotional lability and control
- Mood swings, anxiety, depression, and agitation

Balsiger, L. (n.d.). *Traumatic brain injury—effects and impacts.* Retrieved from http://www.bendlanguageandlearning.com/Traumatic-Brain-Injury-Effects-and-Impacts.pdf

Another primary concern about children with TBI is their school reentry. It is critical that effective collaboration occur between hospitals, therapists, families, and the school system to reintegrate the child. The reintegration process must be highly individualized and tailored to the child's personal medical, physical, cognitive, and social-emotional needs. Depending on the location of the injury of the brain, there might be problems with executive functioning, self-regulation, goal setting, initiating, and inhibiting behavior. Students might also have memory problems and language disturbances. There is a likelihood that their educational and emotional needs will be distinctly different than before their injury. In addition, children who have experienced a TBI can often remember their functionality prior to their trauma, which can result in a myriad of emotional and psychosocial problems. The school must also recognize that the child's educational placement must be based on the student's current academic performance, as opposed to the one he or she maintained prior to the accident or injury.

There are several research-based strategies that have proven effective for students who have TBI. These include the following:

1. Experiential learning (using concrete objects to solve mathematical problems, building a bridge to learn physics, etc.)

2. Using a multimedia approach instead of lecturing

3. Maintaining frequent communication between home and school for students who are having difficulties

4. Providing repetition and consistency

5. Giving verbal and written instructions

6. Providing examples to illustrate new ideas and concepts

7. Avoiding figurative language

8. Checking for understanding

9. Keeping the environment distraction-free

(Disability Law Center of Alaska, 2008)

Another support available for those with TBI is assistive technology. This can take the form of AAC (augmentative and alternative communication) devices, electronic spellers, timers, alarms, visual checklists, calendars, planners, and photograph clues, to name a few. Common adaptations might also include large-print books, books on tape, and graphic organizers. Accommodations that can be helpful include allowing more time on tests, reducing the amount of written work required, and multiple-choice format instead of recall format on tests (Bowen, 2018).

Check Your Understanding 13.5

1. Indicate the various potential causes of TBI.

2. In your own opinion, what challenges would a typically developing child in general education experience if he had a TBI and, following his return to school, was placed in a special education setting due to his cognitive losses resulting from his injury? Why do you think this could be difficult for him, educationally and socially speaking?

3. List the different medical tests that might accompany the diagnostic process for TBI.

Multiple Disabilities

Students with multiple disabilities are those students with the most significant cognitive, physical, and communicative needs. Many have an intellectual disability, significant mobility issues, and limited communicative abilities. They will require intensive and ongoing support at both home and school. Students with multiple disabilities comprise a very small number of students being served under IDEA—somewhere around 2%.

IDEA Definition

[Multiple disabilities are] concomitant [simultaneous] impairments (such as intellectual disability-blindness, intellectual disability-orthopedic impairment, etc.), the combination of which causes such severe educational needs that they cannot be accommodated in a special education program solely for one of the impairments. The term does not include deaf-blindness.

(§ 300.8(c)(7))

This definition will be used as the basis for the chapter's definition of multiple disabilities.

Causes

There are several causes of multiple disabilities, which can occur during the prenatal, perinatal, or postnatal period. Examples are chromosomal abnormalities, malnutrition, lack of oxygen supply to the brain, and lead poisoning.

Comorbidity

By definition, multiple disabilities are a combination of two or more disabilities, according to IDEA. A term commonly associated with multiple disabilities is comorbidity, meaning to coexist. In the event of multiple disabilities, there are at least two disabilities that are simultaneously present. When an individual has comorbid conditions, this almost always means that his or her disabilities are more severe in nature and, as a result, will almost always have implications for all aspects of his or her education.

A child who has been classified as having multiple disabilities may demonstrate:

1. problems transferring or generalizing learning from one situation to another, one setting to another, and one skill to another;

2. limited communication ability;

3. difficulties with memory;

4. need for supports for many of life's major functions (domestic, leisure, community participation, vocational); and

5. need for services from many different service providers.

(Smith & Tyler, 2010, p. 438)

There is a chance that at some point in your career as a special education teacher, you will teach students who have more than one disability. Some of the more common comorbid conditions are intellectual disability, cerebral palsy, severe hypotonia, motor-control disorders, secondary motor impairments, epilepsy, sensory impairments, somatic disorders, autism, and deaf-blindness.

Primary vs. Secondary Diagnosis

In education, a primary diagnosis refers to the disability that has the greatest impact on the child's learning and development. A secondary diagnosis is a disability that is comorbid but whose impact is not as significant as the primary diagnosis. For example, a child might come to school with a primary diagnosis of ASD and a secondary diagnosis of epilepsy. It is relevant to note that a child's IEP may state only one of his or her disabilities, or it may state all of them. This typically varies from state to state.

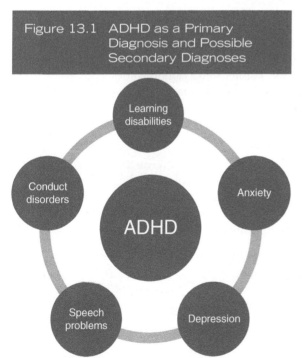

Figure 13.1 ADHD as a Primary Diagnosis and Possible Secondary Diagnoses

The following are examples of primary conditions with secondary diagnoses:

The diagram above shows ADHD as the primary diagnosis. The disabilities surrounding ADHD depict some of the possible secondary diagnoses that might occur with this disorder (see Figure 13.1). These include anxiety, depression, speech disorders, conduct disorders, and learning disabilities. A child may experience one or more secondary diagnoses to his or her ADHD. It is also possible that a child might have a learning disability (or other secondary diagnosis) as a primary diagnosis, and ADHD as a secondary diagnosis. It is relevant to state that not all children will have a secondary diagnosis. Having a secondary diagnosis can have a distinct effect on a child's educational needs. As mentioned, the more disabilities that the child has, the more complex his or her needs will be—because, in addition to attending to one disability, the special education teacher will have to consider both disabilities in ensuring that the student's educational needs are equally met.

Below is another example of a primary diagnosis and possible secondary diagnoses to this disorder. In this example, ASD is the primary disorder, and OCD, ID, epilepsy, depression, and anxiety serve as common secondary diagnoses (see Figure 13.2).

Diagnosis

The diagnostic process will differ for this student population when compared to others, due to its complex nature. When diagnosing a student with multiple disabilities, each separate disability must be considered and evaluated on its own. Table 13.9 contains a list of assessments and processes reflecting how a child with multiple disabilities would be diagnosed:

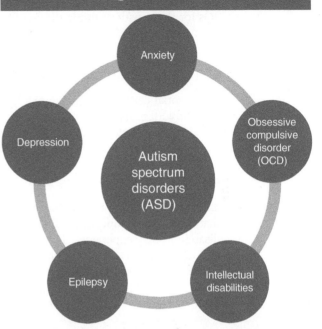

Figure 13.2   ASD as a Primary Diagnosis and Possible Secondary Diagnoses

Table 13.9   Assessing for Multiple Disabilities

- An observation by a team member other than the student's general education teacher of the student's academic performance in a general classroom setting; or, in the case of a student less than school age or out of school, an observation by a team member conducted in an age-appropriate environment

- A developmental history, if needed

- An assessment of intellectual ability

- Other assessments of the characteristics of speech and language impairments, if the student exhibits impairments in any one or more of the following areas: cognition, fine motor, perceptual motor, communication, social or emotional, and perception or memory. These assessments shall be completed by specialists knowledgeable in the specific characteristics being assessed.

- A review of cumulative records, previous IEPs or IFSPs, and teacher-collected work samples

- If deemed necessary, a medical statement or health assessment statement indicating whether there are any physical factors that may be affecting the student's educational performance

- Assessments to determine the impact of the suspected disability

American Academy of Special Education Professionals. (n.d.). *Chapter 9: Multiple disabilities.* Retrieved from http://aasep. org/fileadmin/user_upload/Protected_Directory/BCSE_Course_Files/Course_5/Chapter-9-Special_Education_Eligibility.pdf

The primary tests for this disability population are IQ testing and tests of adaptive behavior. Assessing a child with multiple disabilities' cognitive abilities can be difficult. Using a standard IQ test will not provide accurate results, because it depends largely on verbal skills that are often lacking in this student population. IQs for those with multiple disabilities typically fall in the 25–40 range, putting them significantly below their typical peers.

Educational Considerations

Educational considerations are extensive when considering the complexity of a student with multiple disabilities. Educational considerations can be identified in the areas of chronic health problems, mobility, technology, and the importance of collaboration between school and home for those working with the child.

Chronic Health Problems

Students with multiple disabilities will often experience chronic health problems that impact their education. Much like students with OHI, students with multiple disabilities may experience daily or extended absences for medical appointments or hospitalizations. They will likely require regular attention from the school nurse to administer medications or monitor various aspects of their health. Although medically necessary, frequent absences and visits from the nurse impact the amount of engaged time a student has for learning.

Mobility

Students with multiple disabilities often experience issues related to mobility or the ability to physically move around the classroom. Some students will have leg braces, while others might require a wheelchair. Many will have significant issues getting around their classroom environments. Special attention will need to be paid to the physical arrangement of the classroom. Special education teachers will need to create an environment where there are wider pathways between desks and accessibility to all parts of the classroom for a child with specific physical needs.

Technology

Technology has been a game-changer for many students with multiple disabilities. Perhaps most significantly, it has allowed individuals with disabilities to express themselves both orally and in written form. Special education teachers will be required to have a genuine understanding of assistive technology (AT) when working with this student population. This is particularly true with respect to augmentative and alternative communication (AAC). Prior to the development of AAC devices, students with significant communication problems, such as those with multiple disabilities, had virtually no way to interact with those around them. If they did use some type of assistive technology, it was often considered "low tech" and, many times, awkward, clunky, and cumbersome to transport. Today there is a plethora of devices available to aid in communication for individuals with multiple disabilities, such as the Pocket GoTalk 5-Level, MegaBee Assisted Communication and Writing Tablet, Proloquo2Go, GoTalk 9+, and iPad. These devices give children with multiple disabilities an avenue through which they can communicate their wants, needs, and desires and has allowed them to participate to a much greater extent in their daily learning at school, home, and the community.

The Importance of Collaboration Between School Personnel and Family

Students with multiple disabilities will benefit from educators, paraprofessionals, therapists, and families who are able to work together to plan and carry out their education. Because various professionals are required to come together in this process of educating a student with complex needs, it is important they be able to work together both harmoniously and productively. Therefore, quality collaboration in the form of home-school communication is particularly relevant. Parents of children with multiple disabilities will want and need increased communication from school to know how their child is doing, from both a health perspective and an educational perspective. They will want to know things such as "How did my child feel today?" "Did he have any significant behavioral problems?" "Was he able to eat?" "How is he reacting during the day to a new medication?" It is recommended that the special education teacher maintain daily communication with families either by email, daily log, or phone conversation. It is through this regular type of communication that teachers and families are able to inform each other of the child's health and educational progress so that his or her time spent at school is the most productive.

Check Your Understanding 13.6

1. What is the difference between a primary diagnosis and a secondary diagnosis?

2. Do you think comorbidity impacts a student's ability levels with respect to learning?

3. If you were the parent of a child with multiple disabilities, what concerns would you have about him at school each day? Provide examples.

4. Summarize the diagnostic process for multiple disabilities.

The following case study focuses on what a typical day is like for a fourth-grader with multiple disabilities and the assessment process that occurs in her classroom.

Case Study 13.3: Tanisha's Day

Tanisha is an 8-year-old girl born with cerebral palsy, an intellectual disability, and sensory problems. Because of the severity of her disabilities, Tanisha attends a separate school for students with more significant educational needs. Each morning, her mother wakes her by 5:30 to get her ready for school. Because of the mobility issues she experiences due to her CP, it takes Tanisha significantly longer to get through her morning routine. Her mother also needs to help feed her and make sure that she has taken all of her medications and has been toileted before boarding the school bus. Although there is a public school just around the corner from Tanisha's house, it cannot provide appropriate educational services for her, so she must travel almost an hour to attend her school that specializes in working with children with multiple disabilities. She requires significant help getting on and off the school bus each morning, and there is a bus aide to help her with her mobility issues.

Once at school, Tanisha is greeted by therapeutic support staff, who assist her off of the bus and into the school. When she arrives into her classroom, with assistance, she puts her backpack and lunch away. After she settles in and the other children arrive, the school day begins. There are six students currently in Tanisha's class. The curriculum that her teacher follows is significantly adapted to meet the developmental needs of the students with multiple disabilities. Currently, all students in Tanisha's class have multiple disabilities with some degree of intellectual impairment. Tanisha's classroom is a busy place. Throughout the school day, there are various professionals helping and working with students. The school nurse stops in at different times during the day to administer medication. The physical therapist and occupational therapist spend time in her classroom working on different gross-motor/fine-motor skills and everyday skills. There is a behavior specialist working with a child displaying significant problem behaviors. A speech-language pathologist works with children on their communication skills and learning how to use their AAC devices. There is one paraprofessional for every child in the class. At any given time throughout the day, there are more adults than children in this classroom.

The following schedule is a typical day in Tanisha's classroom:

TANISHA'S DAILY SCHEDULE

1. The teacher reviews the daily communication notebook that was completed by Tanisha's mother the night before.

2. The teacher posts and reviews the daily schedule with the class.

3. Morning Work (e.g., name recognition)

4. Snack and Recess

5. Restroom Break

6. Circle Time Activities (e.g., greeting classmates)

7. Gross-Motor and Fine-Motor Activities (e.g., balance work or stringing beads)

8. Gross-Motor and Fine-Motor Activities (e.g., balance work or stringing beads)

9. Sensory Bins (e.g., exploring different textures)

10. Lunchtime

11. Restroom Break

12. Music (e.g., singing/listening to music)

13. Math (e.g., counting)

14. Exercise (varies according to individual child)

15. Instruction on how to play (e.g., playing simple games)

16. Instruction on Routines and Procedures (e.g., using the restroom)

17. Playtime (e.g., kicking or rolling a ball)

18. The teacher completes communication notebooks to be sent home to parents.

19. Restroom Break

20. Class is dismissed.

21. Students are taken to buses to return home.

At this point in the school year, it is time to assess the progress that the children are making in Tanisha's class. Most students cannot be effectively assessed through the use of standardized assessments. For most children with severe and multiple disabilities, growth is slower than it is for typical children, and assessments that have been designed for typical children rarely consider the various complexities caused by having more than disability. In order to accurately determine the progress that Tanisha has made, her teacher uses a form of authentic assessment which enables her to gain information about Tanisha's growth in her school environment by completing routine activities. This will involve conducting informal observations of Tanisha during the school day in various settings, such as the classroom, the lunchroom, and even the bathroom, demonstrating her progress on her IEP goals. For example, one of Tanisha's annual IEP goals

this year is hand-washing. Her progress on this goal can be informally observed at three different times during the day when she takes her bathroom break. Her teacher will also collect data on her ability to interact socially, participate in classroom activities, and express her needs and wants. In addition, her teacher will conduct structured observations to elicit some certain responses from her that she could not obtain from her informal observations. Tanisha's physical therapist and occupational therapist will also conduct their own assessments, measuring her growth on the goals that they have been working on with her. One annual goal that her physical therapist has been working on with her is independently pulling down her pants when she uses the toilet. Measuring Tanisha's progress is important, because it determines whether the teaching methods and strategies used by her teacher are effective in helping her learn the necessary skills as set forth in her IEP.

1. How might Tanisha's limited mobility affect her ability to get around at school? Provide an example.

2. Which of the activities listed in her daily schedule address her sensory problems?

3. If you were a new special education teacher in this class, what concerns might you have about working with this student population? Teaching this class?

Section 504 and Health-Related Disabilities

There might be instances when a child who has a health-related disability is not in need of special education services but whose needs can be met through a Section 504 service agreement. As previously discussed, a Section 504 service agreement is used when a child with a disability does not require specially designed instruction and can be educated in general education but does require accommodations in order to both ensure academic success and access the learning environment. There are various types of accommodations (e.g., classroom, organizational, behavioral, presentation, assignment, evaluation) that a child with a health-related disability might benefit from. It is relevant to note that any accommodation that a student with a health-related disability will need ultimately depends on the individual needs of the student. In other words, it would be inaccurate to state that all children with a particular disability would require the same set of accommodations even if they had the same disability. In order to give you an idea of what such accommodations might look like, Table 13.10 shows examples of classroom accommodations that would be appropriate for a student with an OI as well as a student with a TBI.

Table 13.10 Accommodations for OI and TBI

- Special seating arrangements to develop useful posture and movements
- Instruction focused on development of gross and fine motor skills
- Securing suitable augmentative communication and other assistive devices
- Awareness of medical condition and its effect on the student (such as getting tired quickly)

Project IDEAL. (2013). *Orthopedic impairments*. Retrieved from http://www.projectidealonline.org/v/orthopedic-impairments TBI

- Minimize extraneous auditory and visual stimulation (use study carrels or room dividers).

- Provide preferential seating.

- Arrange seating to allow for more space between students.

- Provide small-group instruction.

- Structure student's activities and schedule to limit number of changes and reduce unstructured time.

- Limit the number of persons whom the student deals with each day.

- Provide the student with a written schedule, and keep the schedule as consistent as possible.

- Provide area to keep supplies, books, etc., away from student's work area.

- Select a classroom buddy.

Dade Schools. (2002). *Traumatic brain injury: Classroom modifications and strategies for TBI students.* Retrieved from http://ese.dadeschools.net/tbi/2classroom.html

CHAPTER SUMMARY

In this chapter, we discussed a diverse group of students eligible for special education services. We examined students with OHI, OI, TBI, and MD. In doing so, we provided overall descriptions of each disability category, common disorders specific to them, symptoms, causes, the diagnostic processes, and educational considerations needed to be made by the special education teacher responsible for children with these diagnoses. The importance of collaboration between school personnel and family and the usefulness of a Section 504 service agreement were also highlighted. Case studies were provided, to give the reader a more authentic idea of what working with children experiencing these disabilities might be like.

APPLY WHAT YOU HAVE LEARNED

1. Select any one of the health impairments discussed in this chapter (e.g., diabetes mellitus, Tourette syndrome, leukemia, epilepsy). Develop a list of questions that you might ask a medical professional about how this disability could impact a person's ability to learn.

2. Multiple disabilities are complex to diagnose. In order to better understand their impact on an individual, research prenatal (before birth), perinatal (during birth), and postnatal (after birth) causes of multiple disabilities. Consolidate the information onto a chart that you can share with your classmates.

3. Interview a medical professional (ER doctor, nurse, paramedic, etc.) about traumatic brain injury (TBI). Create a list of specific questions

to ask him or her about the diagnostic process, tests, and procedures used to make this diagnosis.

4. Imagine you are preparing a student with a health-related disability for postsecondary life. Write a brief essay detailing some of the considerations that would need to be addressed with respect to job opportunities, further education, community involvement, and independent living.

REFERENCES

American Association of Neurological Surgeons. (2018). *Traumatic brain injury: TBI symptoms.* Retrieved from https://www.aans.org/Patients/Neurosurgical-Conditions-and-Treatments/Traumatic-Brain-Injury

American Lung Association. (2019). *Asthma.* Retrieved from https://www.lung.org/lung-health-and-diseases/lung-disease-lookup/asthma

American Academy of Special Education Professionals. (n.d.). *Chapter 9: Multiple disabilities.* Retrieved from http://aasep.org/fileadmin/user_upload/Protected_Directory/BCSE_Course_Files/Course_5/Chapter-9-Special_Education_Eligibility.pdf

Balsiger, L. (n.d.). *Traumatic brain injury—effects and impacts.* Retrieved from http://www.bend-languageandlearning.com/Traumatic-Brain-Injury-Effects-and-Impacts.pdf

Bowen, J. (2018). *Classroom interventions for students with traumatic brain injuries.* Retrieved from https://www.brainline.org/article/classroom-interventions-students-traumatic-brain-injuries

Brazier, Y. (2018, January 19). What you need to know about spina bifida. *Medical News Today.* Retrieved from https://www.medicalnewstoday.com/articles/220424.php

Centers for Disease Control and Prevention. (2019). *Frequently asked questions about epilepsy.* Retrieved from https://www.cdc.gov/epilepsy/about/faq.htm#What%20causes%20epilepsy?

Cleveland Clinic. (2019). *Leukemia.* Retrieved from https://my.clevelandclinic.org/health/diseases/4365-leukemia

Dade Schools. (2002). *Traumatic brain injury: Classroom modifications and strategies for TBI students.* Retrieved from http://ese.dadeschools.net/tbi/2classroom.html

Disability Law Center of Alaska. (2008). *Educating students with traumatic brain injury.* Retrieved from http://www.dlcak.org/files/pdf/Publications/EducatingStudentswtihTBI.pdf

Encyclopedia of Children's Health. (n.d.). *Tics.* Retrieved from http://www.healthofchildren.com/T/Tics.html

Epilepsy Society. (2016). *Causes of epilepsy.* Retrieved from https://www.epilepsysociety.org.uk/causes-epilepsy

Felman, A. (2017). Leukemia: What you need to know. *Medical News Today.* Retrieved from https://www.medicalnewstoday.com/articles/142595.php

Individuals With Disabilities Education Act, 20 U.S.C. § 1400 (2004).

Lava, N. (2017). What are the types of epilepsy? *WebMD.* Retrieved from https://www.webmd.com/epilepsy/guide/types-epilepsy#3

Martel, J. (2017). *Muscular dystrophy: Types, symptoms, and treatment.* Retrieved from https://www.healthline.com/health/muscular-dystrophy

Mayo Clinic. (2018a). *Asthma—diagnosis and treatment*. Retrieved from https://www.mayoclinic.org/diseases-conditions/asthma/diagnosis-treatment/drc-20369660

Mayo Clinic. (2018b). *Cerebral palsy—symptoms and causes*. Retrieved from https://www.mayoclinic.org/diseases-conditions/cerebral-palsy/symptoms-causes/syc-20353999

Mayo Clinic. (2018c). *Diabetes—symptoms and causes*. Retrieved from https://www.mayoclinic.org/diseases-conditions/diabetes/symptoms-causes/syc-20371444

Mayo Clinic. (2018d). *Muscular dystrophy—diagnosis and treatment*. Retrieved from https://www.mayoclinic.org/diseases-conditions/muscular-dystrophy/diagnosis-treatment/drc-20375394

Mayo Clinic. (2018e). *Spina bifida—symptoms and causes*. Retrieved from https://www.mayoclinic.org/diseases-conditions/spina-bifida/symptoms-causes/syc-20377860

Mayo Clinic. (2018f). *Tourette syndrome: Diagnosis and treatment*. Retrieved from: https://www.mayoclinic.org/diseases-conditions/tourette-syndrome/diagnosis-treatment/drc-20350470

Mayo Clinic. (2018g). *Tourette syndrome: Symptoms and causes*. Retrieved from https://www.mayoclinic.org/diseases-conditions/tourette-syndrome/symptoms-causes/syc-20350465

National Association of Special Education Teachers. (2019). *Comprehensive overview of other health impairments*. Retrieved from https://www.naset.org/index.php?id=2278

Project IDEAL. (2013). *Orthopedic impairments*. Retrieved from http://www.projectidealonline.org/v/orthopedic-impairments

Project IDEAL. (2018). *Traumatic brain injury*. Retrieved from http://www.projectidealonline.org/v/traumatic-brain-injury/

Smith, D., & Tyler, N. (2010). *Introduction to special education* (7th ed.). Upper Saddle River, NJ: Merrill.

Traumatic Brain Injury.com. (n.d.a). *Diagnosis*. Retrieved from https://www.traumaticbraininjury.com/diagnosis

Traumatic Brain Injury.com. (n.d.b). *What are the causes of TBI?* Retrieved from https://www.traumaticbraininjury.com/what-are-the-causes-of-tbi

WebMD. (2019). *Asthma diagnosis and tests*. Retrieved from https://www.webmd.com/asthma/diagnosing-asthma-tests#1a

Making Connections Between Diagnosis, Eligibility, and Instruction

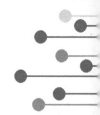

CHAPTER 14

Making Connections Between Diagnosis, Eligibility, and Instruction

Mary A. Houser, EdD, and Tara S. Guerriero, PhD

Learning Objectives

After the completion of this chapter, you should be able to:

- Describe the major components of a comprehensive evaluation report: Demographic Information, Referral, Administration and Collection of Assessment Data Indicating Student Performance, Conditions of Administration, Determining Factors, Present Levels of Student Performance, Conclusion, Recommendations.

- Differentiate between accommodations provided by a Section 504 Service Agreement under Section 504 of the Vocational Rehabilitation Act of 1973 and specially designed instruction provided by an IEP under IDEA.

- Distinguish between present levels of performance and present levels of academic performance and functional performance.

- Give examples of annual goals, short term objectives, and benchmarks.

- Summarize the components of an annual review.

- Discuss how an educational re-evaluation occurs and its components.

Key Terms

annual goals (p. 432)	present levels of performance (p.429)
annual review (p. 440)	referral (p. 419)
demographic information (p. 419)	short-term objectives (p. 434)
educational reevaluation report (p. 441)	specially designed instruction (SDI) (p. 435)
present levels of academic and functional performance (PLAAFP) (p. 430)	

Introduction to the Chapter

The complexities associated with assessment and the overall diagnostic process has been highlighted throughout the text. Part I of the text provided the background in assessment that is necessary for comprehending and applying the components of a comprehensive diagnostic evaluation that would be included in evaluating a student for special education services under IDEA.

- Chapter 1 provided an understanding of both the history of assessment within special education as well as the legislation that informs assessment decisions. Further, it helped to bridge an understanding of assessment and eligibility for special education services as it relates to special education and civil rights legislation.

- Chapter 2 included an overview of assessment, assessment-related terminology, and ethical considerations surrounding assessment.

- Chapter 3 included a description of assessment types that are commonly used in educational settings and comprehensive diagnostic evaluations.

- Chapters 4 and 5 described six areas of student characteristics (intelligence, areas of academic achievement and language, behavior, social/emotional characteristics, and health and medical status); connections were also made to the assessment types discussed in Chapter 3, and examples of specific measures were included throughout the chapter.

Parts II and III provided a description of the diagnostic and eligibility criteria and the assessment process associated with the IDEA categories of disability. While Part II focused on those disabilities that may be diagnosed in an educational or a private setting, Part III focused on disabilities and disorders that are diagnosed not in an educational setting, but rather in a medical setting. The purpose of the chapters in Part III was to facilitate the understanding of medically diagnosed disabilities and to promote an awareness of the diagnostic criteria and their relevance to eligibility for special education services under IDEA. Further, they focused on the impact that each disability may have on education, as well as differences that may occur based on the age of onset or diagnosis (prenatal, perinatal, and postnatal).

In this chapter, you will learn how to translate everything that we have discussed throughout the text into criteria that will be used to make educational decisions for a student.

- We will examine the components of a comprehensive evaluation report and focus on the analysis and interpretation of assessment results.

- We will bridge the gap between assessment and instruction by illustrating how all the information that you have learned about the assessment process fits together with the diagnostic criteria of each disability to determine the need for special education services.

- We will examine the process of providing accommodations under Section 504 of the Vocational Rehabilitation Act of 1973 (often referred to as Section 504) should it be determined that a student has a disability but does not need special education services.

- We will discuss how the evaluation information can be used to inform the individual student's education in the development of an individualized education program (IEP) should it be determined that a student is eligible for special education services.

- We will delve into the process of planning for special education programming.

- We will further examine the role of ongoing assessment (e.g., progress monitoring, annual reviews, and reevaluations) to guide instruction.

Analysis and Interpretation of Assessment Results

In order to truly understand the determination of need for special education services, it is first necessary to look at the actual components of a comprehensive diagnostic evaluation and how it is used to reveal learning strengths and needs that a child may have.

Data Collected for a Comprehensive Evaluation

The comprehensive evaluation is often completed by a school psychologist or another individual who is able to administer and interpret assessments. Each state has its own criteria for who is qualified to complete a comprehensive evaluation, so the actual person will vary by state. Regardless of who primarily completes the evaluation, information will be obtained from multiple assessment types (as discussed in Chapter 3), areas of student characteristics (as discussed in Chapters 4 and 5), and sources or people (teacher(s), parent(s), student, medical professional, behavior specialist, etc). The following are all components of a comprehensive evaluation:

1. *Demographic information.* Personal demographic information (child's name, address, phone number, chronological age, grade level, teacher's name, etc.) will be collected and included in the report.

2. *Referral for an evaluation.* A discussion of the referral process serves as an explanation of why the evaluation is taking place. It typically

includes information about when the referral was made, who referred the student for an evaluation (e.g., teacher, parent), the reason for referral (e.g., academic difficulties, a diagnosis of a medically related condition, behavioral difficulties), and a hypothesis for diagnosis (if it is an educationally related disability, such as a learning disability). While the diagnostic process associated with many disabilities (e.g., learning disability) is directly related to the student's education, that is not the case for disabilities that are medically or health-related. In those instances, the educational system does not diagnose; instead it determines whether the student is eligible for special education services based on need. In this instance, the referral would not relate to diagnosis.

3. *Administration and collection of assessment data indicating student performance.* The principal expectation of the comprehensive evaluation is to gather data related to the student characteristics highlighted in Chapters 4 and 5 (i.e., intelligence, academic areas of achievement and language, behavior, social/emotional characteristics, and health/medical status) using multiple means (as highlighted in Chapter 3).

4. Conditions of Administration: There are many assessment types that must be administered under standard conditions to be considered valid. Typically, a comprehensive evaluation includes a statement indicating whether the assessments were conducted under standard conditions. If they weren't, the nonstandard conditions must be taken into consideration when interpreting the results.

Check Your Understanding 14.1

1. Why would demographic information be included in the comprehensive evaluation report?

2. Describe the purpose of a referral and what should be included in the referral.

3. Give a scenario in which assessments may not have been administered under standard conditions and how that might impact student performance and results.

Analysis of Assessment Results to Determine the Need for Special Education Services

Following the collection of data, an extensive analysis of the assessment data will be completed. As part of this analysis, the following will be determined.

Determining Factors

The team will rule out difficulties resulting from a lack of appropriate instruction in reading and math, as well as limited English proficiency.

Present Levels of Student Performance

Present levels of student performance will be determined, to indicate the student's current level of proficiency in all the areas of student performance that are evaluated as part of the comprehensive evaluation.

Conclusion

The team will come to a conclusion as to the results of the comprehensive evaluation and determine whether the student is eligible for special education services. As part of the conclusion, the following questions will be answered:

> *Does the child have a disability?* The team will evaluate the data in relation to the eligibility criteria for the disability/disabilities in consideration to determine whether the child qualifies for a diagnosis of a disability/ disabilities. If the student has a disability, disorder, condition, or syndrome that has already been diagnosed by another professional, such as a medical professional or psychologist (e.g., ADHD, physical impairment, sensory impairment, mental disorder, autism), the team will determine whether the disability qualifies for services based on the eligibility criteria for each of the 14 disability categories covered under IDEA.

> *Does the child need specially designed instruction?* The team will evaluate the student's present levels of performance in the educational system and determine whether the student needs specially designed instruction in order to receive an appropriate education. If a student doesn't need specially designed instruction or modifications (changes to educational expectations) to receive an appropriate education, he or she won't be eligible for special education services under IDEA.

If it is found that a student needs specially designed instruction based on evidence from the comprehensive evaluation, the team will move toward planning for special education programming, which will be covered in depth below. Alternatively, if a student is diagnosed with a disability, disorder, condition, or syndrome either through the comprehensive evaluation or by another professional, but not found to be eligible for special education services through IDEA based on educational need, he or she can receive accommodations under Section 504 of the Vocational Rehabilitation Act of 1973 (discussed in Chapter 1). This civil rights legislation aims to provide access to students in federally funded programs (such as the public school system) to prevent discrimination. The accommodations that are provided under Section 504 do not change the content that students are expected to learn or expectations for what students will accomplish. Instead, they involve changes in the input/output processes that are involved in learning, to enable access to the educational system. Accommodations can take many forms. For example, accommodations may be physical (seating arrangement in the classroom, proximity to the teacher, access to an elevator, a distraction-free environment for testing, etc.), organizational (checklists for organization, an extra textbook at home, providing a written list of homework, etc.), instructional (extra time to complete an activity, graphic organizers to assist with written language, simplifying directions to assist with understanding, etc.), or behavioral (using a fidget to assist with attention, allowing breaks to accommodate for attentional or emotional needs, using verbal or nonverbal cues to assist with attention, etc.). The following scenarios are examples of instances in which a Section 504 service agreement may be used to provide accommodations that may facilitate access to the educational system for a student:

- If a student has memory deficits that make it difficult to remember multiplication facts, an alternative means of learning multiplication facts may be taught that will help the student be able to determine an answer to multiplication facts. The student is still expected to know the facts; however, he or she is given an accommodation that attempts to minimize the memory deficit.

- If a student has difficulties with organization, he or she may have difficulties with keeping a binder organized. A checklist may be provided as an accommodation to help the student with organizational skills. The student is still expected to maintain an organized binder, but the checklist will enhance the student's ability to accomplish that task.

- If a student has a visual impairment that hinders him or her from reading text, changing the input to incorporate a different sensory system, such as the sense of touch (e.g., through Braille) or the sense of hearing (e.g., auditory enhancements, such as talk to text) may be used as an accommodation.

- If a student has a physical impairment that prohibits him or her from walking, a wheelchair and access to an elevator may be provided as an accommodation to prevent discrimination to the individual.

- If a student has attentional deficits, taking a test in an environment that has many other students may be distracting for the student and may limit the student's ability to perform at his or her best. Allowing the student to take a test in a distraction-free environment may minimize the effect of his or her attentional deficits.

All of these types of accommodations may be incorporated into a Section 504 service agreement to ensure that the student has equal access to the educational system as he or she would if he or she didn't have a disability.

Recommendations

The team will provide recommendations for the continued and future education of the student. If the student has been found eligible for special education services, the recommendations will provide a starting point for the IEP team when developing the student's individualized education program (IEP). If it is determined that the student is not eligible for special education services, the recommendations will serve as ideas for enhancing the student's education in the general education system.

The following two case studies serve as examples of two different students, one of whom was found to be eligible for special education services based on need, and one who was not found to be eligible but instead received accommodations under a Section 504 service agreement:

1. Matthew was found eligible for special education services based on a diagnosis of a speech and language impairment and a demonstrated need for specially designed instruction.

2. Jennifer (whom you met in Chapter 11) was diagnosed by a medical professional with attention-deficit/hyperactivity disorder–combined type but was not found eligible for special education services because she did not demonstrate a need for specially designed instruction.

Case Study 14.1: Matthew

Matthew is currently 9 years old and in the fourth grade. During kindergarten, he was diagnosed with an expressive language disorder in oral language; however, his parents decided to seek private services from a speech and language therapist as opposed to seeking services from the school district. During his third-grade year, his parents requested a comprehensive diagnostic evaluation through the school system, and he was diagnosed with a speech and language impairment that resulted from an expressive language disorder that manifested itself in both oral and written language.

Background

During his early developmental years, Matthew's receptive and expressive vocabulary development was fairly typical of his age, as he could understand and use many different words. Examples of his first words were "ball," "mom," "dada," "goggy (doggy)," As he got older, he seemed to understand what was being said to him, but he had difficulties putting together words at an age-appropriate time. When he did put words together, his utterances didn't conform to typical grammatical structures; such as "me go," "more milk," "want that," and "dada up." He tended to put high-content words together—for example, "mommy goggy" or "room light." He didn't appear to be demonstrating appropriate grammatical constructions. As he got older and entered kindergarten, it became apparent that other children his age were beginning to speak in much more lengthy sentences while Matthew was still struggling to produce shorter

(Continued)

(Continued)

utterances. He seemed to become much more quiet and often listened more than he spoke. Throughout his early elementary years, he continued to be a quiet child, but his responses and actions indicated that he understood what others said to him. He continued to produce short sentences that were often grammatically incorrect, and, when he did use longer sentences, he didn't seem to be able to organize his thoughts and express them clearly. For example, when describing a recent family vacation, he said, "We went to beach." When asked what he did at the beach, he said, "We did swimming and things. I like to have bucket and sand." During the second and third grade, he began to do a lot more writing. He showed difficulties in written language similar to those he showed in oral language. He showed deficits in the content of his ideas (semantics), the organization of his ideas, and grammar. He could write down or say the words that he wanted to use, but he couldn't find what he called the "right" way to put them in a sentence. For example, when asked to write down words to describe his dog, he wrote the following: "Cooper, little, fun, friendly, white, playful, fluffy." He was then asked to write a story about his dog, and he wrote the following: "My dog name cooper. He play over there and he like bone in the grass. There is white and black." Despite his difficulties with oral and written language, he learned to read at an early age (4 years) and developed a love for reading; his parents often asked him questions about what he read, and he demonstrated that he understood.

Diagnostic Procedure, Findings, and Services

Matthew began receiving speech and language services from a private therapist for an expressive language disorder in oral language during the end of his kindergarten year. He continued to have difficulties, and during the end of his third-grade year, Matthew's teacher suggested that he be tested for difficulties in language that extended beyond his oral language difficulties. The school psychologist conducted a comprehensive psychoeducational evaluation and found that he had above-average intelligence and achievement in the areas of reading and mathematics; however, aspects of his oral language and written language performance were lower. He performed in the above-average range on both receptive and expressive vocabulary measures, and his spelling was above average. However, he demonstrated achievement at the low end of the average range on measures of expressive oral language and written language that required higher levels of productivity (sentences of greater length and content). Both formal and informal measures indicated that his receptive language was good, while his expressive language was not progressing as it should. These findings were consistent with the behavior that he was demonstrating both at school and at home. He was diagnosed with a speech and language impairment—more specifically, a global expressive language disorder that extends to both oral and written language. It was clear that his deficits were impacting his ability to achieve up to his potential academically, and the team decided that he should begin to receive special education services from both the school's speech-language pathologist and the special education teacher to improve his expressive communication skills (in both oral and written language). The speech-language pathologist comes into his general education classroom during language arts and works with him for 45 minutes, three times per week. He also receives learning support from a special educator for 30 minutes, two times per week, with a small group in the learning support classroom to improve his written language skills.

1. Matthew was initially diagnosed with oral language difficulties during kindergarten and began receiving services. Why do you think that his general education teacher referred him for an evaluation during his third-grade year? What happened at that time that prompted the referral?

2. Why was it determined that he was eligible for special education services based on need?

3. Describe how deficits in expressive language could impact Matthew functionally, both as a child and as an adult.

4. What are some strategies that a teacher could use to assist Matthew with his expressive language? Why would those strategies be helpful?

5. Describe how you could use his strong vocabulary and receptive language skills to improve his expressive language.

Case Study 14.2: Jennifer

Jennifer, a 12-year-old girl, is currently in seventh grade and has recently been diagnosed with attention-deficit/hyperactivity disorder (ADHD)–combined type. She is currently receiving accommodations through a Section 504 service agreement and is showing progress as a result of her newly implemented service agreement. You may recall meeting Jennifer and her brother John in Chapter 11.

Family Background

Jennifer lives with her biological mother and father as well as a brother, John, who is three years older than she. John was diagnosed with ADHD–hyperactive/impulsive type when he was 7 years old. His diagnosis was fairly straightforward, as he showed many hyperactive behaviors and was very impulsive. For example, he talked over others (often yelling at them), constantly fidgeted or played with things, often threw objects at inappropriate times,

hit his parents and sister, and had a really difficult time sitting still. He has taken medication for his disorder since the age of 9. Additionally, he has been receiving special education services through the school system as well as private behavioral services to help him control his hyperactive and impulsive behaviors. The combination of medical and behavioral therapy has proven to be highly beneficial for him. Both he and his parents decided that he had developed the coping skills necessary for him to be successful in high school. He learned metacognitive strategies that helped him control his impulsive and hyperactive behaviors by thinking through the potential consequences before acting. For example, instead of throwing a pencil in the classroom, he learned to predict what might happen if he did throw his pencil and, instead, tell himself to put the pencil down. As another example, instead of talking over others (or yelling) while they were talking, he

(Continued)

(Continued)

would purposefully wait until his conversational partner(s) had stopped talking for at least three seconds. The family, with input from John's pediatrician and behavioral therapist, made the decision to take him off of medication during the summer before he started ninth grade. He transitioned well into ninth grade and is currently finishing his ninth-grade year with much success.

Behavioral and Educational Background

When Jennifer was young, she was considered a "shy" child, and her parents described her as often being "in a world of her own." They noticed that she didn't seem to be listening when they would talk with her. She also had a lot of difficulty keeping her room organized and often lost her belongings. When playing, she frequently switched activities or toys very quickly. She also had a habit of snapping her fingers while she was playing. As she became older, her parents noticed that she was starting to seem less "shy" and would often jump into other people's conversations or cut them off while they were talking. For example, when they were at the dinner table, talking about their day, she would often interrupt them to say something that was unrelated. Her brother had a very boisterous personality, so her parents assumed that she was seeking attention.

Throughout her elementary years, Jennifer was generally successful in school and was typically described by her teachers as polite and well-behaved. Her second-grade teacher noted that she often stood up during class instead of sitting in her seat, but she seemed to be learning and was so well-behaved in other ways that the teacher didn't focus on it. Her third-grade teacher described her as well-mannered and a joy to have in class. However, that same teacher noted that she was having a lot of difficulty paying attention during class. She seemed

to have difficulty remembering to write down her homework in her assignment notebook, and she often forgot her homework at home. The teacher noted that Jennifer often looked out the window or had a "blank" look on her face when the teacher was talking. Additionally, her desk was always a mess. As Jennifer got older, her fourth- and fifth-grade teachers noted similar behavior. Her fifth-grade teacher reported that she often shouted out answers in class without raising her hand or waiting to be called on. She also tapped her pencil and bounced her leg a lot during class. When asked to stop, she said that it helped her think about what she was learning. In sixth grade, Jennifer began to show much more difficulty with school. She struggled when changing classrooms and often failed to get to each class on time; she often forgot her materials in her locker or at home; and she had difficulties keeping her binders and notebooks organized. During the sixth-grade parent-teacher conference, her team of teachers said that her disorganization, forgetfulness, and lack of attention in the classroom were really hindering her academic progress. The teaching team and Jennifer's parents worked out an organizational system that included a checklist that would be signed by each teacher and the parents. This seemed to help, and Jennifer showed improvement in her organizational skills and her ability to turn in her homework.

Diagnostic Procedure and Findings

During her sixth-grade physical, Jennifer's mother mentioned to the pediatrician the difficulties Jennifer was having in school, and the doctor indicated that perhaps Jennifer should be tested for ADHD. Jennifer's mother replied that she didn't think Jennifer had ADHD, because her brother John had it and his symptoms didn't resemble Jennifer's behavior at all. They talked about the different subtypes of ADHD, and Jennifer's mother realized that

Jennifer did demonstrate many of the signs associated with the inattentive type. Jennifer's parents, soccer coach, and sixth-grade teachers completed a rating scale, and their responses were fairly consistent. Jennifer presented with multiple symptoms from each of the three categories associated with ADHD (inattention, hyperactivity, and impulsivity) and was subsequently diagnosed with ADHD–combined type. Jennifer's parents met with the sixth-grade teachers and guidance counselor to discuss the diagnosis and determine how to move forward with Jennifer's education. They decided to complete a comprehensive evaluation to see whether she was eligible for special education services as a result of her ADHD. The comprehensive evaluation showed that she was performing well academically, that her behavior really wasn't interfering with school, and that she was socially getting along well with her peers. Her most prominent difficulties were related to organization. The team determined that she was not eligible for special education services, because there didn't appear to be a need that required specially designed instruction or a modification to her education. Instead, they determined that she should receive accommodations under a Section 504 service agreement. The school developed a Section 504 service agreement with input from the parents that included various accommodations, such as keeping an extra set of books at home, receiving additional time for getting to each class, using checklists for organization, being encouraged to ask for clarification regarding directions, being provided a weekly schedule of assignments, and being allowed the use of a stress ball during class. These accommodations have proven to be beneficial for Jennifer, and, through discussions with the pediatrician, Jennifer and her parents have decided not to seek treatment through medication but to continue to monitor her progress with the accommodations that are in place.

Check Your Understanding 14.3

1. Why didn't Jennifer's parents suspect that she had ADHD even though she presented with symptoms at an early age?

2. Why was it determined that Jennifer was not eligible for special education services?

3. What suggestions could you give to parents/teachers about how to identify characteristics of ADHD at an earlier age?

4. What additional accommodations could you suggest to help Jennifer, academically?

Concluding Thoughts on Analysis and Interpretation of Assessment Results

The analysis and interpretation of the assessment results is as important or even more important than the actual scores themselves. As was mentioned several times previously in the text, the diagnostic evaluation is a giant puzzle that needs to be solved before a true picture becomes evident. This process leads to the determination of whether a student is eligible to be diagnosed with a disability that is covered under IDEA and whether the student shows evidence of need for specially designed instruction. Consider the following outcomes:

- If the answer is no to both, the student will move forward in the general education system.

- If the answer is yes to eligibility for a diagnosis and no to the need for specially designed instruction, the student will also move forward in the general education system. However, in this scenario, the student may be eligible for accommodations under Section 504 of the Vocational Rehabilitation Act of 1973.

- If the answer is yes to both eligibility for a diagnosis and the need for specially designed instruction, the team will move forward with planning for special education programming.

It is necessary to truly understand that accommodations provided through a Section 504 service agreement are not the same as special education services provided under IDEA. There is a different underlying premise that is guiding their implementation and usage.

- A Section 504 service agreement is implemented within the context of the general education system; the IEP is implemented within the context of a special education system in combination with general education.

- A Section 504 service agreement only provides accommodations, but not specially designed instruction or modifications, while an IEP provides specially designed instruction, modifications, and accommodations.

The remainder of the chapter will focus on the process that takes place once it has been determined that the student is eligible for special education services (and subsequently an IEP) as a result of both being diagnosed with a disability and showing evidence of need for specially designed instruction.

Check Your Understanding 14.4

1. What is the difference between a Section 504 service agreement and an IEP?

2. List and give a brief description of each of the four parts of the comprehensive diagnostic evaluation that focus on the analysis and interpretation of the assessment results.

3. Explain the difference in educational outcomes for Jennifer and Matthew following the comprehensive diagnostic evaluation.

Planning for Special Education Programming

Once a child has been evaluated and the diagnostic team has determined that a student is eligible for special education services because (1) there is a disability present and (2) there is a need for special education services, it is time to share the information with the parents and commence special education programming. Most states have specific guidelines as to when parents must be given the evaluation results and when the IEP must be developed (check your own state's Department of Education for specific timelines).

Using Information From the Comprehensive Diagnostic Evaluation to Inform Instruction

Planning for special education programming occurs before and during the IEP meeting(s) and requires input from all the IEP team members (parents, special education teacher, general education teacher, school psychologist, speech-language pathologist, etc.) to create the best possible program for the child who has been found newly eligible for services. The comprehensive evaluation plays a critical role in the development of the student's educational programming. The IEP team closely examines the diagnostic evaluation for planning purposes, as quality programming must be derived directly from the comprehensive evaluation report. One of the first things the IEP team will do is examine the child's strengths and area(s) of need, as these will serve as a baseline for where instruction should begin.

Present Levels of Student Performance

Present levels of performance (also referred to as present levels of educational performance) serve as a starting point for where special education services begin. It is important to know where the child is currently performing, so that we are able to gauge his or her progress when intervention begins. For example, a fifth-grade child with a specific learning disability in reading might be performing at a first-grade level in reading at the time of his baseline assessment of reading comprehension. His present level of performance in this academic area is therefore first grade (or approximately four grade levels below what is expected of a student in his grade). Knowing this information provides the teacher with a place to begin his reading comprehension instruction moving forward. Present levels should be indicated for each of the child's qualifying areas in special education. It is important that the child's present levels be clearly written, observable, and measurable, so that relevant data can be taken and understood and applied by educational professionals.

Present Levels of Academic Performance and Functional Performance

Delineating the present levels into specific areas is referred to as **present levels of academic and functional performance (PLAAFP)** and is the result of a revision to IDEA (2004). In essence, this is an extension of the student's present levels of performance. This provides more relevant and precise information to help educators more clearly understand the child's baseline abilities. It will refer to the following age and grade-level expectations:

1. The impact of the disability

2. Statement of academic strengths

3. Statement of academic need/weaknesses

4. Statement of functional abilities and needs

(Cohen & Pullen, 2010, p. 3)

For example, consider the student mentioned earlier who is in fifth grade yet has a first-grade reading comprehension level. This baseline score indicates that his present level of performance is on the first grade level, or several years behind his peers. This is important information when planning for instruction, because the IEP team will need to begin his reading comprehension instruction at the first-grade level in order for him to continue to develop this skill.

The following is an example of an adolescent who is already receiving special education services and whose present levels are being reviewed. Additionally, annual goals (discussed in detail in the next section) and progress toward goals (discussed in detail later in the chapter, under "Ongoing Assessment") are also included, as a means of showing the full cycle of assessment as it relates to each PLAAFP.

PLAAFP Example: Jacob

Jacob is 16 years old and attends the STARs Program, a program for adolescents with autism at a public school specifically for children with disabilities. This program focuses on independent living skills, functional communication, functional academics, and job readiness.

Academic

Jacob's relative academic strengths include spelling and math computation. His academic need is in the area of oral fluency when reading. Given an oral reading fluency passage at the seventh-grade reading level, Jacob is currently reading at a baseline of 13 words per minute (WPM).

Annual goal: Given oral reading fluency passages at the seventh-grade reading level, Jacob will apply learned decoding and word-analysis strategies to improve within one academic year from a baseline of 13 WPM to an average of 70 WPM across five consecutive assessments.

Progress toward goal following specially designed instruction for 1 year: When given an oral reading fluency passage at the seventh-grade reading level, Jacob is able to read an average of 75 WPM across five consecutive probes. Jake's last five data probes are 84, 79, 60, 80, and 71 WPM.

Functional

Jacob's relative functional strengths include signing in/out of work and managing a weekly budget. His functional needs are responding appropriately when denied access to preferable tangible objects or preferred activities. Currently, in the presence of an identified antecedent (denied access to preferred items, objects, or activities), Jacob has demonstrated a baseline in which he has engaged in problem behavior 70% of the time.

Annual goal: In the presence of an identified antecedent (denied access to preferred items, objects, or activities) that has previously resulted in problem behavior, Jacob will engage in replacement behavior (request a quiet break) or continue with his scheduled activity with 80% independence in 8 out of 10 data-collection opportunities.

Progress toward goal following specially designed instruction for 1 year: Jake engaged in replacement behavior (request a quiet break) with verbal prompting or he continued with his scheduled activity 80% of the time on five out of eight data-collection opportunities. His last eight data-collection points were 90, 90, 70, 100, 100, 70, 70, and 100

Check Your Understanding 14.5

1. What is the difference between present levels of performance and present levels of academic performance and functional performance?

2. Describe Jacob's current a) academic strengths and b) functional strengths.

3. What type of improvement do his teachers want him to make in reading fluency? With regard to his replacement behavior?

Annual Goals, Short-Term Objectives, and Benchmarks

Once there is a clear picture of the present levels, one of the most important steps is to determine the annual goals. The cornerstone of any quality IEP is the annual goals and the short-term objectives that are included for each of the child's qualifying areas. **Annual goals** are defined as those skills that can be reasonably accomplished by the child in a particular academic, social, or behavioral area within a 12-month period. Annual goals should refer directly to the child's present levels of performance when being written so as to predict what can reasonably be accomplished. If a child is struggling with reading comprehension, with proper intervention, it might be appropriate to predict that he can gain one year's grade level in reading comprehension in one year's time, or the team might determine that the child is only able to reasonably make six months of progress in one year's time.

Annual goals must adhere to specific criteria, so that they are valid and useful. One method of writing annual goals is known as the SMART method (Mind Tools, n.d.). The SMART method states that annual goals must be written is a specific way so that they are:

S—Specific

M—Measurable

A—Achievable

R—Relevant and Results-Focused

T—Time-bound

The following is an example of a baseline and annual goal that demonstrates the use of the SMART method:

- Baseline: Sarah is currently able to solve computation problems that require the addition of decimals to the tenths place, with 35% accuracy.

- Goal: By March 15, 2021, Sarah will be able to solve computation problems that require the addition of decimals to the tenths place with 80% accuracy on four out of five consecutive measures.

  1. Specific: The annual goal must specifically state the behavior that is to be measured so that both the student and the teacher are clear regarding the expectation. It must be written clearly and be observable. For Sarah's math goal, we know what we want her to do (solve computation problems that require the addition of decimals to the tenths place) and to what degree of accuracy (80% on four out of five consecutive measures) and by when we want her to achieve this goal in order to be successful (March 15, 2021).

2. Measurable: The annual goal must measure the student's growth on a particular skill or behavior. Therefore, the goal must be written in such a way that the performance can be measured to result in accurate data. In Sarah's math goal, the special education teacher will be able to measure Sarah's success at computing decimals by reviewing her completed decimal problems over several administrations to determine whether she scored an 80% or above.

3. Achievable: Goals must be achievable. The team should have high but realistic expectations for student achievement. This means creating mastery goals that are attainable for students. For Sarah's math goal, the IEP team must also consider whether she has all the prerequisite skills she needs to achieve her goal before finalizing the goal and planning for instruction. For instance, we need to know whether Sarah is able to add whole numbers with more than one place value.

4. Relevant and results-focused: Sarah's math goal must be aligned with what she is expected to learn as set forth by the IEP team and in combination with learning standards. For this goal, the IEP team determined that decimal computation was a necessary skill for Sarah to have, based on grade-level expectations. Additionally, in considering the concept of mastery, 80% was determined to be an appropriate percentage for Sarah's goal.

5. Time-bound: The goal must indicate when it should be mastered. This informs both the student and the teacher how long they are allowing for the progress to take place. The date for annual goals will differ, depending on the implementation date of the IEP. The IEP is in effect for exactly one calendar year (this will be discussed in more detail when we cover the annual review). For Sarah's math goal, it is indicated that she has until March 15, 2021 (one calendar year).

Examine the following SMART annual goals and identify the key criteria in each: specific, measurable, achievable, relevant and results-focused, and time-bound:

1. By the end of semester, following the silent reading of a third-grade-level narrative, Lauren will accurately respond to four out of the five wh- (who, what when, where, why) questions, across three consecutive sessions with her speech-language pathologist.

2. When presented with a pattern of colored blocks, Jamie will produce a copy of the given model with 100% accuracy, in three out of four trials, by May 19, 2022.

3. By February 18, 2021, when presented with a task that requires the completion of a set of three steps (presented orally), Carrie will accurately complete all three steps of the given task in three out of four trials.

Examine the following SMART annual goals and (1) determine what is missing in order to make them quality annual goals and (2) rewrite each goal to make it a SMART goal:

1. Emily will independently complete all steps required for brushing her teeth.
2. Willie will demonstrate conversational turn-taking by the end of the semester.
3. By April 2022, Juanita will button her coat.
4. Frank will show improvement in reading.

Short-term objectives are intermediate steps that a student completes in the process of achieving his or her annual goals. Short-term objectives give educators an idea of the progress that a student is making toward the annual goal. Short-term objectives are helpful because without them, the IEP team might not be aware of adaptations or modifications that may be needed to achieve an annual goal. Students will often have a few short-term objectives for each annual goal, although there is no required number of short-term objectives. Short-term objectives typically include the name of the learner and the skill or behavior to be achieved. These objectives are written in the same way as annual goals. Short-term objectives are not a requirement by all states, so it is necessary for special education teachers to be cognizant of what their state requires.

Let's look at the following annual goal (behavioral) and its short-term objectives. In this example, a girl named Susie, a child with ASD, is having difficulties independently greeting her peers. This problem is characteristic of child with ASD and was identified during her psychoeducational evaluation. Her baseline indicates that, at the present time, she does not greet at all unless she is prompted by the teacher.

By May 12, 2022, Susie will independently greet a peer by saying "hi," in three out of four opportunities, as evidenced in the teacher's log.

- Susie will identify five peers whom she would like to greet by October 2021.
- Susie will approach peers, maintaining appropriate personal space, by December 2021 in four out of five trials.
- Susie will maintain an acceptable speaking volume when greeting her peers in four out of five trials by February 2022.

As you can see, it is necessary that Susie achieve all the short-term objectives in order to be successful in reaching her annual goal.

As discussed in Chapter 2, *benchmarks* are major milestones that a student needs to achieve in the process of achieving annual goals. They occur when measurable standard(s) are put in place for learning. Benchmarks should be attained in sequential order. They are similar to short-term objectives in that they include a timeframe, condition, and behavior, yet they differ from short-term objectives because they do not include a criterion for mastery.

The following are examples of benchmarks:

- By the end of the first trimester, Sally will independently greet one peer.

- By the end of the second trimester, Sally will independently greet two peers.

- By the end of the third trimester (school year), Sally will independently greet three or more peers.

Check Your Understanding 14.6

1. Define the terms "annual goal," "short-term objectives," and "benchmarks."

2. How do annual goals differ from short-term objectives?

3. What does the acronym SMART stand for, when referring to SMART goals?

Developing Specially Designed Instruction

Specially designed instruction or SDI refers to the essence of what special education can provide to a child with a disability. It is the teaching methods, strategies, and adaptations to the content used to deliver appropriate instruction. SDI is highly individualized and unique to each student. It is through the design and delivery of SDI that a child with a disability can effectively move toward achieving his goals as set by the IEP team. Providing students with SDI is a requirement under IDEA.

According to IDEA (2004), SDI provides some valuable assurances to students with disabilities.

1. It ensures access to the general education curriculum so that a child with a disability can meet the educational standards that apply to all children (34 Code of Federal Regulations (CFR) § 300.39(b)(3)).

2. It enables students with disabilities to be involved in and make progress in the general education curriculum (34 CFR § 300.320(a)(2)(i)).

3. It provides opportunities for free appropriate public education for students with disabilities in the least restrictive environment (34 CFR § 300.17).

In order to implement SDI, it is important to understand the types of changes that can occur to a student's instruction when implementing this specialized type of instruction for a student with special needs. The following are changes that can occur to instruction in order to meet a child's needs:

1. The purpose and appropriateness of the task
2. The complexity of the task
3. The size of the task
4. The time allotted
5. The pace of instruction
6. The environment
7. The order of learning
8. The instructional procedures and routines
9. The resources and materials
10. The application and demonstration of knowledge
11. The level of support/assistance from specialists
12. Student independence, participation, and motivation

(Kansas State Department of Education, 2017, p. 6)

In addition to making changes to a child's instruction, the teachers implementing such instruction take on specific roles. Both the general education teacher and the special education play distinct roles in implementing SDI. These roles can vary, depending on the educational placement of the student with a disability (see Table 14.1 and 14.2).

Table 14.1   General Education Setting

General Educator	Special Educator
• Integrates SDI into the lesson planning process and considers SDI when creating learning activities, assignments, assessments and projects	• Designs and implements SDI with students receiving special education services as per their IEPs
• Implements SDI as appropriate on an individualized basis as defined by the IEP, including frequency, duration, and location	• Supports the general educator in understanding the details of the student's IEP so that they can effectively integrate the SDI that is necessary to support the student's learning

Adapted from Education Service Center, Region 20 and Texas Education Agency. (2016). *Specially designed instruction: A resource for teachers.* Retrieved from http://acentral.education/assets/uploads/docs/SpeciallyDesignedInstruction-AResourceforTeachers.pdf, p. 31.

Table 14.2 Special Education Setting	
General Educator	**Special Educator**
Collaborates with special educator regarding curriculum and how to effectively modify that curriculum so as to maintain its integrity	Designs and implements SDI with students receiving special education services as per their IEPs

Adapted from Education Service Center, Region 20 and Texas Education Agency. (2016). *Specially designed instruction: A resource for teachers.* Retrieved from http://acentral.education/assets/uploads/docs/SpeciallyDesignedInstruction-AResourceforTeachers.pdf

Know that paraprofessionals may also deliver SDI. The SDI, however, must be designed by certified special education teachers, and the paraprofessionals must be under the supervision of a certified special education teacher while delivering the instruction.

Let's take a look at how SDI can support students with special needs. There are many different adaptations that teachers can implement when working with students with special needs, depending on their specific disabilities. The following are specific examples of SDI adaptations for a student with ASD:

1. Allow for sensory breaks throughout the school day.

2. Provide clear, consistent rules for behavioral expectations, with advance warning provided when possible if a change is to occur.

3. Use a visual schedule of daily classroom tasks, including breaks and end-of-work completion reward.

4. Use a choice menu to represent the options that are available during a task break.

5. Use a script (to be eventually faded) for engaging in conversational turn-taking.

Determining the Least Restrictive Environment (LRE)

In Chapter 1, the concept of least restrictive environment (LRE) was discussed as a key principle of IDEA. When thinking about the least restrictive environment, data gathered during the comprehensive evaluation can help in determining the LRE. The following are examples of sources that might inform LRE:

- Information collected through a direct observation on a student's behavior may be very informative when determining where a student will receive his or her education.

- Information provided through an interview by the general education teacher may give insight into the student's educational needs and what might be the best placement for a student.

- Information related to health and medical status may be necessary when thinking about the best placement for a student.

Concluding Thoughts on Planning for Special Education Programming

One of the most important points to remember is that the benefits of a comprehensive evaluation don't end with a diagnosis and determination of eligibility. Instead, the comprehensive evaluation should be used heavily to inform instruction and a course for special education services. The first IEP should really be a reflection of student performance according to the comprehensive evaluation. The summary of present levels from the evaluation should tie directly into the present levels in the IEP and subsequently lead to the development of goals. Further, information about student strengths and needs that was gathered throughout the evaluation should help inform specially designed instruction and LRE.

Check Your Understanding 14.7

1. Compare and contrast the roles that general educators and special educators may play in providing specially designed instruction.

2. How can the comprehensive evaluation inform LRE?

3. Why must you know a student's present levels before determining his or her annual goals?

Once an IEP has been developed and a student has started receiving special education services, ongoing assessment continues to provide needed information about the student's learning, strengths, and needs.

Ongoing Assessment

Assessment in special education is an ongoing process and should not be considered a "once and done" thing. In Chapter 2, we discussed the concept of the assessment loop. This occurs once the student has learned content and is assessed on what he or she has learned. If the student performs well on the assessment, new material will be presented. If the student performs unsuccessfully on the assessment, the special education teacher will reteach the content using an alternate strategy. A key concept in assessment, therefore, is determining whether the student is making adequate progress.

Progress Monitoring

As we have previously mentioned, progress monitoring is an essential component in any child's education and particularly relevant to the education of a child with a disability, due to his or her academic, social, and/or behavioral challenges. It is a core component of RTI and required under IDEA to determine how a child is responding to instruction. It is the process of making periodic checks on student progress to ensure that the student is making adequate strides toward his or her goals. This is particularly relevant, because, as educators, we want to ensure that we make the most of our instructional time. By keeping abreast of how our students are performing, we are able to maximize the time that we have to provide them with quality instruction. If there are changes that need to be made, as educators, we want to be aware of them so that the child can continue to progress. If students are doing well, we will want to proceed with a similar pace and intensity of instruction. The concept of progress monitoring differs significantly from year-end assessment, which aims to:

1. estimate a growth in knowledge and skills from one year to the next;

2. identify academically at-risk students; and

3. evaluate students' progress against national norms.

(Vanderbilt University, 2018, p. 1)

We have determined that the purpose of progress monitoring is to assess students' academic performance, to quantify a student rate of improvement or responsiveness to instruction, and to evaluate the effectiveness of instruction. This provides the special education teacher the necessary information to determine whether the student's SDI is appropriate to make the necessary progress at school. Furthermore, progress monitoring can be used to:

1. estimate the rates of student improvement, allowing comparison to peers;

2. identify students who are not making adequate progress, so that changes can be made to their instruction; and

3. compare the efficacy of different types of instruction.

(National Center on Response to Intervention, n.d., p. 2)

1. What do you call the instruction that students with special needs receive at school that is highly individualized and unique to each student?

2. List three examples of changes that can occur to instruction when implementing SDI.

3. What is the role of the special educator when implementing SDI in the general education setting? What is the role of the special educator when implementing SDI in the special education setting?

Annual Review of the IEP

The annual review of a child's IEP is another way that special education teachers and the IEP team monitor how a child has performed during the course of a year's time. Annual reviews are a requirement under IDEA. In the case of an annual review, a child's progress is determined by the gains that he or she has made during one calendar year (12 months) since his or her last annual review in relation to the annual goals. This does not necessarily correspond to the academic school year. For example, if a child was determined to be eligible for special education in November and began receiving special education services at that time, the annual review would occur one year from the date that his or her services began: in November of the following year. A child's IEP can be reviewed more frequently, however, if there is a reason to believe that the student's needs are not being met as defined by the current IEP.

At the annual review or the IEP meeting, the IEP team members gather to discuss the child's progress. Typically, all members of the IEP team, such as the special education teacher, the general education teacher(s), the parent(s), the speech-language pathologist, and the occupational therapist, provide a report on the child's progress in relation to the annual goals and short-term objectives that have been set forth for the child over the past year. Often these education professionals will present examples of the child's work as evidence, or they will report on test scores or other progress-monitoring assessments that have been implemented. At this time, the team determines whether the child has met his or her specific goals and new ones should be created or whether the child has not made sufficient progress and alternate strategies should be implemented. A progress report for each qualifying area of special education and related service should be given at the annual review meeting. Other considerations regarding the child's educational programming may include:

1. parental concerns or requests,

2. adding or removing test modifications,

3. transportation or additional related service needs,

4. the child's desires (if at the age of transition), and

5. consideration of ESY (extended school year).

As part of the annual review process, a new IEP is developed that will be implemented for the following calendar year.

Educational Reevaluation Report

Educational reevaluation is a process by which schools determine whether a child requires continued special education and related services. Reevaluation of the student's eligibility for special education must occur every three years, unless the school district and the parents agree that this is not necessary (IDEA, 2004, § 300.303). Some states require a more frequent reevaluation, particularly in the case of intellectual disabilities. A reevaluation may also occur more frequently if the teacher and the parent deem it necessary. The educational re-evaluation report includes all data that has been previously collected through the annual review(s), progress monitoring, and classroom-based performance. However, the team may also determine that additional assessments are necessary.

Parents must be informed in writing that a reevaluation will take place. This is referred to as the Notice of Reevaluation. Very specific guidelines have been developed and are enforced to ensure timeliness and compliance to these binding procedural standards. For example, parents may be given 15 calendar days to respond to the school's request to reevaluate. If additional assessments are proposed at the time of reevaluation as part of the process, parents must agree to such assessments before they are performed. The only exception to this is if the school has requested permission in writing to perform additional tests and the parents do not respond. A reevaluation reexamines several important aspects of the child's programming. It looks at whether the child continues to have a need for specially designed instruction; evaluates the effectiveness and/or appropriateness of the child's current special education and related services; begins future planning for transition; or even considers the cessation of special education services (IDEA 2004). An IEP meeting will then occur to discuss the results of the assessment and either the continued need for or cessation of special education services.

Check Your Understanding 14.9

1. What is an annual review of the IEP? What occurs during an annual review IEP meeting?

2. What other types of considerations might be made during an annual review IEP meeting?

3. How often does a reevaluation occur? Why is a reevaluation conducted?

4. What aspects of the child's programming are assessed in a reevaluation?

The following is a sample reevaluation report that provides information on reading and cognitive assessments only.

Sample Reevaluation Report: James

Review of Records

In September 2020, the Peabody School District completed a reevaluation on James when he was a seventh-grade student at High Mills Middle School. Based on the records, the reevaluation included a review of existing data (attendance, IEP progress, and summary of previous assessments). The reevaluation report concluded that James continued to be a student with ASD. His IEP goals focused on speech and language, social skills, reading, writing, and math.

James's parents initiated a private evaluation in June 2020; this evaluation was unrelated to the reevaluation that was to be completed later that fall (see previous paragraph). Ashley O'Brien, BCBA, of Progress ABA, Behavioral Consulting & Therapy Services, completed a reevaluation on James. Data was collected from numerous sources. The following is a score report of test results.

Measure of Intelligence: Comprehensive Test of Nonverbal Intelligence, Second Edition (CTONI-2)

Testing Observations

The examiner and James's PCA both escorted James to the testing room. James followed the examiner's direction and sat down at the testing table. The examiner immediately began the first subtest of nonverbal intelligence. James began pointing to the correct answers. He seemed to find the correct answers very fast. During the presentation of the pictures, James sometimes mumbled under his breath after providing his answers. He also occasionally started reciting *SpongeBob SquarePants* episodes. Again, this behavior did not seem to impede his ability to respond to the presented items. Overall, this assessment is believed to be a valid estimate of James's current level of nonverbal cognitive functioning.

Results of the Comprehensive Test of Nonverbal Intelligence, Second Edition (CTONI-2)

The Comprehensive Test of Nonverbal Intelligence, Second Edition (CTONI-2) was administered as a measure of cognitive functioning in order to gain information regarding James's nonverbal problem solving abilities. The CTONI-2 minimizes the role of language and fine motor skills. Therefore, it is useful in assessing those who have linguistic difficulties or those with a cultural difference. The rationale for administering this assessment to James came as a result of his difficulties with language-heavy tasks.

James's overall performance fell in the below-average range of intellectual functioning (Nonverbal IQ = 78; 7th percentile). James's Pictorial IQ of 73 (3rd percentile) was within the well-below-average range, while his Geometric IQ of 87 (19th percentile) was within the lower end of the average range. There was a statistically significant difference between his Pictorial IQ and Geometric IQ.

Subtest	Scaled/Standard Score	Percentile	Range
Pictorial Analogies	5	5th	Well Below Average
Geometric Analogies	7	16th	Average
Pictorial Sequences	6	9th	Below Average
Geometric Sequences	10	50th	Average
Pictorial IQ	73	3rd	Well Below Average
Geometric IQ	87	19th	Average
Nonverbal IQ	78	7th	Below Average

The Pictorial Analogies subtest (Scaled Score = 5) and the Geometric Analogies subtest (Scaled Score = 7) measure analogical reasoning ability, or the ability to determine the relationship of two objects or geometric designs and then find the same relationship between two different objects or geometric designs. The Pictorial Categories subtest (Scaled Score = 7) and the Geometric Categories subtest (Scaled Score = 7) measure categorical classification ability, or the ability to determine the relationship between two stimulus figures and to select the item that shares the same relationship with the stimulus figures. The Pictorial Sequences subtest (Scaled Score = 6) and the Geometric Sequences subtest (Scaled Score = 10) measure sequential reasoning ability, or the ability to determine which item completes a sequence of actions shown in three pictures/designs.

Measures of Academic Achievement

Woodcock-Johnson IV (Standard Battery)

Area of Achievement	Test	Standard Score	Range
Reading	Letter-Word Identification	73	Well Below Average
Reading	Word Attack	77	Below Average
Reading	Oral Reading	88	Average
Reading	Sentence Reading Fluency	75	Below Average
Reading	Passage Comprehension	43	Well Below Average

Written Language	Spelling	90	Average
Written Language	Writing Fluency	82	Below Average
Written Language	Writing Samples	54	Well Below Average
Mathematics	Calculation	82	Below Average
Mathematics	Math Facts Fluency	74	Well Below Average
Mathematics	Applied Problems	57	Well Below Average

AIMSweb One-Minute Timed Reading Fluency

- Seventh grade: 92/94 words correct per minute (wcpm)
- Eighth grade: 76/77 wcpm, 67/69 wcpm

Test of Word Reading Efficiency (TOWRE)

- Sight Word Efficiency: raw score 66, age equivalence 10, grade equivalence 4.6, Standard score = 79 (Below Average Range)
- Phonemic Decoding Efficiency: raw score 40, age equivalence 11.9, grade equivalence 6.0, Standard score = 86 (Average Range)

Brigance Silent Reading Comprehension (Reading Assessment)

- Lower second grade: 60% (questions answered wrong—sequence, main idea)
- Upper second grade: 80% (questions answered wrong—main idea)
- Lower third grade: 75% (questions answered wrong—main idea)
- Upper third grade: 60% (questions answered wrong—literal, vocabulary)
- Fourth grade: 80% (questions answered wrong—main idea)
- Fifth grade: 40% (questions answered wrong—literal, vocabulary, main idea)

Brigance Comprehensive Inventory of Basic Skills (CIBS): Listening Comprehension (Oral Language Assessment)

- Unsuccessful at upper first grade and lower second grade

Classroom-Based Assessment in Reading

James was given a paragraph on the third-grade level, with eight literal questions that followed. James read the paragraph out loud. James was then asked to read each question. James either knew the correct answer automatically or used "look back" strategies to give the correct answer. He scored 100% on two probes at the third-grade level.

When James was given multi-paragraphs at the fourth-grade level, he was unable to independently find his answers. If the paragraph where the answer can be found is given, he can independently then answer the question with success.

Check Your Understanding 14.10

1. Identify any three subtests on the WJ-IV, and indicate how well James performed on them.

2. List a strength and a weakness found in James's student work samples.

3. What was the result of James's performance on the CTONI-2? What does this suggest about his current intellectual abilities?

4. Based on the results of James's reevaluation, it was determined that he should continue to receive special education services. Explain why.

CHAPTER SUMMARY

Throughout the course of this text, you have learned about the assessment process that is associated with special education as defined by IDEA. The focus of this chapter was to demonstrate how important that process is in determining how a student with special needs will move forward in the educational process. The comprehensive diagnostic evaluation not only serves as a means for diagnosing a disability and determining eligibility for special education services, it also serves as a starting point for how to plan for special education programming. During the course of a student's education, his or her special education services will be monitored and evaluated constantly to ensure that the student is receiving the best possible services to ensure a free and appropriate education, as required by IDEA. Assessment is as much a part of the monitoring process as it is in the initial diagnostic evaluation. As you move forward and think about assessment as it relates to special education, continue to think about the many facets of assessment (assessment types, areas of student characteristics, diagnostic criteria associated with each disability, etc.) and how you can use them throughout your educational career for all students with special needs.

APPLY WHAT YOU HAVE LEARNED

1. Look back at the reevaluation report for James. For each area of achievement in which James was tested (oral language, reading, written language, and mathematics), make a chart of the assessments that were given and his performance on each of the assessments. Summarize his performance in each area of achievement.

2. Compare and contrast the two case studies based on Matthew and Jennifer, and provide evidence for why one child was eligible for special education services and the other was not.

3. Choose any one case study from any disability chapter (Chapters 6–13), and discuss how what you learned about the student can help inform instructional planning.

REFERENCES

Cohen, S., & Pullen, P. (2010). *EDIS 5141: IEP and transition planning*. Retrieved from http://faculty.virginia.edu/PullenLab/EDIS3020_5000/Mod4/IEPPart15.html

Education Service Center, Region 20 and Texas Education Agency. (2016). *Specially designed instruction: A resource for teachers*. Retrieved from http://acentral.education/assets/uploads/docs/SpeciallyDesignedInstruction-AResourcefor-Teachers.pdf

Individuals With Disabilities Education Act, 20 U.S.C. § 300.305 (2004).

Kansas State Department of Education. (2017, August). *Considerations for specially designed instruction*. Retrieved from https://www.ksde.org/Portals/0/SES/pubs/ConsiderationsForSpecial-lyDesignedInstruction.pdf

Mind Tools. (n.d.). *SMART goals: How to make your goals achievable*. Retrieved from https://www.mindtools.com/pages/article/smart-goals.htm

National Center on Response to Intervention. (n.d.). *Progress monitoring*. Retrieved from https://rti4success.org/sites/default/files/Transcript%20What%20is%20Progress%20Monitoring.pdf

Vanderbilt University. (2018). *Classroom assessment (Part 1): An introduction to monitoring academic achievement in the classroom*. Retrieved from https://iris.peabody.vanderbilt.edu/module/gpm/cresource/q1/p01/#content

Name Index

Ageranioti-Bélanger, S., 217
Anderson, N. B., 269
Apel, K., 284
Appelbaum, A., 357
Arthaud, T. J., 300 (table)
Ashcraft, M., 138
Asher, S., 307
Austin, J., 105

Bailey-Joseph, J., 188
Balsiger, L., 401
Barton, P., 274
Battaglia, A., 218
Beaujean, A., 180–182
Benasich, A. A., 274
Benner, G. J., 284
Ben-Porath, Y. S., 299 (table)
Bergan, John Richard, 38
Bergan, John Robert, 38
Bergeron, R., 203
Berko, J., 103
Bernard, M. E., 306
Berninger, V., 332
Bernstein, D. K., 285
Best, A. M., 292
Bloom, L., 101–102, 268, 270
Bos, C. S., 120, 303
Bowen, J., 402
Boyd, K., 358
Braden, J. P., 354
Bradley, R., 9
Brazier, Y., 395
Brown, L., 280, 300 (table)
Burnette, J., 41
Burnham, C. G., 38
Burns, M., 178
Butcher, J. N., 299 (table)
Butter, E. M., 218

Caldwell, J., 188
Carlson, C. L., 304
Carr, E. G., 284
Carroll, J. B., 98
Choudhury, N., 274
Clark, G., 230
Cohen, S., 430
Cooter, R., 123
Coutinho, M. J., 292
Cowin, C., 229
Cronbach, L., 75
Cullinan, D., 300 (table)

Dahlstrom, W. G., 299, 299 (table)
Darley, J., 77
Dart, E., 218
Dave, M., 248
Davis, R., 219
Dee S., 368
DeKlyen, M., 307
Deno, S., 78
Desrochers, M. N., 368
Dietel, R., 39
Dixon, S. G., 96
Dombeck, M., 203
Dubov, J., 304
Dunn, L. M., 6
Durand, M., 284
Dutton, G. N., 358

Easterbrooks, S. R., 354
Eisenman, L, 229
Ellis, A., 306
Ely, R., 367
Epstein, M. H., 297, 300 (table)
Estrada, R., 333
Evely, M., 208

Farmer, W., 369–370
Feldman, H., 329, 333
Felman, A., 388
Feuerborn, L., 284
Finegood, E. D., 274
Fisk, J. E., 273
Flanagan, D. P., 96
Floyd, R., 203
Freedman, B., 229
Frey, B., 80
Friend, M., 5, 11, 346

Gage, N. A., 297
Gallaudet , Thomas Hopkins, 343
Gallistel, C. R., 135
Ganim, Z., 208
Garcia Winner, M., 306
Gardner, H., 96
Geary, D., 135–136
Gelman, R., 135
Geyer, E., 328
Gibbon, F. E., 284
Gillon, G. T., 268
Giuliano, K., 328
Glaser, R., 77
Gleason, J. B., 103
Goldstein, A. P., 306
Graham, J. R., 299 (table)
Green, C., 143
Guerriero, T., 135–143

Hale, J., 180–181
Hall Lueck, A., 356
Hammill, D., 123, 280, 300 (table)
Hargis, C., 78–79
Harris, S., 252
Hass, M., 180

Raymond, E., 165–167, 171, 173
Reed, V. A., 284
Reid, D. K., 123
Reiff, M., 329, 333
Reutzel, D. R., 125
Reynolds, C. R., 299 (table)
Reynolds, T., 203, 205, 210
Roberts, T. G., 300 (table)
Rollins, Paula, 368
Romaniec, M., 251
Rosenberg, M. S., 25, 216
Rosenthal, R., 75
Rowland, C., 369
Roy, S., 229

Salako, O. O., 304
Sarris, M., 246
Schmitt, V., 80
Schumm, J. S., 305
Schutte, K., 331
Schwartz, H. D., 267, 278–279

Serna, L., 188
Shames, G. H., 269
Shapiro, E., 86
Shemmassian , S., 333
Shorter, E., 294
Shriberg, L., 285
Smith, D., 404
Smith, T. E. C., 285
Spivey, K., 284
Styck, K., 180
Sukhodolsky, D. G., 217
Sulkes, S. B., 213
Sullivan, A., 178
Swain, J. E., 274
Swanson, J. M., 304
Swenson, A. M., 367

Taggart, L., 219
Teigerman-Farber, E., 285
Tellegen, A., 299, 299 (table)
Torreno, S., 206
Trout, A. L., 297
Tyler, N., 404

Ullman, M., 273

van Schrojenstein Lantman-de Valk, H., 219
Vaughn, S., 120, 303, 306
Vicker, B., 257
Volpe, R., 86

W. Cousins, 219
Wareing, M., 273
Weaver, B., 53
Welch, T. R., 371–372
Westen, D., 75
Westley, D. L., 216
Westling, D., 25
Wilbur, R. B., 354
Winfree, L., 38
Winzer, M. A., 343
Wolk, L., 271

Yell, M. L., 6, 9

Zebron, S., 268
Zupanick, C. E., 203

Subject Index

inattention, 324, 325 (table)
intelligence and, 332
other health
impairment, 323
overview, 322
primary vs. secondary
diagnosis, 404–405,
405 (figure)
professionals to diagnose,
330–331
social/emotional status,
332–333
specialized teaching
methods, 333–336
Tourette syndrome
and, 386
treatment, 333–336
types of, 322
Auditory blending, 172,
171 (figure)
Auditory closure, 172,
171 (figure)
Auditory discrimination,
171–172, 171 (figure)
Auditory figure-ground
discrimination, 172,
171 (figure)
Auditory memory, 172,
171 (figure)
Auditory perception,
171–172, 171(figure)
blending, 172, 171 (figure)
closure, 172, 171 (figure)
discrimination, 171–172,
171 (figure)
figure-ground discrimination,
172, 171 (figure)
memory, 172, 171 (figure)
Auditory processing (Ga), 98
Augmentative and alternative
communication (AAC),
259–260, 390, 402, 406

Authentic assessment,
79–80, 370
Autism, 12
IDEA definition of, 236
Autism Diagnostic Interview,
Revised (ADI-R), 241
Autism Diagnostic
Observation Schedule
(ADOS), 241
Autism spectrum disorder
(ASD), 30, 40, 236
assessing areas, 245–250
augmentative
and alternative
communication,
259–260
case studies, 252–254
characteristics, 237–238,
238 (table)
common learning
characteristics, 246,
246 (table)
comorbidities to, 248–249
daily living/adaptive
behavior domains, 259
diagnosing methods,
238–245
diagnostic criteria,
236–238
educational placements
and, 247–248,
247 (figure)
evaluating components,
242 (table)
evidence-based practices,
255–259
family, impact on, 250–252
genetic syndromes with, 249
health and medical status,
248–249
intelligence assessment,
245–246

postsecondary life, 260–261
primary vs. secondary
diagnosis, 404–405,
405 (figure)
professionals in diagnosing,
240–242, 241 (table)
screening instruments, 240
sensory processing
difficulties, 249–250
severity levels for,
244–245, 244 (table)
social skills training, 261
specialized teaching
methods, 254–261
test administration and, 243
tools, 241
Autistic disorder, 236
Average (mean), 69

Basal rule, 66–67
BASC. See Behavior
Assessment System for
Children (BASC)
Bayley Scales of Infant
Development (BSID),
205, 225
Beery-Buktenica
Developmental Test of
Visual-Motor Integration
(Beery VMI), 173
Behavior, 148–149
Behavior Assessment System
for Children (BASC), 148,
217, 299, 299 (table),
302, 326
Behavior disordered.
See Emotional
disturbance (ED)
Behavior Evaluation Scale,
300 (table)
Behavior Rating Profile,
300 (table)

Behavior rating scales (BRS), 88, 217

Behavioral and Emotional Rating Scale, 299 (table)

Behavioral characteristics
of hearing impairment, 354
of intellectual disabilities, 216–218
of learning disabilities, 184
of speech/language impairment and, 284
of visual impairment, 368

Behavioral Evaluation Scale (BES-2), 302

Behavioral interventions, 304–306

Behavioral manifestations
externalized, 297
internalized, 297

Behavioral programs, 304

Bell curve, 59
with intellectual disabilities, 204 (figure)
normal, 60 (figure)

Benchmarks, 311, 435

Benefits available for
intellectual disabilities
home and community-based waiver services, 220
social security administration benefits and Medicaid, 220–221
special education services, 220

Bilateral hearing loss, 345

Blending, phonological awareness, 121

Blindness, 356–357
IDEA definition, 356
See also Visual impairment

Blood sugar. See Diabetes mellitus

Bookshare (www.bookshare.org), 369

Braille system, 357, 367–369

Breadth of vocabulary, 103–104

Brigance Inventory of Early Development, 225, 444

Brigance Life Skills Inventory (LSI), 207

Brigance Silent Reading Comprehension, 444

BRS (behavior rating scales), 217

CAI (computer-aided instruction), 257

Cardinality, mathematics skill, 135–136

Case studies
analysis and interpretation of assessment results, 423–427
for attention-deficit/hyperactivity disorder, 333–336, 425–427
autism spectrum disorder, 252–254
emotional disturbance, 302
intellectual disabilities, 221–223
mathematics learning disability, 194–198
multiple disabilities, 408–409
nonverbal learning disability, 190–193
other health impairment (OHI), 391–392
overview, 185–186
reading learning disability, 186–189
specialized teaching methods, 188–189, 192–193, 196–198

speech or language impairments, 285, 287, 423–424
syllable types, 189 (figure)
traumatic brain injury, 398–400
written learning disability, 186–189

CASL. See Comprehensive Assessment of Spoken Language (CASL)

Cattell-Horn-Carroll model, 96, 180

CBAs. See Curriculum-based assessments

CBCL. See Child Behavior Checklist (CBCL)

CBM. See Curriculum-based measurement

Ceiling item. See Stopping points

Ceiling rule, 67

CELF. See Clinical Evaluation of Language Fundamentals (CELF)

Center for Deaf and Hard of Hearing Education, 345, 355

Centers for Disease Control and Prevention, 327, 342

Cerebral palsy (CP), 393
causes, 393
diagnosis, 393
symptoms, 393, 394 (table)

Cerebral visual impairment (CVI), 358

Change problems, mathematics, 140

CHC model. See Cattell-Horn-Carroll model

Checklists, 87–88, 207, 299–290

social characteristics, 218–219, 218 (table)
specialized teaching methods, 223–231
syndromes, 214–215
teaching methodologies, 227–229

Intelligence
attention-deficit/ hyperactivity disorder (ADHD) and, 332
auditory processing (Ga), 98
autism spectrum disorder, 245–246
comprehension-knowledge (Gc), 97
defined, 96
emotional disturbance and, 301
fluid reasoning (Gf), 97
language and, 100
learning disabilities and, 160–161, 176
long-term storage and retrieval (Glr), 97
processing speed (Gs), 97–98
reevaluation report, 442–443
short-term memory (Gsm), 97
speech/language impairments and, 284
test, 96–99
visual processing (Gv), 98

Intelligence quotient (IQ), 96
and ID, 203, 205

Interim alternative education setting (IAES), 304

Internalized behavior, 297

International Phonetic Alphabet, 279

International Statistical Classification of Diseases (ICD), 294

Inter-rater reliability, 74

Inter-response time, 87

Interrogative sentences, 133

Interval recording, 86

Interviews, 83–84, 149
with primary caregivers, 210
with teachers, 210

IQ test, 99

ITSP (infant/toddler sensory profile), 249

Kaufman Functional Academic Skills Test (K-FAST), 207

Kaufman Test of Educational Achievement (KTEA), 55, 119

Keller, Helen, 355

KeyMath, 139

KTEA (Kaufman test of educational achievement), 119, 139

Language, 267 (figure), 268
assessment of, 279–280
complexities with, 105
components of, 101
content, 101
defined, 100
elements of, 101
form, 101
model of, 102 (table)
morphology, 103
oral, 116, 118–122
phonology, 101–103
pragmatics, 105
related academic achievement, 117–118

semantics, 103–104
syntax, 103
use, 101

Language and literacy technology, 286 (table)

Language delay, 106

Language difference, 106

Language disorder, 106

Language impairment, 267, 269–270

Latency recording, 86

Learning disabilities, 156, 158–160
academic achievement, 161–162, 176
behavior, 184
case studies and instructions, 185–198
diagnosing methods, 177–181
diagnostic criteria, 158–160
emotional characteristics, 188
health and medical status, 188
intelligence, 160–161, 176
processing deficits, 156–157
psychoeducational evaluation for, 176–177
psychological processing (See Psychological processing)
Section 300.309 of IDEA, 158–160
social characteristics, 185
subtypes, 183
See also Auditory perception; Visual perception

Learning media, 359

Least restrictive environment (LRE), 6, 9–10, 226, 248, 437–438